ALL OR NOTHING

ALL OR NOTHING

The Axis and the Holocaust
1941–1943

Jonathan Steinberg

ROUTLEDGE
London and New York

First published 1990
by Routledge
11 New Fetter Lane, London EC4P 4EE
29 West 35th Street, New York, NY 10001

Typeset in 10/12 Palatino by
Mayhew Typesetting, Bristol
Printed in Great Britain by
Richard Clay Ltd, Bungay, Suffolk

British Library Cataloguing in Publication Data
Steinberg, Jonathan
All or nothing : The Axis and the Holocaust, 1941–1943.
1. Jews. Genocide, 1939–45. Historiography
I. Title
940.53'15'03924
ISBN 0-415-04757-9

Library of Congress Cataloging in Publication Data
Steinberg, Jonathan.
All or nothing: the Axis and the Holocaust, 1941–1943 /
Jonathan Steinberg. p. cm.
Includes bibliographical references.
1. Holocaust, Jewish (1939–1945) – Balkan Peninsula. 2. Holocaust,
Jewish (1939–1945) – France. 3. World War, 1939–1945 – Jews –
Rescue – Italy. 4. World War, 1939–1945 – Diplomatic history. 5. Italy –
Foreign relations – Germany. 6. Germany – Foreign relations – Italy.
I. Title.
D804.3.S75 1990
940.53'18'09496 – dc20   89-70241

For Jacob M. Kaplan
1891–1987

CONTENTS

ILLUSTRATIONS

MAPS AND DOCUMENTS

MAPS

DOCUMENTS

ACKNOWLEDGEMENTS

Several public bodies have generously supported this work. The Leverhulme Trust elected me a Research Fellow for 1987–88 and helped to cover my travel and research expenses. The Shelby Collum Davis Center for Historical Studies at Princeton University invited me to present a paper on this research before what must be the most exacting and serious historical jury in the world. Their comments and criticisms have transformed the argument and I want to thank Professors Lawrence Stone and Harold James of the Department of History for arranging the invitation. While in America I lectured at Harvard, Brown, the University of Pennsylvania, the University of Connecticut and the State University of New York at Stony Brook. I am grateful to Professors Wallace MacCaffrey, Volker Berghahn, Thomas Childers, James O. Robertson and Ms Kim Reynolds, my hosts in those universities.

The German Academic Exchange Service granted me a travel award so that I could visit the University of Tübingen and work in the archives at Freiburg im Breisgau. Dr Peter Alter of the German Historical Institute invited me to lecture in their series of afternoon seminars. Dr Wilhelm Deist, director of the Militärgeschichtliches Forschungsamt, Freiburg im Breisgau, gave me his help. his friendship and, together with his wife Ursula, much hospitality. Fregattenkapitän Dr Gerhard Schreiber of the MGFA gave me valuable documents and shared his expertise generously. The British Council paid for a trip to Australia where, as a guest of the Frederick May Foundation in the University of Sydney, and of the Departments of History at the University of Western Australia and The Flinders University of South Australia I talked about the Italian plot to save Jews. I am enormously grateful to Professor R.J.B. Bosworth of the University of Western Australia who made the arrangements to get me there. I am grateful to colleagues in all these places who listened to my ideas and offered criticisms and comments. If I had any doubt that research and teaching belong together, the experience of these past few years has dispelled it. What I owe to the Master and Fellows of Trinity Hall for nearly twenty five years of conviviality and support cannot easily be imagined. The Hall has been *alma mater*.

My debts to individuals have accumulated over the years I have worked on the project. I should not have survived in Rome without Piero and Joan Fitzgerald Boitani, who put up with me as an almost permanent house guest, and I should not have completed the research without the help of Consigliere di Stato Professor Guglielmo Negri, Ambassador Umberto Vattani, Professor Pietro Pastorelli, and Professor Pino Arlacchi. I am grateful to the Hon. Senator Giovanni Spadolini, President of the Senate, and His Excellency Bruno Bottai, secretary general of the Italian Foreign Ministry, for writing letters of recommendation for me.

I owe a special debt to Mr Imre Rochlitz and his son Joseph Rochlitz. What began as a family trip to the island of Rab by the Rochlitz family to see where Mr Rochlitz had been interned by the Italians in 1943 became in time Joseph Rochlitz's moving documentary film *The Righteous Enemy*. Joseph Rochlitz helped me in every way, providing me with introductions to people he had filmed, producing an invaluable collection of documents which he kindly sent me and publishing the Merci diaries.

Dr James Walston turned himself into my assiduous Roman historical agent, furnishing me with the names and addresses of former Italian officers to interview and tirelessly hunting down references when I was not in Italy. Mr Martin Brown drew my attention to the captured Italian files in Washington and Assistant Archivist Linda Brown of the National Archives, Washington, DC, got me essential microfilms by return of post. Mr Michael Ryder of the Foreign Office acted as host during an exceptionally productive week at the Berlin Document Centre and cut through much red tape for me.

I am grateful to all those people who let me interview them: Mr Paul Bandler, Mr Camillo Boitani, General Carlo Casarico, Mrs Evi Eller, Dr G.C. Garaguso, Professor Salvatore Loi and Ambassador Guelfo Zamboni. I am grateful to His Excellency Ambassador Antonello Pietromarchi for permission to quote from his father's unpublished diaries and Dr Gianludovico De Martino for help with a crucial text from the Senate Library.

The following people helped in ways that they will remember and I want to acknowledge: Giacomo Becattini, Piero Bevilacqua, Steven Bowman, Francesco and Barbara Calvo, Andrew Cohen, Joe Cremona, Ginny Crum-Jones, Anne de Bruyne, Miri Erez, Peter Fluck, Rita Goldberg, Lothar Hilbert, Sir Harry Hinsley, Patricia Hilden, Dganit Iserles, Priscilla Dale Jones, Tanya Luhrmann, Toni Meier, Richard Mitten, Jonathan Morris, Milivoje Panic, Luise Rinser,

Alessandro Vaciago, Anita Warburg, Eric Warburg, Ingrid Warburg Spinelli and Morton Yarmon. I remember with gratitude the conversations I was privileged to have with the late Professors A.D. Momigliano and Uberto Limentani and the late Dr Wolfgang von Tirpitz. Miss C.B.A Behrens, who died in January 1989, listened to a set of lectures on the issues in this book and applied her exacting standards of coherence to them.

I want to thank the staffs at the Uffico Storico, Stato Maggiore dell' Esercito (especially Ten. Col. Fernando Frattolillo); the Archivio Storico Diplomatico of the Italian Foreign Ministry; the Archivio Centrale dello Stato; the Istituto Gramsci; the Centro di Cultura Ebraica, Rome; the library of the Associazione Nazionale dei Partigiani Italiani; the Berlin Document Centre, the Bundesarchiv-Militärarchiv (especially Frau Müller and Herr E. Moritz who ran the reading room so generously), the University Library, Cambridge (especially Mr A.G. Parker of the Accessions Department), and Miss A.C. Cunninghame of the Seeley Historical Library, Cambridge.

The following kindly granted permission to reproduce the pictures in the book: Collins Publishers, London gave permission to reproduce Illustration no. 1 from their book *The Rome Berlin Axis: A Study of the Relations between Hitler and Mussolini*, by Elizabeth Wiskerman (1966); Illustrations 2–7 were reproduced by permission of Verlag Kurt Desch, Munich, from their book *Der Faschismus von Mussolini zu Hitler Texte Dokumente*, by Ernest Nolte (1968); Illustration 8 was reproduced by permission of the Paul Popper Photographic Agency; Illustration 9 was reproduced by permission of Atlantis Verlag, Zürich from their book, *Berlin* by Martin Hurliman (1981); Illustrations 10–14 were reproduced by Ufficio Storico, Stato Maggiore Esercito Italiano, Italy; and Illustration 15 was reproduced by permission of the Archivio Centrale Dello Stato who hold the picture.

Andrew Wheatcroft of Routledge, Chapman and Hall encouraged me when I needed it. Jill Steinberg read the manuscript in all its variants and would have saved me much trouble and discomfort if I had listened to her.

The late Mr Jacob M. Kaplan and the J.M. Kaplan Fund backed my foolhardy decision in 1961 to give up merchant banking and to begin an academic career. Jack Kaplan supported me with enthusiasm for twenty five years. He knew that I wanted this to be 'his' book. I regret only that it took so long that he never lived to see it. It is with gratitude and in loving memory that I dedicate it to him.

ABBREVIATIONS

The following abbreviations have been used in the notes. For full
archival references, see the bibliography:

ACS   Archivio centrale dello stato
B   Busta
BA   Bundesarchiv
BDC   Berlin Document Centre
CC   Control Commission (Allied)
CR   Carteggio riservato
DS   Diario storico
f.   fasicolo
GAB   Gabinetto Armistizio e Pace
HGr   Heeresgruppe
Kdo   Kommando
KTB   Kriegstagebuch
MA   Militärarchiv
NA   National Archives, Washington, DC
NMT   Nuremberg Military Tribunal
PS   Pubblica Sicurezza
OB   Oberbefehlshaber
OKW   Oberkommando der Wehrmacht
sf   sotto-fascicolo
SME   Stato Maggiore del Esercito
SPD   Segreteria particolare del Duce
TWC   Trials of War Criminals (Nuremberg Tribunal)
US   Ufficio Storico

All translations, unless otherwise indicated, are my own

Die Vergangenheit ist in die Gegenwart eingeschlossen, ist untrennbar eins mit ihr. Gegenwart und jede andere Gegenwart, die wir Zukunft nennen, sind nichts anderes als das Ergebnis unserer Vergangenheit. Sie sind das Gericht über alles Geschehene. Man kann sich eine Weile einbilden, man sei aller Vergangenheit ledig. Doch eines Tages richtet sich die Vergangenheit vor einem auf und erweist sich als ein Engpass, durch den – und nirgendswo sonst – der Weg in die Zukunft führt. Scheut man die enge Pforte, gewinnt man nie das Freie.

Luise Rinser

Bisogna scrivere questi fatti . . . Gli uomini sono uomini. Bisogna cercare di rendergli migliori e a questo scopo per prima cosa giudicarli con spregiudicato e indulgente pessimismo. In quasi tutte le mie azioni sento un elemento più o meno forte di interesse personale, egoismo, viltà, calcolo, ambizione, perchè non dovrei cercarlo anche in quelle degli altri? Perchè ritrovandolo dovrei condannarlo severamente?

Emanuele Artom

Names which hoped to range over kingdoms and continents shrink at last into cloisters and colleges. Nor is it certain that even of these dark and narrow habitations, these last retreats of fame, the possession will long be kept.

Dr Samuel Johnson

THE PROBLEM

The thing is just not possible. They [the Jews] have put themselves under our protection. The Croatians have asked that they be handed back. Naturally I flatly refused. They said that they would have to ask the Germans to ask for them. Now there's an order of the Duce.'[1]

In the late summer of 1942 a small group of Italian diplomats and senior officers decided to save the lives of a few thousand Jews. The Jews, mostly from Croatia, had fled to the parts of Yugoslavia which the Italian army occupied during 1941 and had since that time lived in peace under the protection of the Royal Italian Army. They had run from the unsystematic butchery of the Croatian fascists, the Ustaši, but by the middle of 1942 they were threatened with the systematic extermination planned for them under the Nazi 'new order' in Europe. In August of 1942 the German government formally asked the Italian government to hand them over. Mussolini agreed; a handful of Italian diplomats and generals said no.

By refusing the German request and disobeying an explicit order of the Duce, the conspirators set a perilous course which in the end crossed not merely the murderous ambition of a nasty, little Axis puppet but that of Hitler, Himmler and the SS. At the start they had no conclusive evidence of what we now call 'the final solution' but the Italian Foreign Ministry had received a broad hint. On 18 August 1942, Prince Otto von Bismarck, minister of state at the German Embassy in Rome, called on the Marchese Lanza d'Ajeta at the Italian Foreign Ministry. He had orders to demand that the Italian government instruct its military authorities 'to actuate those measures devised by the Germans and the Croatians for a transfer in mass of the Jews of Croatia to territories in the East.'[2]

Prince Bismarck let slip the fact that the measures would lead to the 'dispersion and elimination' of such Jews. Indeed, in the original text d'Ajeta had recorded the word 'liquidation'. Mussolini was perfectly

1

Ministero degli Affari Esteri
Gabinetto

APPUNTO PER IL DUCE

Bismarck ha dato comunicazione di un telegramma a firma
Ribbentrop con il quale questa Ambasciata di Germania viene
richiesta di provocare istruzioni alle competenti Autorità
Militari italiane in Croazia affinchè anche nelle zone di
nostra occupazione possano essere attuati i provvedimenti
divisati da parte germanica e croata per un trasferimento
in massa degli ebrei di Croazia nei territori orientali.

Bismarck ha affermato che si tratterebbe di varie mi-
gliaia di persone ed ha lasciato comprendere che tali provvedimenti tenderebbero, in pratica, alla loro dispersione
ed eliminazione.

L'Ufficio competente fa presente che segnalazioni della R.Legazione a Zagabria inducono a ritenere che, per desi
derio germanico, che trova consenziente il Governo ustascia
la questione della liquidazione degli ebrei in Croazia sta-
rebbe ormai entrando in una fase risolutiva.

Si sottopone, Duce, quanto precede per le Vostre deci-
sioni.

Roma, 21 agosto 1942-XX

Document 1 Mussolini permits Jews to be deported from the Italian zone,
1942

prepared to grant his Nazi ally the bodies of a few thousand Croatian Jews. In his large hand he wrote 'nulla osta [no objection] . . . M' (see Document 1) across the memorandum.[3] The Duce apparently did not care what happened to the Jews of Croatia or refused to believe Bismarck's hint. It was that 'order' of the Duce that the conspirators decided to disobey.

It was not until early November 1942 that the Italian authorities had the proof they needed. The Carabinieri General Pièche. who had been sent on a secret mission to assess the Balkan situation, reported on 4 November 1942 that 'the Croatian Jews deported from the German zone of occupation to the eastern territories have been 'eliminated', by the use of toxic gas in the train in which they were enclosed.'[4]

The chief of the department of 'Confidential Affairs' in the Italian Foreign Ministry, Luigi Vidau, wrote 'evidence' on the memo and the stamp shows that it had been seen by the Duce. Two days later, Mussolini made one of his crude jokes to the industrialist Alberto Pirelli, who recorded it in his diary: 'With regard to the Jews, Mussolini said, "they're letting them emigrate . . . to another world".'[5]

Hence by saying 'no' to the Croatians in August 1942 the Italian conspirators interfered with the smooth operations of the holocaust and eventually were forced to do the same on behalf of the Jews in Italian-occupied Greece and southern France.

How and why the conspirators behaved as they did is the main story told in this book. Why did senior figures in the fascist regime risk their careers to save Jews who were not even Italian? In Vichy a puzzled Pierre Laval, Prime Minister of the French puppet regime, summoned the Italian Ambassador on 14 January 1943: 'Laval expressed himself to the effect that, while he could understand our interest in favour of those Jews with Italian nationality, he could not exactly account for our intervention "in favour" of foreign Jews.'[6]

The Germans could understand and tolerate it even less. The SS complained; German civilians and army officers complained. Ribbentrop called the Governor of Dalmatia, Giuseppe Bastianini, 'an honorary Jew'[7]. The Italians replied evasively. They pretended to comply with German wishes. In November 1942 the Italian Army rounded up the Jewish refugees who had fled into their zones of occupation in Yugoslavia. As the trucks loaded with Jews trundled along the Dalmatian coast road the Jews, mostly Croatians, waited to see if they took the right or the left forks. The right fork meant that the convoy would leave the coast and head for Croatia and certain death. If they took the left fork the Jews would remain under Italian protection and live.[8] The trucks took the left fork and delivered them to Italian concentration camps. What would happen there?

To tell them, His Excellency General Mario Roatta, commanding general of the Italian Armed Forces in Slovenia and Dalmatia, paid a visit on 27 November to the internment camp at Kraljevice (Porto Re in Italian) on the Dalmatian coast to which the majority of the Jews had been sent. The following day five senior internees, all former Yugoslav bankers or industrialists, sent the general an indication of their gratitude.[9] A survivor who was there, Imre Rochlitz, seventeen at the time, told me that General Roatta had said that if he had submarines in his command, he would transport them all to Italy where they would be really safe.[10]

Think of the date, the place, the characters involved. The internees were Jews and this was the Europe of the holocaust. In the summer and autumn of 1942 the extermination of Jews had gathered momentum. In the middle of August the Jews of Sarajewo had been rounded up[11] while further east during the same week Jews from more than twenty communities in eastern Galicia were deported, including more than 40,000 from Lvov alone, turning the place 'into a city of nightmare and blood'.[12]

In effect what had begun as a conspiracy to disobey an order of Mussolini had become a wider conspiracy to deceive and frustrate Nazi Germany's determination to destroy the Jews of Europe. In March 1943 the German Ambassador had a private audience with the Duce in which Mussolini promised to take a tougher line with his generals in the future.[13] Nothing changed. Until the sudden armistice on 8 September 1943 ended the Axis partnership no Jew under the protection of the Italian forces was ever surrendered to the Germans, the French, the Croatians or anybody else.

Pierre Laval was not the only contemporary puzzled by the paradox. Italy, a fascist state committed to anti-semitic policies at home, allied with Nazi Germany abroad, and utterly dependent on the Germans for raw materials, more or less openly thwarted Hitler's will. What were Mussolini's motives? Did he connive at the behaviour of his generals and diplomats or was their behaviour a genuine mutiny?

Jews who benefited from Italian protection were the first to try to answer these questions. Isaac Schneersohn, first president of the now world-famous *Centre de Documentation Juive Contemporaine* of Paris, described its establishment:

> It was under the Italian occupation at Grenoble that I assembled my first collaborators. In the midst of the summer of 1943, at the very moment when Italy was about to be defeated and Germany at the point of taking over . . . the first meeting of the Center was held.[14]

It was hardly surprising that among the early documentary publications of the Centre in 1946 was Leon Poliakov's *La condition des Juifs en France sous l'occupation italienne* and that the centre should extend its study to the Jews of the other two zones of occupation in Leon Poliakov and Jacques Sabille, *Jews under the Italian Occupation* of 1954. Poliakov and Sabille provided documentary evidence that the Italians had behaved as they were alleged to have behaved. Since then a trickle of historians writing in English, Italian and Hebrew have asked the basic question: why did the Italians save Jews?[15]

It is an astonishing story, occasionally told but never satisfactorily explained. Susan Zuccotti in her *The Italians and the Holocaust* has made the most recent attempt. In the end, she has to admit 'But when all is said, something still seems missing.'[16] The official documentary history of the Vatican during the Second World War makes the same point, 'Berlin ran into an opposition which the official documents have never entirely explained.'[17]

One reason for the feeling that 'something is missing' is that only half the question has been asked. Why did the Italians save Jews? Why did the Germans let them? If the Germans had really wanted to do so, they could have exerted pressure on supplies, without which the Italian war effort could not proceed. We know what Hitler could do when enraged and we know what he did do to Vichy France after 8 November 1942, to Italy after 8 September 1943 and to Hungary after 19 March 1944. What held Hitler, Himmler and the rest of the German armed forces from forcing Italy to surrender what were, in the end, a handful of saved among the millions of damned?

The question goes to the very core of the greatest crime in human history but in a way which links the holocaust directly both to the Axis partnership and to the course of the war. In order to understand the set of circumstances which allowed at most some 50,000 Jews in the three Italian zones of occupation to escape the gas chambers (some only for a while), the historian has to consider the whole interconnectedness of the Second World War. Extermination of Jews was not a random part of the Nazi war effort but its very heart and *raison d'être*. To understand how and why these Jews survived is to grasp the essence of the war itself.

In 1962 F.W. Deakin published his great study of the Axis partnership, *The Brutal Friendship*.[18] He caught the essential features of the personal relations, the diverging objectives and the inevitable frictions of a war-time alliance between two totalitarian dictatorships superficially so similar but structurally so different. Yet he never mentioned the holocaust as a factor in Nazi-fascist relations. He failed to see the connection between the extermination of the Jews and the collapse of the Axis, because the true Italian attitude to the holocaust remained a deep secret. By 1943 the Italians realized that their conspiracy to frustrate it might cost them their lives so they hid the documents which recorded their share in it. Deakin caught the spirit of the Axis but missed its most extraordinary episode, the Italian determination to have no part in the German 'final solution'.

At the same time that Deakin published *The Brutal Friendship* the Eichmann trial in Jerusalem uncovered much, but not all, of the story of Italian behaviour towards the Jews in Italian zones of occupation. In the heart of Nazi-occupied Europe, in the midst of the fury of destruction, witnesses told of Italian officers, diplomats and civil servants who simply refused to be part of the crime: consuls who forged passports, generals who bent rules, ambassadors who disobeyed orders, ordinary citizens who broke their country's strict racial laws. Hannah Arendt, who attended the trial, wrote in her famous *Eichmann in Jerusalem*:

> What in Denmark was the result of an authentically political sense, an inbred comprehension of the requirements and responsibilities of citizenship and independence . . . was in Italy the outcome of the almost automatic general humanity of an old and civilized people.[19]

Arendt's book, like Deakin's, has become a classic. To it we owe the now familiar concept of the 'banality of evil' which she saw unfolded in the thousands of German bureaucratic decisions to murder the entire Jewish people. Yet as Deakin missed the holocaust, Arendt missed the Axis. In effect, she never noticed the 'banality of the good', the semi-official character of Italian behaviour. Her eye caught the dark but missed the light. Hence she could see the remarkable story but not the problem of policy. Armies act on orders. Civil servants give and receive directives. Ambassadors carry out the instructions of their superiors. Fascist Italy was a totalitarian state and a pillar of the Axis. Italian policy toward the Jews took place in the midst of a war under a regime caught in the tangles of its own complex and contradictory nature and tied to a partner more complex and still more brutal. The full story has to put the Italian behaviour, the Axis and the holocaust into the context of the war and the course of events.

Much of this book tries to tell that story: how the Italians got involved, almost by accident, in protecting Jews, first in Croatia, later in Greece and France; how what began in the turmoil of ethnic struggle in Yugoslavia ended by making the Italian 2nd Army the protector of Jewish refugees in Croatia and Dalmatia; and how in their turn the Germans put more and more pressure on their Axis partner to surrender that handful of Jews. The story itself, a moment of light in the darkest night of the human soul, deserves telling for its own sake but it raises wider, insistent and more complicated issues. Why did the principal Italian conspirators act as they did?

No other fascist regime behaved this way. It is true that the Rumanian regime, to the consternation of Eichmann, suddenly ceased deporting Jews in October 1942, but the Rumanian 2nd Army had slaughtered Jews in southern Russia so promiscuously and shoved Jews out of their zone so brutally that even German butchers like Martin Luther of the German foreign office spoke of 'illegal . . . wild deportations'.[20] The Bulgarian regime refused after March 1943 to surrender 'its' Jews, that is, the Jews of 'old Bulgaria', but the Jews of the Bulgarian zones of occupation in Thrace and Macedonia, that is, alien Jews, had been delivered without protest to the SS. Admiral Horthy in Hungary made a clear distinction between Magyar Jews, 'who are as good Hungarians as you or I',[21] and the alien Jews who could be deported. Other regimes and ethnic groups participated with varying degrees of enthusiasm in the extermination of the Jews. The Nazis needed help to collect and to murder six million people and they got it from Latvians and Lithuanians, from French policemen and Croatian priests, from Rumanian colonels and Hungarian gentlemen. The Italians not only refused; they made no distinction between 'their' Jews and the rest. Indeed in the spring of 1943 the Italian 4th Army in France housed refugee Jews in some of the best resorts along the Riviera while the more anti-semitic Italian Ministry of the Interior in Rome made lists of Italian Jews for forced labour.

Arendt explains Italian behaviour as the result of an 'almost automatic general humanity of an old and civilized people' and there is much truth in that observation. But it's too simple. It's not the way the fascist regime looked to Italian socialists, trade unionists, liberals and other victims of its violence, to thousands of prisoners in the regime's jails, to the people of Ethiopia, to Spanish villagers, to the Slovene civilians interned or shot as hostages and to the victims of Italian reprisals in Greece. Many of those active in saving Jews committed acts later judged to be war crimes. After October 1943 Hitler established Mussolini in a puppet regime in northern Italy known as the 'Republic of Salò'. The new regime adopted a charter which deprived Jews of citizenship and declared the Jews to be an 'enemy nationality'.[22] Italian police and militia rounded up Jews with as much ferocity as the most rabid anti-semites in Hungary. Fossoli was an Italian concentration camp but a real one. There were Italians who hated Jews; Salò put them in power.

Even before Salò there were paradoxes in Italian treatment of the Jews. Those Jews saved by the Italians in their zones of occupation owed their lives to a fascist state which prided itself on its brutality and which claimed to be, and in some ways was, a totalitarian dictatorship. The state which ruthlessly deprived patriotic and distinguished Italian Jews of rights, property and position under the 'racial laws' of 1938 turned into the saviour of alien Jews by 1941. The story is much, much more complicated than Hannah Arendt supposed and cannot be explained by large strokes with a broad brush.

An adequate explanation needs to weave a single narrative thread, the fate of the handful of Jews under Italian protection, into a much broader fabric: the character of Hitler's relations with Mussolini; grand strategy in the Russian and Mediterranean theatres; the progress of the war in North Africa and on the Russian front; the complex, bloody rivalries among the populations of the Balkans; the instability of Nazi and fascist puppet states; the rise of conflicting guerrilla and resistance movements; Allied moves and counter-moves; the action and inaction of the Christian and Muslim communities; the role and intervention of the Vatican and the Catholic hierarchy; and the constant struggles among generals, diplomats. bureaucrats, party bosses and favourites for power and position at the courts of the two fascist dictators. Above all, it has to get the timing right. Acts, even acts of virtue, depend on what the clock says.

The Germans watched the same clock as their Italian ally. Their forces operated in the same zones, often, as in Russia or Africa, under joint command. In the Balkans the Axis had clearly marked zones of operation but the anti-partisan campaigns needed joint staff work. As I used German and Italian documentary sources I kept stumbling over the contrasts. In the files of the German general who represented the *Wehrmacht* in Croatia I found many letters, mostly private, in which German officers and civilians described Italian behaviour toward Jews in Italian-occupied Yugoslavia. I found no document, not even a private, hand-written note, in which any German officer or NCO ever expressed the slightest sympathy with Italian behaviour to the Jews. In the entire enormous file of the German armies in the Balkans, I only saw one German document in which the word 'ethical' appears. Italian documents use such vocabulary all the time. And then there was the stark fact that every Jew who fell into the hands of the *Wehrmacht* went to a concentration camp. No Jew under Italian protection did.

Comparison between German and Italian behaviour must be made – indeed the story of how Italians saved Jews while Germans murdered them cannot be told in any other way – but easy generalizations about national character will not do. Jewish policy in Italy and Germany, as was true of all other policy, arose from a complex matrix of institutions, traditions, habits, customs, unspoken assumptions, conflicts both structural and personal, laws and their evasion, leadership, order and chaos; in short, out of the almost infinite complexity of the interrelations we call for short 'reality'.

This has not been an easy book to research. It reminded me of a huge jigsaw puzzle on which the player works without the picture on the box, without an idea of the number of pieces and without even knowing if they are all there. I am certain, even as I write, that part of the puzzle will always be missing. That part of policy-making which rests on the unspoken assumption, on winks and nods, on the exchange of glances, can never be recaptured. I am convinced that the gradual awareness of the German intention to exterminate the entire Jewish people made a profound difference to the way the Italian political class behaved, not least because, as I shall try to show, that knowledge reached it at the moment when a series of crises in North Africa and on the Russian front suddenly brought the prospect of defeat and the end of the regime into view. Such feelings did not have to be put on paper. All insiders knew what was at stake.

It has been equally difficult to write. The interaction of so many factors at different levels poses exceptionally challenging problems of historical narration. Everything affects everything else but not always at the same time in the same way or with the same force. The themes intertwine. There ought to be a sort of historical polyphony in which all the themes develop independently but the listener hears them as a whole. Instead, like all writers, I have to put one word after another. I have to set out each chain of events separately and trace it line by line and sentence by sentence.

Just telling the story was not enough. Again and again I found myself explaining Italian or German behaviour or reading documents in the light of what I knew about Italian and German history. Culture, understood widely, made clear to me why the two allies, confronting the same crises and crimes, behaved so differently. Culture is not merely that bit of life described in the arts pages of daily papers; it is a thick, if invisible, amalgam of historical experience, political institutions, social practices, personal habits, language, values and norms.

After many false starts, I finished by dividing the book into 'The Problem', 'Events', 'Explanations', and 'Conclusions'. 'Events', as the name implies, traces the course of the war, the evolution of the Axis and Italian treatment of the Jews from June 1940, to 8 September 1943, the day the Allies announced an armistice with the kingdom of Italy. 'Events' finishes on the day after the armistice when Roberto Ducci, head of the Croatian department and one of the original conspirators in the Italian Foreign Ministry, disobeyed instructions to burn the secret files on the Jews and removed them to his home for safe-keeping. His rash act would have meant death for his fellow conspirators had the Gestapo found the documents; it also made it possible to tell this story. Actors in great historical dramas frequently turn and asked to be judged by historians; few are good enough to supply documents as well.

There is a certain artificiality in making such a sharp distinction between narrative and explanation. Narratives 'explain' too. In ordinary life we respond to a question about the cause of something by saying, 'well, it happened this way' and telling the story of how the thing 'came about', but I saw early on that such a natural procedure would not work. I knew that my account was incomplete. Certain crucial files did not survive the war; certain crucial actors left no diaries or private letters and some of the most important truths were never recorded, especially the sorts of knowledge, feeling or assumption which people at the time simply took for granted. Hence a part of my account, and I don't know how much, depends on guesswork or 'feel'. This is true of all chronological history and is not in itself unusual.

What bothered me was something else. I could not escape the nagging feeling that simply telling the story, no matter how well, would never be enough. In my first draft I tried to thicken the narrative with comment but that merely clogged the flow of the narration and annoyed the readers. 'Thick narrative' failed both to tell the story clearly and to isolate causation. I wanted to exploit the parallels between German and Italian behaviour in the face of the same stimuli. Conventional narrative does not lend itself to comparative analysis.

Finally I saw that this book was really, if indirectly, about the holocaust and that it, the research that went into it, and indeed the life of its author, have all been dedicated to the question, 'How could Nazism and the holocaust have happened?' Ever since that icy February morning in 1956 when from the deck of an American troop ship I could just see the spires of Bremerhaven through the freezing fog, I have been obsessed with Europe, its cultures, its languages, its variety, its wars and its disasters. I learned German quickly, and as a GI and later as a trainee banker in Germany I read, listened and absorbed. None of it was part of my past. I had spent the war safely in the United States. My grandparents had emigrated in time from Eastern Europe but there I was, an American Jew in Germany, in a place where my right to exist was denied only a few years before. More than thirty years later the question still haunts me. The motto of my life has been that Heine phrase,

> Denke ich an Deutschland in der Nacht,
> Dann bin ich um den Schlaf gebracht.
> (If I think of Germany in the night,
> Then I am robbed of my sleep.)

I learned Italian and studied fascism for the same reason, to understand 'how it could have happened'. I took up this research because it gave me a chance to try to answer the same question. Here were, after all, a small group of people who said 'no'. 'The thing', said General Roatta, 'is just not possible.' Why did he say it when his German opposite number *Generaloberst* Löhr said 'yes'? Was it because of their persons, the states they served, the uniforms they wore? If I knew the answers to these smaller questions, I might know a little more about the larger ones.

Attentive readers may feel uneasy that, on the one hand, I justify the peculiar layout of the book by reference to the holocaust and, on the other, offer the model of historical discussion and disagreement as the way to understand it. The holocaust, they may feel, is not an historical subject like others. The right response is awe, mourning and repentance. The rest should be silence. I reject that view. Controversy – informed, humane, open controversy – is one of the very few worthy responses that this generation can give to the horror of the holocaust. Its bestial contempt for all that is lightest, freest, most playful and hence most human cannot be met by mourning only. We must affirm those very qualities that Hitler and his dark legions wished to destroy, the free exercise of the human intellect and the imagination.

As witness in my defence I call on Primo Levi who for millions, Jew and non-Jew alike, became the interpreter of the holocaust. There is a section in his book *If This be a Man* called 'the Song of Ulysses' in which Levi and a young French Jew, known as 'Pikolo', have to fetch the slops for the lunch-time 'meal' for a work gang. They take their time and in the long walk there and back Levi becomes obsessed with the need to remember and interpret for his French comrade the great passage in Dante's *Inferno* which stands for the whole human quest, the final journey of Ulysses:

It's late, it's late, we're already at the kitchen. I have to finish:

> Tre volte il fe'girar con tutte l'acque,
> Alla quarta levar la poppa in suso
> E la prora ire in giú, come altri piacque.

I hold Pikolo back, it's absolutely necessary and urgent that he listen, that he understand that 'come altrui piacque', before it's too late. Tomorrow he or I could be dead, or never see each other again. I have to say it, explain the middle ages, the anachronism so human and so necessary and so utterly unexpected, and much more, something gigantic which I have only now seen, in the intuition of a second, perhaps the why of our destiny, of our being here today.[23]

11

It seems to me that this passage, one of the greatest hymns to literature ever written, stands as a permanent monument to the strength of the human spirit. Poetry, art, thought itself, outlive the butchers of Auschwitz. By remembering fragments of Dante, a medieval epic poem, Primo Levi, an Italian Jew with a number tattooed on his forearm, saved his humanity in the midst of the dark night of human history.

I have spent my adult life as a professional historian; as Goethe once observed, 'in the service of a clock whose hands are forever motionless'. I used to give a seminar course on the Nazi seizure of power. Every May in spite of my best efforts the Nazis came to power anyway. I could not stop the 'March on Rome' no matter how eloquently I lectured on it. All I could do – have attempted in this book – is to understand and, having understood, to explain it to others, not because I believe that we learn lessons from the past, which is unique and unrepeatable, nor because great laws of human nature can be deduced from a close examination of past events, but because the act of understanding is itself valuable. Out of the deepest tragedies of mankind, out of the stuff of history itself, what Gibbon once dismissed as 'little more than the register of the crimes, follies and misfortunes of mankind', I can try to make sense, to comprehend, to understand. This book records in the end what a few good men did in an evil time. It is a modest monument to them and to those whom they could not save, but it is also a work of history. Is history any use? About as useful as Auden thought poetry was, as he wrote in his 'In Memory of W.B. Yeats':

> For poetry makes nothing happen: it survives
> In the valley of its making where executives
> Would never want to tamper, flows on south
> From ranches of isolation and the busy griefs,
> Raw towns that we believe and die in; it survives,
> A way of happening, a mouth.[24]

PART I
THE EVENTS

PHASE ONE

UNSYSTEMATIC MURDER: WAR IN THE BALKANS

April 1941 to June 1942

Germany invaded Poland on 1 September 1939 without consulting its Axis partner. Italy remained neutral. It was not an heroic posture and the Duce found the situation extremely embarrassing. The swift German victory over Poland turned embarrassment into humiliation. Germany needed no assistance from Italy and Europe no longer required the Duce's mediation. As he said to his generals on 31 March 1940,

> If the war continues, to think that Italy can remain outside it to the end is absurd and impossible . . . Italy cannot remain neutral for the whole duration of the war without resigning from its role, without disqualifying itself, without reducing itself to the level of Switzerland multiplied by ten.[1]

Precisely what Italy would do in the war had not been deeply considered. In August of 1939 Mussolini announced to his military chiefs that in the event of an Anglo-French attack on Italy, he would order a defensive position around metropolitan Italy tied to a double offensive: one 'certain' against Greece and one 'probable' against Yugoslavia. Fortunato Minniti in a recent article remarks mildly, 'This orientation is difficult to interpret . . . you respond with an offensive approach but the offensive is directed against third countries and not against the aggressors.'[2]

Italy was unprepared for war. Colonel Antonio Gandin attended the military parade on 9 May 1939, the birthday of the Empire, and went back to his office deeply depressed:

> infantry: of four grenadier and infantry regiments only one (81st) has the complete new equipment . . .
> motorized infantry: one regiment with automobiles for infantry of the new type, one with vehicles of the old type . . .

15

artillery: practically all old material. . . . In conclusion it is easy to sum up: prevalence of antiquated equipment, shortage of new material.[3]

Italian war preparations amounted to bluff and bluster. Mussolini talked about 'eight million bayonets'. Ciano recorded in his diary on 29 April 1939, after a Council of Ministers:

The military make great play with a lot of names. They multiply the number of divisions, but in reality these are so small that they scarcely have more than the strength of regiments. The ammunition depots are short of ammunition. Artillery is out-moded. Our anti-aircraft and anti-tank weapons are altogether lacking. There has been a good deal of bluffing in the military sphere, and even the Duce himself has been deceived – a tragic bluff. We will not talk about the question of the Air Force. Valle states that there are 3,006 first-line planes, while the Navy information service says there are only 982.[4]

Three days before the Italians declared war on France and Britain in the intoxication of the German victories of April and May 1940, a senior general, Quirino Armellino, recorded his sense of foreboding:

So we are about to be thrown into a war with the hope that it could finish tomorrow with a victorious peace but could also be long and hard – in an incredible, terrible situation which could end by submerging us all entirely. If the history of this is ever done, our successors will see the card that we are playing and judge us harshly.[5]

Strategic thinking had not advanced much beyond general gloom by April 1940. Italy was still not prepared for war. The Chief of the General Staff reckoned that Italy had reached about 40 per cent of its wartime requirements but Mussolini was becoming impatient. During 1939 and 1940 the Duce had managed to achieve complete command over the Italian armed forces and by May 1940 had established a command structure 'on the German model (alien, however, to Italian traditions)'.[6] Mussolini, as First Marshal of the Empire, commanded the Royal Italian armed forces as delegate of the King and used a Chief of the General Staff, who coordinated the staffs of the three services, to do so. Mussolini stood to Badoglio and his successors as Hitler did to Keitel.

On 11 April, Marshall Badoglio put the position to Mussolini quite clearly:

Our forces, even if the preparation were complete, would always be inadequate for a decisive impact in any sector whatever . . .

unless a ponderous German action had really so prostrated the adversary's forces to justify any audacity. Such a decision, it is clear, is reserved to you, Duce. We carry out your orders.[7]

By the end of May, the enemy seemed prostrate enough for Mussolini to add a kick or two. In a series of lightning strikes unparalleled in the history of warfare, the *Wehrmacht* had overrun Denmark, Norway, Holland, Belgium and Luxemburg and broken through the impregnable French defences. Mussolini decided to act before the Germans won the war without any Italian participation. On 29 May 1940 the Duce explained to his senior generals 'the geometric logic' which revealed to him, the great strategist, that 'we absolutely cannot avoid war'.[8] Renzo De Felice, Mussolini's biographer, writes: 'Nobody made objections. A very brief discussion followed the words of the Duce but limited entirely to a few technical aspects.'[9]

Italy entered the Second World War without clear objectives, without adequate preparation and without honour. On 10 June 1940 Italy declared war on the Allies, an act which the French President, Paul Reynaud, described in a broadcast as 'a stab in the back' and others in even less complimentary similes.

The fortnight of hostilities added to Italian embarrassment. Against a French Army which the Germans had defeated and demoralized, the Italian armed forces got nowhere. The French held the frontier along the Alps and the Riviera and even threatened to break the Italian lines. The official German history of the Second World War describes the two weeks of fighting on the Alpine front as 'a débâcle'. The figures of dead and wounded speak for themselves: the Italians: 631 dead, 2,631 wounded, 616 missing and 2,151 victims of frostbite; the French: 32 dead, 42 wounded and 150 missing.[10] In spite of that, Hitler – and not for the last time – covered the shame of his ally and granted the Italians a status in the armistice negotiations to which their military accomplishments had not entitled them.

Hitler also conceded substantial chunks of the globe to his Axis partner with the generosity of the gambler who has just won a jackpot. When Ciano visited Berlin in early July the Führer told him, as Ciano reported, 'Everything which concerns the Mediterranean, that includes the Adriatic, is a purely Italian question into which he [Hitler] does not intend to involve himself, approving *a priori* whatever decision and whatever action could be accomplished by the Duce.'[11]

In July 1940 generous impulses could be indulged. A complete German victory seemed near. No sensible British government would carry on the fight after the fall of France. It cost little to concede spheres of influence to Italy which would fall to the Axis in any case.

On the other hand, Hitler had a shrewd idea of Italian strength and a week after Ciano returned from Berlin he declined 'in a definite and courteous way the offer to send an Italian expeditionary force' for the invasion of Britain. The Duce was 'very much annoyed' but could do nothing.[12]

The summer and early autumn of 1940 was a difficult time of waiting for both dictators. In spite of constant hectoring the Italian forces in North Africa made slow progress on the route to the Suez Canal. Russian troop movements alarmed Hitler and the Battle of Britain began slowly and perceptibly to turn against the *Luftwaffe*. The German naval attaché in Rome reported to Berlin that the Italian navy showed lack of offensive spirit, and the early engagements against the Royal Navy had not encouraged it to develop any. On 19 September 1940 the German Foreign Minister, Joachim von Ribbentrop, visited Rome and told Mussolini that Greece and Yugoslavia remained 'exclusively Italian interests'. In return Mussolini promised von Ribbentrop that 'militarily he would not undertake anything for the time being'.[13] At a meeting between the Führer and the Duce at the Brenner Pass on 4 October, the Germans offered the Italians armoured units for the attack on Egypt. Badoglio replied evasively. He wanted to reserve that theatre for an exclusively Italian triumph on the banks of the Nile.[14]

On 6 October, Mussolini ordered the demobilization of 600,000 out of the 1,100,000 who had been called to the colours.[15] On 15 October, while the army was disbanding its units, Mussolini announced to his supreme army commanders and his commanding generals in Italian-occupied Albania his intention to attack Greece. The official minutes of the meeting at Palazzo Venezia read as follows:

> The purpose of this meeting is to define the means of the action
> – in its general character – which I have decided to initiate against
> Greece . . . Having defined the question thus, I have stabilized
> the date which in my view must not be delayed even by an hour:
> that is, the 26th of this month.[16]

Mussolini left his generals less than two weeks to prepare an operation in mountainous, difficult terrain, at the wrong time of year, with no secure means of transportation, with port facilities inadequate to the number of men, horses and guns soon to pass through them, with notional forces of 70,000 men to the supposed 30,000 of the Greeks, and with the army at home demobilizing. No military operation has ever been more absurdly conceived and disastrously executed than the Italian attack on Greece. The generals at the meeting who knew the truth said nothing and those who talked could no longer tell truth from rhetoric. There was no opposition, no strategic planning and, above all, no German help. Mussolini intended to have his revenge. This time it would be Hitler who read of Mussolini's bold stroke in the newspapers.

The result was chaos. A typical experience was that of the crack Alpine division 'Pusteria' which was hastily ordered to join the 9th Army in Albania on 16 October. It finally got there on 24 November, and was assigned to the 11th Army under General Geloso. On 2 December 1940, Geloso reported to General Soddu, Vice Chief of the General Staff, that the 'Pusteria' had,

> lacked its commanding officer and the entire headquarters staff, the greater part of the baggage train and pack animals, all its supporting services . . . and by a true miracle of manoeuvre on the part of the few vehicles available had been put into the line anyway.[17]

In the four and a half months which followed the attack on Greece at the end of October the Italians eventually deployed over 300,000 men and succeeded – just – in not losing the Albanian territory from which they launched the attack. The Greeks, inferior in numbers and equipment, fought the Italian army to a bloody standstill and inflicted deep wounds on the national psyche. The Royal Navy inflicted real wounds on the Italian capital ships, sinking the *Littorio*, *Duilio* and *Cavour* while they were riding at anchor at Taranto on the night of 11 November, and on 9 December the British counter-attacked at Sidi-el-Barrani, which began a headlong retreat by Marshall Graziani's African army.

Mussolini reacted to the defeats hysterically and issued an 'order' on 10 November that every Greek city with more than 10,000 residents be razed to the ground.[18] This was the first of a series of violent orders born of frustration which turned the Balkans into a bloody nightmare. Both German and Italian forces issued such orders. The difference between them was that the Germans carried theirs out.

Next he fired everybody he could think of in the first instance of what came to be known as 'Changing the Guard' and finally he lost his nerve completely. His only hope was to beg Hitler for help. 'There's nothing to be done here. It's grotesque and absurd, but that's the way it is.'[19]

Hitler had 'raged' when he heard the news of the Italian attack on Greece and announced that he had now 'lost any desire for further military cooperation'.[20] Grand Admiral Raeder saw Hitler a week later and told his staff that 'on no occasion was authorization for such an independent action given to the Duce by the Führer'.[21] Goebbels was utterly disgusted by the spectacle. 'Our Allies are turning tail and running. A shameful sight. The English are crowing with triumph.'[22]

As Hitler and the German army watched the Italians flounder in the mountains of Albania their sentiments changed from contempt to alarm. Neither the German nor the Italian High Commands gave any serious thought to the geographical implications of Italy's declaration of war in June 1940. Before 1939 the Axis partnership existed on paper and in speeches from balconies. No combined operations were ever planned. Only one serious meeting of staffs took place: on 19 March 1940, at the Brenner Pass. General Enno von Rintelen, German military attaché in Rome from 1936 to 1943, explained to his American captors after the war:

[The Germans] had apparently not fully taken into account that by Italy's entry into the war, the entire Mediterranean area would automatically become involved in the war and thus the theater of war greatly extended . . . . Significant for this is the fact that Italy entered the war on 10 June, 1940 without the effects of such a step having been discussed beforehand and without the German General Staff knowing anything about Italian intentions.[23]

Before Mussolini's sudden attack on Greece in October 1940 von Rintelen went to see Marshall Badoglio and General Roatta to ask the significance of troop movements which the Germans had observed in Albania. Both lied about the Italian intentions. Roatta later apologised by observing that 'Mussolini had strictly forbidden us to give any information to the German Army about Italian intentions.'[24]

Italy invaded Greece on 28 October 1940. The following day the first British troops landed on Greek soil. The RAF now had forward bases close to the Rumanian oilfields at Ploesti, which, as *Luftwaffe* General Alexander Löhr declared, 'would have been catastrophic for Germany, since they were the most important, indeed the only really effective, oil sources for us.'[25]

By October 1940 Hitler had in any case begun to turn his attention from west to east. The German air force had not subdued the RAF. Landing an army in Britain during the winter of 1940 could not be imagined, so Hitler considered an attack on the Soviet Union instead. Since September 1940 General Friedrich Paulus, first Quartermaster General in the Army High Command, had been assigned the co-ordination of German strategic planning for a war against Russia and on 5 December reported the results. Hitler took the occasion for a grand review of the strategic position. European hegemony required a struggle against Russia but not quite yet. First the Mediterranean mess must be cleared up, Gibraltar seized and Greece occupied. The generals concluded that Hitler had not yet finally made up his mind.[26] A few days later he issued Führer Directive No. 20 for Operation Marita:

1) The outcome of the battles in Albania cannot be foreseen. In view of the threatening position in Albania it is doubly important that the English be prevented from forming a Balkan alliance which would provide them with a dangerous basis for air operations against Italy and the Rumanian oil fields.
2) My intention is therefore:
    a) to build up in the next few months a strong battle group in southern Rumania
    b) after the improvement in the weather, probably in March, to deploy this battle group through Bulgaria to seize the north coast of the Aegean and – should this be necessary – the whole of continental Greece.[27]

Hitler reassured his army command that the Greek operation would be a side-show and not interfere with planning for the Russian campaign.

By the end of December 1940 the Greek counter-offensive had ground to a halt. Hitler breathed a little easier. If the Italians could just hold the line, his attack on Greece would relieve them and chase the British planes away from the oilfields. Unfortunately, the Italians had collapsed in North Africa while Hitler had been worrying about Greece. Sidi-el-Barrani fell on 10 December and the British took Bardia on 5 January 1941. The Italian high command had already begged the Germans for air support in Libya but after the fall of Bardia they asked for an armoured corps as well.[28] On 11 January Hitler issued 'Führer Directive No. 22' which promised help.[29]

Mussolini had problems at home too. The humiliation in Albania 'surprised [Italian] public opinion all the more forcefully', wrote the police superintendent in Forlì, 'in view of the strength of the illusion of an easy war'.[30] The collapse in Africa began to erode Mussolini's own self-esteem. He told his generals in Albania in tones of resignation: 'The situation is not and cannot be brilliant . . . as far as we are concerned it is not possible to do great things because of our training. On the other hand, war will train the troops.'[31]

Worst of all he had to face Hitler. The two dictators met at the train station in Puch on 19 January 1941, and made their way to the Obersalzberg. Mussolini was frightened by the prospect of being told off for his failures and for once allowed a military delegation led by General Alfredo Guzzoni, Deputy Chief of the General Staff, to accompany him. Ciano was appalled: 'I don't like him. He is a man who stirs up trouble, he is untrustworthy, and, besides, it is humiliating to present to the Germans such a small man with such a big paunch and with dyed hair.[32]

Guzzoni had another embarrassing defect, an outspoken Hungarian Jewish mistress who made 'defeatist remarks',[33] but that seems to have been no obstacle to his career in fascist Italy. In spite of his appearance and compromising social habits, he was in General Rintelen's view, 'a practical soldier who stood his ground ably in all the discussions'.[34]

Mussolini's fears were soon dispelled. Ciano could scarcely believe it:

> The meeting is cordial and, what surprises me most, spontaneously cordial. There are no hidden condolences in the air – condolences that Mussolini feared . . . Hitler talked for two hours on his coming intervention in Greece . . . with unusual mastery. Our military experts are impressed. Guzzoni, wth his tightly stretched paunch and little dyed wig, according to Alfieri, made a poor impression on the Germans . . . Mussolini is elated as he always is after a meeting with Hitler.'[35]

Hitler genuinely liked Mussolini. A few months later, when Italy's performance as an ally was certainly no better, he told his entourage that, 'a meeting with the Duce is always a special joy; he is a very great personality'.[36]

That affection was sorely tried over the next few weeks. Early in February 1941 General R.N. O'Connor drove his 7th Armoured Division across 200 kilometres of desert and on 7 February cut off the retreat of the Italian 10th Army along the coast of Cyrenaica. The Italians fought furiously to break the ring. The British had precisely twelve operational 'Cruiser' tanks at the end but the Italian 10th Army had been destroyed. Since 9 December 1940 the British XIII Corp, composed of two divisions, had defeated ten Italian divisions and captured 130,000 prisoners, 180 medium and 200 light tanks. Its own losses amounted to 500 dead, 1,373 wounded and 55 missing.[37] General Rommel, who arrived in Libya on 13 February with the first German troops, summed up the Italian defeat simply:

> The failures of Graziani were caused principally by the fact that a large part of the Italian Army, not being motorized, in the open expanse of the desert, was in the power of the British, who were weaker but completely motorized.[38]

On the same day Goebbels wrote gloomily:

Reports from Italy mention profoundest defeatism. These days, the Führer is their only hope. Ciano is absolutely finished, and the Duce's popularity is approaching zero level. Added to this are disorganization, corruption, in short, a state verging on chaos. We must soon make a move, or Italy will crumble into nothingness.[39]

By mid-February 1941 Italy had ceased to be a great power; it could no longer make independent foreign or military policy. If fascist Italy were to win the war, Nazi Germany would have to win it. Everybody in Italy at every level of society knew that truth, whether they talked or kept silent. It posed a dilemma for most Italians which worsened as the war grew more brutal and knowledge of German atrocities began to trickle along the channels of communication: was it not better to lose the war and be rid of Nazi Germany than to win it and live in the Nazi new order? Marshall Caviglia summed it up in April 1941, in the midst of further brilliant German victories in Yugoslavia and Greece:

> Strange the situation in Italy. The greater part of the population outside of the fascist clique, that is 99 per cent of the Italians, desire that the Axis lose the war and expresses its real wishes in the following play on words: 'se la va male, la va bene; se la va bene, la va male' [if things go well, they go badly; if they go badly, they go well][40]

In any community the members take certain things for granted, often the most important things. The generation of Englishmen who fought the Second World War never seriously entertained the thought that they would lose it. They knew that they were superior to all foreigners and would win in the end. The generation of Italians who fought the same war had no such certainty; after February 1941 they knew Italy must lose whatever the outcome.

At 5.15 a.m on 6 April 1941 the *Wehrmacht* crossed the frontiers of Yugoslavia and Greece from the north and the east. The 2nd Army under *Generaloberst* von Weichs invaded Yugoslavia from the north; the 12th Army under Field Marshall List and the 1st Armoured Group under *Generaloberst* von Kleist invaded from Bulgaria and headed west into Yugoslavia and south into Greece; the Hungarian 3rd Army occupied the Banat in the north while the 4th German Air Fleet under General Alexander Löhr used its 400 bombers, 210 fighters and 170 reconnaissance planes to destroy the Yugoslav air force on the ground. The Italian 2nd Army under General Ambrosio moved south from Istria along the Dalmatian coast, while the Italian 9th and 11th Armies looked up from their precarious positions on the Greek and Albanian fronts and prepared to advance against a Greek army under attack from the rear.[41]

Zagreb fell on 10 April, Belgrade on the 12th and six days later Yugoslavia capitulated. On 27 April German troops, after unexpectedly fierce resistance from the Greek and British forces, finally entered Athens.[42]

The Germans and their allies redrew the Balkan map.(See Map 1, p. 26) Yugoslavia ceased to exist. On 13 April 1941 the Independent State of Croatia was proclaimed with its capital in Zagreb, its frontiers from the Drau and Danube in the north-east to those parts of the Dalmatian coast left it by the Italians in the south. A line running north-west to south-east divided the new state into German and Italian spheres of influence. Slovenia was split on the same basis with the southern part, including the capital Ljubljana, annexed to Italy, the northern part to Germany. Hungary occupied the Banat and the Voivodina. Bulgaria 'redeemed' what it had always regarded as its ancient provinces of Macedonia and Thrace. Serbia was put under direct German miltary rule and Serbs and their officers were, according to OKW (High Command of the *Wehrmacht*) instructions, 'to be treated exceptionally badly'.[43]

A terrible chapter of misery began for the Balkan peoples amidst the confusion of demoralized but not disarmed military units, changed borders, new authorities, laws and languages and accompanied by fatal miscalculations. Hitler made the first and most fateful. As always careful to prop up the prestige of his friend Mussolini, he left Italy to administer huge tracts of the Balkans because he thought that once the Yugoslav and Greek armies had been defeated, there was nothing for the *Wehrmacht* to do. As he put it, talking of Greece on 10 May 1941,

> Our effort must be directed at getting out of Greece as quickly and with as many units as possible and leaving the security of the entire region to Italy. . . . Whether Italian occupation troops get into conflict with the Greek government does not concern us. A military threat which could have as a consequence a renewed intervention by German troops no longer exists after the defeat of the Greek army and its weapons.[44]

Hitler imagined that the Italians, good for little else, could at least sit on a conquered people, thus releasing German troops for the real battle for European hegemony in Russia and at the same time giving Mussolini the appearance of handsome achievements. To be sure, there were embarrassments such as the Greek refusal to sign an armistice with an Italian army to which they had not surrendered and some absurd claims by Mussolini, as Goebbels noted, in 'a telegram to General Cavallero, in which he claims the victory in Greece as his own . . . . Our people feel something close to hatred for the Italians.'[45]

24

Hitler was wrong and for two reasons. Italian force was always too weak to govern such large areas and the war in the Balkans had only begun. On the same day that Hitler waved his hand over the map and gave Greece to Italy, a Yugoslav colonel called Draza Mihailović, who had not accepted the capitulation of the Yugoslav army, began guerrilla operations in south-west Serbia in the Rawna Gora district. Mihailović and his *cetniks* (a Serbo-Croat word for band) were to go on fighting Germans, Italians, other *cetniks*, partisans (after the invasion of Russia on 22 June 1941) and each other until the war ended. The confusions, divisions and complexities of Balkan politics burst into open warfare among armed bands. The terrain suited guerrilla warfare. There were long traditions of *hajduks* (Turkish: *haydud*, bandit) and *uskoks* (pirates) who went to the woods to wage guerrilla warfare against the Turks. They had never died out, not least because reactionary regimes were prone to use and misuse such people. Now they turned the former territory of Yugoslavia into a permanent source of unrest.

The second miscalculation was Italian. Italy had no real basis for annexing large areas inhabited by Slavs other than the politics of illusion and bluff. Oddly enough Slovenia was inhabited by Slovenes and not even D'Annunzio, the poet of limitless Italian claims, had ever imagined that Ljubljana was an Italian town. Ciano and Ribbentrop, according to General Mario Roatta, at a meeting in Vienna on 21 April 1941, had divided Slovenia and picked out the frontier between Italy and Croatia on a large map

> which showed a border marked in pencil not very clearly, to which a small piece of paper had been attached with a few lines of notes also in pencil. That was it. In such conditions the Italo-Croatian frontier at certain points was absurd. . . . It was an error on Italy's part to have 'annexed' the regions of Yugoslavia assigned to it and yet worse to have introduced immediately Italian civil administration and fascist institutions. . . . In order to make a bit of froth for Rome the fascist hierarchy resorted to *bluff* [English in original] so much so that partisans captured in battle were frequently found to have fascist party membership cards, perfectly authentic ones. distributed to anybody without distinction, even to people who didn't speak a word of Italian, just to augment the number of converts.[46]

Alberto Pirelli, the tyre manufacturer, got the same impression on a visit to Rome in mid-May 1941. The division of Slovenia made no economic sense. The frontier passed so close to the city of Ljubljana that it lost 'its economic rationale. The aqueduct and electricity plants have ended in German hands, the mines and cotton plants too . . .

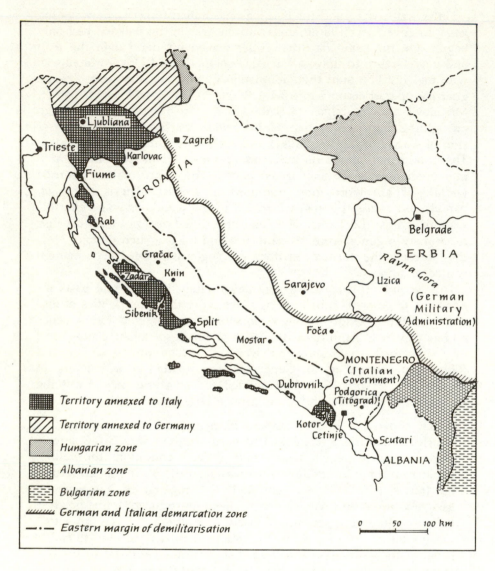

Map 1 German and Italian zones of occupation in Yugoslavia, 1941–43

[there is] widespread discontent with Germany'[47]

Negotiations between Italy and the new Croatian state produced no easy agreement. Ante Pavelić, its leader or *Poglavnik*, modelled himself and his *Ustaši* movement on Mussolini and fascism; indeed, he owed his and its survival to fascist protection and support during the 1930s when Pavelić and his followers were in exile in Italy. In spite of his debt to Italy and to Mussolini, he was appalled when

26

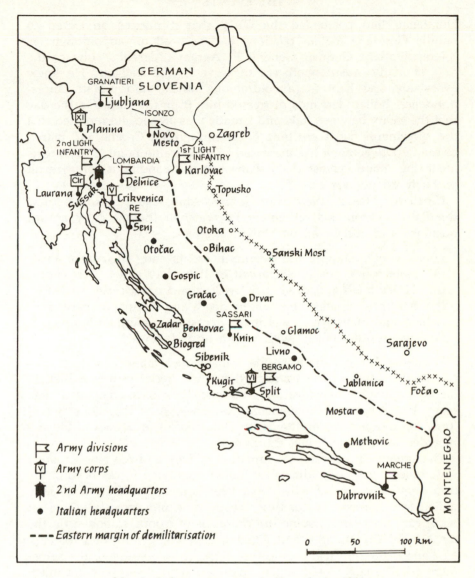

Map 2   Italian army units in Yugoslavia, 1941

the Italians annexed historic Croatian lands on the Dalmatian coast. Most of the coast with its beaches, the Dalmatian islands, the cities of Zara, Dubrovnik, Split and the city and bay of Cetinje became provinces of metropolitan Italy. Hitler refused to intervene and Pavelić had no choice but to sign a state treaty on 18 May 1941 in Rome.

The distinguished Austrian military historian Edmund Glaise von

Horstenau had persuaded the OKW that it needed an expert to handle German-Croatian relations and secured an appointment as 'plenipotentiary German General in Agram [Zagreb]',[48] one of the first of many Austrian officers to serve in the Balkans. He knew everybody and kept up a voluminous official and private correspondence. Italian demands distressed him from the start. On the day that the treaty between Italy and Croatia was signed, he reported that the agreement 'had a crushing effect throughout Croatia and hatred of the new hegemony has increased to an extreme point. . . . Threats are being made against the Italians but the conditions for a revolt probably do not yet exist.'[49]

Ulrich von Hassell, the former German Ambassador in Rome, knew the Italians. From his retirement he watched them occupy absurd positions and speculated on Hitler's motives:

> Border construction in the Balkans nears its end. Their form and the protectorate positions granted to Italy defy belief. It is clear that Hitler has fulfilled all their wishes and consciously so with the thought that later there will be death and damnation between Italians and Slavs which will make necessary a German intervention against the Italians with whom he is furious.[50]

Whatever Hitler's motives, the Italians had made a serious miscalculation. Most of the territory they now declared Italian had no Italian population whatever. It had once been Venetian at a time when lordship had no nationalist overtones. As a local joke put it, 'only the monuments are Italian in Dalmatia'. The politics of illusion recorded another and final triumph.

The agreement between the kingdom of Italy and the new Croatian state called for the withdrawal of Italian occupying forces beyond the thin strip of the coast which had been annexed and from 20 May Italian forces ceased to 'possess the powers and prerogatives of an occupying force and assume the character of troops stationed on the territory of the friendly and allied independent state of Croatia.'[51] No serious thought had been given to the consequences of the agreement. The Italians would be left holding a strip of territory not much wider than a few kilometres in some places. The main rail and road links passed beyond their control for long stretches. If the Croatians made difficulties, the Italians could be seriously embarrassed.

Early in June 1941 Giuseppe Bastianini and his staff arrived at Zara to establish the grandly named Governorship of Dalmatia. Bastianini, a handsome and vigorous man in his early forties, had been a fascist 'of the first hour' and had a reputation for telling Mussolini the truth, something few did by 1941. Like Dino Grandi and several other leading fascists he had stepped sideways from the party into the diplomatic service and served with distinction abroad. Bastianini ordered his staff to put on their dress uniforms of *orbace*, the choicest Sardinian wool, to impress the locals and organized a fine parade to mark his arrival. None of that dispelled the fears of the tiny, resident, Italian-speaking minority. Egidio Ortona, Bastianini's foreign policy expert, noted in his diary that his Italian-speaking, local landlord was full of 'pessimismo',[52] more than justified as events were to show.

A Balkan empire was a poor substitute for the loss of Africa but Mussolini accepted his bit of territory eagerly. Neither the Greek nor Yugoslav armies were properly disarmed and the Italians lacked the forces to repress a rising if it came. What neither Hitler nor Mussolini nor anybody else could have foreseen was that the first threat would come not from the enemies of the Axis but its friends in the new Croatian state. Glaise von Horstenau surveyed its prospects in a long report of 12 May 1941:

> the Croatian revolution is largely the revolution of old men and former imperial Austrian officers. . . . A heavy burden, alongside the Italian mortgage, is the deep conflict with the Serbians, a consequence to a considerable extent of the unholy policies of the Magyars in the last years of the Danube Monarchy.[53]

The new state lacked everything. It scarcely had enough cars to drive its cabinet officers about but it soon developed legislation to please Hitler. Within three weeks of its establishment it passed legislation defining Jews in racial terms. In the months of May and June 1941 it rapidly passed the laws that the Nazis had taken years to work out, prohibiting inter-marriage and employment of Aryan female servants by Jews, and providing for the marking of Jewish stores and persons, registration of property, removal of Jews from the bureaucracy and professions and the 'aryanization' of Jewish capital. As early as May 1941 some of the Jews of Zagreb were rounded up and sent to the Danica camp and later in the summer to the infamous Croatian camp in Jasenovac. The eighty thousand Croatian Jews had been sentenced to death as had the thirty thousand gypsies.[54]

Croatia joined the Nazi New Order and happily paid its dues. When the *Poglavnik* Ante Pavelić called on Hitler on the Obersalzberg in early June, he had a warm welcome.[55] None of this was extraordinary in Hitler's empire. What happened next was unique to Croatia. In early June, the Carabinieri in Split reported streams of Serbian and Jewish refugees crossing into Italian territory with tales of atrocities and massacres carried out by the *Ustaši*, the militia of the Croatian revolution.[56] By 28 June Glaise von Horstenau reported that 'according to reliable reports from countless German military and civil observers during the last few weeks in country and town the *Ustaši* have gone raging mad.'[57]

Serbian and Jewish men, women and children were literally hacked to death. Whole villages were razed to the ground and the people driven into barns to which the *Ustaši* set fire. There is in the Italian Foreign Ministry archive a collection of photographs of the butcher knives, hooks and axes used to chop up Serbian victims. There are photographs of Serb women with breasts hacked off by pocket knives, men with eyes gouged out, emasculated and mutilated.[58] At one point the *Ustaši* had thrown so many corpses into the River Narentva near Matkovic that the government began to pay peasants 100 *kune* for each body hauled out, lest they float downstream into the Italian zone.[59] A Serb friend of mine remembers being on board a ferry on the River Sava as a child and seeing chopped-up human remains floating downstream from Jasenovac.

Neighbours murdered neighbours, as Menachem Shelach points out, people whose families had lived side by side for generations.[60] The Croatian militia unleashed an unsystematic campaign of murder, often egged on by local priests. When an Italian junior officer asked a Croatian priest for his authorization, the priest replied, 'I have one authorization and only one: to kill the Serb sons of bitches.'[61]

Nobody can say to this day how many Serbs the *Ustaši* murdered but it must have run into hundreds of thousands, nor can anybody say why. Traian Stoianovich argues that the *Ustaši*, like other extreme nationalists in the Balkans, came from 'marginal elements of all classes' while the leadership came from what he calls 'middle sectors'.[62] The sociology is familiar; the extreme brutality is not.

Observers within the German army disapproved of what they saw as uncontrolled violence. Early in July Glaise reported with dismay that the Croatians had expelled all Serbian intellectuals from Zagreb. When he went to see the *Poglavnik*, Pavelić promised humane treatment for them. The fact that they were only allowed 30 kg of luggage made Glaise suspicious.[63] He had good reason. On 10 July he reported the 'utterly inhuman treatment of the Serbs living in Croatia', the embarrassment of the Germans who 'with six battalions of foot soldiers' could do nothing and who had to watch the 'blind, bloody fury of the *Ustaši*.'[64] On 19 July he wrote:

> Even among the Croatians nobody can feel safe in this land any more. . . . The Croatian revolution is by far the harshest and most brutal of all the different revolutions that I have been through at more or less close hand since 1918.[65]

The Italian representative in Zagreb, Casertano, reported with dismay that 'persecutions of Jews are continuing. Foreign influence [i.e. German] is clearly visible in the recent decree prohibiting Jews from circulating in the city before ten in the morning and at any hour in markets or banks.'[66]

Small communities were not spared. The adjutant major of the 32nd Infantry Regiment stationed in Bileca recorded in the unit's war diary on 16 June that 'searches and arrests are continuing day and night. Numerous murders have taken place. Jews and Serbs are being robbed of all their goods by the *Ustaši* who are profiting from that in their greed for personal enrichment'.[67]

A few days later he recorded an incident that was soon to become all too common. Two lorries of fascist militiamen, 55 blackshirts, 2 officers and a doctor had set out from Bileca for Gacko when, 35 km from Bileca, the transport was caught in a storm of automatic fire and explosions. The militiamen threw themselves to the ground crying, 'siamo italiani! siamo italiani!' [we are Italians!], at which point the firing suddenly stopped and a group of sheepish Serbs emerged from the undergrowth to apologize for mistaking the fascists for *Ustaši*. They also reported that in the next village they had found 200 Serb corpses.[68]

The situation was rapidly becoming intolerable for the Italian occupation forces. As the Serbs took to the hills and fired back the Italian army got caught in the crossfire. In the meantime they had to watch as the 'friendly and allied independent state of Croatia' committed atrocities in front of their barracks. On 24 June Bastianini wrote a strong letter to Rome. Italians troops were

> constrained to stand-by inactive in the face of such acts carried out under their very eyes. . . . I cannot guarantee that in reaction to some act of violence carried out in our presence there will not be an energetic intervention which could collide with the sensibilities and sentiments of the local 'lords and masters'.[69]

Unsystematic murder was about to reach a much larger zone of Europe with consequences for the Balkans and the whole of mankind. At 3.15 on the morning of 22 June 1941, Operation Barbarossa went into effect and German troops crossed the frontiers of the Soviet Union. The communist parties of all the Balkan states now joined the anti-fascist front and in time came to dominate those movements.

Wholesale murder began behind the advancing German lines. Within two days the first Russian Jews had been murdered in Lithuania, as the infamous *Einsatzgruppen* under orders from Reinhard Heydrich spread out.[70] In the eastern Galician town of Drohobycz, SS Sergeant Felix Landau recorded in his diary,

> things it is impossible to describe. . . . Eight hundred Jews have

been herded together; they are to be shot tomorrow. We drive further along the street. Hundreds of Jews with bloodstained faces, with bullet holes in the head, broken limbs and gouged-out eyes run ahead of us. One of the Jews carries another one who is bleeding to death. . . . Covered with blood, they collapse on top of one another – they scream like pigs – we stand and look on.[71]

Hitler's greatest crime was no doubt the premeditated attempt to exterminate the Jews but no less evil was his cynical manipulation of human bestiality in all its forms. The New Order sanctioned the murder of one people by another. He demoted Jews, Russians. Serbs – '*ein Rattenvolk* [a people of rats]' SS *Gruppenführer* Meyszner called them[72] – and gypsies to the status of animals and encouraged historic enmities. Hitler never wielded an *Ustaši* knife on a Serbian child but his hand was no less bloody than that of the Croatian murderer. The guilt of the good Germans, men like Edmund Glaise von Horstenau, who showed in von Hassell's words 'manly courage'[73] by his protest to the *Poglavnik* at Croatian murders, lay in their failure to protest at the murders they themselves permitted. Von Hassell had no doubt that these terrible events should:

at last be enough to open the eyes of the army leadership to the spirit of the regime for which they are fighting. . . . Brauchitsch and Halder have already allowed themselves to be manipulated by Hitler into burdening the army with the odium of crimes that the SS bore alone before. They have taken the responsibility and by a few little additional clauses which preserve the appearances (necessity, keeping control of discipline) have deceived themselves and others. Hopeless subalterns![74]

The Jews, unarmed and surrounded by hostile local populations, could do little to save themselves. Russian prisoners of war died in their tens of thousands in the same way. The peoples of Yugoslavia were different; the ancient traditions of the bands, the *cetniki*, and of the heroic brigand, the *hajduk*, had never died out. Arms were like hoes and rakes, part of a peasant's stock of tools. Mountains were high and crossed by donkey tracks. Sporadic fighting had already broken out as Serbs resisted the Croatians. Now, partly under the influence of organized communist cadres, formal revolt began, on 13 July in Montenegro and on the 27th in the Lika, the zone between the Dalmatian coast and the mountains.

In Montenegro, the Italian governor rapidly lost control of the situation and announced that Italy had as much chance of suppressing the revolt as of 'ploughing the sea'.[75] Local garrisons were overrun and columns of troops ambushed in the high valleys. In the Lika the headquarters of the Sassari Division recorded, rather to its surprise, that 'it appears that the bands of *cetniks* intend to avoid any action which might justify our reaction or intervention.'[76] Two days later. it reported even more astonishing news:

the population of the Lika beg the Italian army to occupy immediately the entire zone of the province being unable to resist or live here because of the Croatian atrocities. The population and the *cetniks* look to us as friends.[77]

Rarely have strategic miscalculations been so swiftly punished as those made by Hitler and Mussolini in April 1941. Hitler's dreams of peaceful withdrawal and Mussolini's of empire without effort lay in ruins. Count Luca Pietromarchi, the diplomat responsible for the occupied territories in the Italian Foreign Ministry, wrote privately to his friend Raffaele Casertano, Italy's representative to the Croatian state, that Mussolini was in an extremely 'bad humour about the Dalmatian question'.[78]

The Serbs had also begun a revolt in old Serbia now under German military government. On 21 July Field Marshall List visited Serbia and demanded action. The OKW ordered its local forces to 'burn out the trouble-makers through the most brutal actions and sharpest reprisals'.[79] The German army began a policy of retaliation, shooting large numbers of hostages for every German killed or wounded. As the German army historian Wisshaupt wrote,

Even with the most unrestricted reprisal measures – up until the end of August a total of approximately 1,000 communists and Jews had been shot or publicly hanged and the houses of the guilty burnt down – it was not possible to restrain the continual growth of the armed revolt.[80]

On 4 September 1941 Field Marshall List ordered a policy of ruthless reprisals. Christopher Browning paints a fascinating portrait of the civilized German general, a lover of opera, a cultivated Hellenophile, who impressed Archbishop Roncalli (later Pope John XXIII) by the simplicity and refinement of his manners, who stopped his troops from plundering synagogues in his command in Poland but who neverthless ordered a brutal campaign of retaliation against the Serbian civilian population for which he was later tried in the so-called 'hostages trial' at Nuremberg. Browning argues that in part the order to shoot hostages 'reflected the frustrations of a professional soldier with little political sense'.[81] Nearly two generations later, after countless examples of brutality by armies coping with such frustrations – the French in Indochina, the Americans in Vietnam, the

Russians in Afghanistan and the Israelis in the Gaza Strip, we recognize how common such behaviour has become. In Europe in 1941 few serving soldiers had practical experience of guerrilla warfare. As General Roatta shrewdly observed in early 1942, the Italian and German forces faced the same sort of unconventional enemy and the same sort of war as that 'in which Napoleonic troops in Spain found themselves in 1808 and afterwards',[82] that is, in those very conditions in which the word *guerrilla*. the little war, had been invented.

There was another motive in List's approach to repression of the Serbian rising. For List it was clear that the Serbs were, if not by nature then by history, a primitive and violent people, who would and could only understand force:

the individual in Serbia is obviously like every other peasant, under normal conditions, but as soon as differences arise, then caused by the hot blood in their veins, the cruelty caused by hundreds of years of Turkish domination erupts.[83]

That view was shared by a great many Italian commanders in the Balkans. General Pirzio Biroli, governor of Montenegro, argued that the Balkan mentality only recognized force and urged extreme measures of repression and retaliation.[84] The shrewd and complex General Mario Roatta, whom we have seen protecting the Jews, told a meeting of his staff at Kočevje, in August 1942, that the Duce intended to eradicate the partisans in Croatia and Slovenia by any means necessary. Roatta recognized the problem that every regular soldier faces in guerrilla war:

I know perfectly well that we would rather fight a proper war. . . . I think of the phrase which somebody used a while ago which compared our work to that of a butcher. Nevertheless I am convinced that we have to do it and in a much more rigorous and bloody way.[85]

Roatta then outlined a new, severe policy for Slovenia of wholesale internment of Slovene villagers suspected of harbouring partisans, which was to include men, women and children, even 'if during the interrogation we have the impression that the people are not dangerous',[86] and concluded by pointing out that internment was no substitute for 'shooting all those elements guilty or suspected of communist activity'.[87] Italian troops throughout Yugoslavia, and after 1942 in Greece, burned villages, shot innocent people and interned or moved civilian populations.

The difference between the Italian and German armies was, however, not just one of degree of brutality. The Italians never made reprisal into a rigid system. Commanding generals like General

Geloso in Greece had the discretion and authority to refuse to carry out wholesale reprisals because they were 'not only useless but damaging and as such to be absolutely forbidden'.[88] Those who carried out more vigorous reprisals like General Mario Robotti, commander of the XIth Army Corps, offered their officers a moral choice:

> either you feel able to proceed as I intend and to apply without false piety my and hence your orders; or you don't feel able to proceed in such a manner and declare it so that you can be destined for other duties.[89]

Many German generals were as convinced as Geloso that reprisals on civilian populations worked against the interests of the occupying army. It drove hitherto neutral and moderate people into the guerrillas' arms. General Glaise von Hortstenau repeatedly urged local commanders and the OKW itself to be cautious in the application of reprisals. In December 1941 he learned that General Franz Böhme, like Glaise an Austrian, had ordered 650 hostages to be brought to Sarajewo for execution as a public reprisal for Germans killed by *cetniks*. The hostages were to be taken from the concentration camps at Sabac and Nis from what the order untranslatably described as '*altserbischen Beständen* [old Serbian supplies]', i.e. people from the territory of the old Serbian kingdom. Glaise was horrified on political as well as moral grounds:

> One can argue about the morality and utility of executing hostages in general but in the present instance by taking the hostages from another state's territory it will be distorted to something grotesque. . . . What will it mean for the inhabitants of Sarajewo if German soldiers march out to shoot a mass of people who not only have absolutely nothing to do with the matter but even with the country in which the acts deemed worthy of reprisal took place?[90]

The difference between Glaise and Geloso was that Glaise confronted a system, Geloso random excesses. By the time Böhme had his 'Serbian supplies' shot in Sarajewo, German commanders in the Balkans had been engaged in such acts for some months. In the words of the indictment of Field Marshall List, Field Marshall von Weichs, General Böhme and ten other senior commanders at Nuremberg in 1947, they had

> executed at arbitrarily established ratios from 50 to 100 for each German soldier killed and 25 to 50 for each German soldier wounded . . . non-combatants arbitrarily designated without

benefit of investigation or trial . . . wholly unwarranted and justified by military necessity[91]

'Supplies' for such operations came from the camps nearby which never ran short of persons to murder. The use of such supplies had been indirectly sanctioned by Field Marshall Keitel in an order of 16 September 1941, which set a ratio ranging from 50 to 100 hostages for every German killed. Böhme expanded the order to include 'all communists, all those suspected as such and all Jews' and fixed the ratio at 100 to 1.[92] Even *SS Gruppenführer* Turner who helped the German army finds its quota of 'supplies' for the hostage executions had doubts, as he observed in a letter to his patron and friend *SS Gruppenführer* Richard Hildebrandt:

in the last eight days I had 2,000 Jews and 200 gypsies shot in accordance with the ratio 1:100 for bestially murdered German soldiers, and a further 2,200, likewise almost all Jews, will be shot in the next eight days. This is not a pretty business. At any rate, it has to be, if only to make clear what it means even to attack a German soldier, and, for the rest, the Jewish question solves itself most quickly this way. Actually, it is false, if one is to be precise about it, that for murdered Germans – on whose account the ratio 1:100 should really be born by Serbs – 100 Jews are shot instead; but the Jews we had in camps – after all, they too are Serb nationals, and besides, they have to disappear.[93]

Turner had recovered enough of his good humour about the matter by the following April to see some unexpected consequences of the execution of the Jews. In a letter of 11 April 1942 to *SS Obergruppenführer* Karl Wolff he remarked,

Several months ago I had every Jew seizable shot and all Jewish women and children interned in camps and at the same time with the help of the SD got hold of a 'de-lousing truck' [inverted commas in the original] which within 14 days to four weeks cleared the camp. . . . Then the moment came in which under the Geneva Convention the Jewish officers in prisoner of war camps would *nolens volens* find out that their relatives were no longer around which might have led to a few little complications. If we release those involved, they will have their full freedom but like their racial comrades, not too long and so the whole matter will be finally resolved. The one slight reservation could be consequences for our prisoners of war in Canada, if it comes out that freed officers are not running about any more. I don't share that view.[94]

The translation fails to catch the jokey, self-congratulatory tone of the letter. After all, *SS Obergruppenführer* Karl Wolff had, as personal adjutant of Himmler, no small say in who rose and who fell in the SS. The little witticism about the Jews came in the midst of a jurisdictional dispute beween Turner and Meyszner, the local Higher SS and Police Leader for Serbia, and was designed to show Turner up as even more brutal and hard-nosed than Meyszner.

We expect now that such behaviour of the SS be declared officially inhuman by civilized people, although even today many elderly murderers live peacfully in Paraguay, Syria and Austria. The German army's role in the execution of 'human supplies' requires a moment's thought. The German army committed atrocities during the Second World War and tolerated many more. In the Balkans, it got involved in a uniquely political war which Hitler as an Austrian understood in his way. General Löhr told his Yugoslav captors after the war that Hitler had appointed him to be Supreme Commander South East, although a *Luftwaffe* General, precisely because he was Austrian.[95] Nor can it be chance that so many of his subordinate army, corps and territorial commanders were also Austrian. They brought to the politics of the region the traditional Habsburg contempt for the 'non-historic' peoples of the Empire, especially for Serbs. They dismissed the pretensions of the Croatian state to independence and Glaise who pleaded with them to respect the appearance of Croatian sovereignty was brushed aside, even by his old school friend Löhr.

It was the civilized and charming General Alexander Löhr who added a clause to the Führer's infamous order of 18 October 1942, to kill all Allied commandos, even if in uniform, by extending it to partisans:

> All enemy groups are under all conditions to be wiped out to the last man. Only when every rebel knows that he will *in no circumstances* [original emphasis] escape with his life is it to be expected that the occupation forces will master the rebel movement. The issue is life and death. There are no compromise solutions. Remarks like 'the heroism of a freedom-loving people' etc are out of place. Valuable German blood is at stake. I expect every superior to take care *by full engagement of his own person* [original emphasis] that this order is carried out by his troops *without exception* and with brutal severity. I shall investigate any *failure* [original emphasis] and call those responsible to a pitiless reckoning.[96]

It is almost as if a kind of centrifugal force spun German commanders away from the central axis of our common humanity. They outdid each other in brutality and reprisal, scrambling to repress a movement which grew by its very repression.

Croatian atrocities and German reprisals pushed the non-communist Serbs and much of the civilian population towards the milder Italians for protection. In the autumn of 1941 strange transformations of relations began to occur. Italy's allies, the Croatians, were turning into enemies, and their enemies, the Serbs, rebelling against German and Italian occupation, were becoming allies. The German brutality to Serb civilians accelerated the process. The old laws of Balkan politics reasserted themselves: the friend of my friend is my friend; the friend of my foe is my foe; but the foe of the friend of my foe is my friend.

None of this was clear at once or ever. The Italians still had a rebellion to subdue and began to send back to Yugoslavia troops withdrawn under the state treaty of 18 May 1941. On 1 August the 6th Regiment of Bersaglieri on its way home received orders to return to Yugoslavia and to proceed to Gracac. Colonel Umberto Salvatores, its commanding officer, found Gracac like Dante's Hell, shots being fired, women and children shrieking and 'arrogant and provocative men with faces like hangmen in *Ustaši* uniform'.[97] His superiors issued orders which added to the confusion. On 17 August General Ferrari Orsi sent a telegram to all commands: 'The Serbs are our enemies . . . the Croatians are our allies. . . . In a situation like the actual one it is possible to make a mistake.'[98]

A young Bersaglieri second lieutenant, Salvatore Loi, had already made one. He, a corporal and two soldiers had intervened to save 400 Serbs about to be massacred in a farm building ouside Gracac and had protected a column of Serbs and Jews fleeing toward a road block which he had set up.[99] Junior officers spread out to save their nominal enemies from their nominal allies. According to Loi, Colonel Salvatores, whose orders clearly required him to do precisely the opposite, turned a blind eye to these acts of humanitarian insubordination.[100]

Italian policy was a hopeless mess. On 10 August Governor Bastianini went to Rome where he saw Pietromarchi at the Foreign Ministry. The position, he argued, 'was by now a true guerilla war . . . the only solution is to let the railway line to Split pass under our military control and to extend our defences beyond the present borders.'[101]

The following day he had a private audience with the Duce and outlined his proposals. The revolt of the Serbs in the Lika had made the coastal strip, which Italy had annexed, indefensible. Italy had to occupy more territory. The Croatians would scream but the *Poglavnik* and his regime would not last long. Besides, Croatia was rapidly turning into a little Austria, a fiefdom of Berlin. Mussolini accepted the argument and observed,

38

it's true. I sometimes ask myself if I have not played the wrong card. . . . I want to ask the Germans what game we are playing given the fact that they are grabbing everything. We talk a lot about comradeship between the armed forces but when it comes to deeds, they leave us with our hands empty. For example, we haven't kept a single mine in Croatia.[102]

On 25 August, at Otric, a few kilometres from Zrmanje, General Fulvio Monticelli, commanding officer of the Sassari Division, General De Blasio, Chief of Staff of the 2nd Army and Colonel Salvatores met a delegation of Serbs and agreed that the Italian 2nd Army would assume full military, civil and political powers in a huge zone of inland Croatia, soon to be known as the 'second zone' or 'zone B'. On 7 September 1941 General Vittorio Ambrosio, Commanding General of the Italian 2nd Army, issued a proclamation announcing that Italy had taken power in the zone. From Fiume to Montenegro the Italian army controlled a zone which stretched from 50 to 80 km inland from the Dalmatian coast.[103] (See Map 2, p. 27.)

Italy slipped deeper into the Balkan bog. The annexation of yet more Croatia enraged the *Poglavnik* and his henchmen. The *Ustaši* swore great oaths and anti-Italian demonstrations took place. Italy had now in effect switched sides. The Roman Catholic Italians supported the Greek Orthodox Serbs against the Roman Catholic Croatians and their German allies, Protestant and Catholic. The Muslim population played for advantage, sometimes siding with the Italians and Serbs, sometimes with the Croatians and Germans. The Serb rebellion turned into a civil war as *cetniks* who followed Mihailović and the Allies fought *cetniks* who favoured the Axis or, more accurately, the Italians. Both categories contained tribal chieftains fighting out local vendettas under the cover of grand causes, allying, betraying and re-allying with alarming agility. Both sets of *cetniks* fought the increasingly numerous and better disciplined communist partisans under Tito and a different communist movement in Slovenia, which, as Edward Kardelje, its leader, explained to Tito, had 'a particular Slovene sensibility';[104] in other words, it was nationalist as much as communist. The Russians frequently had only the vaguest idea of the personalities involved and exercised little control. There were the 'green *cetniks*' or Montenegrin separatists, not to mention the surviving politicians and political groupings of the old Yugoslav state, never a model of unity and self-discipline.

The rebellion spread and partisan activity pushed both Germans and Italians on to the defensive. Hitler became seriously worried about an area which he regarded as the right flank of the Russian front. In late September 1941 he ordered the German military attaché to approach the Italians with a new plan. The Italians, General von Rintelen told the High Command in Rome, should push their occupation forward to the demarcation that divided the German from Italian zones of influence in Croatia. The Duce, who could resist neither Hitler's flattery nor his own greed, issued orders to General Ambrosio:

> In Serbia the Germans have initiated a large-scale action to repress the communist rebellion. Since the rebels could penetrate into non-occupied Croatia, you are directed to enter with your troops the territory between the demilitarized zone and the demarcation line with the German occupation until contact is made with the Germans.[105]

Ambrosio issued orders to units of the Vth and VIth Army Corps to enter what came to be called the 'third zone' or 'zone C' but the High Command had no reserves to spare. To occupy a territory as large as zones A and B put together (and exceptionally mountainous) the 2nd Army received three battalions of Alpini and one of mountain artillery. On paper they controlled half Croatia; in reality they held a variety of isolated fortresses. By the end of October 1941 the formal occupation was complete.

The breakdown of the unity talks between Tito and Mihailović allowed the Italians a little relief. At least they fought a divided enemy; there might be deals to be made. Hitler grew impatient. He pressed the Duce at a summit meeting in December to join with him in a serious combined operation to put an end to the rising. Mussolini had no choice but to accept for the Italians had got themselves into a desperate situation.

Italian units faced impossible operational difficulties. They had orders to carry out a regular *rastrellamento* (raking up) of guerrillas in their zones. Colonel Antonio Pignatelli, commanding officer of the 55th Infantry Regiment in the Marche Division, reported on a typical *rastrellamento* in the summer of 1942. Three columns set out to clear the area around Ljubomir of a unit of partisans estimated to be 300 strong. The 55th moved out in force. Each column numbered over 700 troops, 20 officers and more than 120 horses and mules. The terrain was rocky and difficult: 'From Jangac to Dubroman the path is scarcely traced and plummets straight down into the plain below. The quadrupeds were compelled to proceed extremely slowly pulled along on ropes.'[106]

When they entered Ljubomir, the communists had long since vanished but would soon be back. The population was friendly but guarded. The Italians could not guarantee their safety. Partisan revenge on collaborators was swift and bloody. Without air support and before the use of the helicopter, conventional army units like the 55th Infantry Regiment fought frustrating ghost battles against guerrilla enemies who simply vanished into the hills or merged with local populations. In valleys the partisans often ambushed them; on hills they waited beyond the next comb of rocks.

Our generation understands the futility and frustration of guerrilla war. It has watched the United States and the Soviet Union, equipped with the highest of high technology, fail to suppress a rebellion of Vietnamese in their jungles and Afghan tribesmen in their mountains. Helicopters, radar, electronic sensing and surveillance, chemical warfare and huge numbers of troops in relation to the number of guerrillas failed to avoid humiliating defeats for both great powers. The slow-moving, clumsy Italian infantry, only as mobile as its mules, had no chance.

The Germans hoped to suppress the guerrillas by terror and by elaborate operations to encircle and exterminate them. The Italians, too weak, slow and sceptical, sought allies. In January 1942 General Mario Roatta succeeded Ambrosio as commanding officer of the Italian 2nd Army in Croatia and Dalmatia. Roatta, undoubtedly one of the cleverest and most experienced Italian commanders, had served as chief of military intelligence, as field commander of an expeditionary corps in Spain and as an army chief of staff. Marshall Caviglia wrote in his diary: 'Roatta is agile, active and full of imagination, maybe sometimes he has shown himself not balanced enough and too aggressive to his inferiors.'[107]

He impressed his German colleagues. Major von Plehwe thought him 'very sharp-witted' and a good negotiator.[108] Glaise von Horstenau watched him in action and wrote a vivid description of a joint Italo-German staff meeting in a private letter to his old school friend *Generaloberst* Alexander Löhr, Supreme Commander South East:

After a glass of vermouth we gathered round the map table: five Italians, Roatta at the head, and four Germans. Roatta put himself at once in the position of a shrewd but kindly school-master who is prepared to meet the wishes of his pupils and played the role brilliantly to the end. His own views he scattered during the 'examination' as afterthoughts. He has a superb gift for putting his finger on weak points and accepted the replies with the expression of somebody who knows everything better but is constrained by the duties laid on him to be retiring. He has mastered the geography of the region down to the smallest nest, makes a show of his detailed knowledge but really does know a lot about mountain and guerrilla war. His reasoning even when he used German was hard to beat . . . Our good old Lüters was not up to him and more than once got handed a 'satisfactory minus' as a grade.[109]

By the standards of the Italian Army Mario Roatta at 55 was unusually young to be given an army command. The secret service commented on the 'luxurious life style' of General and Mrs Roatta, on the fact that the Signora considered herself 'well informed and talks a great deal about politics'. She was, the report continues, 'feared' at the Ministry and a word from her 'opened doors'. The couple lived 'according to free principles' in their private lives. The General had told a friend that after the first five years of married life he had declared his wife 'out of fashion'.[110]

General Roatta moved in the world of high society. As former head of the Italian military intelligence and as attaché in Berlin he knew his way round the corridors of power and the secret rooms off the corridors. After the war he was accused of war crimes. Among other accusations he was charged with having arranged a political murder when he had been head of the secret military intelligence. In 1937, at Bagnoles de l'Ornes, Carlo and Nello Rosselli, the two Italian Jews who founded the leading non-communist, anti-fascist resistance group 'Justice and Liberty', had been murdered and Roatta, it was alleged, had given the orders.[111] In short, Roatta was a political general.

Roatta understood from the beginning what Glaise preached in vain to the German High Command, that 'politics and warfare can never be separated in anything to do with the Balkans. The smallest move in one district affects every other.'[112]

Before formally assuming his command on 20 January 1942, he made a lengthy inspection tour of the 2nd Army's zone of occupation in Croatia, Slovenia and Dalmatia. What he found depressed him. In the first place the Italians had 'broken up' their zone of occupation into the province of Lubiana, the province of Fiume, the governorship of Dalmatia, the governorship of Montenegro, and the two zones of military occupation, the so-called zones B and C:

> if one adds the diplomatic, political and military missions, both German and Italian in Zagreb and the *'missi dominici'* who arrive from time to time . . . it is not surprising that the population in any case diverse in race, religion and tendency, is disorientated.[113]

The terrain posed the classical dilemma for a commander fighting a guerrilla war. Roatta saw clearly that to hold the country he had to occupy the main centres which were 'numerous, far from one another and connected only by mountain roads'.[114] To keep lines of communication open he had to guard the roads and the precious rail links. Large partisan detachments then overran the small garrisons guarding the lines of communication and by the time cumbersome large units came out from the strongholds, like the 55th Infantry in Ljubomir, the communists had disappeared and the road or railway had been damaged anyway. Sending more men to patrol the roads weakened the strong-points, (the Italians called them *presidios*) and invited partisan attacks on the garrisons. The rebels had recently used the heavy snowfalls in the mountains at Korenica to do a double, both to ambush a garrison and the relief column and then to besiege the stronghold which the survivors, forcing their way through snow up to their chests, had just managed to reach. Korenica was under siege from late December until the snows melted in March.

There were three options: first, large combined operations by joint German-Italian-Croatian task forces; second, withdrawal to defensible lines leaving the Yugoslav mountains to turn into a Soviet state; or third, 'reducing significantly the number of *presidios*, concentrating our forces and guarding only the most important and indispensible lines of communication'.[115]

Lyndon Johnson or Mikhail Gorbachev would have recognized Roatta's options. Guerrilla warfare always places the political leadership of the occupying state in difficulties. Arms alone can never subdue a rebellion if the terrain is favourable and the guerrillas supported by the local population; there must be a political solution. The occupying power takes a while to see that. It first sends many more men. It then makes elaborate plans for joint operations as the Germans and Italians did in the summer of 1942. Finally it admits defeat and seeks to withdraw under the least humiliating of conditions.

The Axis got caught in a double squeeze. The Italians could not do the former; the Germans the latter. The Italians lacked the men, munitions and transport for combined operations, and the Germans never considered a political solution. Hitler's view of the world required *Alles oder Nichts*, and that is not a negotiating position. Moreover, Hitler's blind racism made it impossible for him to accept the reality, let alone the rights, of certain peoples like Serbs or Jews.

Italy had in real terms only one, feeble option: to find a native ally, the Balkan equivalent of the Army of the Republic of Vietnam. There was one, ready, armed, only too eager to fight – the *cetniks*. By the end of February 1942 Glaise von Horstenau reported to the OKW that the *cetniks*

were parading in every village occupied by the Italians fully

armed. . . . In the Herzegowina it has even come to the point
where the Italians actually handed over a Croatian military
column to the *Cetniks*. Croatian 'independence' is being trodden
under foot.[116]

In order to carry on the fight against the mainly Serbian
communists in Tito's movement, the Italians armed and encouraged
non-communist Serbs to fight on their side. But these Serbs had their
own battles to fight – against each other but mainly against the
Ustaši and the hated Croatian regime. The Italians undermined the
political structures on which their German allies placed their hopes
and did so by using 'human supplies' whom Hitler had earmarked
for destruction.

Friction between Italy and Germany on the *cetnik* issue was constant
and irritating. By comparison disagreements on the Jewish question
were spasmodic. Besides, the Italians pretended to meet their ally's
demands on Jewish matters. They simply could not do so on the
question of the *cetniks*. Their occupation of Croatia made the
Croatians hate them. Since in the Balkans 'the foe of my foe is my
friend', the Serbs had to be allies.

But which Serbs? The Royal Yugoslav government in exile had
nominated Draza Mihailović a brigadier general in December 1941,
and recognized his *Jugoslavenska vojska u otadžbini* as the official army
of Yugoslavia in the fatherland. The *cetnik* movement had spread to
old Serbia, to Montenegro, to Bosnia, Herzegovina, the Sandjak of
Noivipazar, the Lika or, in short, everywhere that Serbs were found,
'often more like bands led by brigands not officers, undisciplined and
without clear directives'.[117] In effect, the Italians proposed to ally
themselves with allies of the British. The friends of my foe are my
foes, and the Italians could never be sure which *cetniks* were which.
The retiring commander of the 2nd Italian Army, Vittorio Ambrosio,
saw only one solution. It was vital

> to reduce to the minimum the number of enemies in the hope
> that one can arrive quickly enough to separate *cetniks* from
> communists. I think it would be opportune to try to arrive at an
> accord with the *cetniks* themselves by means of regular negotia-
> tions conducted at the centre.[118]

What Mihailović failed to achieve, the Italians could not do either.
The very nature of the guerrilla bands made central agreements
impossible. Each *cete* or band was a law unto itself. The Germans
would in any case never have agreed to negotiations with the *cetniks*.
In the summer of 1942 the headquarters of *Kampfgruppe Bader*, the
operational task force set up to surround and crush Tito's partisans

44

in the so-called Operation Trio, actually sent out two officers, 'one specialized in Balkan affairs', to try to convince commanders of Italian divisions, one by one, that the *cetniks* 'represented a latent menace to the Axis'.[119] This extraordinary sales trip by the Germans failed.

So did other attempts at every level right up to the Führer. The *Poglavnik*, Pavelić, summoned Roatta to a meeting in September 1942 and tried to convince him to disarm the *cetniks*, but Roatta replied that he had to use them 'in spite of the dangers mentioned'.[120] At a crucial summit meeting in December 1942, when the Russians had broken the Italian line on the Don, when Paulus' 6th Army had been surrounded at Stalingrad, when the Afrika Korps had been driven from Libya, Hitler and his generals still found time to take up the *cetnik* issue. General Ugo Cavallero, chief of the Italian general staff, wrote in his diary: 'Roatta is the object of a pitiless offensive on account of the *cetniks*. They want to disarm them and get them out the way.'[121]

Ribbentrop raised the issue with the Duce at their meeting on 25 February 1943, a meeting at which the German Foreign Minister pressed the Duce to force his army commanders to cease protecting Jews.[122] It made no difference. In June of 1943 the Supreme Commander South East, General Löhr, complained that in spite of promises the Italians still had not disarmed the *cetniks* and that this

> contradicted fundamental instructions of the OKW and that therefore no agreement to engage German troops in the proposed common operation in the Lika can be given unless the disarming of the *cetniks* has been carried out before the operation begins.[123]

The *cetniks* were not disarmed before the operation; they were never disarmed. As Roatta put it in a meeting with senior staff chiefs in Rome in early January 1943, 'the *cetniks* are the only marbles we have left in that sector and we had better hold them in our hands.'[124]

The Jews were not 'marbles' but the Italian military authorities kept them in hand too. When the Italian army moved into zone B to repress the *Ustaši* atrocities and restore order, General Ambrosio, as commanding general of the Italian 2nd Army, issued a proclamation in which he announced that Italy had assumed military, political and civil powers. The last paragraph declared: 'All those who for various motives have abandoned their country are herewith invited to return to it. The Italian armed forces are the guarantors of their safety, their liberty and their property.'[125]

That clause became the Magna Charta of Italian policy towards the Jews. It took on the status of a sacred oath. When during 1942 German pressure added its weight to Croatian demands for the surrender of Jews who had sought protection under the Italian flag, the office of civil affairs at 2nd Army headquarters underlined the 'moral aspect' and, with reference to the proclamation of 7 September 1941, argued that to hand over Jews would be

a violation of a word of honour given by us with damaging repercussions in relation to all those who having put their trust in us will justly fear their abandonment from one moment to another. Our prestige will be seriously reduced.[126]

The more the Germans insisted, the more the Italians stiffened in defence of their 'honour'. It may be that the series of military defeats and humiliations in 1941–42 left them with little else, but at least they had that. Both senior and junior officers in the 2nd Army observed Ambrosio's proclamation solemnly.

By the time Italian troops reoccupied zone B, the Germans could report with satisfaction that the Jewish problem in their part of Croatia was making progress. In Belgrade, as Glaise von Horstenau wrote, it had been 'relatively completely solved' but not yet in Sarajewo and smaller centres.[127] The Independent State of Croatia with its *Ustaši* butchers and its concentration camps had the makings of an exemplary ally.

The same could not, alas, be claimed for the Italians. During the last few months of 1941 disturbing stories reached Zagreb. The German Ambassador to Croatia, Siegfried Kasche, a high Nazi party functionary,[128] wrote to Berlin that the Croatian mayor of Karlovac had told him that

about 500 Jews live in Karlovac. A great many of them have housed Italian officers. Measures against the Jews have been obstructed or prevented by the Italians. As a result he is not in a position to carry out measures against Jewry [*das Judentum*].[129]

A distinguished German geographer on a research trip in the Italian zone was horrified to see how the Italian army disarmed the Croatian militia and led Serbs and Jews back to their homes under military protection.[130] In December 1941 *Oberleutnant* Weiss of the military-economic section reported from the Italian zone that in Dubrovnik

the relationship between Italian officers, Jews and Serbs, is an absolutely undeniable fact. Italian officers are often seen with Jewish women in the Café Grodska. . . . In Dubrovnik there are about 500 Jews. Most of them came from Sarajewo and were brought here with Italian help. 10,000 to 50,000 *kune* is the normal price for smuggling across the border with false passes. . . . In Mostar things are cruder still. The Italians simply revoke all Croatian orders and let the city overflow with Jews. . . . The director of the German Academy in Dubrovnik, Herr Arnold, was invited together with some Croatian officials to a reception . . . and was outraged by the arrogance of the Italian General Amico. . . . With regard to Croatia he said that the Italians were there to protect the poor and persecuted – Jews and Serbs – from brutality and terror.[131]

The SS officer attached to the German Embassy in Zagreb reported on 30 May 1942 that General Amico had been even more explicit in a recent conversation. According to a witness, the General said publicly: 'The Croatian anti-Jewish laws are strict; the German one still stricter. To send those poor Jews who have fled to Ragusa [Dubrovnik] back to Sarajewo, would mean sending them to their deaths.'[132]

The files of General Glaise von Horstenau began to fill with reports from the Italian zone of occupation which told the same story. In July 1942 *Ministerialrat* (civil service equivalent of colonel) Schnell of the Reich Ministry for Armament and Munitions made a formal protest. The chief of staff of the Division 'Murge' had refused to comply with Herr Dr Schnell's reasonable request to throw Jews in Mostar out of their homes so that German mining engineers could be housed because it was 'incompatible with the honour of the Italian Army to take special measures against Jews'.[133]

Those Jews who could – and only a few were lucky enough – headed for the Italian zone. The Germans assumed contemptuously that the Italians took bribes to let Jews in. Why else would anybody help a Jew? Many Italians did so but, as Mr Imre Rochlitz told me, he and his family resorted to a trick worthy of the Marx brothers. Each member of the family got off the train in Dubrovnik saying that another member further back had their papers and the last member said that the first had them. The carabinieri simply shrugged and let them all off the train.[134]

The office of civil affairs of the Italian 2nd Army calculated in the summer of 1942 that before the war there had been about 150 Jews in Dubrovnik and 50 in Mostar. After the German occupation of Serbia in 1941 and the Croatian pogroms the numbers in Dubrovnik reached over 1,000 and nearly 200 in Mostar. Early in January 1942, just before leaving his command, General Ambrosio 'assured the Jews that they would not be molested'.[135] Indeed, Consul General Mammalella welcomed an influx of mostly *sephardic* Jews, 'who by tradition, culture, relationships and knowledge of Latin languages – all the *sephardi* speak Spanish as their official language – [were] a mass to manoeuvre . . . in the eventuality of a plebiscite'.[136]

The Axis partners had moved apart by the winter of 1941–42 but not so far that Hitler considered action against them. The mess in Africa might still be redeemed. There would be a spring offensive on the Russian front and now that Japan had attacked America, both English-speaking countries had a formidable new enemy in the Far East. The trouble in the Balkans was certainly a nuisance. The Axis partners disagreed on a whole range of issues from the use of *cetnik* volunteers to tactics in the field but not beyond hope of agreement. Indeed, in mid-December, Hitler offered Mussolini the whole of Croatia to the dismay of Kasche and Glaise von Horstenau in Zagreb. The Italians, for once, recognized realities and declined.[137] In March 1942 German and Italian commanders met at Sussak to plan a huge joint operation which would put an end to the partisan threat once and for all.[138] On 20 April Operation Trio began with General Roatta as overall commanding officer but the German General Paul Bader in tactical command of a special *Kampfgruppe*.[139]

Relations between the Italians and Croatians improved. As Glaise reported by telegramme to the OKW, the visit of Marshall Cavallero, chief of the Italian General Staff, to the *Poglavnik* on 25 April 1942, went 'most amiably' and Cavallero, who spoke perfect German, had a 'comradely' private talk with Glaise that evening in which he expressed

> great confidence especially with regard to the situation in the eastern Mediterranean. Special praise for Rommel. . . . The war will be decided during this year; preconditions: the smashing of Russia and the liquidation of British hegemony in the eastern Mediterranean.[140]

Cavallero was right. For Italy the war was decided by the end of 1942 but it was Italy which was to be smashed and liquidated. In the spring defeat seemed far away. The Italian army could afford to pursue its own policy in the Balkans for the time being. The collapse in Africa and Russia later in the year which ought to have shaken Italy's protection of the Jews had the opposite effect. The reasons for that change lay beyond Italian control and in the spring of 1942 beyond even the wildest Italian imagination.

Outside Berlin there is a series of marvellous lakes. On one of them, Grosser Wannsee, there is a sedate villa set back from the lakeshore drive, number 58 am Grossen Wannsee. In that comfortable but inconspicuous house on 20 January 1942, *SS Gruppenführer* Reinhard Heydrich, head of the *Reichssicherheitshauptamt* (the Reich Main Security Office) presided over a meeting of representatives of several German ministries to plan 'the final solution of the Jewish question'.[141] The consequences of that meeting forced the Italians to face a new question. It was one thing to resist the primitive brutalities of the Croatians, a very different thing to resist the orderly activities of the Germans. From the beginning of 1942 Europe moved from an era of unsystematic murder to the systematic, bureaucratically organized, extermination of an entire people. No crime like it had ever been envisaged in the history of mankind. No parallel can be found for it. Even today the holocaust stands absolutely unique; the only instance in which a modern technologically advanced society has been programmed to exterminate an entire human community. The era of systematic murder had begun.

PHASE TWO

SYSTEMATIC MURDER: THE ITALIANS OBSTRUCT THE FINAL SOLUTION

June 1942 to November 1942

Knowledge of the holocaust spread slowly during 1942, in part because Hitler and his entourage took care to conceal it. They used euphemisms and made sure that only those who 'needed to know' did. Any mention of the murder of the Jews was expressly forbidden. In July 1943 Martin Bormann, head of the party apparatus, issued a directive to all party leaders 'by order of the Führer': 'In public discussion of the Jewish question any mention of a future total solution must be avoided. However, one may discuss the fact that all Jews are being interned and detailed to purposeful compulsory labour forces.'[1]

Knowledge of the holocaust spread slowly, in addition, because people simply refused to believe the evidence. Nothing like it had occurred before. Certainly Croatians murdered Serbs. That was regrettable but normal. Peoples had always used the sword on each other. The holocaust was different. Ordinary human beings found it hard to accept that the bloodless apparatus of a modern state had become a machine for collecting, processing, transporting and then efficiently murdering an entire people. Even Goebbels could not believe at first. On 27 March 1942 he wrote:

Beginning with Lublin, the Jews in the General Government are now being evacuated eastward. The procedure is a pretty barbaric one and not to be described here more definitely. Not much will remain of the Jews. . . . No other government and no other regime would have the strength for such a global solution of this question. . . . Fortunately a whole series of possibilities presents itself to us in wartime that would be denied us in peacetime.[2]

Holocaust records show that Jews themselves often refused to believe what was happening in spite of the evidence of their own

50

eyes. Italian Jews in particular went on assuming that it could not happen to them even after they had been warned. Evi Eller told me that when the Badoglio government made peace with the Allies on 8 September 1943, and the Germans occupied Italy, her mother, who was then living in Trieste, went to the local synagogue and begged the officers of the Jewish community to destroy the lists of members. They refused.[3] The records of the Roman Jewish community had not been hidden when the SS came for them on the 'black sabbath', 16 October 1943, the day when the Jews of the Roman ghetto were rounded up. The rabbi of Florence, Nathan Cassuto, was one of the very few who understood at once that 8 September 1943 meant death to the Jews and, as his sister testified at the Eichmann trial, he 'went from house to house to warn them to hide themselves in convents or in little villages, under false names.'[4]

If the Jews themselves could not believe the menace that faced them in the autumn of 1943, the Italian Army, the Foreign Ministry and the diplomatic corps, cannot be blamed for not reading the signs more than a year earlier. Something was clearly happening but what? The evidence suggests that from August 1942 onwards, hints by accommodating Germans and Croatians, reports from eye-witnesses in the east and investigations by the Italian secret services made it hard to deny that the phase of un-systematic murder was giving place to something more ominous, but it could still be plausibly interpreted as a new Croatian tactic. On 22 September 1942 Vittorio Castellani, the Italian Foreign Ministry's diplomatic advisor at the the headquarters of the Italian 2nd Army in Sussak, a man both well informed and committed to saving Jews, still believed that 'the Croatian authorities, meeting time and again a clear refusal on our part, have now changed their position and are asking for German intervention.'[5]

The Italians were never told about the Wannsee Conference of 20 January 1942, nor the subsequent meetings. Officially they knew nothing about the final solution. Hitler kept it from his 'dear Benito Mussolini' in spite of the fact that the decision to murder the entire Jewish people transformed the nature of the war and affected Italy as an Axis partner. Once the Wannsee decisions began to operate, the Allies could never contemplate a separate peace with Germany. The pathetic attempts made by Italian diplomacy in the late spring of 1943 to convince Hitler to negotiate a peace with the Russians reveal how little they grasped that fact. Hitler and Goebbels understood perfectly what their 'global solution' implied. The final solution made sure that it would be *Alles oder Nichts*.

The plotters of 20 July 1944, who let the bomb off in Hitler's headquarters knew about the final solution. Many of them had seen the truth as senior officers in the East and the rest, like Ulrich von

Hassell, had no difficulty in finding out. They too for all their courage misunderstood what it meant for Germany. For, as the news of Auschwitz and Treblinka spread to the Allied peoples, the entire German nation came to stand for a barbarism without parallel in the history of mankind. The courageous generals and civil servants who gave their lives for 'another Germany', as von Hassell put it, were too little and too late. General von Hammerstein knew that when, as he lay dying, he told my friend, Wolfgang von Tirpitz, 'we shall never get rid of these guys until we have a one hundred percent defeat'.

The story of the Italian official reaction to the holocaust needs that perspective. The reader has to remember that the Italians knew nothing officially; they knew some things unofficially but never the full extent of the programme of mass murder. When they asked questions of German officials, they got evasive replies. Throughout 1942 and 1943 German generals, SS officers and diplomats persisted in discussing the deportation of the Jews in the usual euphemistic terms: Jews were a threat to security; they were to be used for labour in the East etc. When sceptical Italians asked if the old, the sick and the babies threatened the Axis or were expected to do forced labour, the Germans changed the subject.

There is a paradox in the story. The more the Italians knew the less they dared to talk about it. The war was unpopular enough; public knowledge of the holocaust would make it much more so. The documents show the paradox perfectly. Reports trickled into Italy. Soldiers returning from the Russian front and war correspondents like Curzio Malaparte brought home tales of unimaginable horrors. The Italian authorities now had reliable accounts of the German atrocities through official channels and grew increasingly nervous. Little tell-tale signs, asides, and marginal comments reflect their embarrassment. They knew that something dreadful was happening. The problem for Italian diplomacy and the armed forces was what to do about it.

In the spring of 1942 the mass deportations from various European countries began. On 26 March 1942 the first Slovak Jews were deported and on the 28th the first trains left France.[6] Between 17 and 20 April the ghetto of Lublin was cleared of Jews and razed to the ground,[7] and at the end of May the Italian Ambassador to the Vichy regime reported that the Germans were pressing the French to force Jews to wear the yellow star.[8]

Governor Bastianini reported in the middle of May 1942 that the numbers of Jews entering the annexed territories had reached such alarming levels that he had given orders to repel them in spite of the dramatic scenes to which they abandon themselves at our check points. Many succeed nonetheless in getting into our cities. I regard it therefore as necessary that an intervention be made with the military authorities of the zone to put an end to the exodus to Dalmatia.[9]

Foreign Minister Ciano had the answer and in a telegram on 1 June 1942 put it to Bastianini: 'This ministry asks if the simplest solution would not be to organize a concentration camp for Jewish elements coming from Croatia choosing a Croatian territory occupied by us.'[10]

The Governor leapt at the idea and proposed it to General Roatta as commanding general of the area of Slovenia and Dalmatia. The trouble was that Bastianini's relations with the 2nd Army and his nerves were both showing signs of wear. His foreign policy advisor, Egidio Ortona, had begun to worry about his chief. After a meeting in late May in which General Roatta suggested that the Italian Army would probably withdraw from the third zone, Bastianini's pessimism spread to the public and formed, in Ortona's words, a general 'psychosis' in Zara.[11] The last thing Bastianini needed was a few hundred extra Jewish refugees in Zara and Split, raising prices and causing shortages. The trouble was that his attempts, as he wired Ciano on 1 June, to send the Jews back had produced 'scenes of violent despair'. The only solution was to force the Croatians to find concentration camps where there would be a 'guaranty of their safety and a minimum of humane treatment'.[12]

Roatta was not having that. His reply to Bastianini in early June made it absolutely clear that

> we have guaranteed them a certain protection and have resisted Croatian pressure to deport them to a concentration camp. It is my opinion that if Jews who have fled to annexed Dalmatia were to be consigned to the Croatians, they would be interned at Jasenovac with the well-known consequences.[13]

Jasenovac was a death camp and by now everybody involved in Italian policy knew it. Roatta suggested vaguely that the Jews might be interned on the islands off the coast of Dalmatia.

There was deadlock among the three authorities responsible for the life or death of the Jewish refugees: the Foreign Ministry, the Governor of Dalmatia and the 2nd Army. In an effort to resolve the differences, on 23 June 1942, Baron Michele Scamacca, the Foreign Ministry's liaison officer at the Supreme Command headquarters in Rome, summed up the position. The persecutions had driven Jewish refugees into Dalmatia which had caused 'serious inconvenience' and had led to Governor Bastianini's request to drive them back into Croatia. For obvious reasons of political prestige and humanity, that is not feasible. The Foreign Ministry, as a contingent solution, has proposed that such refugees be concentrated at Cirquenizza or in a zone of Croatia under our military control. . . . His Excellency Roatta has not shown himself favourable to such a project.[14]

Scamacca's reaction to Bastianini's proposal sums up the core of the Italian position on the Jewish question. It was 'obvious' that both 'political prestige' and 'humanity' required the Italian forces not to surrender the Jews to the Croatians. It was, of course, not obvious to Bastianini nor to all Italian officials always and everywhere but to most of them most of the time. Young Lieutenant Loi and his bersaglieri had not hesitated to protect people from their persecutors in the summer of 1941; now his superiors, faced with the same choice, behaved in the same way. This 'obvious' reaction of Italian officialdom at all levels is a chapter of glory in the history of modern Italy which makes up for a good many defeats on the battlefield.

Resisting the Croatians was one thing; resisting the Germans another. A day after Baron Scamacca wrote his memorandum, his equivalent in Croatia, Vittorio Castellani, the Foreign Ministry's liaison officer to the 2nd Army, wired something very alarming. A visiting German engineer had told the commanding officer of the Division 'Murge', stationed in Mostar, that the German and Croatian governments had reached an agreement for 'the transfer to Russian territory occupied by the Germans of all the Jews of Croatia, including those of Herzegovina.'[15]

Castellani, who worked closely with Roatta and shared his views on the Jewish question, urged the Italian Foreign Ministry not to allow the agreement to be extended to the Italian zone of Croatia. It was not known at the time but a particularly grotesque element of the agreement lay in the arrangements to cover the costs of the deportations. After much haggling the Croatian government agreed to pay the Germans 30 marks for each Jew delivered.[16] Can the German Ambassador in Zagreb, Siegfried Kasche, have been so insensitive that he missed the biblical resonance of 'the thirty pieces of silver' or so cynical that he had specially chosen that precise sum? The documents give no answer. The Italians, no less familiar with the Bible than the Germans, will not have missed the fact that Judas sold Jesus for thirty pieces of silver. It is a bizarre footnote to the story of the holocaust how often German SS and army reports make ironic references to the 'chosen people', the 'promised land' and the like. Hitler's paganism could not eradicate the hours spent in Sunday School from the heads of all his hangmen.

Early in July General Roatta again visited Governor Bastianini to try to reconcile their growing differences. Bastianini emphasized his 'constant worry' about the Jewish refugees.[17] Besides, the rebels were picking off presidios one by one and had now reached a position a mere 40 kilometres from Zara itself. Roatta's forces seemed incapable of defending the province and the general was apparently unwilling to help with the refugees. A few days later, Ortona wrote in his diary

> What happened today can be defined as the complete break with the military authorities. . . . From now on a harsh and bitter skirmish has opened with drawn swords in which the Governor is ready to take the worst consequences and the military will not distinguish themselves in tenderness.[18]

The numbers of Jews reaching Italian territory rose at the very moment that Italian arms looked less and less capable of protecting them. As the news spread through Croatia that the Italian army intended to withdraw from the third zone or zone C, garrisons reported from Bihac, Drvar, Kalinovik, Konjic, Karlovac, Petrova Gor and other places that there was 'panic' among Jews and Serbs and, 'in some zones, a mass exodus of the population too terrified to intend to remain in localities solely controlled by the Croatians.'[19]

The Italians could neither advance nor withdraw without getting ever deeper into the quagmire of Balkan ethnic hatred and the Jewish problem. On the last day of July the Duce travelled to Goriza to meet his generals and to reveal to them his deep thoughts on the Balkan campaign, among which were meeting violence with violence but without employing more force, as he put it: 'we cannot keep so many divisions in the Balkans'.[20] More withdrawals would mean more panic and more refugees.

Sometime in the middle of August, the monthly foreign news survey prepared and distributed by the army's counter-intelligence organization reached the King, the Royal Princes, the High Command, 2nd Army HQ and some hundred other offices and commands. It reported the latest stages of German persecution of Jews in France, the round-up of 20,000 foreign Jews in the Paris region and their forthcoming transportation to Poland. It also described the latest restrictions on the Jews of Holland, the limits on their movements, use of public transport, post and telephone, and the prohibitions on their exercising certain professions.[21] The Jewish question was moving into a new phase, and the Italian authorities would have to find a policy.

At precisely that moment, while Bastianini still insisted on getting rid of 'undesirables from the province of Split',[22] the Germans emerged from behind the Croatians and put their ace of spades on the table. The Minister of State at the German Embassy, Prince Otto von Bismarck, the grandson of the Iron Chancellor, whom von Hassell regarded as 'friendly to the Nazis',[23] and the SS officer Dollmann, suspected of exactly the opposite,[24] called on Count Ciano's chief of cabinet, Blasco Lanza d'Ajeta with a request from Italy's ally. Bismarck was not popular in the Italian Foreign Ministry. Roberto Ducci, responsible for Croatia under Count Pietromarchi, thought him both arrogant and snobbish.[25] Yet on 18 August he did something unusually honourable. He presented a telegram signed by Ribbentrop which asked the Italian government to instruct its military authorities in Croatia to adhere to the measures agreed between the Croatian and German governments and to arrange for a 'transfer in mass' of the Jews from the Italian zone as well: 'Bismarck stated that it was a question of several thousands of people and led me to understand that such measures would lead, in practice, to their dispersion and]liquidation ["annihilation" in the original but lined out]'[26]

Italy now faced the holocaust squarely. Bismarck himself had whispered the truth to the cabinet chief of Count Ciano. The Jews were not being transferred to the east to work but to die. The Italian government had to reply. The first person to have to do so was d'Ajeta himself and the tortured prose of his memorandum suggests how hard it was. 'Apart from any consideration of a general character' (i.e. humanity), he pointed out that to surrender the Jews would run counter to previous policy and directives recognized even by the Croatians. Messages from the legation in Zagreb indicated that the Jewish question had now entered 'the phase of resolution'. What should the Italian response be?

> If on our part it were thought proper not to adhere to the German request it might be opportunely made clear that one of the bases of our policy of pacification, tirelessly pursued in our zone of responsibility, has consisted in the suspension of drastic measures against any ethnic or religious community whatsoever. . . . It could eventually be added that the 5 or 6 thousand Jews residing in our zone of occupation – that appears to be the maximum number – would be subjected more than ever to severe control.[27]

The memorandum contains several arguments for not surrendering the Jews; none for surrendering them. Count Luca Pietromarchi, a very senior official in the foreign ministry, recorded in his diary two days later that Bismarck had asked the Italian Foreign Ministry to surrender the Jews from the occupied zones in Croatia 'in order to destroy them. He was given a dilatory answer by our chief of cabinet'.[28]

56

While the Italian Foreign Ministry prepared a memorandum on the issue for the Duce to decide, on 20 and 21 August 1942 the Jews of Sarajewo were rounded up and readied for deportation.[29] The holocaust had reached Croatia in its systematic German uniform. On 21 August 1942 Ciano presented Mussolini with a shortened version of Lanza d'Ajeta's memorandum. It contained the clear reference which Bismarck had made to the 'dispersion and elimination' of the Jews. Mussolini wrote in his large, unmistakeable handwriting across the upper right hand of the memorandum *'nulla osta . . . M'*. (I reproduce the document on p. 2.) Mussolini had 'no objection' to condemning the Jews in the Italian zone to death.[30]

There is no record either in the official files or in his diary to tell us how Ciano reacted to the Duce's heartless decision. Nor do we know how Lanza d'Ajeta or his associates took the news. Count Pietromarchi simply recorded in his diary a few days later: 'The Duce has ordered the surrender to the Germans of the Jews who find themselves in Croatian territory occupied by us.'[31]

Any lingering doubt about the meaning of Mussolini's *'nulla osta'* would have been dispersed by a dispatch from the Italian minister in Zagreb, Raffaele Casertano, of 22 August. In it he reported that Jews were being sent to Poland in special trains and not to some unspecified area 'in the East'. He also mentioned that the representative of the Vatican in Zagreb, Monsignor Ramiro Marcone, had intervened to try to halt the deportations but had failed. He reported the fee of 30 marks paid by the Croatians and added that the German ambassador

> had remarked in a recent conversation on the desirability of proceeding to the removal of the Jews who had fled to the second zone occupied by Italian troops and asked how many there were. He added that according to his information the main nuclei were found at Mostar, Ragussa and at Cirquenizza. Finally he referred to an official step which the Reich government would soon be undertaking to ask that these Jews, together with the other Croatian Jews, be sent to Poland.[32]

For a week nothing happened. On 28 August 1942 d'Ajeta wrote to the Supreme Command of the Armed Forces informing them that the Germans had made a request for the surrender of the Jews and that 'the *nulla osta* of the Royal Government has been given'. He asked the Supreme Command to provide him with the exact numbers of Jews involved and with 'any other useful information on the modalities which it is thought might be followed in this regard'.[33]

By the end of the month of August, as the 2nd Army reported, the Jews in the German zone of Croatia and those in concentration camps at Stara Gradisca and Giacovo had already been deported; those at

57

Jasenovac and Labor-Grad were next. Military intelligence had found out that

> the recent mass arrest of the Jews has produced the worst sort of impression on the population of Zagreb provoking unfavourable comments . . . to show their opposition to the measures a great number of people have gone to the prisons to bring food to the detainees. It seems that many of them have tried to take their lives.[34]

The German foreign ministry looked on with satisfaction. Franz Rademacher, a councillor in the Section *Deutschland* which dealt with Jewish affairs at the Wilhelmstrasse, reported to Under Secretary Martin Luther, his chief, on 4 September 1942, that while there were small difficulties in Greece – the Italian ambassador was unwilling to make Greek Jews in the Italian zone of occupation wear the yellow star – elsewhere things were moving along nicely, as he wrote, 'in a similar case with regard to removal of Jews from Croatia, the Duce has decided that the Jews in the parts occupied by Italy should be treated exactly as in those occupied by German troops.'[35]

What happened next stands out in the entire history of the Second World War and deserves a place in the wider awareness of mankind. Italian soldiers, diplomats and civil servants simply refused to obey those orders. Whereas the early reaction to the *Ustaši* massacres in 1941 had been the result of spontaneous responses by junior officers to awful things happening before their eyes, the decisions of August-September 1942 were the considered responses of senior people, men in the diplomatic service trained to be professionally cautious, and of high ranking generals and colonels with responsibility for thousands of troops. It was a silent mutiny of the mighty and the well-connected; in that respect it had certain similarities to the 1944 plot to kill Hitler. The German *Widerstand* enrolled the same class of people: field marshals, ambassadors and permanent under-secretaries.

The Italian 'resistance' of 1942, if one can call it that, differed in one fundamental respect; it was not a grand plot to change the leadership of the state. The Italian 'resisters' just could not bring themselves to act in the inhuman way that their allies demanded. A few thousand foreign Jews became the cause on which many of them risked their careers and in time even their lives. There were certainly strong practical motives for behaving well to the Jews and these became increasingly apparent in 1943 by which time the Italian chapter of the war had been written. In 1942 with Rommel pressing ahead in Africa and the German armies within sight of the Caucasus mountains, such considerations seem to have played a small part. They did what they did because it was right.

Count Luca Pietromarchi was one of the first to act. He was the senior diplomat responsible for all the territories occupied by the Italians. A handsome and imposing man, Pietromarchi had the very best of connections. His sister had married Bernardo Attolico, long-serving Italian Ambassador in Berlin, and he himself had contacts throughout the Italian establishment. As former head of the economic warfare section of the Foreign Ministry, he knew many industrialists, men like Alberto Pirelli, who regularly called to see Pietromarchi on trips to Rome. A week after the Duce surrendered the Jews to the Germans, Pietromarchi decided to do something about the decision, as he recorded it in his diary: 'I sent for Castellani, who serves as liaison with the 2nd Army, and agreed with him on the ways to avoid surrendering to the Germans those Jews who have placed themselves under the protection of our flag.'[36]

The reaction in the Army was equally adamant. Colonel Cigliani, the colonel in charge of the Office of Civilian Affairs at HQ of the VIth Army Corps, independently of Pietromarchi and at the same time, prepared a summary of the 'situation of the Jews' on 27 August in which he set out the argument

> that our entire activity has been designed to let the Jews live in a human way. . . . [It was impossible to surrender the Jews] because we would not be true to the obligations we assumed . . . they have given us no trouble of any sort.[37]

The best tactic available was one deeply rooted in the Italian bureaucracy: to do nothing in the most officious possible way. The Office of Civilian Affairs of the 2nd Army had already drafted a memorandum outlining eight points showing how to seem to comply without actually doing so,[38] and, when Vittorio Castellani returned from Rome, he received a copy. On 11 September Castellani wrote a personal, private letter to Pietromarchi in which he set out how the campaign of obstruction was going:

> As soon as I got back from Rome, I went to see General Roatta about the question of the Jews. He shares completely our point of view. Supersloda [the Supreme Command Slovenia-Dalmatia] will therefore respond (without too much haste) to the Supreme Command. . . . Naturally the criteria for judging the pertinence [pertinenza in Italian] of persons in the territory of the first zone will be rather elastic.

The news that the Croatians were paying 30 marks to the Germans merely reinforced Castellani's determination to sabotage the surrender of the Jews: 'Apart from any other consideration of a moral character, this is an ignoble traffic in which it is extremely humiliating to have to share, even indirectly.'[39]

The bases had now been laid for an activity in which the Italian state is European champion: surrounding inaction with a gauze of active words. *Pertinenza*, according to the dictionary, means 'appurtenance, a right belonging to a property or estate, competence, belonging'. Presumably it was in the last 'rather elastic' sense that *pertinenza* applied to Jews. While the Italian Consul General in Dubrovnik denied that he had invented the term and tried to claim an ancient pedigree in Austro-Hungarian law,[40] *pertinenza* really meant that Croatian Jews with no claims to Italian citizenship (the Jews of the second zone or zone B) somehow 'belonged' in the annexed territories of Dalmatia (the first zone or zone A), part of metropolitan Italy administratively and hence not under Croatian control. This smokey use of language has an honourable history in Italian politics. It is normally used to cover irreconcilable differences and reached its apotheosis in the description of Communist-Christian Democrat cooperation in the 1970s devised by the late Prime Minister Aldo Moro: 'converging parallels'.

A day after Castellani wrote to Pietromarchi, Roatta flew to Rome for military discussions with the Supreme Command. Pietromarchi recorded in his diary for 13 September 1942, that he met General Roatta on Via Veneto, which under the circumstances is not likely to have been a chance encounter. Roatta asked him how the business with the Jews was going and then said:

> The thing is out of the question. They have placed themselves under our authority. The Croatians have asked us to give them back. I naturally opposed it with a flat refusal. They said that they would then have to ask the Germans. Now there's an order from the Duce.[41]

Roatta and Pietromarchi still evidently believed that the Croatians were behind the demands not the Germans; in other words they knew nothing yet about the final solution. They parted having agreed to exchange letters and 'to draw things out'.

But the General was not in Rome to worry about Jews; the Italian state had begun to show the first signs of its terminal illness. When on 13 September Mussolini made one of his regular telephone calls to General Cavallero, his chief of staff, the general told him that 'unpleasant things' had happened at Zara and that he had summoned Roatta to explain reports of 'ferment among the troops and unwillingness to obey orders'.[42] A few days after his return from Rome Roatta went to investigate a presidio in Yugoslavia overrun by partisans. In the course of his investigation he observed that in the period between 24 August and 2 September there had been fifteen acts of sabotage on the road and rail lines betwen Fiume, Ogulin and Karlovac and that he no longer had the force to repress them because his units were

> poor in quality by age and training; tired because of heavy duty for months without the possibility of rotation; insufficient in number (instead of 25–30 men per kilometre of line, as was judged necessary, there are only 10–15). [underlined in original][43]

At that very moment the Greek guerrillas began to make an impact. Compared to Roatta's 2nd Army in Yugoslavia, General Geloso's 11th Army in Greece had enjoyed a relatively peaceful time. Although the Greek army had been disarmed in the same casual manner as the Yugoslavs, the Greeks lacked the widespread traditions of banditry and self-defence which made the emergence of *cetniks* inevitable in the north. The peculiar paralysis of Greek life brought about by the pre-war Metaxas dictatorship, the uncertain loyalty of the Greek people to the King and Queen in exile, the deep divisions among the bourgeois parties, the relative weakness of the communists and the absence of a unified political leadership combined to slow the growth of a Greek armed struggle.[44] By the middle of September 1942, for the first time, 11th Army HQ reported that the guerrillas had begun to fight in large formations and that one had wiped out an entire Italian battalion.[45] On 22 September Geloso too was in Rome explaining to Cavallero the poor condition of his troops.[46]

Another crisis, a personal one, became increasingly clear in the autumn of 1942. Ortona had confided in his diary that when the Duce was absent, Rome was 'paralysed'.[47] By early September 1942, even on the rare occasions when the Duce was physically present, he was spiritually absent. Pirelli wrote:

> Actual situation full of enigmas and contradictions; permanent excess of power of the chief and recurring criticism: 'he's a weakling!' (with regard to Hitler; his inability to get rid of certain collaborators etc). Discontent very widespread but on the other hand enthusiastic crowds if he appears on a balcony or speaks.[48]

The Duce spoke less and appeared less because during the summer months of 1942 he stayed away from Rome. Apart from three brief visits to Rome he was either at Riccione or in his retreat in the Romagna at la Rocca delle Caminate.[49] Rumours about his health began to circulate; by early October they had become fact. Bottai saw his *capo* for the first time for weeks when Mussolini returned to Rome on 7 October:

The face grey, ashy, the cheeks drawn, the gaze tired, the mouth fixed by an expression of bitterness, all indicate clearly the illness which, as rumour says, has taken over again. The old ulcer! Or, according to the investigations of Castellani, amoebic dysentery.[50]

The story spread throughout Mussolini's shrinking empire. As Console Scalchi, commander of the fascist militia in Dalmatia, emerged from the Governor's office in Zara a day after Bottai had seen Mussolini, he told Ortona that all he and Bastianini could talk about was the Duce's illness.[51] The prefect of Zara, who returned to Dalmatia from an official visit to Rome on 10 October, 'spoke of the heavy atmosphere, cynicism, exhaustion, disorder and above all the rumours about the state of the Duce's health.'[52]

In his *The Brutal Friendship* F.W. Deakin has a marvellous image to explain Mussolini's method of government:

In a sense, Mussolini governed Italy as if he were running a personal newspaper single-handed, setting the type, writing the leaders, interviewing everybody, chasing reporters, paying the informers, sacking staff incessantly . . . and basically ignoring the supreme responsibility of political power as extraneous to the business.[53]

As in Hitler's Reich so in Mussolini's 'Roman Empire', no provision had been made for the succession. The Duce had no deputy and trusted nobody. The generation which had made the fascist revolution, men frequently of great ability like Bottai, Bastianini, or Grandi, had reached their forties or early fifties and no longer enjoyed Mussolini's confidence. The Duce had never trusted his son-in-law Galeazzo Ciano and the Mussolini children, except for Edda Ciano, were nonentities. The fascist youth movement and the student organizations had become cheap ways to enter the civil service or make careers. Perhaps no single fact more sharply describes the intellectual bankruptcy of fascism than the absence of a younger generation within the movement. Throughout September and October 1942 the Italian authorities could pursue their delaying tactics on the Jewish question because Rome was gripped by a creeping leadership crisis. Nobody dared to take a major decision on anything when the Duce was away.

Roatta replied to the Supreme Command on 22 September, telling them that he had given orders to establish the 'pertinence' of some 3,000 Jewish refugees as a first step to turning at least some of them over to the Croatian authorities. Roatta was not the sort of general who simply saluted and obeyed. He took the opportunity to raise two objections to the *consegna* (consignment) as the surrender of the Jews was now generally called:

> My own point of view is that consigning the Jews to the Germans or the Croatians would end in practice by harming our prestige because, even if only tactically, we have put them under our protection and because it would cause grave repercussions among the armed voluntary *cetnik* militia who might be induced to believe one day they too might be given over to the *Ustaši.*[54]

Roatta had now found an argument which made military sense. The 2nd Army could not fight the guerrilla war on its own. He had just supplied Supreme Command with all the evidence they needed. Without the aid of the *cetniks* there was no hope of holding on to territories now occupied. Roatta had fought German pressure to disarm them. He knew how volatile and uncertain their loyalty was. The London government-in-exile made soothing noises to them. It would take a lot less than the consignment of a few thousand Jews to the Croatians to cause the friendly, local *cetniks* to disappear into the hills. After all, Italian forces had become the protectors of both Serb and Jew in 1941 because the Croatians threatened both; if that protection ceased, the Serb *cetniks* would look elsewhere for shelter.

General Mario Roatta had to be careful. Castellani, who, as Foreign Ministry liaison officer with Roatta's headquarters, had actually drafted the letter of 22 September, wrote privately to Count Pietromarchi a few days later enclosing a copy of the reply and adding that

> the report is rather laconic and does not, perhaps, develop sufficiently all the points which would have been useful to mention. Still, all the ideas are there and can be used, if one wants, to serve as a point of departure to try to provoke an attenuation of the decisions taken by higher authority on the matter.
>
> I might add that I prepared a much more detailed and precise reply but the compilation of the reply has been exceptionally hard work and we only arrived at the formula finally adopted after six successive versions. Besides, one has to bear in mind that the position of General Roatta is extremely difficult and that he is constantly worried (and perhaps with reason) that he may be offering his 'friends' in Rome the chance to present him as a rebel who doesn't obey orders or to let him slip on the customary banana skin.[55]

The chief Roman 'friend' and the one most likely to strew banana skins in General Roatta's path was Marshall Ugo Cavallero, Chief of the General Staff of the Armed Forces known as *comando supremo*

(Supreme Command). Of all the figures in this curious story of virtue and intrigue Cavallero remains the hardest to get into focus, although paradoxically he left the largest volume of paper. Cavallero anticipated Nixon by installing in his desk in the Supreme Command a listening device which went through to a next door office where literally every official word spoken was transcribed. The same stenographer transcribed every word spoken outside the office when the Marshall travelled on military business. Cavallero's *Diario Storico*, the war diary kept by all commands in the Italian army above regimental level, reads like a play with the actors' words full of the vitality of living speech, for it is just that. After the war his son published a part of those diaries and the rest are being issued by the Historical Section of the General Staff of the Italian Army. Few modern generals have left such dense source materials.

The man Cavallero remains in the shadow in spite of the diaries. Normally a historian gets a feel for those characters whose letters and handwriting have become familiar. I find myself saying that I 'know' Castellani or Bottai. I would never say that about Cavallero. He reveals extraordinarily little about himself. He studied pure mathematics at Turin University and in the words of the Italian national biographical dictionary was a man 'of vast culture'. He spent part of the 1920s and 1930s in industry, thus anticipating the modern military-industrial general, and enjoyed the respect and friendship of Alberto Pirelli. Ciano loathed him and made that clear on every occasion they met and there were those in the navy (the Italian Supreme Command controlled all three services) who thought he had Bonapartist ambitions.[56]

He gained Mussolini's respect for the cool way he assumed command of the Italian forces in the early stages of the Greek war and turned what might have been a rout into a stalemate. There was no one who doubted either his military or administrative abilities. The record shows that throughout 1942 he spent seven days a week in the office fending off impossible telephone calls from the Duce and impossible demands from his three service chiefs, field commanders and German allies. General Enno von Rintelen, the long-serving German military attaché in Rome, had a high regard for him as an 'active soldier, full of ideas with a sound operational sense and strategic view. He had a good, perhaps too developed, capacity for adapting himself to situations . . . and was always ready to follow the demands of the OKW'[57]

That was the rub. Cavallero, a small dapper man with a pince-nez, spoke fluent German and worked hard to avoid friction between the Axis partners. The well-informed SS agent Eugen Dollmann writes that Field Marshall Kesselring, German commander in the zone, found Cavallero 'absolutely submissive' and saw Roatta 'as the true chief among Italian senior commanders whose acute intelligence, if without scruples, made a great impression.'[58] There is no doubt that Kesselring and Cavallero enjoyed a close working relationship. During critical periods Kesselring called at Supreme Command at least once and often several times a day and both generals spoke extremely frankly to each other.[59] The 'feel' of those meetings never gave me the impression that Cavallero 'submitted' to Kesselring but that there was genuine respect between them.

The mystery around Cavallero can never be resolved and covers the strange circumstances of his death. Cavallero was arrested after the fall of fascism in July 1943, along with Buffarini Guidi, Teruzzi, Gravelli, Interlandi and several other representatives of the pro-German wing of fascism, and was imprisoned at the famous Regina Coeli jail on the banks of the Tiber. After the armistice and the flight of the royal government to Brindisi, the Germans ordered their friends to be released. On the night of 13 September Marshall Kesselring entertained Marshall Cavallero, General Soddu and several other senior commanders to dinner at his villa in Frascati. Earlier that day, on his release from Regina Coeli prison, Cavallero had visited his wife who was seriously ill in hospital. He told her that the Germans had offered him the command of a new pro-Nazi Italian army then in process of formation and that he intended to say no. His wife feared that they would kill him if he refused. Early in the morning on 14 September the body of Marshall Cavallero was found in the garden of Marshall Kesselring's villa, a bullet through his head. Was it suicide or murder?[60]

Cavallero's fellow prisoners in Regina Coeli such as Buffarini Guidi and Interlandi were well known anti-semites as was Farinacci whom the Germans had already whisked to safety in the Reich. All three played an evil part in the destruction of Italian Jewry in 1943–44 under the puppet republic of Salò. I have never found the slightest evidence in his own papers nor in comments by others that Cavallero hated Jews. He certainly knew about the persecution of the Jews of Europe. The SIE (Italian Military Intelligence) collected information on it and circulated it monthly to High Commands. Just before Cavallero lost his post in January 1943 his daily diary records: '0950 hours: telephones General Vercellino. Subject: publication in foreign journals of a proclamation which deplores the war on the Jews'[61] By January 1943 such reports contained many accurate details of the final solution, so Cavallero must have known a great deal.

If a man is judged by the company he keeps then Cavallero, who worked closely with the Germans, must have belonged to the anti-semitic wing of the Italian military-political establishment. As the vacuum opened around the empty throne of Mussolini, rumours of a Farinacci-Cavallero plot began to circulate. About Farinacci's rabid anti-semitism and pro-German sentiments there was no doubt. Marshall Caviglia noted in his diary: 'Farinacci and Cavallero seem to be in close accord. The other fascist chiefs are worked up against Farinacci, and they fear him because he has the Germans with him.'[62]

At the end of October 1942 General Hazon, commanding officer of the carabinieri, a force which combines both military and police functions, told General Puntoni that

> the illness of the Duce has let loose the appetites of the competitors for his succession, some of whom have revealed their hands to Cavallero to find out what he thinks and how he would behave if Mussolini should disappear or in the event of a *coup d'état*. . . . His attitude would be that just as he had also loyally served the Duce so he would be prepared to serve the head of the government who would be appointed by the King.[63]

The verdict on Cavallero remains 'unproven'. The anti-semitic, pro-German wing of the fascist establishment looked to him as 'their' general. Yet Cavallero never seriously impeded Roatta in his policy of saving Jews, and, of course, he could easily have done so. He knew, I suspect, more about the holocaust than anybody at the top of the regime; yet he worked hard and plausibly to help the Axis win the war. The shadowy uncertainty about his real thoughts explains the extreme delicacy of Roatta's position on the consignment of the Croatian Jews. General Vittorio Ambrosio, Roatta's predecessor at *Supersloda* and now Chief of the Army General Staff, noted anxiously in his diary on 17 October 1942: 'Must hold one's tongue. Spies on the staff. . . . Political situation not clear. Duce ill.'[64]

Italian policy toward the Jews emerged out of the murky atmosphere of Rome in the autumn of 1942, an atmosphere full of tension, rumour, intrigue and fear. It was one of many policies and decisions which the historian cannot follow as it disappears into the darker corners of the collapsing regime. A few figures stand out in the gloom by their frankness. There is no doubt where Count Pietromarchi or General Roatta stood because they said what they thought and left evidence of it in writing. What Cavallero thought, what Ciano thought, indeed what Mussolini himself really thought about the Jewish question, can only be guessed. My hunch is that they tolerated the subversion of orders because saving the Jews came to seem a rational policy as the war began to go badly. If Rome had to seek a separate peace with the Allies, it would be a good idea not to have helped the Germans to murder Jews. It was, perhaps, not an ace up a sleeve but might be a joker.

In early November 1942 Pirelli went to see his old business associate Ugo Cavallero and found him in a depressed mood. The news from the North African front was bad. Cavallero said that Rommel was 'defeated'. In this frame of mind, Cavallero told Pirelli that Mussolini would have to make clear to their German ally 'our disagreement on three points: treatment of the occupied countries, excesses towards the Jews, and relations with the Papacy. One ought to try to create a true European federation respectful of each nationality.'[65]

The Chief of the Italian General Staff, as late as November 1942, had not yet grasped the nature of the war nor the real aims of his Axis partner. With hindsight his ideas seem childishly naive. In 1942, in view of what Italians then knew of the holocaust, it is just possible to believe that Cavallero took his proposals seriously. In any case his remarks to Pirelli point neatly to the opportunistic link between defeat and fastidiousness on the Jewish question. Whatever his real feelings, a little mildness to the Jews of the second zone in Croatia might be useful in some future final reckoning.

The vacuum at the centre of power made the conspiracy to help the Jews easier. The Duce's order to surrender them to the Croatians existed and in a totalitarian state could not be openly ignored. On the other hand he was ill and not seeing as many despatches. Checking the 'pertinence' of Jews in Croatia might take months as requests for documents often do in Italy. The famous Padre Tacchi Venturi, the Pope's most reliable private representative, complained to the Under-Secretary at the Ministry of the Interior, Buffarini Guidi, that the Cardinal Secretary of State, Maglione, had been kept waiting for nine months because of the 'slowness' of the bureaucracy.[66] Padre Tacchi Venturi spoke unofficially for the Pope. If His Holiness could not get an answer from the Ministry of the Interior in less than nine months, the 2nd Army could expect to wait years for its requests on behalf of lesser mortals.

Meanwhile Hitler had become impatient with the slow progress achieved in the Balkans. In August he appointed the 57 year old Austrian *Luftwaffe* general, *Generaloberst* Alexander Löhr, Supreme Commander South East with responsibility for the entire Balkan peninsula and headquarters at Salonica-Arsakli. Hitler made Löhr's assignment very clear, as Löhr told the German Ambassador Kasche a few months later: 'He was to make things quiet, even if it was the quiet of the cemetery.'[67]

A few weeks later Löhr inspected his new empire and found conditions not much to his liking. The squabbling authorities in Serbia operated 'alongside one another, and sometimes against each other'. The SS behaved as law unto itself and tolerated no 'interference' from the Army's military police but at least 'in Serbia there are no more

Jews'.[68] He turned to the Italian problem and received in mid-September a summary of the 'disagreements with the Italians' which contained sixteen recent examples of Italy's toleration of the *cetniks* and hostility to the Croatians.[69] The mess needed decision at the highest level and on 25 September 1942 Hitler accompanied by Reich Foreign Minister von Ribbentrop, and Field Marshal Keitel received the *Poglavnik* of the Independent State of Croatia, Ante Pavelić, accompanied by the German Ambassador at Zagreb, Siegfried Kasche, the German Plenipotentiary General Glaise von Horstenau (a school friend of Löhr's and his source of confidential information) and Minister Hewel from Belgrade.

The Führer began the meeting by saying that Germany had only transportation interests in the area and not political ones. *Cetniks* were 'dangerous' because they were Serb chauvinists. If the Italians could not deal with the rebels without *cetnik* help, he would generously relieve Croatia of the need to send more units to the Russian front and expand the Croatian army in the area. On the Jewish question the *Poglavnik* assured Hitler that in most parts of Croatia it had largely been resolved but they could not get at 'Jewish centres' like Mostar and Ragusa because the Italians declared that

> it was part of a larger problem which could not be prematurely decided from case to case. Besides they cited consideration of the Vatican and even the honour of the Italian army in reply to Croatian wishes to solve the Jewish question. . . . The Reich Foreign Minister drew attention to the instruction given by the Duce on the Jewish question [the *'nulla osta'* of 21 August 1942] about which the Rome Embassy had been informed. Apparently this had not yet been carried out on the spot. It appeared that the 2nd Army under General Roatta was pursuing its own policies.[70]

The Reich Foreign Minister had got his facts ominously right. Hitler reacted vaguely by saying that he hoped soon to see the Duce to talk things over.

When the German party returned to Zagreb, they began to review the whole situation in the theatre of operations and prepared a report for the Führer. It was completed on 1 October and signed not only by Kasche and Glaise but by the Supreme Commander South East *Generaloberst* Alexander Löhr himself, one of the very rare occasions when German military and diplomatic representatives attempted any sort of coordination. It is a long document which covers the military and political situation in Croatia, the opposition of the Italians to German wishes, and on page 6 finally deals with the Jewish question:

> The implementation of the Jewish laws of the Croatian state are

being hindered by Italian officials to such an extent that in the coastal zones, especially in Mostar, Dubrovnik and Crkvenica [Cirquenizza in Italian], many Jews stand under Italian protection and many others are being helped over the border into Italian Dalmatia or Italy. Thus the Jews gain help and can continue their treasonable activities and especially those directed against our war aims. To be sure, according to a report of our Embassy in Rome of the beginning of September the Duce has decided that the Jews are to be treated according to the Croatian laws. Up to today neither the Italian Minister Casertano nor the Supreme Commander of the 2nd Army General Roatta has received direct instructions.[71]

The German Foreign Ministry reacted at once and sent a councillor at the German Embassy, Johann von Plessen, to see Lanza d'Ajeta and to tell him that in spite of the Duce's orders, according to reports reaching the German authorities, the Italian military commands had received no instructions. D'Ajeta scribbled across the memorandum that Count Pietromarchi would have to devise 'some reply' especially to 'the point regarding our soldiers'.[72] A few days later Ciano himself sent a cable to the Supreme Command to ask what instructions had been given to the commands in Croatia about delivering Jews 'to the Germans'.[73] As Daniel Carpi writes, we cannot tell if the phrase 'to the Germans' was intentional or a slip, for technically the Jews were to be delivered to the Croatians.[74]

A flurry of activity followed. The Supreme Command sent a telegram to 2nd Army HQ; the Foreign Ministry asked its liaison officer Castellani whether orders had or had not been received, and the 2nd Army replied a little disingenuously that no orders had ever been received to hand Jews over to the Germans.[75] 'Drawing things out' no longer seemed to be an adequate response to mounting German pressure. Himmler himself came to Rome to add his dark prestige to the urgent German request for the Jews under Italian protection. The Duce received the *Reichsführer SS* in the Palazzo Venezia at 5 pm on Sunday, 11 October 1942, and was 'very friendly'. The Duce explained his political difficulties. In Italy he was only 'one of three: himself, King and Pope'.

Himmler told Mussolini the usual lies. Jews were being deported to the east but only to prevent sabotage and, yes, it had been necessary in Russia to have some shot, men, women and children, because they all worked for the partisans:

The Duce said on his part that was the only possible solution. I said to the Duce that we had brought Jews who had been implicated politically to concentration camps, that we were using other Jews to build streets in the east, where, to be sure, they died rather quckly because they were not used to work.[76]

It is not clear if Mussolini believed such stuff but what was only too clear was the mounting level of pressure. On the 14th Pietromarchi wrote in his diary:

The Germans behave with their usual arrogance towards us. They have renewed several times their request to consign the Jews of Croatia to them, stating that they have learned that the command of the 2nd Army has not yet received instructions in that sense.[77]

In the meantime the German Ambassador in Rome, von Mackensen, had been to see Lanza d'Ajeta at the Italian Foreign Ministry to press him to allow the Germans to deport to 'the East' Italian Jews living in France, Belgium and other countries occupied by German troops. D'Ajeta refused. Italian Jews were 'regarded as Italian citizens, who had rights to the same protection as any other citizens'.[78] This was yet another irritating point of friction between the Axis partners. It annoyed the SS and German Foreign Office to see Italian Jews not wearing the yellow star and living normally in a Europe rapidly becoming *judenrein*. It seems in retrospect an odd thing for a senior Italian diplomat to say of a group of persons whom Italian racial laws had deprived of rights, position and property. Mussolini's Italy at least still conceded Italian Jews a right not to be murdered.

At the very moment of maximum pressure, the German Foreign Office suddenly changed its course. On 17 October von Ribbentrop replied to Siegfried Kasche, ambassador in Zagreb, rebuking him for his constant carping at the Italians and reminding him that 'the German-Italian alliance is the basis of our foreign policy and we cannot allow ourselves to be brought into conflict with our ally because of Croatian interests.'[79]

Even the Jew-baiting Martin Luther, head of the section responsible for extermination of Jews in the German Foreign Office, urged his officials to respect the 'special position' of the Italians and to be careful of their sensibilities.[80] On 22 October Luther prepared a long report entitled 'Italy and the Jewish Question' in which he noted with regret how 'little understanding' the Italians had shown for the operation 'to cleanse Europe of Jews' and how dangerous it was that the Axis had 'no united policy in these matters'. After reviewing Italian failings in their treatment of Jews at home, of Italian Jews abroad, of non-Italian Jews in third states under Italian protection, he concluded that

Italy must adapt its measures and legislation to match the

principles and measures we have taken. . . . The appearance of Italy as the protector of the Jews gives our opponents a welcome opportunity to disturb the good understanding between the Axis partners.[81]

The force of these words was much reduced by the conflict which had broken out within the German Foreign Office between Joachim von Ribbentrop, the Reich Foreign Minister, and his former protégé, the ex-furniture remover, Martin Luther. The *Abteilung Deutschland* (German Section) had been established in 1940 and, as Christopher Browning has shown in his fascinating study *The Final Solution and the German Foreign Office*, it had rapidly become Luther's empire. The five German Ambassadors who came from the SA (the *Sturmabteilung*, the Brownshirts of the Nazi Party) had made careers in the diplomatic service under Luther's protection and were understood to be his men. One of them was Siegfried Kasche in Zagreb. Luther's influence spread as the Jewish question became more central and by 1942 through his direct relations with SS functionaries like Eichmann he was operating an ambitious, independent Jewish policy. He over-reached himself in the case of the Rumanian Jews and got caught. Ribbentrop called him to order and from that moment on Luther began to fight for his life. He hoped to drive a wedge between Ribbentrop and Himmler. The Italian question offered the perfect occasion. As Browning writes,

> Luther calculated that if he succeeded in pushing Ribbentrop into making sharp demands upon the Italians in the Jewish question, and the pressure worked, he would get part of the credit. But if the Italians put up the expected resistance and refused to give in to the German demands, Ribbentrop would be discredited by the failure . . . if Ribbentrop showed his usual reluctance to confront the Italians, the foreign minister's hesitancy would stand in marked contrast to Luther's zeal.[82]

Ribbentrop outsmarted Luther. He adopted the same delaying tactics which the Italian authorities had used on him and hence avoided exposing himself as too 'hard' or too 'soft' on the Jewish question. He stayed his hand while Luther's initiatives failed everywhere. In Rumania, the Antonescu government suddenly halted the deportation of the Jews of Bucharest after they had been rounded up. The Jewish poet and physician, Dr Emil Dorian, recorded in his diary on 14 October that

> those present at the moment of liberation witnessed scenes of almost unbearable delirium. People jumped out of windows throwing their luggage into the street, handing babies into

71

outstretched arms, shrieking with the happiness of freedom. Some fainted with joy, unable to bear the emotion of having survived the most agonizing of shipwrecks. And they hugged one another, they kissed, asking over and over if it were really true, their hands fondled the air of freedom, they kissed the ground. Within minutes the city had heard the news of their liberation. And everyone hurried to share it with family, with friends, with acquaintances.[83]

These were intolerable scenes in the eyes of the Germans. They put every conceivable pressure on the Rumanian government but it refused to deport any more Jews from 'old Rumania'. It ought to be said that there is no comparison between Italy and Rumania. The Rumanian authorities had vigorously deported Jews from its conquered territories and had allowed its soldiery to slaughter 160,000 Russian Jews in their zone of occupation in southern Russia known as Transnistria. Curzio Malaparte in *Kaputt* describes Rumanian soldiers, shouting 'rats! rats!', as they fired at Jewish men, women and children hiding in haystacks or bushes.[84] For sheer brutality the Rumanians are only exceeded by the Croatians and the *SS Einsatzgruppen*. It was too much even for Martin Luther who tried to stop the 'wild deportations' of the Rumanians.[85] Fear of Allied retaliation, not humanitarian sentiment, halted the deportation of the Rumanian Jews. The Rumanian army on the Russian front had already begun to buckle; in a few months it would collapse completely. Now was not the moment for enthusiastic participation in genocide. Antonescu was the first Axis ally to leap off the band-wagon almost before it stopped rolling forward.

Martin Luther lost prestige over the Jews of Rumania. The ambassador there was one of 'his' men and he had intrigued with the SS to get credit for the destruction of Rumania's Jews. He grew desperate. In February 1943, when Glaise von Horstenau visited Berlin on military business, he was astonished to find, as he wrote his 'dear friend' General Löhr on his return that

In Berlin my most valuable confidant hitherto, Under-Secretary Martin Luther, one-time shipper and property agent of Ribbentrop and for many years his closest political assistant, is under lock and key in the Gestapo headquarters on Prinz-Albrecht-Strasse, allegedly for mounting a palace revolution against his chief.[86]

Luther went from there to Sachsenhausen concentration camp from which he never emerged. Ribbentrop's caution in dealing with Luther in the autumn of 1942 was clearly justified. The affair had a direct effect on the German Foreign Office's handling of the Jewish question and, in Browning's words, 'left the Italians free to flaunt German desires'.[87]

The Italians did not know that they were free. All they could see was constant pressure. On 20 October the Croatian Ambassador Perić went to see Roberto Ducci, desk officer responsible for Croatia at the Italian Foreign Ministry, to tell him that the Croatians had an interesting new idea. The refugees in the second zone should all be transported to Italy with the proviso that they surrender all claims to property in Croatia. Ducci's memorandum concludes:

> Perić added, as a man, that he hoped we would be able to accept such a proposition. He had come to have a very good idea of what fate awaits the Jews transported by the Germans to the eastern territories.[88]

The Italians were embarrassed by the proposal and even more so when on the next day Prince Bismarck again called to insist that the Jewish refugees be handed over to the Croatian authorities 'as soon as possible'. In response the Foreign Ministry drafted a memorandum summing up the situation and concluding that

> In such a state of affairs it would seem opportune that Supersloda receive orders to intern immediately all the Jews in the zones occupied by us, roughly 2,500; those who are Croatians to be consigned; those with title to Italian citizenship not to be consigned [underlines in original][89]

Roberto Ducci drafted a reply to the Croatian Ambassador which went to the Chief of Cabinet Lanza d'Ajeta and then to Mussolini who approved it. On 28 October the Croatian minister was told its contents. The Jews were to be interned and processed. Those found to be Croatian would be turned over to the Croatian authorities for what was now clearly understood to be 'elimination',[90] while the Italian Jews would be spared. Ambassador Perić replied that since his government only acted in the interests of public order the proposal would be highly satisfactory.[91] That evening d'Ajeta informed the German ambassador von Mackensen that the Italian government had flatly rejected the Croatian suggestion to take the Jewish refugees to Italy 'since Italy was no Palestine'. He then explained to the German Ambassador the Italian counter-proposal to intern all Jews in the second zone, divide them into Croatian and non-Croatian and 'to give them over to the Croatian authorities who would from that moment assume responsibility for them'.[92] That same evening Supreme Command instructed Supersloda (Italian army command in Slovenia and Dalmatia) to proceed to intern all Jews in the jurisdiction of the command and to provide for their sorting on the basis of pertinence, or rather into Croatian Jews and Jews having title to Italian citizenship, and to send to this Supreme Command, when selection has been made, lists of Jews belonging to both categories.[93]

The Chief of Staff of the 2nd Army, Brigadier General Clemente Primieri, wrote on the bottom of the dispatch, 'The foreign ministry was right?!' It certainly looked that way. A few days earlier Castellani had rung him from Rome to say that *consegna* was now firmly decided and there was nothing to be done about it.[94] Primieri wrote angrily,

it's a violation of our word which we gave them and will have terrible repercussions on our relations with all the others who have fairly put their trust in us. They will be afraid that we will abandon them from one moment to the next. Our prestige will be greatly reduced.[95]

An order was an order, and on 29 October Supersloda sent wires to the three corps commanders ordering them to provide for the internment of all Jews in their zones of operation.[96]

What actually happened next is far from clear. One explanation has been offered by the Italian Foreign Ministry in a report prepared after the war on its efforts to help Jews and in an account written by Roberto Ducci under the pseudonym Verax, published in 1944.[97] The Israeli historian Daniel Carpi who is the greatest authority on Italian attempts to save Jews, accepts their arguments. All three suggest that the *consegna* was never seriously intended, and that internment was yet another Italian ruse to keep the Germans off their track. Carpi believes that the furious reaction of people like Brigadier Primieri arose because 'apparently none perceived the true intentions of the new orders, which they had received, and they all expressed their anxiety as to what would happen to the Jews.'[98]

That reading seems to me unlikely. Castellani rang Sussak from Rome on 24 October, that is, while policy in the foreign ministry was being made but after the memorandum proposing consignment had been drafted. He asked his brother, a general, to call at 2nd Army HQ to fill in details presumably too confidential to be discussed on the telephone. We know that Count Pietromarchi regarded Vittorio Castellani as his agent in the struggle to save Jews. Since Castellani was actually in Rome for the decision, it seems much more likely that the decision had genuinely gone against Pietromarchi and Castellani and in favour of the group who wanted to comply with the Germans. Otherwise it is hard to explain General Primieri's outburst which took place before the formal order to consign the Jews reached Sussak and must have been a reaction to the bad news that Castellani had given him. It is no blemish on Italian honour that not all diplomats were equally zealous in saving Jewish lives. Italy contained a fair number of convinced anti-semites and a much larger number of opportunists. What distinguishes the Italian record is that it had such a large number of Pietromarchis, Castellanis and Roattas. It does the good men a disservice to make reality neat and simple; it is never either.

The reaction of the Italian army in Croatia was extremely hostile to the idea of internment. The commander of a mobile machine gun battalion sent a friend a memorandum he had received from 'responsible elements in the 2nd Army' which expressed the army's attitude to the rounding up of the Jews:

> The concentration precedes their consignment to the Croatians who in turn will consign them to the Germans. The Germans do not conceal that their object is to arrive at the violent suppression of these people. . . . The Italian army should not dirty its hands in this business.[99]

The commanding officer of the Carabinieri in the Vth Corps zone, Lt Col Pietro Esposito Amodio, reported that anti-Italian rumour mongers were using the detention of the Jews to weaken Italy's position. They whispered that Italy had been shown to be 'a small country that has been reduced to the status of a vassal of greater Germany'.[100]

These issues, while certainly significant, would by themselves not have tipped the balance towards the Pietromarchi-Roatta camp. What seems to have done so was the mission of the Carabinieri General, Giuseppe Pièche, in early November. The carabinieri occupy a dual position in Italian life, as part of the armed forces, (in the military order of precedence the 'senior service') and as part of the domestic police force which shares responsibility for the maintenance of law and order with the 'public security' services under the Ministry of the Interior. The border between them is complex and overlapping and can only be understood by experts. Carabinieri General Casarico has twice patiently explained it to me at length but it disappeared from my understanding by the time I left his apartment.

General Pièche was an important figure. The Duce and Cavallero consulted him on matters of order in the occupation zones and in early 1943 Cavallero discussed giving him the post of commanding officer of 'the arm', as the carabinieri are always known.[101] This was an unusual mark of respect, for custom and prudence normally require that the commanding officer of the carabinieri not be from 'the arm'. Its combination of military and police functions, its strong sense of identity, and its interesting secret archives could make it a 'state within the state'. In fact, Pièche later commanded 'the arm', one of the few carabinieri to have done so this century.[102]

No record exists in the carabinieri archive of Pièche's mission nor is there any indication in the Supreme Command files that he went on army business. My guess is that either Cavallero or Mussolini himself sent Pièche to Croatia in order to help decide Italian policy and to report what carabinieri agents could uncover about the fate of the Jews. Pièche's long 'Report on Croatia' bears the date 1 November and begins as follows: 'The *Ustaši* regime has recited its "mea culpa! mea culpa!" for the murder of the Jews, "mea culpa!" for the massacre of the orthodox, "mea culpa!" for the fight against Macek and his party [Croatian peasant party].'[103]

Pavelić knows, continues Pièche, that such outrages brought the regime to the edge of 'ruin'. Now he has changed his cabinet and weakened the position in Zagreb of the German general Glaise von Horstenau, 'that master of intrigue'. Since the Führer continues to declare that Croatia is 'a vital space for Italy', now 'would be an opportune moment to clarify the strange divergence beween German central directives and what happens on the periphery . . . and to reinforce our collaboration with the Pavelić regime.'[104] The Jewish refugee question

> seems to be resolved with the order to concentrate them and to consign them to the Croatians. The means of handing them over which have not yet been decided seem rather delicate. The business has awakened everywhere the fear that it will end in a proper 'butchery' which would be repugnant to our Latin sensibilities. According to notices from Zagreb, Pavelić is disposed to limit himself solely to putting them in concentration camps so long as the Jews declare themselves willing to renounce their fixed assets in the second zone. Between murder and robbery it is, perhaps, preferable to put our money on the second. It is certain that by liberating ourselves from these Jews, if possible in a humane way, we shall remove the eyes and ears of London and people at the very least not favourable to the cause of the Axis.[105]

The senior carabinieri general on active duty had not yet learned the true destination of the Jews of Croatia. As a result he sees no real objection to *consegna*. A majority in the Italian Foreign Ministry apparently took the same view. Three days later he wired Rome to report an important new fact. I have not found a copy of the original telegram but it is reproduced in the files of the Foreign Ministry and can be seen on p. 78. It reads very simply:

> General Pièche reports that he has found out that the Jews of Croatia deported from the German zone of occupation to the

eastern territories have been 'eliminated' by means of toxic gas in the train in which they were enclosed.[106] (See Document 2, p. 78)

At last, as Luigi Vidau wrote on the bottom of the dispatch, there was 'evidence', hard, reliable evidence, to show the Duce, and the stamp on the top of the document shows that the Mussolini saw it. Pièche was clearly deeply shaken by what he had found because in his next report to Rome he reversed his position on the issue of consigning the Jews of the second zone. On 14 November he began,

the decision to consign the Jews would be the equivalent of condemning them to death and has provoked very unfavourable comments . . . among the troops . . . and among the rest of the orthodox and muslim populations who fear that they too will be exposed in future to some similar provision whereas today they stand confident under the shadow of our flag. . . . At this particular moment, perhaps, an act of clemency would, in the opinion of most people, be very opportune[107]

The copies of Pièche's reports were in the files of the Office of Civilian Affairs of 2nd Army HQ, an agency which had long taken the same view. It seems plausible to me that General Pièche's conversion tipped the balance finally in favour of resistance. When, two days after Pièche's crucial telegram, Alberto Pirelli went to complain about the 'inhuman excesses' of the Germans against the Jews which he had just seen on a business trip to Paris, Brussels and Berlin, Mussolini replied that 'they are letting them emigrate . . . to another world'.[108]

The summit of the fascist state could no longer evade the truth. The Germans, not the Croatians, were the murderers now. Their Axis partner was engaged in something unheard of in the history of mankind: systematic extermination by modern means of an entire people. The documents suggest that from that point in early November 1942 the Italian authorities in the Foreign Ministry and the armed forces knew that they must not surrender those few thousand Jews.

The Jews themselves had no such certainty. Mr Imre Rochlitz remembers the sudden round-up and the anxiety as the trucks which bore the Jews away from the Dalmatian cities made their way along the coast. Everybody knew that each fork in the road meant life or death. If the convoy took the right fork, it would head to the interior, into Croatia and to death. Every left fork meant that the convoy would stay in Italian territory and the Jews would live.[109] In Mostar, on the other hand, the Jews seemed to have known very early that they were not to be 'consigned'. The Civil Affairs Office of the Division 'Murge' reported on 9 November that

Ministero degli Affari Esteri
Gabinetto A.P.-Croazia

VISTO DAL DUCE

A P P U N T O
——————

Il "enerale Pièche riferisce risultargli che gli
ebrei croati della zona di occupazione tedesca deportati
nei territori orientali, sono stati "eliminati" mediante
l'impiego di gas tossico nel treno in cui erano rinchiusi.

Roma, lì 4 novembre 1942.XX°

Document 2 General Pièche reports the gassing of deported Jews, 1942 on the afternoon of the 6th instant in the local Jewish church, the head of the community of Israelites in Mostar, Hajon David, convoked a meeting of his co-religionists to inform them of the measures which will shortly be adopted with respect to them about the transfer to a new place under direct and exclusive control of the Italian military authorities. Attendance was total and the news was received with lively expressions of pleasure.[110]

The evacuation of the Jews of Mostar began on 19 November and was completed by 3 December; 445 persons altogether were evacuated in four different convoys. Panic broke out on the 20th when a unit of regular Croatian troops, the *Domobrani*, arrived unannounced in Mostar and spread rumours that the Italians were about to withdraw. This caused, in the words of the official report 'lively apprehension'. The panic led to the 'appearance of a group of persons who wished to claim similar treatment to that recently accorded to the Jews'. A delegation of muslims went to see General Paride Negri, divisional commander, to make sure that the Italians would stay to protect them.[111] When the Croatian local authorities asked that eight Jewish doctors, dentists and pharmacists, the only medical personnel in the community, be required to stay at their jobs, the Italians replied that 'said persons prefer to follow and will follow the fate of the other Jews not considering themselves sufficiently protected by the Croatian authorities.'[112]

The Vatican also apparently had not understood the purpose of internment. On 5 November Raffaele Guariglia, Italian Ambassador to the Holy See, addressed a letter to Count Ciano in which he reported that the Cardinal Secretary of State had received news that Germany had requested the consignment of two or three thousand Jews, 'mainly old people, women and children' who were living in the part of Croatia occupied by Italian troops: 'The office of the Secretary of State has asked me to intervene with Your Excellency for the purposes of avoiding if possible the consignment of these persons.'[113]

This is not the place to say much about the Vatican and the Jews, a subject which has generated much bitterness and controversy, mainly about the silence of Pope Pius XII on the immediate question of the deportation of the Roman Jews in 1943 and the larger issues of the holocaust. The German authorities had no such doubts in 1942 and 1943; the Vatican was the single most important obstacle to the extermination of the Jewish people. At the weekly *Chefbesprechung*, the meeting of the Chief of Staff of the Supreme Commander South East in Salonica-Arsakli at the end of September, 1942, Lt Colonel Pfafferoth reported on the conflict between Pétain and the Vatican which had been pressing for 'mildness in the Jewish question'.[114] One of Glaise von Horstenau's regular informants among senior Croatian officers told him in October 1942 that

> the Archbishop Stepanic [of Croatia] and his entourage are '*juden-freundlich*' [friendly to the Jews], and therefore enemies of National Socialism. The same Archbishop had been the protector of Jewish emigrés under the Yugoslav regime, although he paid no attention to the misery of his own people. . . . In August of 1942 at the *Vlaška* Church in Zagreb, a priest named Pietker preached among other things this: the Jews are the chosen people and have remained so to this very day. There is no other leader than God who has chosen the Jews.[115]

Himmler told Glaise on the occasion of a visit to Berlin in February 1943 that he hoped to create an SS division composed of Bosnian Muslims. As Glaise wrote to his friend Löhr in early March, 'Christianity he rejects entirely because of its weakness. The hope of paradise is to be encouraged among the Bosnians because it strengthens their heroic complexes.'[116]

The Vatican acted consistently and intensively to save Jews. As a sign of solidarity, the Papal Nuncio to the Italian state, Monsignor Borgonicini Duca paid not one but two visits to the largest concentration camp for foreign Jews in mainland Italy at Ferramonti-Tarsia in Calabria.[117] He interceded with Bastianini who succeeded Ciano in February 1943, to save the Jews of Split in mid-February 1943, and the following month to prevent the Jews of the Italian zone of France being consigned to the Germans.[118] Archbishop Roncalli (later Pope John XXIII), Papal Nuncio to Turkey, had extensive contacts with the Jewish Agency and worked to save Jews in every way possible.[119] The German authorities were not wrong to see the hand of the Vatican in Italy's Jewish policy but what the hand actually grasped is not easy to reconstruct. Even the official history of the Vatican's intervention on behalf of 'the victims of the war' admits that the reasons for the change of Italian policy on the Jewish question cannot be easily reconstructed: 'at this point Berlin encountered an opposition which the official documents have never entirely explained.'[120]

The Vatican official history cannot trace, nor can I, the effectiveness of its intervention on behalf of the Jews. There is certainly no evidence that it affected the policy on consignment in October-November 1942. Its influence was there, a presence in the background, an alternative source of authority in the state, the last centre of international contact open to Italy and Italians.[121] The Italian government frequently cited the Vatican as a reason for behaving as it wanted to behave anyway but did not, I think, make or unmake a single policy as a direct result of Vatican intervention.

Events achieved what the Pope could not. On 21 August 1942 the German standard was planted on the highest mountain in the Caucasus but the *Wehrmacht* got no further. Hitler became restless, dismissed Field Marshall List and took command of *Heeresgruppe* A himself. Meanwhile the German 6th Army under General Paulus had reached the Volga and in early September they entered the city of Stalingrad. Chief of the Army General Staff Franz Halder warned Hitler that the Stalingrad position exposed the German flanks but was dismissed for his pains on 24 September. By early November it was clear that the single most important battle of the Second World War was being fought out.[122]

On 23 October 1942 the British 8th Army under an energetic new commander, Lieutenant General Bernard Law Montgomery, opened a massive attack on Rommel's lines at El Alamein and hurled the Afrika Korps backwards. The battle of El Alamein lasted until 4 November. On that day, Mussolini, now genuinely anxious, telephoned Marshall Cavallero every hour to find out how things were going. General von Rintelen called in person at 5.15 p.m. to relay the Führer's decision to let

Marshall Rommel have a certain freedom to manoeuvre. He in turn intends to retreat to Fuka. The Chief of the General Staff points out that it . . . will lead to the loss of all the units on foot. Make clear that if he retreats the army is lost.[123]

And it was lost, not immediately but by spring 1943. The battle of El Alamein and the simultaneous struggle on the banks of the Don can, in retrospect, be seen as the turning points of the war in Europe. For Italy it was the beginning of series of defeats which led to the fall of Mussolini, the end of the fascist regime, and ultimately ten months later to the capitulation of the Badoglio government to the Allies on 8 September 1943. In the small story of the 3,000 Jewish refugees of Croatia it marked a change too. Defeat came at the very moment that Mussolini and the Italian authorities accepted for the first time that their Axis partner had begun to murder Jews as part of a system. It greatly concentrated the collective mind on the issue.

On 8 November a large Allied convoy, which German and Italian reconnaissance had been shadowing for several days, arrived off the coast of French North Africa and Allied troops landed at several points in Morocco and Algeria. What would the puppet French government in Vichy do? In his diary Cavallero noted: 'The French fleet is ready to put out from Toulon in an hour. I do not dare to hope, but if this collaboration comes off, we have won the war.'[124]

The French fleet did not fight nor except for sporadic skirmishes did the French land forces in North Africa. At 10.15 that morning, Cavallero received von Rintelen and said:

It is necessary to do something to give the country the sensation that there will be some sort of possible compensation for the probable loss of Libya. Asks that the OKW be requested to authorize the application of O2 . . . the eventual occupation of unoccupied France.[125]

The fascist regime was going down still puffing clouds of illusion and phoney prestige from funnels already full of holes. There were certainly serious strategic problems. The Allied landings caught the Axis off balance. 'Algeria', Cavallero told Rintelen, 'is outside the range of our aviation.' The Allies intended – that was clear – to finish off the Axis forces in Africa by crushing them in a giant pincer movement, the 8th Army from the east and the Anglo-American force from the west. But was that all? Algeria and Morocco provided jumping off points for landings on the continent of Europe and there were a large number of possibilities. Mussolini was convinced that it would be Corsica. The OKW became obsessed with the idea that it would be Greece and as late as the following May, when General Löhr went to Berlin for a conference on strategy, as it was reported at the weekly *Chefbesprechung*,

found once again the conviction of the OKW as firm as ever that within a short time an enemy attack on mainland Greece (Peloponnese and its islands) is to be expected. The Chief does not believe that it will be a large attack but is convinced that it will be large enough to provide a basis for air operations in the Greek theatre.[126]

The initiative in the Mediterranean had passed to the Allies, but Hitler was not finished. Operation 'O' (*Esigenza Ovest*), an operation to occupy parts of France, had begun to interest the Italian General Staff in September. As Cavallero put it, 'if we move, we have to arrive at the Rhone at the first leap. For the spring we have to prepare a second leap to get to the Pyrenees. Excellency Ambrosio points out that the means don't exist.'[127]

A familiar story with a familiar outcome. When Hitler decided to occupy unoccupied France, Cavallero scrambled to get the 4th Army to make its first 'leap'. At 10.55 p.m. on 10 November, the General Staff of the Army ordered the 'actuation of operation 'O' to begin at 700 hours on 11 November'. It did not quite work out like that. General Mario Vercellino, commander of the the Italian 4th Army, noted the 'material impossibility of reaching by the prescribed hour the demarcation line given the previous ban on moving units from their zones of winter disposition.'[128]

Once again Italian staff work had failed. The troops were not ready to move out in an organized way. Cavallero became wild with impatience. On the night of 11 November he rang Vercellino to ask:

How far have our light units advanced? It's necessary to get to Marseilles. The concept is to advance. Projects are to be put in the drawer. They are obsolete. Now we advance in all directions. I have given a clear, categorical order. We have agreed with our friends that the demarcation line will be fixed at the points which we reach. Go forward day and night. Projects are to be treated as if they had never existed. . . . Put your people on trains and march to Grenoble. Don't worry about your supply lines.[129]

The 4th Army and General Vercellino were incapable of such sudden excitements and continued to clatter slowly along the cobbled streets of French towns on horseback. In the end the Italian zone was much smaller than Cavallero had hoped. The Italians never reached Lyons but they did hold six departments of southern France and became inadvertently the protectors of a large population of Jews some of whom had fled south in any case. Richard Cohen reckons that about 150,000 French and foreign Jews had reached unoccupied France by the autumn of 1942.[130] The Vichy regime, however horrible, was preferable to direct rule by the Germans. Now, as many as could do so sought to get across the Rhone into the Italian zone of occupation. The Allied landing had, as an unforeseen consequence, pushed the Italians more directly into the business of saving Jews.

Saving Jews still depended on reversing Mussolini's casual order of 21 August to 'consign' them to the Croatians. Bastianini hurried to Rome to see the Duce, accompanied by Ortona, who found the atmosphere 'terrifying'. Bastianini took the occasion of his audience with the Duce to shift the conversation from the affairs of Croatia and Dalmatia to internal conditions within Italy. The people were unprepared to resist an Anglo-American invasion: 'There's no unity, nor can one say that any one sector is more anti-fascist than any other. Everywhere there reigns perplexity, discomfort, discord.'[131]

General Roatta came to Rome on 17 November. General Löhr arrived on the same day. There were meetings with the Duce, with Cavallero, with Ambrosio. General Löhr brought up the extremely 'unsatisfactory conditions in Croatia, especially the growth of the numbers of *cetniks*' but was told that, if anything, the Italians intended to withdraw yet more troops and retreat from much of the second zone. As Löhr reported, General Roatta told him that for a permanent cleansing [of guerrillas] he was too weak. He wanted to avoid a repetition of the situation of the previous winter in which Italian occupation units were like islands being shot at from all sides and just keeping them supplied had caused great difficulties. . . . In my view we must not be satisfied with this purely defensive posture but make life impossible for the enemy by attacking his supply bases in terrain which makes supply very difficult. Destruction of winter quarters and supply bases must be a main goal.[132]

There was no hope of that. Roatta and the Italian 2nd Army lacked the means and the will to fight an active guerrilla war. Besides there was still the Jewish problem to resolve. During his visit Roatta saw Mussolini alone and explained to him the link between the *cetnik* volunteer force, which was vital to the Italian war effort, and the Jewish refugees. The argument was the familiar one developed by Roatta, the Office of Civil Affairs at 2nd Army HQ and enlarged by Pietromarchi, Castellani and Ducci at the Foreign Ministry: there would be 'repercussions of a military and political character' if the Jews were consigned to the Croatians. The argument was familiar but the situation of Italy had changed. The Duce himself saw that and revoked his earlier '*nulla osta*'. The report of the meeting continues:

The Duce has disposed:
1) all said Jews are to be held in concentration camps;
2) that in the meantime, beyond determining the pertinence of every internee, there will be a procedure to collect – analagous to the requests contained in the proposals of the Croatian government referred to above – the formal applications of the interested parties themselves who might wish to renounce freely their Croatian citizenship by also renouncing all title to any property possessed in Croatia.[133]

Since Croatian law number 192-2502-2-1942, published at the end of October 1942, had robbed Croatian Jews of their fixed assets anyway,[134] the hardship was not great. Croatian citizenship had come to mean little more than a passport to a death camp. Behind the bureaucratic language and apparent compliance with Croatian wishes, the Duce had reversed his previous decision. *All* Jews were to be interned. The 3,000 Croatian and other foreign Jews were safe and on 27 November General Roatta went to the largest of the Jewish concentration camps at Kraljevice (Porto Re) and told them so. The elders of the camp expressed their very great relief.[135] Italy had now formally committed itself to obstruct the final solution in Europe.[136]

PHASE THREE

THE NET WIDENS:
THE ITALIANS DEFEND JEWS IN
GREECE AND FRANCE
November 1942 to July 1943

'Meanwhile', wrote Count Pietromarchi at the end of November 1942, 'the Germans continue imperturbably to massacre Jews.' His diary quotes reports via Radio Londra (Italian service of the BBC) that the Jews of the Warsaw ghetto were being deported at the rate of six or seven thousand a day and that on arrival at concentration camps they were being exterminated. By now the Germans had already murdered a million Jews.[1]

A few days later Alberto Pirelli had an audience of the King 'who showed himself to be well informed'. They talked about the 'repugnance of the neutral countries and the occupied countries because of the excesses against the Jews'.[2] On 10 December Pietromarchi asked:

Is this the civilization installed by the new order? Is it surprising if nobody believes in an Axis victory? It repels anybody who still has a feeling for human dignity. So it is that the Axis alienates the greater part of public opinion.[3]

The critical moments of the war coincided exactly with the spread among the Italian elite of the true facts of the holocaust. For those who dismissed Radio Londra, Curzio Malaparte, the writer and journalist, returned to Italy in late November 1942, and could provide eye-witness confirmation of the horrors of German rule in Poland and Russia, later published in *Kaputt*, his masterpiece.[4]

The terminal convulsions of fascist Italy took place under the shadow of the gas chamber. The news spread in whispers. In April 1943 Mussolini summoned the directorate of the fascist party to deny the stories:

Events in Russia have led to a notable recrudescence of hatred towards the Germans and Germany. All kinds of rumours are

abroad. Now there is talk of atrocities happening in Russia. . . .
We must react against this habit of thought. . . . The Party must
stop this kind of talk.[5]

Italian diplomats and soldiers must have found official encounters
with their German ally very uncomfortable. In the midst of the deportation of the Jews of Salonica in December of 1942, General Carlo
Geloso, commander of the Italian forces in the Greek theatre, paid a
courtesy call on *Generaloberst* Löhr, his German opposite number, at
the headquarters of the German forces in the south-east. There was
a frosty moment when the cordial Austrian general asked his Italian
colleague

> to use similar methods on the Jews in the part of Greece occupied
> by Italian forces. The proposal in the form of a simple idea
> thrown out in the course of one of our conversations was actually
> put to me by *Generaloberst* Löhr himself and by a German general
> staff officer to my chief of staff General Tripiccione. I replied . . .
> that I could not carry out such acts without an explicit order of
> my government and since I had no such orders, I could not
> possibly follow them on that road.[6]

Germans constantly startled Italians by moments of unexpected
brutality. Göring on one of his many visits to Rome suggested to
Count Ciano that Roatta invite Mihailović

> one of these mornings to breakfast and after the coffee hang him.
> . . . Count Ciano replied that the commanding general of the
> army had never had the least contact with Milhailović and that,
> apart from that, 'denied that it was one of his characteristics to
> have his guests hanged.'[7]

The Nazi leadership grew more and more dissatisfied with the
Italians. They had failed militarily. Hitler and Jodl agreed at the
beginning of December 1942 that no more Italians were to be in
charge of joint operations.[8] Goebbels expressed his disgust a few
weeks later on a different but no less important matter:

> The Italians are extremely lax in the treatment of Jews. They
> protect the Italian Jews both in Tunis and in occupied France and
> won't permit their being drafted for work or compelled to wear
> the Star of David. This shows once again that Fascism does not
> really dare to get down to fundamentals, but is very superficial
> regarding most important problems. The Jewish question is caus-
> ing us a lot of trouble. Everywhere, even among our allies, the
> Jews have friends to help them, which is a proof that they are still
> playing an important role even in the Axis camp.[9]

In this atmosphere of mutual recrimination, distrust and repugnance Goering arrived in Rome on 1 December for high level talks on the war. Goering took the chair. Rommel had been summoned from Africa. Admiral Weichold represented the German navy and Marshall Kesselring the *Luftwaffe*. Cavallero headed an Italian delegation representing the three services. The situation was undoubtedly difficult, Goering began, but for the first time Axis troops were only 'a panther's spring' from their supplies.[10] Everything now depended on supplying Rommel, as Kesselring told Cavallero, with 'petrol, munitions, food and uniforms', but Cavallero, 'making the greatest possible effort could send only 200 cubic metres of petrol a day.'[11]

In an effort to strengthen ties, Bottai paid an official visit to Berlin later the same month. The experience depressed him:

> We arrive at one. But instead of the light of noon, a livid *Dämmerung*, a dusk, without gods. The hosts await us in a squalid station. The city is black, gloomy. Somebody recalls the line in Goethe which says that the night in Italy is clearer than the day in Germany. And it's true. The eternal night in this plain without end gives one an urge to escape, to scream, to free oneself.[12]

Bottai noted a 'slight fall' in the position of Göring but 'a constant rise in the power of Himmler, in the shadows . . . his adepts and followers have their own doctrine and culture. In the almost general silence . . . the new order is incubating in the dossiers of the police.'[13]

What the new order had in store for mankind was revealed in a remarkable speech by Himmler to SS leaders in Poznan later in 1943. The SS man must be guided by one principle: 'loyalty to those of our blood'. What happens to other people is

> a matter of total indifference to us. If good blood of our type is to be found among other nations, we will take it, if need be by taking their children and bringing them up ourselves. Whether other peoples live in plenty or starve to death interests me only insofar as we need them as slaves for our culture. . . . Whether 10,000 Russian women keel over from exhaustion in the construction of an anti-tank ditch interests me only insofar as the ditch for Germany gets constructed.

The killing of lesser peoples was part of the SS man's routine activity. The really 'glorious page of our history', Himmler continued, was being written in the blood of Jews:

> I want to tell you about a very grave matter in all frankness. We can talk about it quite openly here, but we must never talk about

it publicly . . . I mean the evacuation of the Jews, the extermination of the Jewish people. It is one of the things one says lightly: 'The Jewish people are being liquidated', party comrades exclaim: 'naturally, it's in our programme, the isolation of the Jews, extermination, okay, we'll do it.' . . . All those who talk like this have not seen it, have not gone through it. Most of you will know what it means to see 100 corpses piled up, or 500 or 1,000. To have gone through this and – except for instances of human weakness – to have remained decent, that has made us tough. This is an unwritten, never to be written, glorious page of our history.[14]

While Himmler and his butchers wrote their pages of history, the Russian winter etched a different one. Along the great bend of the Don four Italian army corps had been strung out forming the Italian 8th Army. By mid-November 1942 intelligence had spotted the gradual massing of the tanks of the Russian 5th Tank Army on the other bank but, as *Oberleutnant* Salazar, the German liaison to the Division 'Cosseria', reported:

In spite of the unfavourable balance of forces – the 'Cosseria' and the 'Ravenna' faced eight to nine Russian divisions and an unknown number of tanks – the atmosphere among Italian staffs and troops was certainly not pessimistic. . . . The Italians, especially the officers of the 'Cosseria', had confidence in what they thought were well built defensive positions.[15]

The Russians had already broken through in mid-November to the Italian right in the sector held by the Rumanian 2nd Army and had established a bridgehead. On the night of 15 December the temperature dropped to forty below zero and the Don froze solidly enough to allow the huge force of Russian tanks to cross safely. By 17 December Italian troops 'flooded back in their hundreds'.[16] On the 20th the Division 'Sforzesca' received orders to destroy everything if the enemy should break through. When the Italian operations officer asked his German counterpart if the 'order meant in effect *sauve qui peut* Major von Wangenheim answered, ''Yes, one could understand the order in that sense.'' '[17]

A terrible ordeal began. Italian, Rumanian and German troops fell back in chaotic disorder, soon ran out of fuel and had to make a 200 kilometre retreat on foot in sub-zero temperatures, harassed by partisans and pursued by the Russians. The German translator officers, in some cases, uniformed civilians, found themselves in command of hundreds of demoralized Italians. As one wrote in the war diary which in spite of hardship he continued to keep:

28 December 1942; With our vehicle we get no further. We have no more fuel. The last bit of our way must be done on foot. A twenty-four hour, almost uninterrupted march begins. The horse-drawn column of Rumanians makes slow progress alongside us because of the deep snow. We pass them. In front we see Italian infantry. Do they still deserve the name? Only every tenth man has a weapon. What the German soldier gives up last the Italian throws away lightly: his gun.[18]

Thousands died of frost-bite and starvation. The losses of the 8th Army, as estimated in early March, amounted to 4,645 officers and 122,400 men.[19] The Italian 8th Army had ceased to exist and in April 1943 was formally disbanded.

The collapse on the Don has been overshadowed by the much more dramatic battle for Stalingrad but it formed a no less important part in the final defeat of the Axis. The Russians had hurled the combined Axis forces back from the great central rivers which constituted the lifeline of the Soviet Union and from that moment on intelligent observers began to realise that the Axis had lost the war.

The Italian political and military leaders happened to be on the way to a summit meeting at the Führer's headquarters at the Wolfschanze deep in eastern Prussia, almost on the old border with Lithuania, when the Don froze. The Duce had not recovered enough to make the long, frigid journey so Ciano led the Italian delegation. Ciano had instructions to tell Hitler that Mussolini thought it vital 'to come to an agreement with Russia'.[20] By the time Ciano, Cavallero and their staffs reached Hitler's forest lair, as Ciano recorded in his diary on 18 December,

no one tried to conceal from me or my colleagues the uneasiness over the news of the break-through on the Russian front. There were open attempts to put the blame on us. Hewel, who is very close to Hitler, had the following conversation (in English) with Pansa: 'Had our army many losses?' Hewel: 'no losses at all; they are running'. Pansa: 'as you did in Moscow last year?' Hewel: 'exactly'.[21]

Hitler was in no mood for arrangements with the Russians. He opened the plenary session by pointing out that the Axis was fighting 'a battle for the civilization of the world' and that it was no longer a question of the existence or not of regimes 'but of the existence of our nations themselves'.[22] Hitler made it absolutely clear, as he always had, that his war would end in *Alles oder Nichts*.

General Cavallero got through on the 19th to General Gariboldi, commander of the Italian 8th Army, who reported that by then the gap in the front had widened to 40 kilometres.[23] That evening he telephoned Rome to say that at the Führer's HQ the situation was 'considered ugly but not in a sense displeasing for us, but as a fact that had happened'.[24] Once again Hitler treated his Italian ally with that exemplary courtesy he had used on the occasion of every previous humiliating defeat.

The following day the summit continued. As Cavallero telephoned to his chief of staff, General Magli, some Germans, other than Hitler, were now trying to make Gariboldi bear the blame because they knew that the fault lay in German plans of campaign not Italian failings:

> And then there's Croatia. They want a decisive action in the spring and have made it into a question of principle. They would have liked to give immediate orders from yesterday. I am glad that they were not given because it needs a lot of thought. . . . Mario [Roatta] is the object of a merciless offensive on the question of the *cetniks*. They want them disarmed and put out of the way. But this too needs to be considered.[25]

By the time Marshall Cavallero got back to Rome he faced a double collapse: in Africa as well as Russia. Kesselring paid his usual daily call on the morning of 22 December and both the Italian and German marshalls agreed that Rommel had begun to find excuses to retreat as far as possible. Kesselring observed sadly that 'Rommel no longer believes in success'.[26] The following day Cavallero presided at the usual weekly meeting of service chiefs and said simply, 'these days are the ten days in which we go under or we win'.[27] Just over ten days later the Italian Supreme Command decided that Libya could no longer be held and the Duce agreed to a gradual transfer of forces to Tunisia 'to continue the struggle'.[28] The Italian dream of empire had come to an end.

At the Führer's headquarters, Hitler struggled for the first time with the implications of multiple collapse. Stubbornly he refused to allow General Paulus to extricate the German 6th Army from the ring of steel closing round it. When General Zeitzler, one of the few commanders with the courage to stand up to Hitler, urged the Führer to let Paulus retreat, Hitler refused. By the end of January 1943 the 6th Army's position had become hopeless, but when General Paulus asked permission to save what could be saved from the encirclement, Hitler telegraphed back:

> Forbid surrender. The army will hold its position to the last soldier and the last cartridge, and by its heroic endurance will make an unforgettable contribution to the building of the defensive front and the salvation of Western civilization.[29]

Shortly before 3 p.m. on 2 February 1943 a German reconnaissance plane flew over the ruined city and reported no more signs of fighting. Over 90,000 German prisoners were taken including Paulus himself whom Hitler had promoted field marshall at the last minute. Hitler flew into one of his rages: 'The man should shoot himself as generals used to fall upon their swords when they saw that their cause was lost. That's to be taken for granted! . . . what does life mean? Life is the nation; the individual must die.'[30]

Hitler then indulged in one of his most persistent, morbid fantasies about the Russians, that they tortured people by putting them 'in their rat-infested cellars' until they all talked. He foresaw with a madman's uncanny accuracy that Paulus, Seydlitz and the other generals captured with the 6th Army would soon be broadcasting on Radio Moscow but like all genuinely paranoid people could not see his own part in driving them to their treachery.

In his extraordinary biography of Hitler, Joachim Fest traces Hitler's deterioration after Stalingrad, his increasing hypochondria, pedantry and retreat from reality. His language crumbled and returned to the crudities of his semi-educated youth. He flew into furious rages at his generals and occasionally burst into tears. He suffered from dizziness, swellings on his legs and depression, and took drugs to counter the effects of the other drugs. Fest argues convincingly that Hitler's nervous system gradually gave way and that the person he had always been became simply more and more manifest:

> From comparable observations during the twenties one of his early followers had drawn the conclusion that Hitler needed self-deception in order to be able to act at all. He craved vastly overblown sham worlds against whose background all obstacles became insignificant and all problems trivial. He was capable of acting only on the basis of false pretences. That note of fantastical overexcitement associated with his personality derived from this disturbed relationship to reality. We might say: only unreality made him real.[31]

Night after night Hitler sat surrounded by his generals and companions spinning his plots to turn Europe into a vast charnel house where German blood was restocked. Dutiful officials carefully recorded his 'thoughts'. As the German armies retreated from their conquests, Hitler could at least take comfort from his one unshakeable achievement. In the presence of Himmler and Heydrich he had said on 31 October 1941:

> Before the Reichstag I prophesied to Jewry [*Judentum*], the Jew will disappear from Europe, if a war cannot be avoided. This race

of criminals has the two million dead of the Great War on its conscience and already hundreds of thousands in this.[32]

On 2 April 1945, with the Reich literally crashing over his bunker as Allied bombs and shells pulverized its grand buildings, he said with grim satisfaction that he had been 'the first to grasp the Jewish problem realistically', that he had 'planted the best seed', and that the world would be 'eternally grateful to National Socialism that I have exterminated the Jews in Germany and Central Europe.'[33]

He could take less satisfaction at the end of 1942 in his Italian ally. The Italians had failed the test in both the desert and on the Don. On 28 December 1942 he issued Führer Order No. 47 which gave to General Löhr, now re-designated as Supreme Commander South East, the power to take over command of the Axis forces in the event of an Allied landing in the Greek theatre but preserved the customary fictions of 'consultation' with the Italian Supreme Command. In reality, as General Hermann Foertsch, Löhr's chief of staff, put it, 'We need to tighten the reins on the Italians. The question of their subordination . . . at the moment of an attack must not be mentioned in their presence; at first the whole thing must be tuned to a coordination.'[34]

Military defeat pushed the Italians into an ever more subordinate role. Matters of prestige came to seem more and more important. On 24 January 1943 Marshall Kesselring called on Marshall Cavallero to tell him that the Führer had now decided that General Löhr was to have command of the Axis forces in the Balkans in the case of an Allied landing. Cavallero blew up:

> he cannot receive orders from the Führer nor can he say to the Duce that the Führer had given orders to the Supreme Command. The Führer had better speak to the Duce. He was not going to say to the Duce we are yielding the command of four armies (Greece, Montenegro, Dalmatia and Croatia). The Supreme Command cannot obey. . . . With the Italian people one has to respect the forms.[35]

The sharp fall in Italian power made considerations of prestige more, not less, prominent. When, in March 1943, the Germans made their heaviest onslaught on the Italian position with regard to the Jews and Mussolini began to vacillate yet again, Bastianini, by now Ciano's successor as Foreign Minister, used precisely the argument from prestige to persuade the Duce not to comply:

> our prestige in France and everywhere else would suffer a very severe shock if in our zone of occupation the protection afforded by our flag to the inhabitants should be limited by any thing

other than Italian law. If all those Jews, including children, are spies, the Germans have only to let us have proof and, law-book in hand, we could deal with them.[36]

On the day Stalingrad fell Count Pietromarchi considered the issue of the consignment of the Jews from a different angle:

In spite of all the disasters that have struck the Germans they continue to insist that all the Jews of the territories occupied by us be consigned to them. They confirm that by the end of 1943 there will not be a single Jew alive in Europe. Evidently they want to involve us in the brutality of their policies.[37]

Relations between the Axis partners were deteriorating and were certainly not improved by the dismissal of Cavallero as chief of the Supreme Command at the end of January 1943. Ciano recorded in his diary that there was 'dissatisfaction among the Germans. Bismarck has become the mouth-piece of the latter and praises the excellent cooperation the Marshall has given. Naturally, I said that the event did not have any political significance.'[38]

For once Ciano was absolutely correct. The dismissal had no political significance but not for the reasons that Ciano imagined. He had always seen Cavallero as a pro-German toady, an obstacle to a more detached foreign policy. With Cavallero out of the way Ciano hoped that he could now collect the strands of a plot to make a separate peace with the Allies before it was too late. Bastianini arrived from Dalmatia on an official visit on 2 February 1943 and, according to Ortona, found Ciano in a 'catastrophic' mood:

He talks openly about counting on an agreement with the Anglo-Saxons. I find the same atmosphere of catastrophe in all the colleagues at the Ministry. Even in the secretariat of the minister they speak openly about him in a hostile way.[39]

Three days later Ciano was gone, removed from office without warning (and without thanks) by his father-in-law, Mussolini, who at least had the decency to show 'that he is very much embarrassed'.[40] Bastianini equally unexpectedly found himself in Ciano's office as his successor. Whatever hostility Bastianini may have shown in 1942 to the 'undesirables' – Jewish refugees who gathered under his governorship – he proved no less firm than Pietromarchi, Ducci and Castellani in the protection of Jews. By early spring of 1943, if there were diplomats and soldiers willing to help their Axis partner in 'solving the Jewish question', they kept quiet.

Prestige, humanity and self-interest fused in the Italian determination not to participate in the holocaust. As the destruction of the Jews of Europe accelerated in 1943, German pressure increased at the very time when Italy's ability to resist diminished. In addition to the tensions caused by Italy's refusal to surrender the Jewish refugees in Croatia, two much larger and more ominous points of friction emerged in the early months of 1943: the German demands for the consignment of the Jews of Greece and France.

The tragedy began in Greece. Early in March 1943 the Jews of Thrace, part of Greece which the Axis had allotted to Bulgaria, were suddenly rounded up, pushed into empty tobacco warehouses and then assembled in concentration camps at Gorna Dzhumaia and Dupnitsa. There the Bulgarian authorities handed them over to the Germans who shipped them to Treblinka where they were all killed on arrival, over 4,000 people in all from eleven communities.[41]

The Jews of 'old Bulgaria' (the pre-war territory of the kingdom) and Macedonia were next on the list but the Germans began to encounter resistance. Bulgarians, as the German ambassador sadly remarked, simply did not understand the importance of murdering Jews: 'raised partly among Greeks, Armenians, Gypsies and Turks, the average Bulgarian does not fathom the significance of the fight against the Jews, especially since he is not too concerned with racial issues.'[42]

Nevertheless the government of Prime Minister Filov had more or less settled the fate of 20,000 Jews (4,000 from Thrace, 8,000 from Macedonia and another 8,000 from 'old Bulgaria'). Following the deportation of the Jews of Thrace, some 5,000 Jews of Macedonia were also deported. That, politically, was the easy bit. Thrace, Macedonia and the Dobrudja had been spoils thrown to the Kingdom of Bulgaria by the Germans, far-off places, remote from Sofia. Now the account had to be settled in old Bulgaria to meet the quota. At that point, Filov, the interior ministry and the SS pulling the wires ran into unexpected resistance. On 17 March 1943 Dimitur Peshev and forty other members of the *Sobranje*, the Bulgarian parliament, signed a petition urging that deportations be stopped. Archbishop Kiril of Plovdiv sent a telegram to the King announcing his intention to lie down on the tracks in front of trains carrying Jewish deportees.[43] Besides, Stalingrad and the retreat from the Don had an immediate impact on a state with a long border with Russia. The Bulgarians realised that deportations would be widely reported. The time for Bulgaria to extract itself from the final solution had clearly arrived. The 50,000 Jews of the kingdom of Bulgaria would survive the war.

Greece presented a very different picture. The political structures of the Greek state had never been very firm. The First World War divided and impoverished the country. Greece then fought a disastrous war against Turkey and by the Peace of Lausanne of 24 July 1923 had been forced to cede all Greek mainland possessions in Asia and absorb over a million Greek refugees from Anatolia. In the four years between 1924 and 1928 there had been eleven governments, military putsches, several elections, and two military dictatorships. The monarchy had become a partisan in the struggle against the liberal Venizelist forces. It tolerated, indeed encouraged, the establishment in 1936 of the dictatorship of General Ioannis Metaxas, and while the Metaxas regime gained popularity by its stiff resistance to Italian invasion, the death of Mextaxas on January 1941 and the shattering impact of the German attack left the country divided, uncertain and prostrate.[44]

The King fled the country and established a government-in-exile, leaving Archbishop Damaskinos as regent. General Georgios Tsolakoglou, the army commander who had signed the armistice with the Germans, became Prime Minister of a quisling regime. Neither he nor his successors, Konstantinos Logothetopoulos and Ioannis Rallis, succeeded in establishing any independence or leverage against the Axis powers. Unlike Bulgaria, Rumania or Hungary, and certainly unlike Mussolini's Italy, which were genuinely, if unequally, the partners of Nazi Germany, the Greek regime of 1941 to 1944 deserved the label 'puppet'. Like the independent state of Croatia, Vichy France or the almost invisible government of Serbia, Greece belonged to those subject regimes in which the occupying powers trampled all over their 'sovereignty' and rarely even observed the fiction that these were 'states' in any serious sense.

The Greek land mass fell under three different authorities. The Bulgarians annexed Macedonia and Thrace. The Germans took the strategically important area on the Turkish border and the main port of northern Greece, Salonica (Thessaloniki). The Italians gained all the rest of Greece including almost all the islands, some of which, the Dodecanese, they held as the booty of an earlier war against Turkey and ruled as if they formed part of metropolitan Italy.

The economy, never self-sufficient, collapsed under the impact of war, the dislocation of trade and the Allied blockade. Monstrous occupation costs imposed on an already feeble economic base produced a colossal inflation, hoarding, black markets and widespread starvation. By the end of December 1941 the Italian consulate in Salonica reported the total destruction of the city's famous tobacco industry, which in normal times produced 8 million kilos and gave high-paid seasonal work to 3,500 male and 40,000 female workers. Now all were out of work.[45]

The winter of 1941–42 saw thousands of Greeks starving to death. The cities of Athens and Salonica were especially hard hit. Refugees fleeing from Bulgarian Thrace and Macedonia flooded into the towns and increased the misery of slums where refugees of 1922 still waited for decent housing. Hagen Fleischer has made a careful study of the claims about the numbers who died in the 'black winter' of 1941–42 and calculates it at about 100,000.[46]

The drachma collapsed. Stravos Thomadakis estimates that between December 1939 and August 1943 the amount of currency in circulation went up 114 times, and prices between October 1941 and August 1943, 42 times. By the late summer of 1943 the average daily wage bought about two-thirds of the daily minimum subsistence ration of food.[47] The situation bcame so desperate that Mussolini himself was moved to compassion, or what passed for it in his case. After a state visit to Athens in July 1942, he wrote to Hitler that the country was 'on the edge of a financial and hence an economic and political catastrophe' and urged Hitler (the old journalist could never resist turning a phrase) 'even amidst the roar of the great victorious battles of your armies to turn your attention to the Greek problem'.[48]

The tragedy of the Greek Jews took place against the background of the national one but it was sharper and more concentrated. There were roughly 80,000 Jews in Greece but unfortunately 50,000 of them lived in the wrong place, Salonica, which the Germans had seized and were determined to hold. They thus captured at one grasp one of the most remarkable Jewish communities in the world. For almost five centuries, since Ferdinand and Isabella had expelled the Jews from Spain, Salonica had been the capital of sephardic Jewry, as the Hebrew phrase put it, *ir ve-em be'Yisrael*, mother city in Israel. The port and its trades had been in the hands of a Spanish-speaking community which with its newspapers, libraries and synagogues preserved a ritual and culture of great beauty and variety. Salonica had not escaped the vicissitudes of Greek politics and in the wake of the defeat of 1922 became a magnet for the Anatolian Greeks who had been traders and middle-men in their old homeland. The sephardic metropolis became a Greek city and with it harsh rivalries, anti-semitism and violence between the communities erupted.[49] By 1941 the population of Salonica was 75 per cent Greek and only 25 per cent Jewish, which reflected both the heavy immigration of Anatolians and the emigration of Jews.[50] The fact that the sephardic leadership was old, traditional and alien did not help them to adjust, nor did their enthusiasm for the Metaxas regime's authoritarian ways endear them to the progressives.

The Jews of Athens, a tiny population of 3,500 out of 1,500,000 residents, were assimilated, Greek-speaking, patriotic, and well integrated. Elsewhere Jewish communities dotted the mainland and the islands, some as on Corfu and Rhodes Italian-speaking, but most either sephardic in origin or descendants of medieval romaniote communities. By the outbreak of the war, most of the younger generation, even in Salonica, spoke Greek and considered themselves as Greeks.

As Steven Bowman has pointed out, the traditional tolerance of the Greek Orthodox Church towards Jewish communities, in spite of the outbursts of anti-Jewish activity at local level, helped to account for the support the church gave to the Jews during the Nazi persecution. Archbishop Damaskinos issued an encyclical ordering his priests to help Jews and authorized them to issue false baptismal certificates, a fact which did not escape the Germans. Some 600 priests and monks were arrested for helping Jews.[51]

Persecution of Jews began in Salonica with the customary outrages. The *Einsatzstab* Rosenberg plundered the synagogues, archives and museums of the sephardic community and took away some of the treasures accumulated over four centuries. The three Jewish papers in Spanish were closed but for the time being Jewish property was not touched. For more than a year nothing happened. Suddenly on 11 July 1942, 9,000 Jewish men between 18 and 45 were ordered to report to Liberty Square in the centre of the city where for hours they were kept standing in the sun and humiliated in all sort of ways by the *Wehrmacht*. Two thousand were subsequently taken for forced labour.[52] The time of travail of the Jews of Salonica had begun.

In Athens, no action was taken against the Jews then or ever by the Italian authorities. This was an awkward fact, as the German plenipotentiary in Athens, Altenburg, pointed out in a despatch to the German Foreign Office a few weeks later. He had met his Italian opposite number, Pellegrino Ghigi, who had raised serious objections:

In view of the importance of the influence which Jews exercise in the Mediterranean zone, especially in Tunis, he would wish to see any move against the Jews postponed. If those authorities in Germany interested in the action were to insist, he considers it advisable that the question be examined jointly in Rome and Berlin. In his view a united Axis policy in Greece is desirable. If agreement were not achieved and the authorities in the German zone were to proceed independently against the Jews, he would have to ask, following his orders, that Jews of Italian citizenship be exempted from such action.[53]

The argument that Italian Jews represented an important outpost of Italian imperial and economic interest in the Mediterranean constituted one of the standard replies that the Italian foreign ministry gave to requests by German authorities to deport Jewish communities. It was used in Tunis, where the Italian government absolutely refused to allow the Vichy regime, only too willing to send Jews, French or Italian, to die in the east, to touch the substantial Italian Jewish community. Germans at every level watched with disgust as Italian Jews enjoyed privileges denied by the Reich to co-religionists elsewhere. As an army counter-intelligence officer in Libya reported in early 1942, the situation there was quite scandalous:

> It becomes clearer every day that the local Jews sit 'in an iron barrel' [i.e. are protected], as the Italians appropriately put it. . . . A closer look reveals that the Italian administrative apparatus itself is 'the iron barrel', which surrounds the Jews protectively and allows them to go on pursuing their dirty business. One frequently hears from Italian officials the astonishing opinion that the Jews of Libya are 'decent chaps'. . . . The police make no distinction between Jews and Italians.[54]

It is worth pausing to notice the clash of culture. The German intelligence officer, not an SS fanatic but an army counter-intelligence specialist, an AO III, simply cannot imagine how Italians could call Jews, any Jews, 'decent chaps'. He is amazed that the Italian police do not distinguish between Italian and Jew and reports with disgust that until 1938 the local commander of the carabinieri was a Jew, the 'notorious' Colonel Levi. Worse still, when the racial laws forced the colonel out, his patron Italo Balbo, governor of Libya and a founder of fascism, got him a job as a director of a local firm where he still was![55] German anti-semitism was not the special preserve of a few fanatics in black uniforms but a pervasive, widespread and fundamental attitude found throughout the entire *Wehrmacht*. In many years of intensive research in German army archives I have found fewer than five examples of German officers expressing anything other than the opinions quoted above. Hitler could never have achieved the great crime which he committed without those attitudes.

The Germans continued to press the Italians to surrender the Jews of the Mediterranean and the Italians refused. As the deportations spread, the existence of Italian Jews unmarked by the Star of David and untouched by the segregation laws became so intolerable that by 1943 the Germans began to insist that Italian Jews be repatriated. Beginning in the spring of 1943 Italian Jews left German-dominated Europe for home. Their sentiments were well expressed by Signora Vittoria Levi who, on 29 March 1943, sent a telegram to the Italian Foreign Ministry: 'In the name of all the Jews repatriated by the convoy of the 27th of this month I send you most heartfelt and grateful thanks for the warm welcome received.'[56]

The Jews of Salonica were next for extermination. Eichmann's agents, *SS Hauptsturmführer* Dieter Wisliceny and Alois Brunner arrived in the city in early February. Soon Dr Max Merten, head of the civil administration, had announced the necessary regulations to rob, ghettoize and deport the Jews. By the end of the month of February the convoys were ready to roll.[57]

The Germans had taken the precaution of closing all foreign consulates in Salonica except the Italian so that the world would not hear of the atrocities.[58] The consul general was a tiny, lively and combative man from the Romagna, the same region from which Mussolini himself came, called Guelfo Zamboni. Zamboni was one of the first candidates for the diplomatc corps not to come from a wealthy background, a beneficiary of Mussolini's decision to abolish the requirement that career diplomats offer notarized statements of their private incomes. After several years in the international treaty section, in the Italian government in Albania and in Finland, he had served under Bernardo Attolico in the Berlin Embassy during the late 1930s. A protégé of Jacomoni, the governor of Albania, he had been offered the governorship of Epiros until the Germans quashed all Italian plans for dismembering Greece. His appointment to Salonica came as a surprise and involved a kind of promotion, for it meant that Zamboni represented the Italian government as its highest official to the German command responsible for the entire Balkan theatre and to the civil administration of Ageis-Salonica, as the Germans called their zone. With General Löhr he had relations sufficiently intimate to learn the general's true feelings about Nazism. One evening at dinner, the General offered the toast of 'the Fourth Reich', a better Germany which would follow Hitler. The trouble was, according to Zamboni, that when the SS arrived, everybody from General Löhr down 'trembled from head to foot'.[59]

The consulate staff contained other extraordinary figures including a mysterious official called 'Riccardo Rosenberg' and some play has been made of the irony of a Jew in that post in Salonica. Professor Salvatore Loi has examined the records of the diplomatic and consular service but found no such name. He suspects that 'Riccardo Rosenberg' never existed but was an ironic, whimsically chosen pseudonym for a member of the Italian secret service.[60] The military liaison officer at the consulate, Captain Lucillo Merci, not only existed but kept a diary from which excerpts have been recently published by Joseph Rochlitz.[61]

Merci recorded on 19 February 1943 that he had been 'kept very busy' and that the consulate had been 'besieged' by Italian Jews seeking to gain exemptions for their relatives with Greek citizenship from the fatal restrictions imposed by the Germans.[62] A battle began between Consul Zamboni and the Italian consulate on the side of the

Jews and the *SS Hauptsturmführer* Wisliceny and Dr Merten on the other, fought out Jew by Jew, to save or destroy lives:

> I accompanied our Consul, Mr Zamboni, on his visit to Dr Merten. We submitted to him the requests we had received for exemptions from the restrictions against the Jews . . . truly heart-rending pleas from people 80 to 90 years old, from orphans, sick persons. . . . 'There is nothing I can do here', replied Merten. 'These directives have been issued in Berlin on behalf of *Reichsführer SS* Himmler. They are clear: everyone is required to wear the Star of David and reside in the ghetto. This applies also to Italian Jewesses married to Greek nationals.'[63]

You have to have a heart first before it can be rent. Merten clearly had none but the SS were worse. Merci's diary conveys the uncanny chill which even somebody protected by diplomatic immunity and a foreign military uniform felt in the presence of great evil. On one occasion Merci was summoned directly to Wisliceny on a matter to be discussed but 'not over the telephone':

> I informed the Consul and set out for the Gestapo headquarters in Via Belisario located in a building surrounded by a fence, with a courtyard and a garden. Access to the building from the street is not at all easy. At the gate the SS sentry enquired about the purpose of my visit. Then he ordered me to wait on the street. A few minutes later *Sturmbannführer* Wisliceny came out and led me to the courtyard with the SS guard watching me.[64]

Italian intervention saved many lives. On 9 July a trainload of 350 Jews with Italian citizenship (interpreted by Consul Zamboni with unusual latitude) left Salonica for Athens, but the great majority of the Jews of Salonica were doomed. On 15 March 1943 the first transport left the city. Eighteen more followed, the last on 7 August. According to the accounts kept at Auschwitz, 48,974 Jews arrived at Auschwitz-Birkenau where 37,386 were gassed on arrival.[65]

The Italians had protested and obstructed in every way and had been allowed to do so. On 10 March 1943 Dr Max Merten made clear that he at least understood why:

> I certainly do understand your tenacious and sympathetic efforts on behalf of the Italian Jews residing here, irrespective of their country of origin. It is clear to me that Italy concerns itself with its special economic and political interests in Greece, above all in Salonica – the city with the largest Italian colony in the country, which includes many affluent Italian Jews wielding considerable economic influence. As far as I understand there are agreements

between Germany and Italy concerning Jews. The Führer has ordered us to respect these agreements which he had approved, and to refrain from damaging the interests of a friendly ally.[66]

There were no formal 'agreements', but Dr Merten was not entirely wrong. On the one hand, there was the relentlessness of the 'final solution'; on the other, the obstruction carried out by Italian diplomats and soldiers had become widely known in the Balkans and elsewhere. It seemed impossible to orderly German officials that such Italian tenacity could go on without an explicit concession made by the Führer. Hitler's tenderness towards Mussolini personally also had a part to play in German attitudes towards the Italians. In May 1942 Himmler rebuked one of his most brutal subordinates, the police chief in Serbia, *SS Gruppenführer* Meyszner:

Bear in mind that you are a Higher SS and Police Leader of Adolf Hitler's Reich, of the Führer, whom a close and cordial friendship unites with the congenial Duce Benito Mussolini. Of course we find a lot to complain about in the behaviour of individual Italians; in a similar way they will object to things we do. That makes no difference. We are allies and only as such strong. Permit no jokes or other criticisms of the Italians but represent the line of the Axis to Germans and above all to foreigners.[67]

On the other side of the demarcation line, in the Italian zone of Greece, Jews went about their business unharmed. The Jewish population of Athens grew by an additional 5,000 as refugees from the German and Bulgarian zones sought the safety of the Italian administration. There were moments of alarm as rumours spread, but, on the whole, as long as the Italians commanded in Athens, the Jews felt safe.

The Germans found the Italians hard to take seriously. After a brawl in an Athenian cafe, a German sergeant, picked up by the carabinieri, was heard shouting: 'That's the bloody end! Now we allow ouselves to be thrown out by these guys. Who won the war anyway?'[68] At higher levels, the Germans complained uninterruptedly about the Italian failure to be severe enough with the Greeks. In his report to the Supreme Command, General Geloso listed six areas of conflict between the Axis partners: the character of the Greek government, the police service ('the German police frequently acted as if we did not exist'), the refusal to shoot hostages according to the German ratios in the German way ('without enquiry, whenever it seemed necessary to set an example . . . an odious practice'), the confiscation of radio receivers, the imposition of forced labour ('a fixed point for our ally from the first days') and the persecution of the Jews.[69]

Geloso was himself the object of much German speculation. 'You're little and ugly', said General Soddu to him when he gave him the command of the 11th Army, 'but you're the smartest general we have.'[70] Cavallero told Kesselring very much the same thing: 'Geloso is, perhaps, the best of our generals, technically prepared, energetic and full of tact.'[71] He had a good civilian education, and unusually among senior Italian commanders, held a university degree in engineering. For a time during the 1930s he went on the reserve list and practised as a civil engineer.[72] He wrote the entry 'Strategy' in the *Enciclopedia Italiana* of 1936, itself a tribute to his 'technical preparation'. Geloso took a relaxed view of the moral standards expected of an army of occupation: 'I have never thought that an officer in wartime ought to be expected to be chaste and pure, the more so as I am firmly convinced that those who are chaste, can neither fight nor command.'[73]

Geloso applied these interesting principles to his own command and chose a lady who gave the Germans a good deal of irritation. An army intelligence officer reported to German Supreme Command South East in May 1943:

General Geloso, whose wife has Greek relations, has a Jewish girl friend, whose connections with anglophile circles have long been known to us. A relative of this girl friend of Geloso was introduced by her to the Italian general staff chief Tripiccione and is known to have been in a relationship with him for about half a year. The two women have access to considerable means. They have given parties in luxurious villas which Geloso confiscated for them to which Italian girls serving with the forces have been invited in considerable numbers as well as young single officers in the Italian army.[74]

A constant German complaint about the Italian military government was its toleration of the black market. German civil and military authorities expected that of Italians. After all, how else could they explain the Italian attitude to the Jews if not as a result of Jewish bribery? The Germans did not invent the stories. There are neutral, Greek sources which indicate that the famine produced widespread and well-organized rings of hoarders and market manipulators. When the Germans intervened in their zone by acting on price levels, rather in the way contemporary central banks intervene in currency markets, they produced a genuine 'bust' and prices halved within a few days.[75]

Italian officers and soldiers participated enthusiastically in such schemes, just as American GIs in Italy did during 1943–44. As that great military figure, ex-PFC Wintergreen of *Catch 22*, explained at one point to Yossarian, 'We all have our jobs to do. My job is to unload those zippo lighters at a profit if I can and pick up some cotton from Milo. Your job is to bomb the ammunition dumps at Bologna.'[76]

For Colonel Ravenni, commanding officer of the 7th Regiment of heavy artillery, known as the 'blue cravats', it was prunes to be unloaded at a profit and, indeed, prunes whch undid him. As Ugo Dragoni writes in his very funny autobiography of his wartime service:

> Ravenni, who had remained uninterruptedly for fourteen months in the zone of operations, had been in constant struggle with [general] Scipione and every time had done the opposite of what the general ordered. He had played with all the colours, from the phoney firing exercises . . . to official letters with the signatures imitated to perfection by the adjutant major. His attempt to export prunes from Croatia to Italy, under army consignment orders, caused the cup to overflow a bit. . . . Scipione sent corps command a detailed report in order to torpedo his promotion to general and get him sent home. The 2nd Army command, having taken due note, transferred him to the army's historical section with the concession of a month's leave for special merit.[77]

Ex-PFC Wintergreen would have understood perfectly but the typical German general staff officer could not. Here were soldiers who were unwilling to fight, colonels who disobeyed orders, exported prunes and consorted with Jews; none of this was excusable behaviour in the midst of a war to defend whatever it was that the upright German staff officer imagined was being defended. Like all the sane characters in *Catch 22*, no sensible Italian had the slightest intention of getting killed unnecessarily in a war which had nothing to do with him. As Yossarian explained impatiently to another officer:

> 'You are talking about winning the war, and I am talking about winning the war and keeping alive.'
> 'Exactly', Clevinger snapped smugly. 'And which do you think is more important?'
> 'To whom?' Yossarian shot back. 'Open your eyes, Clevinger. It doesn't make a damned bit of difference who wins the war to someone who's dead.'[78]

The trouble was that Colonel Ravenni and his men were also losing the war. General Geloso summed it up in a long report to the chief of the Army's general staff in mid-October 1942. The Supreme Command of the Italian armed forces in Greece had no coastal artillery, no bombers, no naval units and 'all my troops, as is well known, have antiquated armament, absolutely no sort of armoured carriers, anti-aircraft equipment or tanks.'[79]

The general thought it unlikely that his 11th Army could contain a raid the size of the one at Dieppe, let alone a serious landing. On the night of 25–26 November 1942, slack Italian guards allowed a team of Greek partisans led by young British officers to blow up the Gorgopatomos bridge. The Germans were understandably furious that the main line of communication from their Greek headquarters had been destroyed.[80] Where Italian and German troops shared duties, the Germans became increasingly exasperated with them. Intelligent Italian officers understood perfectly the superiority of the Germans. Giovanni Pirelli listed the factors in a letter to his father. After discussing the excellence of German strategic planning, he notes several other factors which account for the superiority of German armies:

1) Perfect logistical organization of the Germans;
2) Organization of communications. The command of an armoured group disposes of a telephone network so good that it can communicate in a few minutes with all commands, even in an advancing phase, down to company commanders and from the Führer's headquarters down to battalion level;
3) Excellent material and personnel perfectly trained. The quality of the personnel is the secret of the stunning successes reported everywhere.[81]

The Italians simply could not compete with that and had become less an ally than a serious burden on the German war effort. Yet the Germans were prevented from doing anything about it. After the summit meetings of military staff in early December 1942, chaired by Göring, Rommel observed bitterly:

Although we had always been forbidden to say a word to the Italians about the shortcoming of their Army and State, or to demand improvements, Göring now began to talk to Cavallero about really fundamental questions, such as the poor Italian armament, their sea strategy and similar thorny subjects. The only result, of course, was that he put their backs up without any hope of getting anything put right. . . . Many Italians felt very deeply that the Axis was a sham and consequently believed that in final victory we would have scant regard for their interests. . . . A great many Italians had had enough of the war, and were considering how best they could get out of it.[82]

Mussolini's strategic miscalculations and the illusions of the fascist regime now had to be paid for. By 1940 Italy had acquired a sprawling, unprofitable Empire in Africa. All of her possessions depended exclusively on the maintenance of control of the sea and from the night of 11 November 1940, when the Royal Navy surprised the Italian capital ships at Taranto riding at anchor and sank the *Littorio*, *Cavour* and *Duilio*, Italy never had that command. As the late Captain Stephen Roskill put it

> Admiral Cunningham had rapidly established a marked ascendancy over the Italian Navy. By a series of successful actions, and by the rising offensive of our Malta-based forces against the Italian supply routes to Africa, he placed the entire overseas land forces of Italy in jeopardy.[83]

Italy lost its empire and the war on what Italian merchant seaman called the 'route to death', the convoy route which plied between Italian ports and Tripoli, Bengasi and Tunis during the war. Between 10 June 1940 and 13 May 1943, when 200,000 German and Italian soldiers, surrounded in Tunisia, surrendered to the Allied armies, Italy lost at sea a million tonnes of shipping, huge quantities of supplies, the lives of 22,735 soldiers of both the Italian and German Africa Expeditionary Corps and an unrecorded number of sailors and merchant sailors.[84] Moreover, as Ralph Bennett has shown, the Allied ability to read the *Wehrmacht*'s top-secret code, 'Ultra', played a particularly decisive role in leading RAF and American planes to the routes of these convoys: 'What the official Italian naval history calls ''the hecatomb of the tanker'' . . . was the chief consequence of the unprecedented amount of logistical intelligence supplied by Ultra during this period.'[85]

The Allied landings in Algeria and Morocco in November 1942 caught the Axis completely by surprise and transformed Italy's strategic position at a stroke. When Hitler occupied unoccupied southern France, Italy rushed troops into the same area for reasons of prestige. It would, Cavallero believed, compensate in some measure for the certain loss of empire in Africa. As an occupying power Italy had unwittingly become directly involved for the first time in the actual day-to-day execution of the final solution of the Jewish question in Europe. In Croatia, there had been an intermediary, the Independent State of Croatia, between the Germans and their Jewish prey. In Greece, the Italians had by Hitler's express order complete freedom to administer their 'vital space' and, in any case, the overwhelming bulk of Greek Jews fell under the German zone of occupation. In France, the Italians faced the SS directly for the first time.

The Allied landing and the subsequent occupation of unoccupied France unexpectedly halted the SS machinery. Up to 11 November

1942, according to Serge Klarsfeld, 'Jewish policy' had moved smoothly. Of the 75,000 French Jews ultimately deported, 42,109 had left France for the East, sometimes as in late August or early November at the rate of nearly a transport a day.[86] None of this was possible without the cooperation of the French government and French police which was, on the whole, willingly offered.

Before November 1942 the work of destroying Jews had been divided between the Vichy government, which still had a vestige of sovreignty in the southern part of France, and the German authorities in the north, where they exercised full powers as an occupying force. By his order of 9 March 1942, which established a Higher SS and Police leadership in the area of occupied France, Hitler had given the SS responsibility

> for all tasks which concern the *Reichsführer* SS and Chief of the German police. . . . In these areas of competence he has the right to order and inspect French agencies and police units. He may deploy the French police forces in the occupied territories.[87]

Given that background, the SS naturally assumed that they could operate as before in the new territories occupied by German and Italian troops. On 16 November 1942 Hitler confirmed that assumption by Special Order Number 1 for newly occupied French territory which declared the area an 'operations zone', the ominous phrase used to describe areas behind the lines where the SS commands could work freely, and by empowering the Higher SS and Police Leader 'to extend' his authority to the new territory.[88]

The Higher SS and Police Leader in France, *SS Brigadeführer* Karl Oberg, had already been involved in mass murder of Jews in his previous post in Radom in Poland. On receiving Hitler's Special Order Number 1, Oberg mobilized his men and prepared to move into the new zones. He ran into an unexpected obstacle and sent an urgent telegram to Himmler:

> I had asked General Field Marshall von Rundstedt to smooth the way for despatch of our *Einsatzkommandos* in the area occupied by Italian troops on the assumption such troops were under his command. The field marshall cannot grant my request because the troops are not under him. . . . Since it is absolutely vital that our *Einsatzkommandos* which were mobilized today, be allowed to operate in the area near Lac Léman, in Marseilles and on the Côte d'Azur, I suggest that on Wednesday I make a personal visit to the Italian divisional commanders in question to make an attempt in your name to settle the matter. Were this to fail the only choice would be that of direct negotiations with the Italian government.[89]

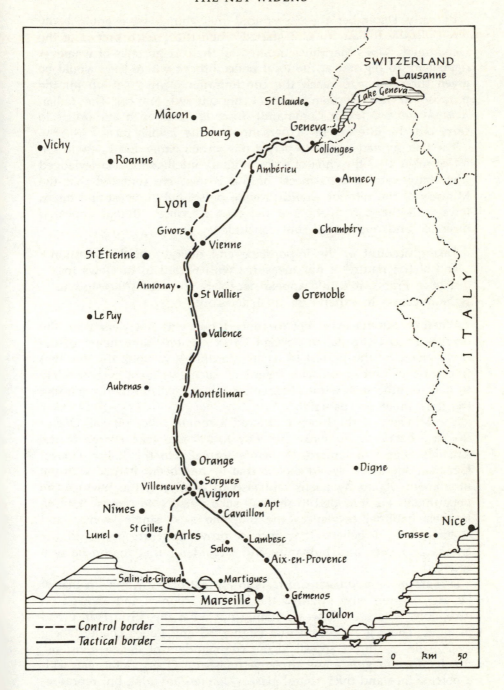

Map 3 German and Italian zones of occupation in France, 1941–43

By early December the SS noticed that things were going badly wrong in the Italian zone. It started when the French prefect of the Department Alpes Maritimes ordered all the foreign Jews of whatever nationality to register at the local police offices where they would be given three days to reach the concentration camps set up for the purpose in the German zone of unoccupied France. The Italian *comando supremo* (High Command) 'forbade the French authorities to carry out the internment of personnel of the Jewish race'.[90]

The Italians had begun to play a dangerous game and knew it. On 8 December 1942 the chief of secret military intelligence acknowledged 'the complexity and vastness' of the issues. He reported that the Ministry of the Interior would provide personnel to arrest and intern Jews with the participation of the French police, 'if that appeared desirable and opportune', but concluded:

Taking account of the importance and delicacy of the question and of the nature of our measures with regard to the Jews resident in France it would appear necessary to entrust the study of the question to experts for final decision.[91]

Whether experts ever met to concert policy is not clear from the documents. At the Italian Foreign Office, when Ciano heard of the order given by the prefect of Alpes Maritimes, he took the line that 'measures of precaution with regard to said Jews must pertain solely to Italian authorities without exception . . . the disposition regarding the Jews must be suspended.'[92]

The Ministry of the Interior ordered a senior police official, Doctor Rossario Barranco, to make his way to Nice to take charge of the situation. Early in January he wrote formally to the Italian Consul General Alberto Calisse to explain that he had been charged with the internment of enemy aliens and also to deal with the Jews of the department. He intended to send all such persons to camps, 'leaving in their habitual residences the old, the sick, single women and children. . . . I believe that such a provision corresponds to the criteria of justice and humanity and should for that reason be well received.'[93]

Dr Barranco's approach contrasts in an instructive way with that of Dr Max Merten who interned the Jews of Salonica and allowed no exceptions whatever. It was certainly not what the SS in France had in mind. There is no record that Higher SS and Police Leader Oberg ever made his direct appeal to the commanders of Italian divisions. It is hard to imagine a less attractive emissary. Oberg, a fat man with a porcine face and thick round glasses, looked anything but representative of a genetically desirable stock of human beings. His subordinate, *Standartenführer* Dr Helmut Knochen, made a very different impression, as an official assessment noted:

> very good appearance, understands how to act in every situation, calm, clear and objective, excellent political tact, ideally suited to be police attaché at an embassy or for special duties abroad. One of the best of the rising generation of leaders in the SD [*Sicherheitsdienst*].[94]

By January 1943 Knochen felt compelled to appeal directly to the head of the Gestapo to get the Italians to stop 'special treatment' for the Jews. It had been bad enough that the Italians prevented the proper treatment of Italian Jews, who, while not numerous, created 'great difficulties'; what the Italians seemed to be doing now was much more serious:

> if the Italians now interfere on behalf of all Jews with foreign citizenship, that will make the continuation of a Jewish policy in our sense impossible, that is, we cannot be certain that we shall get the Jews of French citizenship handed over to us in the next few months and get them shipped off.[95]

The French government might use the occasion to wriggle out of its collaboration in the final solution. On 14 January 1943 Pierre Laval, Prime Minister of the Vichy puppet government, summoned the Italian Ambassador to ask what the Italians were up to:

> Laval expressed himself in the sense that, while he could understand our interesting ourselves in favour of Israelites of Italian nationality, he could not exactly grasp our intervention 'in favour' of foreign Jews, also because this put the Jews of French nationality, as a consequence, in a position of disadvantage with respect to foreign Jews. He added that he would prefer to see the Italian Jews and maybe the foreign Jews transferred to Italy.[96]

Laval's wish to be rid of Italian and foreign Jews was hardly surprising. There were limits to his powers to cooperate with the Germans. If foreign Jews went free while Vichy rounded up genuine citizens of France, some decorated as war heroes, he would be finished.

The Italian 4th Army which took up its positions in the south of France looked formidable on paper: three Army corps and several crack divisions. The Alpine Division 'Pusteria' occupied Grenoble, the Division 'Legnano' entered Nice, the 'Lupi di Toscana' Marseilles and the 'Taro' Toulon.[97] In reality it had not much more fighting power than Geloso's 11th Army in Greece. A German report in the spring of 1943 declared: 'The 4th Army has no planes, no naval protection, no heavy artillery, no anti-aircraft. In addition they are short of cement and iron in order to carry out coastal fortfifications.'[98]

When the Germans provided cement and iron, the Italians

apparently used them for other purposes. According to General von Neubronn, the German military representative to the Vichy government, no German officer, not even the liaison officer to 4th Army HQ, ever saw a single blockhouse built with German cement. What they did see and noted with dismay were the roadblocks on the inland roads. As von Neubronn put it,

> it was not easy to understand what these obstacles to traffic had to do with preventing an enemy landing. One got the very distinct impression that these remarkable installations were directed against us Germans, especially since the cars of German officers were frequently stopped and controlled at these points.[99]

Even more unsatisfactory from the German point of view was the chain of command. Formally the Italian 4th Army came under the command of the Supreme Commander West, Field Marshall von Rundstedt, who, according to von Neubronn, never managed to gain 'any influence over the Italians until the end of Italian participation in the war'.[100] The German military, divided into a dozen overlapping authorities, made less fuss about this mutinous behaviour than it might have for fear that Hitler might explode in irritation and do something rash. The Inspector General actually ordered his staff in late November 1942, to be especially careful with counter-intelligence and public opinion reports: 'Highest places already suspicious enough. Through unfavourable reporting the situation with regard to the French can change with lightning speed and good, that is, usable porcelain be smashed.'[101]

In other words, the moderates in the army command in France hoped to preserve a Vichy regime with at least the shreds of authority as long as possible. Their dilemma resembled that of Glaise von Horstenau in Croatia and for the same reason. Hitler's contempt for his puppets could barely be restrained and Himmler's treatment of them even less so. If the puppets were to be swept away by an outburst of the Führer's rage, the German army would have to govern France or Croatia directly and hence further spread its stretched resources. It was prudent not to be too critical of the Italians in 'highest places' because such criticism might have the same effects on the Führer's patience with his Axis partner.

Franco-Italian relations at the beginning were not good. General Vacca Maggiolini, head of the Italian Armistice Commission, reported 'the long face' that his French opposite number wore after the occupation. It had been humiliating enough to have to sign an armistice with the Italians who had got nowhere in 1940 but even more so, two years later, to suffer an occupation by Italian troops which their feats of arms hardly justified.[102]

The course of the war, the news of Stalingrad, the behaviour of the German forces, especially the Gestapo, in the German zone, played into the hands of the Italians. Italian occupation was embarrassing but not brutal. The Germans by contrast largely ignored the wishes of the French state. General Walter Warlimont of the German general staff put it neatly to a high level meeting of various German agencies concerned with France just before Christmas 1942: 'The French government should preserve a certain sovereignty, but only in so far as it is useful for our purposes.'[103]

After the first period of friction, the Italians treated the French with courtesy. By May 1943 the German liaison to the joint Axis control delegation in Toulon was able to report that

> the Italian policy of annoying the French has since the occupation of southern France undergone a complete transformation. The occupation forces have evidently got instructions to operate with special tact, considerable thoughtfulness, understanding and help-fulness. Until recently the Italian tri-colour was not flown even on official buildings. . . . By contrast the French attitude to Germany has been transformed into mistrust and rejection because of our encroachments, mistakes and the often tactless behaviour of mostly subordinate but independently operating organs.[104]

The Germans seemed to be going out of their way to alienate the French population. Early in February 1943 the German security police suddenly decided to blow up a part of the old quarter of Marseilles because its winding streets provided a good refuge for members of the resistance. A splendid old neighbourhood was turned into a pile of rubble and 6,000 arrests made, which, as the Italian consul reported, 'increased hatred against the Germans especially for the way they use the French police'.[105]

The brutality of the SS caused problems for the army authorities and for those units of the *Wehrmacht* whose business brought them into contact with French authorities. Colonel von Rost of the German military mission to the Vichy government made a plea for more considerate treatment in a report at the beginning of February 1943:

> One forgets that one is not dealing with half-savage Asiatics but with a people with a sensitive feeling for their honour and a self-conscious temperament. Besides the French are subject to constant enemy propaganda. With the best will in the world the French government can do nothing about that. Without wishing to plead for a false softness, I do think it would be right if the French government were informed with suitable safeguards when large scale arrests are carried out and why they are necessary.[106]

The truth was that by 1943 nobody could stop the SS and the police doing what they pleased. In June 1943 von Rost's superior, the German general representing the Reich in Vichy, General Freiherr von Neubronn, received orders to go to the French Ministry of Defence and search the place. Hitler and Himmler had decided that the French were building a secret army and wanted proof. The aristocratic general found the exercise acutely embarrassing but, good officer that he was, he took charge of the operation himself. As he wrote in a letter to von Rundstedt, the French officers and civil servants were understandably worried that this might be the first step leading to a wave of arrests.[107]

The Italian occupation thus frustrated the SS in several ways. The Italian 4th Army seemed to be beyond the control of the Supreme Commander West, who for reasons of his own was neither able nor willing to exercise authority over it. The Italians were busy winning the sympathy of the French population by courteous treatment, while refusing to allow Vichy's police to act against the Jews.

As time passed things worsened from the SS point of view. In the middle of January 1943 the *comando supremo* announced in a letter to the Italian military attaché to Vichy, the Duke of Avarna, that the Italian army intended 'to exercise . . . all the rights of an occupying power'.[108] Italian military law thereafter superceded French domestic law. When the French authorities tried to impose the wearing of the Star of David on the Jews of the Italian zone, the Italian military government intervened and forbade it. This time the story was published by *The Times* in London on 21 January under a headline which read 'Jews' Badges in France':

Last week in the Italian-occupied departments of Savoie, Haute Savoie, Basses Alpes, Hautes Alpes, Alpes Maritimes and Var, the Italian commanding generals notified the Prefects that it was irreconcilable with the dignity of the Italian army that in territories occupied by Italians, Jews should be compelled to appear in public with this stigmatizing badge, and consequently notified the prefects that Vichy's orders were to be cancelled.[109]

This was another risky aspect of Italian policy. In Croatia, Western intelligence knew a good deal about the intricacies of genocide in the northern Balkans (for example, Churchill had firm information about the divisions between the Axis partners on the *cetnik* question[110]), but the newspapers could not easily get such information. France was different. It was within easy reach and through Free French and other underground sources newspapers in Britain could report with complete accuracy a story like the one above within days of the event. The story then got recycled by the Italian service of the BBC and the

Italian military authorities began to realise that their policies in occupied France had made world news. A few days after the report in *The Times*, Marshall Cavallero rang General Mario Vercellino, commanding general of the 4th Army, to tell him about the story.[111]

Early in February the police attaché at the German Embassy in Paris informed *Obersturmführer* Röthke of the Security Police that the measures planned on the Jewish question had not been carried out because the Italians had not worked 'in conformity' with German policy. Now the Foreign Office in Berlin had given orders to go ahead with the 'planned measures':

> If the French government runs into difficulties caused by the Italian High Command in the implementation of the measures, you are to report in precise detail each concrete instance, so that these special cases can be taken up with the Italian government.[112]

Italian policy toward the Jews put the two Axis partners on a collision course. The Consul General in Marseilles reported that the German police in Marseilles were taking a census of the population, always a first step in segregating the Jews.[113] The Italians countered by adopting the policy they had tried in Croatia: internment. On Sunday 14 February orders went out from HQ 1st Army Corp to all divisional commanders ordering them to prepare to

> initiate operations by the 20th of this month for the assignment to forced residence of the subjects of hostile states and of all foreign Jews resident in the department of Alpes Maritimes. . . . This command has notified the prefect of the department of Alpes Maritimes to have the hotels in St Martin Vesubie and Vence reopened and to secure the victualling of the interned. . . . As a general rule persons aged 60 or above and women living alone [underlined in original] are not to be interned. The assignment of persons to the various localities will be carried out in agreement with Dr Barranco bearing in mind the nationality of the persons involved and the degree of danger they represent.[114]

Part of the justification for internment had always been that Jews favoured the Allies and represented a source of enemy propaganda and spying. The Italian authorities with varying degrees of sincerity insisted on this point both to Jews and to Germans. Those Jews interned had as little doubt in France as they had in Croatia that internment protected them. As one survivor, Albert Sharon, told Joseph Rochlitz in an interview reproduced in the documentary film *The Righteous Enemy*, St Martin Vesubie was a kind of idyll for harassed Jews from central and eastern Europe. They were allowed a synagogue and the local *maresciallo* of the carabinieri, an opera buff, loved to come to services to hear the splendid voice of the cantor.[115]

Approximately 1,100 foreign Jews were assigned to forced residence at seven sites in the areas controlled by the I and XV Army Corps,[116] but internment failed to impress either the SS or the Vichy regime who continued to try to get their hands on the Jews of Italian-occupied France. On 22 February 1943 the commanding officer of the Alpine Division 'Pusteria' and the HQ 20th Ski Regiment stationed at Chambery reported that the prefectures at Valence, Chambery and Annecy had begun to carry out arrests of foreign Jews under 'direct orders' of the Vichy government. When the Italian army intervened, the prefects replied that they had no choice but to carry out explicit orders of their government. When he got the news, General Vercellino, commanding general of the 4th Army, asked permission of the *comando supremo* to order the French prefects to cease and desist from further arrests and in the event of their refusal to arrest them.[117] A stalemate followed as Italian troops prevented French police transporting Jews whom they had arrested. A few days later, the Italian general in charge of the Franco-Italian armistice commission devoted a part of his monthly report to the crisis. He reported that the prefects continued to try to arrest Jews:

without our knowing it and have tried, again without our knowledge, to send such Jews into the zone occupied by German troops. Such an attitude may be due to Vichy's desire to send foreign Jews to work in the Reich rather than French workers. The foreign Jews have naturally welcomed our explicit intervention in their favour with much gratitude and, when the rumour spread around Nice that the Italian authorities were enrolling Jews to work, many presented themselves and asked to be allowed to go to work in Italy. . . . In local Catholic circles our intervention to impede the transfer of the Jews to other zones was known at once and has been interpreted as an act of favour towards persecuted Jews and much appreciated.[118]

For the first and only time during the Second World War Italian policy towards the Jews moved to the centre of the stage. Both the *comando supremo* and the Foreign Ministry had to shape a policy and quickly. Colonel Cesare Cremese, chief of the office of general affairs at the High Command, wrote to the Foreign Ministry on 1 March 1943, on orders of General Ambrosio, the chief of staff, to provide the details of recent activities by the French prefects. He went on to argue that measures of law and order with regard to Jews resident in Italian-occupied France must be reserved to our military authorities and that without discrimination as to the nationality of the Jews concerned, be they Italian or French or foreign. I request you to take the necessary steps with the Vichy government to affirm the above principle and require the government of Vichy to revoke arrests and internments already carried out.[119]

This was strong stuff. The Italians now claimed authority over *all* Jews irrespective of nationality. Later the same day *comando supremo* informed the Foreign Ministry that it had given instructions to the Italian military liaison officer at Vichy, the Duke of Avarna, to state the Italian position to the French government.[120] On the following day Avarna saw Admiral Platon, Vichy Minister of Defence, and carried out his instructions.[121] General von Neubronn reported the meeting to German army headquarters. There is a revealing phrase in his report. Whereas the Italian note merely stated that Italian authorities were to be responsible for the surveillance of all Jews, von Neubronn reported 'that in the area occupied by Italy neither Jews of Italian nor of French or foreign nationality may be pursued [*verfolgt* in the original][122]

Freiherr von Neubronn had inadvertently let the truth slip into an official document. 'Verfolgt' is a strong word. It means chased or pursued but is also the standard expression for persecution as in *Verfolgung der Juden*, the persecution of the Jews. Whatever euphemisms the Nazi regime may have imposed on itself and its servants, truth always seeps out. General Alexander Freiherr von Neubronn, an opponent of Nazism, knew the truth, as did most others of his social class. As the late Herr Wolfgang von Tirpitz once said to me, 'if anybody from my class tells you that they did not know what was going on, they're lying'. Italian policy in southern France put a stop to the 'persecution of the Jews' and everybody involved recognized that.

The SS watched these developments with mounting impatience. Eichmann himself came to Paris. Helmut Knochen appealed to *Gruppenführer* Heinrich Müller, head of the Gestapo Section of the *Reichssicherheitshauptamt*. Something had to be done urgently. Not only was Pétain resisting the German demands to surrender the Jews but the French had begun to feel certain that Germany would lose the war and hence had adopted a 'waiting position' on the final solution. Besides the French were now using the Italians as an argument:

They declare – and these are facts which have been reported and underscored by security police units and other German service agencies – that the Italians intervene on behalf of Jews east of the Rhone. It is not only that official Italian authorities send notes to the French government in which they forbid the marking of Jews and thus act on behalf of Jews of all nationalities but in addition the relations between the Italians and Jews are excellent. Italians live with Jews, allow themselves to be invited out and paid for by Jews so that in the area the impression gets out that German and Italian attitudes are absolutely different. . . . In order to carry out the measures for all of France the precondition is that they are executed in the Italian-occupied zone. Otherwise the already considerable migration of Jews into the Italian-occupied region will assume ever greater proportions and we shall end with half-measures.[123]

Half measures were clearly intolerable. Some Jews might survive on French territory. The final solution might not be final. It was time to apply pressure at the summit of the Italian government. The SS approached the German Foreign Office with what by now had become a long list of complaints. Minister Helmut Bergmann prepared a memorandum summarizing them which he sent by telegram to the special train 'Westfalen' carrying the Reich Foreign Minister to a meeting with the Duce in Rome. Bergmann listed SS reports of Italian obstruction of the final solution in Greece and France. The Foreign Office's section DIII, Bergmann continued, 'can only confirm the correctness of these statements'. The *Reichssicherheitshauptamt* had been asked 'to concretize its wishes and agreed to do this by the 25th of February'.[124]

The Duce flanked by his new Foreign Minister, Giuseppe Bastianini, and by the Italian Ambassador to Berlin, Dino Alfieri, received von Ribbentrop and the German Ambassador von Mackensen at the Palazzo Venezia. They had much to discuss, none of it agreeable. Although Ribbentrop had taken General Walter Warlimont, the very able deputy chief of the German general staff, he went to meet the Duce without him and soon found himself engaged in a lengthy defence of Hitler's strategy in Russia which he did in his usual optimistic and plausible way. Then he turned to the Yugoslav situation and the continuing Italian reliance on the *cetniks*. Bastianini and Ribbentrop disagreed on the reliability of the Italian-armed units and on whether they would or would not immediately join the Anglo-American allies in the case of a landing in the Balkans. It was an old source of friction and not easily smoothed.

The Reich Foreign Minister then turned to the *Judenfrage*. It was well known to the Duce that the Reich had adopted a 'radical' approach to the question and that the enemy had branded the German measures to transport the Jews to 'reservations' in the East as 'gruesome'. Experience had shown how necessary such measures were. Ribbentrop continued:

Even the French had taken measures against the Jews which were extremely useful. They were temporary because the ultimate solution would consist in the transport of Jews to the east. He (the Reich Foreign Minister) knew that in military circles in Italy, as indeed occasionally in military circles in Germany, the necessary understanding of the Jewish question was not to be found. Only thus could he explain the way *comando supremo* had revoked orders for the Italian zone of occupation which the French authorities upon German insistence had begun to carry out. The Duce denied the correctness of the statement and explained it as a French manoeuvre to spread disunity between Germany and Italy. . . . Nevertheless he granted that the Reich Foreign Minister was correct that the army lacked the proper feeling in the Jewish question which he attributed to their different intellectual and spiritual formation.[125]

The discussion then moved on to Stalin, then to the forthcoming collapse in Africa and other issues of strategy. Nothing had been decided but for the first time the conflict between the Axis partners on the Jewish question had become an issue of first-rate importance to be discussed on the same level as military operations in Russia or Africa. It must have been a hallucinatory experience to sit on the Italian side of the table listening to the dapper, grey-haired man chat about 'reservations' for Jews in the East, knowing what those reservations really were. Did Ribbentrop know that the Italians understood where Jews 'sent East' ended up? There is no evidence that I have seen to suggest that he did; on the other hand, he must have been as aware as they of the contents of Allied broadcasts. If he knew that they knew the truth, did they know that he knew?

Pietromarchi recorded the visit of Ribbentrop in his diaries. He learned that Ribbentrop had raised the Jewish question but believed that the Duce had 'cut him off' sharply which the German stenographic account does not support. In conversation afterwards, Pietromarchi wrote down the following dialogue between Bastianini, the under secretary for foreign affairs, and Count Leonardo Vitetti, director general of European and Mediterranean affairs in the Foreign Ministry:

'It is to be hoped', observed the under-secretary, 'that Bismarck himself does not come back to dwell on the subject.' 'To Bismarck', Vitetti said in reply, 'I have made it clear that his grandfather would have been ashamed to discuss questions like this to which he answered that I was right.'[126]

The visit was not a great success. Ribbentrop refused to pay a call on the new Italian Foreign Secretary on the grounds that he was, after all, technically only an under-secretary. The fact that Ciano had been no more but always received the full diplomatic courtesies did not escape Bastianini.[127] Ribbentrop had long since dismissed Bastianini as an 'honorary Jew'[128] and that may have explained his rudeness.

Outside the charmed circle, former ministers waited anxiously for news. Bottai, one of the fallen idols, entered in his diary for 1 March 1943:

> Ribbentrop has been in Rome for four days. Beyond the official communiqué nothing has leaked. Ansaldo, [Giovanni, editor and proprietor of il Telegrafo of Livorno] came to visit me and tells me of a request for an accentuated anti-Jewish policy on our part; in order to compromise us, he thinks, in their policy of persecution and to remove any possibility of discrimination with respect to us. In fact, in today's communiqué there is the formula about the 'Jewish plutocracy', which consecrates, I think for the first time as far as official Italy is concerned, the anti-semitic character of the struggle.[129]

Bottai and Ansaldo were not the first figures I have cited who advanced that argument: the Germans wanted the Italians to cooperate in order to implicate them in their crimes. No German evidence supports that view. Official Germany had always been committed to the 'anti-semitic character of the struggle' in Bottai's words, and if murdering Jews was a crime it was not officially admitted to be one. For Himmler and the SS it was a glorious achievement. For Hitler exterminating Jews remained the one achievement which neither defeat nor death could deny him, as he reminded the world in his testament of April 1945.

Ribbentrop's aim was simple. He wanted what Himmler and Oberg and Röthke and Eichmann wanted. He wanted to get hold of those Jews under Italian protection so that they could be sent to die in the east. It was, after all, a modest request. By comparison with the millions who had already died, a few thousand here or there hardly seemed worth a fuss. The danger, as Helmut Knochen pointed out, was not that a few Jews might escape the net but that the Italian example might encourage the assistant murderers in France, Croatia or Slovakia to think again. That would be serious for the Germans because – it cannot be emphasized enough – the Germans needed the help of their allies to destroy the Jews. It was the French police, not the SS, who did most of the dirty work in France. Their collaboration was vital.

Reports of massacres in Poland continued to reach well-placed

Italians. Pietromarchi wrote that the Italian Embassy in Berlin had provided 'macabre details of the mass execution of Jews in occupied countries'. He then outlined what Italian troops had done in France, Croatia and Greece to help Jews:

> The Germans are showing real annoyance about it. Ribbentrop did not hesitate to send us a note of 26 February in which are listed all the activities of our authorities in occupied countries on behalf of the Jews. He added that such attitudes will encourage other countries to behave in a similar way. I said to my colleagues that we must guard that document jealously as irrefutable proof of our way of acting, precious testimony before history which will redeem us from numerous acts of baseness.[130]

On 6 March 1943 Monsignor Konrad von Preysing, Catholic Bishop of Berlin, wrote to the Pope imploring him to save the Jews being deported from Berlin. 'Their likely fate', wrote the Bishop, 'was hinted at by Your Holiness in your Christmas Message on the radio.'[131] Monsignor Burzio, Papal Nuncio in Slovakia, reported from Pressburg (Bratislava) the imminent deportation of the remaining 20,000 Slovak Jews and the fact that the entire Slovak episcopate had signed a pastoral letter protesting the persecution of the Jews.[132] The next day Sister Margherita Slachta, co-foundress with Edit Farkas of the Congregation of Social Mission, came to plead the cause of the Slovak Jews in person and had an audience of the Cardinal Secretary of State.[133]

The Vatican response was weak. When in the middle of March 1943 the Archbishop of Westminster, Cardinal Hinsley, died, the British Ambassador to the Holy See, D'Arcy Osborne, recalled him with real regret in a diary entry:

> He was a great patriot, though perhaps more courageously outspoken regarding Nazi persecution of the church and other offences against the laws of God and man than would please the hypersensitive neutrals of the Vatican. They probably do not realize how much he has done to counteract the unfavourable effects abroad of their neutrality.[134]

D'Arcy Osborne for Britain and Harold Tittmann for the USA had been pressing the Pope and Cardinal Maglione, the Secretary of State, for months to attack the Nazi extermination of the Jews but had failed. Nor had Osborne minced words. In a confrontation a few months earlier he told the Cardinal Secretary of State 'that the Vatican, instead of thinking of nothing but the bombing of Rome, should consider their duties in respect of the unprecedented crime against humanity of Hitler's campaign of extermination of the Jews.'[135]

Whether a clear statement by Pius XII would have altered the course of events cannot be assessed. It would, conceivably, have strengthened the hands of those prelates in occupied countries where puppet governments still preserved a semblance of independence, such as Cardinal Gerlier of Lyons in France or Cardinal Stepinac in Zagreb. It would have made crimes a little more difficult to commit in Catholic states like Slovakia and Lithuania. I doubt if it would have halted the German murder machine. The men who ran the Nazi state seemed unreachable by appeals to humanity; they had none. Here is Goebbel's reaction to the deportation of the Berlin Jews, very different from that of Monsignor von Preysing:

We are now definitely pushing the Jews out of Berlin. They were suddenly rounded up last Saturday and are to be carted off to the East as quickly as possible. Unfortunately, our better circles, especially the intellectuals, once again have failed to understand our policy about the Jews and in some cases have taken their part. As a result our plans were tipped off prematurely, so that a lot of Jews slipped through our hands. But we will catch them yet. I certainly won't rest until the capital of the Reich, at least, has become free of Jews.[136]

No Vatican appeal would have touched the emotions of a soul so twisted and evil as that of Joseph Goebbels. What it might have done was to reach those 'better circles', as Goebbels called them, who 'failed to understand' Nazi policy about the Jews, to send a message to those thousands of good Christians who were ready in small ways to act against the crime they watched unfold before them, those courageous Slovak bishops and lay people who in the heart of Hitler's darkness lit a candle of humanity. It would have given encouragement to others, even in Germany, to resist, men like Cardinal Count Galen, Bishop of Münster, who in three vigorous sermons in 1941 condemned the whole apparatus of Nazi brutality and by his open attack brought a halt to the Nazi murder of the feeble-minded. 'Why does Rome let Galen fight all by himself?' asked Ulrich von Hassell.[137] The question had no answer then; it has none now.

German pressure on Italy did not let up. The Italians had scarcely rolled up the red carpet for Ribbentrop when on 5 March they had to unroll it for Göring, who, as Ambassador von Mackensen reported, had come on a visit of 'purely military character' but wanted to be briefed 'in broad outlines on the conversations between the Reich Foreign Minister and the Duce'.[138] In the 'war of all against all' at Hitler's court, knowledge of what rivals were up to was vital for survival. A few days after Göring's departure, Ribbentrop returned to the offensive. Italy was, after all, his terrain and, now that he had rid himself of Martin Luther, he too wanted to make successful Jewish policy. On 9 March he ordered von Mackensen to go to see the Duce 'personally'. The Ambassador was to present him with a memorandum which summarized the facts in France: that

at the prompting of the German government an action to arrest all Jews without regard to their citzenship has been undertaken by the French police in the entire territory. President Laval has informed our chargé d'affaires in Paris that on the 2nd of March the representative of the Italian high command in Vichy, General Avarna, submitted a note in which the revocation of all arrests and internments of Jews hitherto ordered was demanded and an instruction to prefects in the territory occupied by Italian armed forces to arrest no more Jews in future.

The full text of the note followed in a long report from the chief of the Vichy police, Réné Bousquet, on Italian behaviour to Jews and on Jewish sentiments in the Italian zone. Ribbentrop then instructed the Ambassador in the sharpest possible way to remind the Duce that in their recent discussions in Rome he had

clearly taken the stand that in Jewish questions there must be unity in adopting very harsh measures. At the time I left the Duce a memo in which the Italian instructions in the Jewish question were manifestly opposed to ours. The Duce then said that he could not believe it, and that it must be an intrigue by the French. . . . Today with the two documents I submit to you we have the clearest proof that Italian military authorities and the *comando supremo* are pursuing policies even in France that are diametrically opposed to the ideas and intentions of the Duce.

There were three possible options which von Mackensen was to present to the Duce:

1) the Duce gives the *comando supremo* clear orders to leave these things to the French police and to stop getting in their way;
2) the Duce withdraws the administration of these matters from the military authorities and transfers them to the civilian police, who in dealing with these issues must be independent of the military authorities. A solution of this kind has been suggested by the *Reichsführer SS*.
3) the *Reichsführer SS* undertakes the management of these matters together with the French police even in the Italian-occupied area so that Italian agencies no longer have anything more to do with them.

The Ambassador was to inform the Duce that in the German view 2) and 3) were preferable but in any case clear orders had to be given to the Italian army. Finally the Ambassador might let slip the fact that the Führer had been informed of the situation and had let his interest in the matter be known by a special telephone call.[139]

The Führer, according to Goebbel's diary for the same day, was more than interested:

The Führer is very angry at the Italians because they are actually doing nothing. They aren't any good on the Eastern Front; they aren't any good for North Africa; they aren't any good for submarine warfare; they aren't any good even for anti-aircraft at home. The Führer is right in asking why they are in the war anyway.

Interestingly the Italians were not the only occasion for an outburst of Hitler's rage on that March day. He began to complain about the low moral qualities of his generals: 'He doesn't believe any general *a priori*. They all cheat him, fawn upon him, furnish him with statistics any child can contradict, and thereby insult the Führer's intelligence.'[140]

The business with the Jews in France united his contempt for Italians with his increasing hatred of the professional soldiers, those men with monocles, titles and crisp upper-class accents who had been right about exposed flanks and supply lines and Russian counter-attacks, while 'the greatest field commander of all times' had been disastrously wrong. The Italian army provided a perfect foil for his irritation. It was full of unreliable professional soldiers who were no good at making war.

While the Germans wanted the Jews of France, they had not forgotten the Jews of Croatia. There is an account in Poliakov and Sabille's *Jews under the Italian Occupation* taken from the post-war testimony of Colonel Vincenzo Carla, chief of the First Bureau of 2nd Army HQ in Croatia, which suggests that Mussolini agreed with Ribbentrop off the record to surrender the Croatian Jews. Carla describes an audience which must have taken place in early March 1943, in which Mussolini told General Ambrosio and General Robotti (Roatta's successor in Croatia) that he had promised Ribbentrop to surrender the Jews of Croatia. According to Carla, Robotti protested so violently that the Duce gave in:

True, I was compelled to consent to the expulsion but you think of whatever excuse you please, so as not to hand over even one single Jew. Say that we have no means of transport to take them to Trieste and that transport by land is impossible.[141]

There is evidence in the files of the Italian Foreign Ministry that some decision had been taken. A memorandum of the Croatian department of 9 March 1943 listed the exact locations of the 2,661 Jews interned in Croatia and another prepared in Luigi Vidau's section, A.G. IV which dealt with confidential matters, that summarizes the state of negotiations.[142] If the Jews of Croatia had been surrendered, there was not much hope to save the Jews in France.

Berlin was clearly losing patience with Rome and, at least in the Jewish question, demanded immediate action. For the first time in the war the Duce and his advisors would have to face concrete proposals to participate directly in the destruction of the Jewish people. They could do it in one of the three ways that the Reich Foreign Minister had generously offered them but an option not to participate was no longer available.

The German military attaché, Enno von Rintelen, who after seven years of service in Rome knew the Italian situation better than any other German official, reported to the High Command on 12 March that the Italian officer corps had surrendered to a certain 'fatalism':

> To this must be added the absence of understanding for the German treatment of the Jews and anti-Catholic policies. The importance and influence of the Church grows the longer the war lasts. The army leadership uses the church more and more to instil better morale in the troops.[143]

The church itself had by now got reliable news of the demand by the German Foreign Minister to surrender the Jews. The day after von Rintelen sent off his report, the Cardinal Secretary of State noted:

> As I wrote in my Note of 22 January 1943, Mussolini has had the deportation of the Jews from Croatia suspended. I now know that the Germans have made new demands for a much firmer attitude on Italy's part towards the Jews(!) One can therefore (without mentioning the above) charge either the Nuncio (or P. Tacchi Venturi) to intercede once more.[144]

Four days later Cardinal Maglione entrusted to Father Tacchi Venturi's 'good priestly heart' the care of the Jews of Croatia and asked him to approach the Italian government with 'his well known tact' to intercede on behalf of persons who otherwise faced 'a very harsh fate'[145] and on 18 March Monsignor Montini (later Pope Paul VI) made a note in which he wrote: 'It is necessary that His Excellency Monsignor the Nuncio ask this very evening of Ortona, the secretary of Excellency Bastianini, for an appointment for tomorrow morning to ask him to intervene on behalf of the Jews in France.'[146]

There was no time to lose. March 17 and 18 were the moments of supreme crisis for Jews under Italian protection. The Vatican clearly knew that on 17 March, in a private audience of the Duce, Ambassador von Mackensen had presented the new demands embodied in Ribbentrop's letter of 9 March. The Holy See knew too how brutal, callous and, above all, unpredictable Mussolini could be. He had condemned the refugee Jews in Croatia to death, then changed his mind and now apparently changed it again. It had taken months and much pressure from military, diplomatic and clerical sources to get the Jews of Croatia reprieved the first time. With the *SS Einsatzkommandos* mobilized there would be no time to work the miracle a second time. The Nuncio had to see Bastianini that 'very evening'.[147]

There are several accounts of precisely what happened when von Mackensen saw Mussolini and what happened afterwards. Von Mackensen himself found the encounter late on the evening of 17 March 1943, highly satisfactory. During the reading of the various documents which Ribbentrop had entrusted to the Ambassador, Mussolini said nothing but showed his agreement by 'approving gestures'. When the Ambassador finished, the Duce requested the Ambassador to convey his thanks to the Reich Foreign Minister and expressed himself disposed to cooperate. He told Ambassador von Mackensen that:

> Our [the German] position of principle on the unavoidable necessity of thorough-going measures against Jews . . . was clear as the sun and undeniably necessary. If his generals had got in the way, it was because with their different mode of thought they had not grasped the extent of the entire measure. It was not malevolent but a logical consequence of their way of thought. In fact the reality was that we should be glad that there was a French government ready to carry out such measures. It was out of the question to get in their way. . . . The behaviour of his generals was not only the expression of the lack of understanding for the significance of the action but a result of a false humanitarian twaddle which had no place in today's harsh world. He would – and I was to report this to the Reich Foreign Minister – give General Ambrosio that very day instructions to let the French police have a fully free hand in their action.[148]

Mussolini had, as the Ambassador noted, opted for Number 1 of Ribbentrop's courses of action: to let the French police get on with the round-up of the Jews.

Vittorio Ambrosio, the chief of the Italian *comando supremo* or High Command, was like so many senior Italian commanders a Piedmontese. He has had a mixed reputation. Von Rintelen thought highly of him as 'a calm, quiet, and competent soldier'.[149] Cavallero, his predecessor, called him a 'cretin'. Acquarone, the Minister for the Royal Household and the King's Chief Advisor, thought him one-tenth as able as Cavallero[150] and Marshall Caviglia noted: 'Ambrosio does not look you in the eyes and does not stand up under direct gaze, but his words are open and frank and I don't want to think it's just a mask.'[151]

Whether Ambrosio stood up under Mussolini's gaze on the Jewish question is not quite clear from the record. He had certainly signed orders forbidding Italian military authorities to surrender Jews to either the French or the Croatians. As the Duce had promised von Mackensen, Bastianini and Ambrosio were summoned to Palazzo Venezia and told of his promise to von Mackensen. According to his account written in the 1950s, Bastianini protested vigorously and demanded that the Duce not give such an order which would deal a dreadful blow to Italian prestige abroad. He proposed instead that the Jews be interned, all the Jews, under the Italian police; in effect, although he does not mention it, he took up Ribbentrop's second option, to give control of the Jews to the Italian police, the method favoured by Himmler who no doubt expected to be able to put more pressure on colleagues from the police than on the Italian army. According to Bastianini, Mussolini 'approved with evident signs of relief and telephoned in person to Senise [chief of police] ordering him to come at once to the Palazzo Venezia and charging him in my presence to consider the possibility of such a transfer'.[152]

Carmen Senise, chief of the Italian police, was a sly Neapolitan, secretive, always dressed in black suits, who had had a long career in the police and was said to have an even longer memory. He had already had a visit from *SS Gruppenführer* Heinrich Müller, the head of the Gestapo, who had come at Himmler's behest to coordinate policy on the Jewish question. The encounter had not gone smoothly. During the course of their meeting, Müller had mentioned with regret that the Germans never succeeded in catching agents parachuted into France alive. They always took poison. Senise remarked that the Italians never had that problem and added maliciously: 'you see that the word about the treatment they can expect from you is such that they prefer to die rather than fall into your hands alive.'[153]

Müller, according to Senise, changed colour and left Rome unexpectedly early that very night. Both Bastianini's and Senise's accounts date from the period after 1945 when high officials of the fascist state had good reasons for pointing out their heroism in the face of the Germans and their steadfastness in defence of the Jews. More reliable, because it was written at the time, is an account which Pietromarchi recorded in his diary. Bastianini apparently told Pietromarchi what he and Mussolini had actually said. According to the Pietromarchi diaries, when Bastianini and Ambrosio entered the Duce's famous office in the Palazzo Venezia, he told them the contents of Ribbentrop's note and von Mackensen's comments. Ambrosio tried to deny that the army had systematically prevented the round up of Jews and tried to blame the French police. Mussolini cut him off by producing the famous 'list' prepared by the *Reichssicherheitshauptamt* at the request of Abteilung DIII of the German Foreign Office on 26 February and sent to Rome by von Ribbentrop on 9 March. Von Mackensen had brought it to the audience the evening before. It contained an irrefutable account of twenty-four cases of obstruction by Italian military authorities of the attempt to round up, mark, transport and murder Jews. Bastianini asked for time to prepare a 'more precise' reply. Pietromarchi's diary note continues:

> In fact he had just received from Vidau [head of Section IV, Confidential Affairs] the latest news from Berlin of the horrifying massacres perpetrated against the Jews and he brought them to the Duce: 'The real reason for the attitude of our officers was not said by Ambrosio, but I am going to say it to you, Duce. Our people know what fate awaits the Jews consigned to the Germans. They will all be gassed without distinction, the old women, babies. And that's why our people will never permit such atrocities to take place with their connivance. And you, Duce, may not give your consent. Why do you want to assume a responsibility which will fall on you entirely?' That was Bastianini's courageous speech. The Duce was shaken.
> 'But I have promised Mackensen that I would give orders to make our military men stop obstructing things.' he said.
> 'With your permission, I'll talk to Mackensen.'
> 'Very well!'[154]

In his memoirs Bastianini recalls that Mussolini smiled with relief, the first time Bastianini had seen him smile for weeks, but that during the audience he seemed to be suffering acute stomach pains which caused him to double up with his hands on his abdomen or to leap from his seat when the griping became unbearable.[155]

On the evening of 18 March, as instructed, the Nuncio Monsignor Borgoncini Duca called on Bastianini and received what he described as 'tranquillizing reassurances' from the Under-Secretary.[156] Bastianini must have been feeling confident that he could handle the situation because he sent to the Italian ambassadors in Paris and Vichy a copy of General Ambrosio's orders of 8 March which made clear that the French government

> must revoke arrests and internments effectuated by prefects in said territories and return elements arrested and deported. . . . I have made it clear that this is not a question of negotiations or requests but of precise notice to the French government that policy towards the Jews in French territory occupied by Italy is reserved to the exclusive competence of Italian authorities.[157]

That was precisely what Mussolini had told the German Ambassador the day before would no longer be the case. Bastianini would have a job to square that particular circle. Early in the morning of 20 March 1943 the Under-Secretary received the German Ambassador at the Italian Foreign Ministry in the Palazzo Chigi. There are two accounts of what happened. The first is one which Bastianini told to Pietromarchi:

> Mackensen came to see him. Bastianini already had a bone to pick with him for going directly to the Duce and thus going over his head.
> 'Mackensen', he said, 'the Duce has given orders that our military authorities are no longer to concern themselves with the Jews of occupied France.'
> 'Yes', the ambassador interrupted. 'The Duce has already told me and that is very good.'
> 'Our police will take over.'
> 'But that's not what the Duce said to me!'
> 'True, but the Duce has changed his mind and I shall tell you the reason. The French police ought not to carry out the rounding-up of the Jews because they are in cahoots with them. They let them know an hour before and let them flee in exchange for compensation. *Elle se fit graisser la patte.* You understand! We shall put them in concentration camps and watch them.'
> The old fox got the picture and found that the Under-Secretary was absolutely right. So the Jews of southern France have been saved by us. They will be concentrated in Savoie where there are plenty of hotels of every category to house them.[158]

Mackensen's own account can be found in a telegram to the Reich Foreign Minister dated the same day. The two accounts begin in much the same way. According to the German Ambassador, Bastianini said that the Duce had now decided for solution 2) and had given the necessary instructions. When the startled Ambassador expressed his 'surprise' since the Duce had in his presence not only opted for solution 1) but supported it with 'compelling arguments', Bastianini explained that Ambrosio convinced the Duce that the French police could not be trusted and that a very senior police inspector, Guido Lospinoso, whom Mussolini had personally chosen from a list of four top police inspectors submitted by Senise, would take over the round-up and internment of the Jews of France. (According to his own account, Lospinoso had been summoned the night before and given his orders.)[159] To each of Mackensen's doubts Bastianini supplied reassurance. All Jews would be interned. Yes, there were enough police agents available to carry out the job and, yes, a very 'sharp' order had gone out to General Vercellino, commander of the 4th Army, warning him of the consequences for any commander who failed to comply.[160]

The Ambassador seems to have accepted that explanation, which, given the picture we have of his character as sketched by Eugen Dollmann, is not surprising. Hans Georg von Mackensen, the son of a famous Prussian Field Marshall, entered diplomatic service after a period as an army officer:

> As a young man he had sworn an oath to the old Prussian monarchy which, when Wilhelm II disappeared, left him with nothing to die for. In the place of that monarchy and that oath there followed Ebert, then Hindenburg and finally Hitler. . . . The political line he followed in Rome was simple and straight. He had sworn fidelity to the Führer and the Führer was tied for life and death to the Duce. Mussolini too had become a new kind of authoritarian concept so that the possibility of secret diplomatic artifices was not to be considered. . . . Anybody who wants to occupy himself with Hans Georg von Mackensen and his activity as ambassador must be aware that it will oblige him to make a serious investigation of Lutheran prussianism and its strengths and weaknesses.[161]

With such a dim but upright ambassador, Italian *furberia* – in this case in a good cause – could celebrate triumphs of deception. Von Mackensen believed what he was told again and again, even when a much less informed person would long since have doubted it. This too in a paradoxical way helped to preserve the thin outer walls of Italian sovereignty in 1943 and hence Italy's ability to help Jews.

Yet much less gullible figures accepted Bastianini's story. 'Gestapo' Müller, a career policeman and the perpetrator of numberless crimes, could hardly be accused of naivety. Yet he was delighted at the decision of the Italian government to assign Jewish matters to the Italian police. On 2 April he wrote that Lospinoso would 'regulate the Jewish problems . . . in accordance with the German conception, and in the closest collaboration with the German police.'[162]

Nor was it implausible. The Ministry of the Interior directed both the police and the enforcement of the Italian racial laws. Under Guido Buffarini Guidi as Under-Secretary it had been the most consistently anti-semitic of all Italian ministries. At the very moment in 1942 when Bastianini and the 2nd Army in Yugoslavia had begun to spin plots to save Jews, Buffarini Guidi's ministry announced a large-scale programme of forced labour for Jews of conscriptable age. It was carried out *alla italiana*, i.e. irregularly, sometimes not at all or with great delay but Roman newspapers for 5 June 1942 headlined stories with pictures of Jewish forced labour units beginning work on the Tiber river banks.[163] Buffarini Guidi went on to justify 'Gestapo' Müller's high opinion by helping the Germans after 1943 to find and deport Jews under the puppet Republic of Salò. The story of Italian anti-semitism, like the story of Italian attempts to save Jews, is not one of good versus bad but of better and worse, of mixed motive and equivocal action. It is a real story of real people; what makes it remarkable is the outcome. Italian diplomats, soldiers and most civil servants could not consciously take part in what they knew to be collective murder.

Inspector General Lospinoso set out for his post and, according to his own account recorded after the war, he paid a courtesy call on his German opposite number in Marseilles. There, to his astonishment, he learned that his government had agreed to intern the Jews before transferring them to Drancy and thence to Auschwitz. Lospinoso claims that he suspected that Mussolini must be playing a double game and decided to evade the German demands by making himself hard to find.[164] It is certainly possible that a senior police official in Italy behaved that way; more plausible, but unwise to confess in the anti-fascist atmosphere of post-war Italy, was that Mussolini or Senise had given him a hint that the orders were not quite what they seemed. Whatever the reasons, Lospinoso became as elusive as he could. On 24 May Helmut Knochen complained that 'we know nothing of [Lospinoso's] possible presence in the Italian zone'.[165] Finally on 26 May *SS Obersturmführer* Moritz could report from Marseilles that a headquarters for the Commissioner for Jewish Questions had been established at the Villa Surany in Nice and that Lospinoso had now established a staff there. Moritz noted that as advisor Lospinoso had installed the 'half-Jew Donati'.The Italians, he continued,

intend to make a coastal strip to a depth of 50 kilometres Jew-free within three months. These measures are being carried out exclusively by the Italian government. According to them Jews are summoned and transported in lorries to the interior.[166]

Jews were on the move in Croatia as well. As early as 18 February 1943 the Civil Affairs Office of the 2nd Army had proposed to transfer the Jews from the existing camps at Kraljevice (Porto Re in Italian) and the islands to a safer place on the island of Rab, where a camp for Slovene civilians already existed.[167] Relations with the internees were less idyllic than they had been. The elders of Kraljevice who had signed the memorandum expressing their gratitude to General Roatta for saving their lives had recently written again, while stressing their gratitude to the Italian army and people, they had gone on to complain about 'the muddy terrain, the absence of sewage canals . . . insufficient toilets technically badly made with very small holes, built too low so that to keep them in a state of necessary cleanliness is almost impossible.'[168]

The Italian authorities were becoming testy. Senise, the chief of police, refused to allow DELASEM, the Jewish refugee relief organization, to visit the camps and there was trouble about the opening of schools.[169] But much more characteristic is the tiny incident of the Strassbergers. Mrs Janke Strassberger, interned on the island of Mezzo, asked permission to have her 18 year old son Branko transferred from another camp, 'since from the moment we fled from the *Ustaši*, my son and I have not seen each other'. The matter went to Brigadier Clemente Primieri, Chief of Staff of the 2nd Army, who gave permission on 28 April, 'given the exceptional facts of the case'.[170]

Slovenes were less lucky and consistently less well treated than Jews. The Italian decision to occupy the southern half of Slovenia and the capital city of Ljubljana had put them in what even Roatta admitted was an absurd position. They had unilaterally declared an utterly alien population and territory a part of Italy. It did not work. When the Italians offered the Slovenes full Italian citizenship, 'very few took advantage of the special provision'.[171] The Germans had a much simpler method of dealing with inconvenient ethnic minorities; they deported the lot. By early February 1943, HQ of the Italian XI Corp reported that the Slovene population of the sector had been 'removed' and the provincial capital 'had assumed the aspect of a completely German place'.[172]

The Italian military authority in Slovenia was neither that ruthless nor that efficient. Nevertheless it had to do something. What it chose was nasty. It began to take hostages 'who will be conducted to and held in prison. They will pay with their lives for the insidious attacks'.[173] In February 1942 a concentration camp for Croatian and

Slovene civilians was established at Buccari near Sussak. The Carabinieri Major who examined the site reported that it had no showers, no mess, the roof leaked and the barracks needed cleaning. Despite the deficiencies, two weeks later the first men, women and children began to arrive.[174] In December 1942 a much larger camp for Slovenes was established on the island of Rab off the Dalmatian coast. Conditions were so awful that the commanding officer of the 14th Battalion of Carabinieri actually complained in early January 1943:

> In the last few days some internees have returned from the concentration camp in such a state of physical emaciation, a few in an absolutely pitiful condition, that a terrible impression has been created in the general population. Treating the Slovene population like this palpably undermines our dignity and is contrary to the principles of justice and humanity to which we make constant reference in our propaganda.[175]

The Slovene historian, Franc Potočnik estimates that over 7,000 Slovene civilians died in Italian camps during the war, mainly in the camp on Rab, to which he himself was sent in December, 1942. He claims that thousands of civilians seized as hostages were shot by Italian soldiers in reprisals.[176] His large numbers rest on large claims and have led to dispute. What cannot be denied is that Slovene partisans and civilians suffered very harsh treatment at the hands of Italian troops. Conditions in the civilian internment camp on Rab were indeed appalling: filthy, muddy, overcrowded and swarming with insects. The sentiments of the Slovenes can be imagined when in June 1943 they watched the nearby Jewish camp set up with proper barracks, sanitation and services. As Potočnik writes:

> The internees in Camp I [Slovenes] could watch through the double barriers of barbed wire what took place in the Jewish camp. The Jewish internees were living under conditions of true internment for their 'protection', whereas the Slovenes and Croatians were in a regime of 'repression'. . . . They brought a lot of baggage with them. Italian soldiers carried their luggage into little houses of brick destined for them. Almost every family had its own little house. . .They were reasonably well dresssed; in comparison, of course, to other internees.[177]

Italian humanitarianism must have seemed hollow to the Slovenes of Camp I and it raises a difficult issue for us looking back at that extraordinary scene. How is one to explain the different treatment of Slovenes and Jews in the same concentration camp? Clearly Jews posed no military threat to Italian political ambitions. Slovenes equally clearly did. They rejected the right of the Duce and his commanders to declare their homeland part of metropolitan Italy and took up arms to resist. In that sense, Italian treatment of Slovene civilians may be seen as the 'normal' reaction of an army of occupation frustrated by the elusiveness of guerrilla war. Random internment always looks attractive; it is easy. The occupier can be seen to be 'doing something' about the guerrillas or terrorists.

Jews were neither. By 1943 everybody knew, including the Slovene inmates of Camp I, that something particularly awful had been marked down for the Jews. The full awfulness did not become clear until 1945 but enough had happened to put Jews in a category of their own. The Jews had come to symbolize for many Italians in some deep, not always explicit, sense the hatred and loathing that they now felt for their German allies. For others it was the last shred of military and political honour to maintain the crumbling façade of Italian sovereignty. That meant treating Jews very differently from Balkan enemies. The Germans wanted those Jews; the Italians would not, dared not, 'consign' them.

By 1 July 1943 the Italian army in Yugoslavia had collected a very large number of civilians whom they were guarding; the official figure was 33,464 of whom 2,118 were Jews. On Rab alone there were 6,646 interned civilians, and the eventual figure grew as final transports of Jews reached the camp.[178] The Civil Affairs Office at 2nd Army HQ had now to issue guidelines for the administration of the camp, and in early July prepared a draft memorandum entitled 'The Treatment of Jews in the Rab Camp'. It is a long document written by Major Prolo of the Civil Affairs Office with marginal comments by Colonel Rolla, chief of the office, and Brigadier Clemente Primieri, Chief of Staff of the 2nd Army. It makes instructive reading in the second summer of the European holocaust. According to Major Prolo, the infrastructure of the camp must be

> comfortable for all internees without risk to the maintenance of order and discipline. . . . Inactivity and boredom are terrible evils which work silently on the individual and collectivity. It is prudent that in the great camp of Rab those concessions made to the Jews of Porto Re [Kraljevice] to make their lives comfortable should not be neglected.

In the margin, Colonel Rolla wrote: 'But naturally! The removal from the peninsula became necessary for us militarily but must not affect the treatment of the Jews which must always be the same.' The Major continued in the draft to suggest that jewels and ornaments not be taken away 'which would recall too atrociously the time that once was' and argued that internal discipline must be exercised 'with a certain tolerance'. He concluded his report with this memorable paragraph:

> In conclusion, the Jews of the Army constitute a mass of 2,700 people who have the duties of all civilians interned for protective reasons, and a right to equivalent treatment, but for particular, exceptional political and contingent reasons, it seems opportune to concede, while maintaining discipline unimpaired, a treatment consciously felt to be 'Italian' which they are used to from our military authorities, and with a courtesy which is complete and never half-hearted.

Rolla wrote in the margin: 'Yes! Yes! Yes! Give a copy to the Liaison Office [the Foreign Ministry's liaison to 2nd Army HQ].' Chief of Staff Primieri added: 'That's fine. All this is in a version of our present dispositions. Major Prolo is to go to the place and check what needs to be done.'[179]

During the summer of 1943, the last summer of the fascist regime, the Italian army and police held 'for protective reasons' some 2,700 Jews in Yugoslavia, five or six times that number in France and allowed many thousands of Greek Jews to live normal lives under the red, white and green Italian tricolour. They protected them because they knew – and that is clear from the words Major Prolo uses – 'exceptional political and contingent reasons' – that their German allies had begun to exterminate the Jewish people. It had become a matter of national honour, perhaps the last shred of honour left, to give such people a treatment 'consciously felt to be Italian'. A long process which began with the spontaneous reaction of individual young officers in the spring of 1941 who could not stand by and watch Croatian butchers hack down Serbian and Jewish men, women and children ended in July 1943 with a kind of national conspiracy to frustrate the much greater and more systematic brutality of the Nazi state. It was a conspiracy which went from Mussolini to the lowest *maresciallo* of the carabinieri. It rested on certain assumptions about what being Italian meant, not always as explicitly stated as in Major Prolo's guidelines, but not the less widely understood.

This remarkable national resistance took place in the face of a great evil and was carried out by people who were, as we have seen, often precisely the same people who interned and tortured innocent Slovene and Croatian civilians. They were not angels nor were many of them free of the guilt of crimes committed in the name of fascism or Italian imperialism. Many of them disliked Jews. Others were indifferent. They agreed out of a mixture of horror, humanity, prestige, sense of honour, military necessity and self-interest that there was a border beyond which they could not and would not go. Certainly, as the Nuncio told Bastianini, there were signs that Italian prisoners got better treatment from the Russians than Germans because the Italians had been humane to the Jews,[180] but the conspiracy evolved before such utilitarian considerations emerged. Certainly the fact that the war was lost made it opportune to put as much distance between the fascist regime and Nazi Germany as possible. But the real explanation goes beyond and below such calculations into the characteristic features of a culture which determine behaviour, which permit certain types of acts and forbid others.

The conspiracy succeeded the more easily because Italy was a totalitarian dictatorship. If the Duce could be persuaded to change his mind, the subordinates could act with wide authority. It succeeded because the Duce never established complete control of the state, the monarchy and the army and he knew it. In 1943 Bastianini and others could say unpleasant things to Mussolini and he might listen. Hitler had long since gone beyond that point in his demented isolation. It succeeded because orders in Italy allow a certain latitude, and it succeeded because conspiratorial actions have a natural fascination in Italian culture, a culture in which Machiavelli and not Hegel has been the dominant figure, in which carbonari, freemasons, Jesuits, mafiosi, nets of clients and patrons have spread webs of intrigue and influence and in which knowing slyness, *furberia*, enjoys prestige. Finally, it succeeded because Hitler let it. How would Hitler behave towards an Italy without Mussolini?

THE LAST ACT

THE FALL OF FASCISM TO THE ARMISTICE

25 July 1943 to 8 September 1943

Hitler and his closest collaborators had always considered Mussolini as the guarantor of the Axis partnership. As Goebbels put it in March 1943, 'The Duce is really our only completely dependable support in Italy. As long as he is in control we need have no fear.'[1]

How long would that be? In early April 1943 Hitler met Mussolini at Schloss Klessheim, a beautiful baroque palace which had once belonged to Mozart's patron, the Archbishop of Salzburg. The two dictators talked mainly in private, appearing more publicly only at the end, as they made their way down the grand staircase. The delegates were shocked: 'They seem like two invalids', said one. 'Rather like two corpses', said Dr Pozzi, Mussolini's personal doctor.[2]

Bastianini, who saw Mussolini frequently, knew how ill the Duce really was. With one exception he took his meals, mostly of milk and biscuits, alone in his private train. His stomach pains had become so unbearable that much of the time with Bastianini he sat with his body rigidly distended supporting himself on his forearms.[3]

Snow fell outside the richly curtained windows during most of the conference; the Italian delegates decided that 1943 would have no spring. The internal atmosphere was no less chilly in spite of elaborate courtesies on the German side. Bastianini had primed Mussolini to raise two issues in the private discussions: a separate peace with the Russians and some sort of 'European League of States' to counter the increasingly effective Allied propaganda. No interpreter accompanied the Duce to his private talks with Hitler but, when he emerged from the first three hour meeting, he told Bastianini with a gesture of disgust that Hitler had done all the talking: 'All he did was to play the same old record. I let him talk but tomorrow I shall talk and very clearly.'[4]

He did not talk the next day or at all. He allowed Hitler, as always, to hypnotize him into cowed silence and said nothing of either theme. Not that it would have done much good with Hitler. The war would end either in total victory or total defeat. Hitler knew no other categories.

On the last day, the Duce suddenly announced that he wished to see Himmler. The SS police attaché at the German embassy in Rome, Eugen Dollmann, was there as interpreter. The Duce's request, he noted, 'was like a bomb going off. Ribbentrop and his people saw red and did everything to prevent the visit, which, however, Hitler had already approved.'[5]

Bastianini watched the SS chief arrive. He was smoking a big cigar and 'always smiling in the cadaverous pallor of his face'.[6] The agenda Mussolini proposed to Himmler contained four unusually revealing questions. The Duce wanted to know the opinion of the *Reichsführer SS* on 1) what measures Himmler planned to cope with domestic unrest if the war were to prolong itself; 2) his opinion of Senise, the Italian chief of police; 3) his impression of the dismissal of Ciano [which had taken place in early February] and the change of the guard carried out then; 4) his information on the attitude of the Italian Royal House and particularly of the Prince of Hesse [married to an Italian princess] and their possible contacts with people abroad.

Himmler reassured the Duce on the first three points. His system of concentration camps and police had proved very effective, as indeed they had. Senise was a competent professional and as to the change of the guard he talked in generalities, not even mentioning the fall of the two strongly pro-Nazi ministers Buffarini Guidi and Ricci. On point four Himmler became agitated and held forth at length on the evils of the corrupt, internationalist, Jew-friendly monarchy and aristocracies in general. As to Philip of Hesse, no doubt he had been of service to Nazism but his 'double nature' came out in his double identity, general in the SA and in-law of the anti-fascist Italian monarchy. The Duce replied: 'My dear Himmler, you will see that the Crown will abstain from undertaking anything serious against me. As you see, fascism and national-socialism have analogous possibilities.'[7]

The questions remained in the air in spite of the Duce's reassurance and tell us something very characteristic about his state of mind. Mussolini trusted nobody. He had the telephones of every important person tapped and spent hours reading the reports of his secret agents. Above all, he distrusted his own police, as Senise himself was well aware:

Mussolini despised even the sentiment of friendship and almost mocked it. He used to say that he had never had a friend in his life. . . . The contempt of Mussolini [was] specially for those who were closest to him in the political hierarchy, including those who most enjoyed or had enjoyed his favour. . . . In the low opinion which he had of all, he had become convinced that one was as good as another and hence to substitute one who had been proved to be of low morality was a waste of time because the next one would be no better.'[8]

This deep cynicism, which had been one of his most abiding characteristics all his life, now left him unable to rely on anybody in his entourage. The faithful Goebbels would not only die with his beloved Führer in the bunker in 1945 but would poison his wife and numerous progeny in a paroxysm of *Nibelungentreue*. Clara Petacci would hang upside down from a lamppost in the Piazza Loretto alongside her lover but, except for her, all the rest of the rats had long since scuttled away. In his growing isolation the Duce turned to the foreign police chief who alone could give him reliable evidence about internal conditions in the state of which he had been dictator for more than two decades. Himmler was too flattered, apparently, to see what a declaration of political bankruptcy the audience revealed.

Hitler left Schloss Klessheim well pleased with his handiwork. As he told Goebbels who had not been with him

The Führer told me that the Duce had been really brought back into form during the four days' discussions. The Führer did everything he could, and by putting every ounce of nervous energy into the effort, succeeded in pushing Mussolini back on the rails. In those four days the Duce underwent a complete change at which his entourage was also amazed. When he got off the train on his arrival, the Führer thought, he looked like a broken old man; when he left again, he was a man in high fettle, ready for any deed.[9]

The Führer's retreat from reality evidently now extended to personal relations as well. Mussolini had not recovered. Admittedly, shortly after his return, he removed Aldo Vidussoni as secretary of the *Partito Nazionale Fascista* and replaced him with the tougher and more ruthless Carlo Scorza.[10] The fascist party stirred momentarily into life. Mussolini appeared on the balcony at the Palazzo Venezia and addressed the crowd for the first time for almost three years, but it was also the last time. A much fitter epilogue to the summit at Schloss Klessheim came unexpectedly from the Reich Foreign Minister Ribbentrop himself, who, according to Bastianini, 'closed the subject with the remark that one would never again get rid of the ghosts which had been called forth.'[11] Whether these ghosts had the form of emaciated skeletons hanging on the wire fences of Auschwitz and Belsen or bloody corpses rising from pits, Ribbentrop never revealed. The remark was not less true, and Bastianini, of all people, knew it.

On his return to Rome Bastianini saw Mackensen and expressed his deep pessimism about the war. The Axis had now lost the diplomatic as well as the political initiative and would never regain it.[12] The Italian armed forces began to crumble. General Wilhelm Speidel reported from Greece that the Italians only operated in 'large actions which promise to be successful' and for the rest showed signs of 'war weariness and fear'.[13] The German plenipotentiary in Athens supported that view and added the observation that it was widely asserted 'by malicious Greeks that every Italian soldier has a civilian suit ready in case the English land and has been issued with gold pounds for flight'.[14]

The surrender of the Axis forces in Tunis on 13 May 1943, as the carabinieri reported from Yugoslavia, 'had unfavourably influenced the morale of the troops and the population'. As the French learned later in Indo-China, the Americans in Vietnam and the Russians in Afghanistan, a successful war against guerrillas is a matter of confidence. The native population must believe that the forces of order will defeat the guerrillas. The carabinieri saw that point perfectly:

> By now everybody is certain that the Axis will lose the war. Such a conviction drives away even those few people who harbour sentiments of sympathy for us, because they fear that they will be the objects of reprisals once the defeat has occurred.[15]

Glaise von Horstenau was having trouble dealing with the Italians in Croatia and he blamed it, in a telegram to the German High Command, on Bastianini whose 'lasting hatred against Croatia' had become even more violent and 'swollen with rage . . . now perhaps influenced by the loss of Tunisia [he] wants to make up for any previous "omissions"'.[16] At the end of May he wrote a private letter to his old school friend *Generaloberst* Löhr:

> Every eye is fixed like the rabbit gazing at the cobra on the enemy in the Mediterranean. As far as our ally is concerned, nobody asks 'whether' but 'when'. Unfortunately on top nobody seems to have given much thought to such not-to-be-excluded eventualities and prefers to play ostrich.[17]

'Whether' and 'when' needed no explanation; they referred to a separate peace. The German Embassy in Rome watched as the number of visitors at the royal palace increased. On 19 May the King said to the head of his military household, General Puntoni:

I am afraid that at any moment the British government or the King of England may approach me direct in order to negotiate a separate peace. Such a move would cause me great embarrassment. If it should happen, I would act without subterfuge. I would speak to the Duce and agree with him a line of action.[18]

Nothing was more unlikely. The King, a silent, devious, 'little' man, had never once in his long reign 'acted without subterfuge'. He always twisted and turned, evaded and dodged. For more than twenty years he had tolerated every sort of usurpation, corruption, brutality and inconsequence. It required the desperate imaginations of men at the end of their resources to think otherwise.

Italy was, of course, not Germany. The old ruling classes had not been butchered in 'nights of long knives' nor terrified by the Gestapo palace of horror on the Prinz-Albrecht-Strasse. Former prime ministers like Ivanoe Bonomi lived peacefully in Rome and in June 1943 emerged blinking from obscurity. Bonomi went to the King and told him that the fascist regime was

the cause of all evil in Italy. The King, who alone possessed the prestige of supreme power and had the support of the Armed Forces, could, whenever he wished dismiss the Prime Minister and Head of the Government. . . . Naturally if the Duce were dismissed, he would have to be placed under arrest to avoid the chance that, backed by the armed Militia of the Party, he might plunge the country into civil war.

There would have to be a military government under Marshall Badoglio, Marshall Caviglia or General Ambrosio, and the first act must be to denounce the alliance with Germany on the grounds that the Axis was an agreement not between states as such but between 'two regimes and two revolutions'. Hence once fascism fell, the alliance ceased to bind Italy.[19]

The incompleteness of fascism sealed its fate. Mussolini had never achieved a 'total state'. His revolution had stopped at Bernini's arcade round the Vatican and at the gates of the Quirinale. The party had never replaced the civil service; indeed the reverse had occurred. Great *Gauleiters* like Dino Grandi, Giuseppe Bastianini, Italo Balbo and Giuseppe Bottai, had gone 'straight', joined the diplomatic corps or taken ministerial appointments. They had merged with the old aristocracies from the regions and the Roman 'black' nobility and had fused with the civilian directors general of ministries and agencies. The Eternal City had absorbed them the way it has always gradually forced new rulers to become 'Roman'. Nor had Mussolini taken care to set up his own, private police force. In the crisis of the regime he

139

had to rely on people like Carmen Senise, career police agents who had risen inside the ministerial hierarchy and were known even to Himmler to be at the best 'non-fascist'. He had no *Leibstandarte* or SS personal guard who would protect him and intimidate the King. In their meeting at Schloss Klessheim, Himmler had again pointed out how dangerous it was for the Duce to be without a proper fascist guard and some attempts were actually made by the SS, with Mussolini's permission, to train such a unit. It was, of course. not ready when it was needed.

Very great power makes strange demands on the psyches of those few human beings who are cursed with it. It ages them prematurely and often produces a kind of suicidal blindness. The shrewdest, most ruthless and cynical of men make mistakes that ordinary people would have avoided. Sometimes when the end comes, it catches the great figure utterly immobile. Robespierre fell from power on the 9th of Thermidor 1794, by a vote in a convention which he had previously dominated, many of whose members he had guillotined and all of whose surviving members feared him. The following day he went to the guillotine himself unprotesting. All over Paris Jacobin clubs loyal to him mobilized and waited for his order. It never came.

Something of that ultimate paralysis of the will afflicted Mussolini during the months of June and July 1943. On 11 June the Allies landed on the Italian island of Pantelleria. Two days later Lampedusa fell. It was now a matter of time before the Allies landed in force somewhere in the Mediterranean. Captain Beck of the *Wehrmacht* had been to Sicily on orders from General von Rintelen to inspect the defences there. For the defence of the island there were nine Italian divisions, plus a brigade, a single German division and one anti-aircraft brigade. The mountainous terrain, the poor road and rail network and the 'air superiority of the enemy' gave the defenders no chance to rush forces to the threatened coast. The Italian troops were of low quality and the Germans were not much better, 'a crowd of soldiers' not a disciplined band of men. There was a shortage of specialists and good junior officers. A landing would succeed.[20]

On 10 July 1943 Allied paratroops landed on Sicily and Captain Beck's prediction became reality. A week later General Ambrosio at the *comando supremo* summed up the situation:

> The fate of Sicily must be regarded as sealed. The main grounds for the rapid defeat are:
> – complete absence of our counter-attack at sea and the weak resistance in the air . . .
> – inadequacy of weapons and structure of the coastal divisions, the small scale and weak capacity to resist of the defensive

implacements, the low fighting quality (armaments) and mobility
of the Italian field divisions.

It is useless to call for the reasons for this state of things; the
condition is the result of three years of war begun with inadequate means. In that time the few stores and sources of energy
reserves were consumed in Africa, Russia and the Balkans.

Ambrosio then outlined the possibilities open to the Axis to defend
the Italian mainland and found them no better than the defence of
the islands. The report concluded:

It behoves the highest political authorities to consider if it might
not be advisable and necessary to spare the country further grief
and ruin and to anticipate the end of the struggle, since the final
outcome will be even worse a year or two later.[21]

The Italian Supreme Command told Mussolini to surrender; there
was no other military option. The war begun frivolously and without
economic or strategic preparation was over. Fascist Italy had lost the
war. To underline the point, five days later, the Allies bombed Rome,
hitting hard the working class district clustered round San Lorenzo
station and market. Giuseppe Bottai took a stroll that July afternoon
to see what it looked like:

I make a circuit: Polyclinic, University, San Lorenzo, Porta
Maggiore. Heavy damage but unfortunately only the beginning.
The reaction of the people, for now, is typically 'romanesque':
disordered but with good humour, amidst the grunts and curses,
still smiling. In the evening on the roads to the hills, the
Tuscolana, the Appia, the Casilina, corteges of poor people with
carts and bicycles, with the occasional rare taxi or truck, or on
foot, who are leaving the city with their household articles and
provisions on their backs. At Pilozzo I still find, in spite of it all,
in my house and within my four walls, a sweet, tender peace,
whose absurdity converts desperation into a faith no longer
human.[22]

Bottai, whom disgrace and defeat had moved from faith in the Duce
to faith in Christ, may have found the peace which 'passeth all
understanding'; few others could do so. Italy was utterly finished,
and it was becoming clearer and clearer that Mussolini was too. The
problem was how to get rid of him.

The threat to Mussolini had aroused Hitler's suspicions. Both
Mackensen and General von Rintelen had been summoned to the
Führer's headquarters; neither had been well received.[23] Hitler no
longer wanted to hear excuses and explanations by those who were

'soft' on the Italians . He decided on Saturday 17 July that he must see the Duce for himself and work his special magic on his flagging Axis partner. Dino Alfieri, the Italian Ambassador to Berlin and a veteran fascist, was startled from his Sunday rest to be told that there would be a meeting the following day. Bastianini. not trusting the telephone, could only hint at the place:

> You know – where there's a large aerodrome, he said. 'Tr—. Tr—. Anyhow, you will find out soon enough from von Steengracht [State Secretary in the German Foreign Office]. I'm looking foward to seeing you – I've got some things to say to you. Until tomorrow morning, then!'[24]

The participants, both German and Italian, had their difficulties in getting to the airport at Treviso where the two delegations would assemble to make the two hour journey to the villa of Senator Gaggià at Feltre. Keitel arrived in a military plane. On seeing General von Rintelen, he hissed: 'All power to the Duce. Exclusion of the Royal House. Strong German intervention under German supreme command.'[25]

The meaning was clear. Behind the façade of Mussolini's titular command, the Germans intended to occupy and control the defence and the domestic politics of the Italian peninusula. The Italian delegation had come up from Rome on a special train. The Duce arrived in his own plane from Riccione. Young Egidio Ortona, who had followed Bastianini from Dalmatia to the Palazzo Chigi as one of his private secretaries, accompanied his chief to the meeting and found Mussolini 'on the whole in form. He immediately began to talk with Marshall Kesselring over a map spread out on the bonnet of a car.'[26]

More planes bearing marshalls and ambassadors arrived at the airport already intensely hot even in the early morning. Finally at five minutes to nine the Führer's plane swept low across the landing strip, rose, circled and circled again. When a puzzled Italian asked von Mackensen what it all meant, he replied: 'it's three minutes to nine. The plane is scheduled to land at nine o'clock precisely.'[27]

Hitler and Mussolini greeted each other warmly and entered the first of a column of cars lined up to take them to the train station. Ortona pushed forward to get a good look at the Führer:

> I find him aged and congealed. He drags his foot markedly. He gives an unsolid and unhealthy impression. . . . I continue to watch Hitler as much as I can. He really does look like a lifeless spectre. He seems somehow unreal. His face is pallid, shape curved; he seems suspended in some unearthly empyrean.[28]

Hitler and Mussolini remained entirely alone for the two hour train journey to Feltre where, as Mussolini later wrote, 'there was a most beautiful, cool shady park and a labyrinthine building which some people found almost uncanny. It was like a crossword puzzle frozen into a house.'[29] Arrangements were hasty and chaotic. The junior members of the Italian delegation had to make do with one of the bedrooms hurriedly cleared out by the family. Bored by the hours of waiting, one of them began to go through the drawers and found a rag doll in the uniform of an American sailor holding a stars-and-stripes. Discussing the fuss the Germans would have made gave them something to do to pass the time. From behind the closed door of the main sitting room they could hear the strident monotone of Hitler who talked without interruption for two hours.[30]

Ambrosio had already told Keitel that Italy would be finished in a fortnight unless the Germans rushed massive reinforcements to its crumbling defence. At the lunch break, Alfieri, who had sat through the fruitless morning session, summoned up his courage and detained the Duce long enough to tell him that he must make clear to Hitler that this was the end. To his surprise, Mussolini beckoned Alfieri, Bastianini and Ambrosio to sit down and replied to them bluntly:

> For the sake of argument, suppose we were to make a separate peace. It looks so simple. One fine day, at a specified hour, we broadcast a message to the enemy. But what would be the result? The enemy quite justly would demand our capitulation. Are we prepared at a single stroke to obliterate twenty years of fascism? to undo all that we have achieved by so much unremitting effort? to acknowledge our first military and political defeat? to vanish from the international scene? It's so easy to talk about a separate peace. But what would Hitler's attitude be? Can you believe that he would allow us to retain our liberty of action?[31]

There were no answers to those questions but Alfieri and his well-meaning conspirators could not see that. With the political sixth sense that made Mussolini the leader and Alfieri, Bastianini, Balbo and company the led, he had grasped what they learned to their dismay a week later: Mussolini *was* fascism. Old Marshall Caviglia had seen in his bitter retirement what the Italian Ambassador to Berlin failed to observe on top of the events:

> There's no doubt that the war is lost but now it's no longer nazi or fascist but Hitlerian and Mussolinian. Hitler and Mussolini cannot yield. If they yielded they would be liquidated for ever. That's why the war will continue and continue to the end. A few months more of oxygen for the two of them and there's life and

where there's life, there's hope. As long as there is a table leg left to burn, Hitler and Mussolini will continue the war.[32]

To make sure that the table legs remained in his hands, Hitler had taken a few necessary precautions. The Italian army could quite clearly no longer be trusted. On the same Monday that the two dictators met in Feltre, the 44 year old *Generalmajor* Heinz von Gyldenfeldt, an able, experienced, Italian-speaking officer, arrived in Athens together with a small staff including *Oberleutnant* Kurt Waldheim who kept the unit's war diary. As Waldheim wrote on that first day in Athens, the General and his officers arrived from Salonica

> with instructions to set up the German General Staff with the Italian 11th Army. . . . In this task of the German general staff the important thing is to increase German influence on the Italian 11th Army in their conduct of the war in Greece.[33]

In other words General von Gyldenfeldt was to supply the nerve centre and ultimately to take control of operations from the slack and demoralized Italians. Field Marshall Rommel received new orders after Feltre. He was assigned to command 'in all of Greece including the islands of Crete and the Aegean'. General Löhr was to take over command of the remaining troops in the Balkans and move his HQ to Belgrade.[34] Details were worked out of the plans later known as Operation Axis to take over from the Italians the war in the Mediterranean. Hitler, Keitel and the OKW watched nervously to see what would happen in Rome.

The Italian delegation returned from Feltre deeply depressed. While Hitler had been holding forth, the air raid had hit Rome. It shattered more than a thickly settled, ancient quarter; it destroyed any illusions left that Rome was somehow exempt from a war which had already destroyed Warsaw, Rotterdam and the City of London. The Allies would not give Italy special treatment. The air raid shattered the general apathy of the holders of posts and wielders of influence. The old fascists began to meet in small groups. Bottai, former Minister of Education, met Roberto Farinacci, the boss of Cremona, at the Grand Hotel on Tuesday morning, 20 July and, although they represented opposite poles in the movement, they exchanged the latest rumours. Together they walked to Palazzo Chigi to find out from Bastianini, their old comrade in arms, what had happened at Feltre. Bottai recorded in his diary that it was 'a pretty sad story'. Bastianini gave them the details of Mussolini's embarrassing failure to speak, let alone to act. The diary entry continues:

> At the end our side wanted no communiqué at all. But now, once returned to Rome, the Duce telephoned to Bastianini that it

would be necessary to issue one in order to explain his absence yesterday from the bombed neighbourhoods, where the Pope, the King and Queen, the royal princes had gone at once. Once again, only his person in question, excuses and even lies not without barbs and personal animosities. Grandi had goaded and pushed him above all with the argumentation about 'a national government' around the King, returned to full command of the armed forces. He resisted.[35]

Fascism had entered its terminal crisis. Twenty years of the regime now hung on the outcome of days and even hours. Everybody at the centre of events, Mussolini and his staff at the Palazzo Venezia and at his official residence in the Villa Torlonia, the King at the Palazzo Quirinale and the officers of the Royal Household, Bastianini and his staff of diplomats at the Palazzo Chigi, General Ambrosio and the *comando supremo* at the Palazzo Vidoni, Count Ciano at the Italian Embassy to the Holy See, von Mackensen, Bismarck, Rintelen and Dollmann at the German Embassy, provincial fascists like Farinacci at the Grand, fallen ministers like Bottai, Buffarini Guidi and Ricci, all talking, telephoning, meeting, waiting. Those who kept diaries began to note the hours at which they came and went so that the historian can reconstruct the movements of many of the players almost hour by hour. It is as if the sense of great events forced each actor to turn to the unknown historian watching him to make sure his deeds were accurately recorded.

While Farinacci and Bottai were listening to Bastianini's 'sad story', Dino Grandi was making his way back to Rome. Grandi has not played a part in the story so far because after 1939 he had left the centre of the political stage, but he had played a very great role in the twenty year history of the movement and regime. A powerful looking man with a Vandyke beard, he belonged in every respect to the fascist inner circle and like Bottai, Bastianini, Balbo, Farinacci and the rest had done his training in the turbulent world of the trenches as a young officer in the First World War. Like most of them and Mussolini himself, he came from petty bourgeois origins, had read the violent literature of irrationalism, admired Nietzsche, Sorel and D'Annunzio. He led the first wave of fascist assault on the institutions of the state in the early 1920s from his stronghold in Bologna, had been the youngest member of parliament, elected on the sufferance of the liberals in 1921, had risen to be Foreign Secretary from 1929 to 1932 and to be Italian Ambassador at the Court of St James to 1939, when Mussolini replaced him with Bastianini because he opposed the Duce's commitment to the Axis. Like Farinacci and the other early fascists he spoke to Mussolini in the familiar *tu* form, the intimate address of family and comrades.

Grandi passed the Second World War successively as Lord Privy Seal and president of the Chamber of Deputies, so that he had a powerful office on paper and access to the King. On 25 March 1943, the King had made him a Cavalier of the Supreme Order of the Most Holy Annunziata and presented him with the golden 'Collar' of office. Very like the Order of the Bath it represented the highest royal favour; the 'Collars' had the right to call themselves 'cousins of the King'. Grandi wrote in his diary: 'I left the Palazzo Quirinale rather emotional. A tepid March morning. Piazza Monte Cavallo bright in the sunshine. Cousin of the King! I think of my poor Dad who wanted to make me a notary'.[36]

Grandi's royal connections had encouraged him to approach the King on several occasions to urge a change of regime, but by that Wednesday, 21 July, no sensible plan had yet occurred to him. Grandi had no idea how Mussolini would react. When he finally got to Rome after a difficult journey, partly by train and partly by car, he learned that the Duce's personal secretariat had been seeking him insistently all day. He replied that he had to see Mussolini urgently, not later than tomorrow and was granted an appointment for the Thursday, 22 July, at 5.30 p.m.:

I shall do my whole duty and am resolved to go the whole way, whatever the menaces or the intimidation which will be made to me. *Basta!* The moment has finally come to act, even if the King will not agree to do so. I shall do it. *I have to do it, by now.* [in the original] It's not possible to go on like this, not one more day.[37]

The next morning at 9 a.m, Grandi went to party headquarters to see another old front-fighter, Carlo Scorza, General Secretary of the party. Scorza told him that Mussolini had decided to convoke the Grand Council of the Fascist Party for the coming Saturday at 5.00 p.m. Grandi entered in his diary:

Finally! Finally. After more than three years he has remembered that there is a Grand Council. So it will be at the Grand Council that I shall attack and give definitive battle. Mussolini will see me again as I was at the 1921 congress at the Augusteo [when Grandi forced Mussolini temporarily to resign from the party leadership] but since I am loyal, I shall go today to tell him everything I intend to say Saturday publicly.[38]

Mussolini had inadvertently played his opponents' card. The Fascist Grand Council had, like so many institutions of the regime, ill-defined powers. Although technically it was the supreme governing body of the party, the fusion of party and state which characterized

146

the fascist regime gave it an authority which no other body could have. It provided a forum for its twenty eight members to air their views and could, as Grandi hoped, be made to function as a kind of large constitutional cloak under which power could be surreptitiously and safely slipped from the Duce to the Crown.

By now Rome was boiling with rumours. Ortona heard that the female personnel at the German Embassy had orders to leave the city.[39] Farinacci, the most violently anti-semitic of the fascist provincial bosses and the most pro-German, decided to call on the Ambassador. Farinacci brought along with him the disgraced Marshall Cavallero, another well known pro-German figure. The Cremona boss filled the Ambassador in on the intrigues and meetings which had taken place, including a stormy one a few days earlier with Mussolini. In his violent and brusque manner he began to recount the Duce's failings. The correct Prussian aristocrat interrupted the vulgar petty bourgeois with a polite warning, as von Mackensen reported in a private telegram to von Ribbentrop:

> I must ask him not to forget when he criticizes the person of the Duce that, although I am a personal friend, I am first and foremost a representative of the Führer who had a boundless respect for the state-making creative energies of the Duce.[40]

Even at five minutes to midnight for the fascist regime, the representatives of the Reich understood the peculiar charm which the Führer's affection had spun round the person of the Duce. Farinacci grumbled that he would bear it in mind and went on to demand the strongest possible Axis military support.

On Friday 23 July Bottai met Grandi to work on a resolution which Grandi had prepared. At 12.30 they went to see Ciano who agreed with the text. Farinacci came in and also agreed although, as Bottai put it, 'we all intuit the sense of his approval, understood as alliance with the Germans jusqu'au bout.'[41] Grandi had become the chief of the fronde. He sent Bottai 'to "work on" the members of the Grand Council one by one, since he knows them better than I. How many can we count on?'[42]

The 'don't knows' and 'uncertains' still made up a majority. Hour by hour he noted the conversions, the conversations and the disappointments. He sent one to talk to another. Alfieri, a member of the Grand Council, arrived from the Berlin Embassy. Ciano took him to be 'worked on' by Grandi:

> We drove down the narrow street that separates Palazzo Chigi and Montecitorio (a distance of, say, 200 metres!) and in a matter of moments arrived at our destination. Ciano went in first, and

after a few minutes I too was invited to enter. Grandi received me most cordially. He was his usual genial and courteous self, and his air of informality was accentuated by the fact that he was wearing a short-sleeved shirt with an open neck.[43]

Saturday 24 July 1943 was, as Grandi wrote early in the morning,

the day that will decide everything. I feel that this is truly and surely the most important day of my life. It is probable that I shall be shot tomorrow morning by Mussolini, that I shall be arrested immediately after the Grand Council. No matter. It has to be done. For the country.[44]

Bottai after a busy morning went back to his house. The day was hot and close with the special Roman *afa*, heat with humidity, that makes the citizens flee it in late July and August. With his elaborate literary sensibilities he recorded those unforgettable moments of stillness in the whirlwind of history: 'I stretch out on the bed and follow in the dense shadow my thoughts which trace their own design, already detached from me; I am, my person is, only that of an actor in the drama.'[45]

As Bottai lay in his hot, darkened bedroom, he took stock of what 'his' fascism had meant, what its values and impulses had been, whether he ought to have acted sooner and how. Like a man awaiting the execution of a sentence, he passed his life in review. At the end he came back to the beginning:

And Mussolini? . . . no longer a personage of my inner life. It's not a question 'to betray or not to betray' but to have the courage to confess his betrayal, consummated day by day from the first disappointment to this moral collapse. Not one idea, not one pact, not one law, to which he has been faithful. Everything was ruined by him, corrupted, distorted in the wake of a presumptuous if shrewd empiricism, founded on contempt for men and their ideals. Within a few hours it will be necessary to pay for all that.[46]

Like the moment in October 1914 when Mussolini betrayed his socialist companions by suddenly rejecting their pacifism and declaring himself for war, Bottai, tortured by guilt and remorse, anticipated the Duce's ultimate betrayal of the fascists. Yet in Bottai's words there was the lingering disillusion of the former lover. As in 1914, so in 1943, above the murmur of the angry crowd the voice of Mussolini could still be heard shouting, 'you hate me now because you still love me!'

Grandi's resolution forced Bottai and his colleagues to vote no confidence in their leader. It aimed to return the functions of government to the ministers who ought to exercise it and to restore supreme command to the Crown. The resolution began:

> The Grand Council declares . . . the immediate restoration of all State functions, allotting to the King, the Grand Council, the Government, Parliament and the Corporations the tasks and responsibilities laid down by our statutory and constitutional laws.[47]

The resolution amounted to a constitutional coup d'état; or, perhaps more precisely, it demanded that Mussolini commit political suicide. The Duce was to ask the King to restore a constitutional order that he had violated for more than twenty years. In effect, the Duce was to declare fascism finished and to slip off the stage of politics. It was not a plausible scenario and members of the Grand Council prepared for the showdown with trepidation. Some took weapons to the meeting. One even had a grenade.[48] Yet they were pleasantly surprised that the Palazzo Venezia had only a light guard when they arrived and took their places in the room next to Mussolini's famous office, the *mappamondo* or map of the world room. Alfieri recalled the scene:

> At five minutes past five when the other members of the Council were already assembled, the Duce strode in with his usual nonchalant, self-confident air. He was wearing the uniform of an Honorary Corporal of the Militia and in front of him walked Novarra, the Chief Usher, carrying his leather briefcase. As usual, Mussolini looked at no one. Scorza's cry of 'Salute the Duce!' was echoed by all present with a ringing 'We salute him!' Mussolini responded by raising his right arm. He stepped up to his table, which was mounted on a dais, and pulled a bundle of papers and notes from his briefcase. As he did so, he turned to Scorza, who was on his left, and ordered him to call the roll. . . . The oppressiveness of the atmosphere was intensified by the fact that the two large windows were shut, while through the faded blue curtains there filtered a pale glimmer of sunshine which contrasted bizarrely with the brilliant light from the chandelier suspended from the middle of the ceiling.[49]

Mussolini spoke first. He dodged, evaded, attacked, threatened. The others followed. Shortly before midnight Mussolini called for a brief adjournment and disappeared into his study to look at telegrams. He summoned Alfieri and asked 'what is happening in Germany?' Alfieri repeated the arguments that he had used at Feltre. Meanwhile, 'Apriliti, who ranked second to Novarra among members of the Duce's personal staff, brought his master a cup of milk, which Mussolini, after adding plenty of sugar, slowly gulped down.'[50]

When Alfieri continued to try to persuade Mussolini to tell Hitler that Italy could fight no longer, Mussolini made a gesture of denial and dismissed him 'coldly'. As Alfieri came out of the study, Grandi approached him with the resolution and Alfieri signed it, the nineteenth and last signatory. There was now an overwhelming majority. Buffarini Guidi, former Minister of the Interior, a strong anti-semite and very pro-German, also had a brief audience in the darkened study. His advice was blunt: 'Arrest them all. It is a plot. There will not be even twenty to put inside. And outside here we should pick up Badoglio and a dozen more.'[51]

Mussolini arrested nobody, allowed the meeting to continue and finally called for a vote. Nineteen voted for, seven against. Suardo abstained and Farinacci voted for his own, pro-German amendment:

> The Duce gathered his papers and stood up. According to his subsequent account he said: 'you have provoked the crisis of the regime. The session is closed.' Scorza attempted to call for the ritual salute to the Duce who checked him saying, 'No, you are excused' and retired to his private study. It was 2.40 a.m. on Sunday 25 July.[52]

The following day Mussolini seemed to assume that business would go on as usual. He went to his office at 8.30, read the incoming telegrams as usual, and saw the Japanese Ambassador for a long and cordial conversation. The only sign that anything special had happened, according to Grandi, was the insistence of Mussolini's Private Secretary De Cesare that Grandi come at once to Palazzo Venezia:

> No, I let him know that I am not in town. *I shall not go to the Palazzo Venezia* [italics in original] . . . 15.00 hours. At Palazzo Venezia they are still trying to find me. 18.00 hours Ciano tells me that Scorza has given orders to the Federale of the City [fascist militia leader] to prepare 'the squads' for tonight to go out to punish the traitors in their homes.[53]

The tension mounted all day but when Mussolini went to see the King at 5 p.m. he took no extra guard and made no special provision. He must have assumed that Victor Emanuel who in more than forty years on the throne had never once showed a scintilla of moral courage would not show any now. After all, Mussolini had browbeaten and humiliated the little King for twenty-two years. The King had always yielded and would presumably do so again. After taking the King through the customary summary of the military events, the

Duce turned to politics. The King interrupted him to say that since the war seemed irrevocably lost, he had appointed Marshall Badoglio as Prime Minister. A stunned Mussolini was arrested, bundled into an ordinary ambulance and taken off to a secret place of detention.[54] Fascism ended without a whimper.

Arrests of others followed, those most associated with an intransigent line or those most markedly pro-German: Scorza, the Party Secretary; Buffarini Guidi, former Minister of the Interior; and Marshall Cavallero, former Chief of Staff. Farinacci fled to the German Embassy for protection and, disguised in a German uniform, was flown to Berlin that night.

At the Foreign Ministry in the Palazzo Chigi, Bastianini and Ortona were waiting anxiously for news. Towards 7 p.m. the minister of the Royal Household, the Duke of Acquarone, informed Bastianini that the new Badoglio government had replaced him with the experienced professional diplomat Raffaele Guariglia who was at the time Ambassador to Turkey. By early evening the situation had become so menacing that Bastianini decided to spend the night at Ortona's flat:

In the darkness we make our way from the Ministry to my house. At 10.45 the radio gives the news of the resignation of the Duce and the nomination of Badoglio. A few minutes later the first voice explodes with a 'Viva l'Italia! Viva Badoglio! Viva l'esercito!' and from that moment on an impressive crescendo of noise. Not a cry about the Duce for an hour or so. Then you can hear the 'courage' rising and then the sound picture is completed with 'Down with the Duce, Donna Rachele, the lover!' I cannot grasp a phenomenon so sudden and immediate. I go to bed at 3 deeply saddened, heart-broken and afflicted.[55]

At his apartment Grandi noted the same events:

An incessant demonstration at the Piazza Colonna and on Via Umberto begins and goes on till late at night. 'Viva Badoglio! Viva l'Italia!'. . . . They curse fascism and Mussolini. The crowd tries to storm the party headquarters in Piazza Colonna.[56]

Grandi and his fellow conspirators in the fascist hierarchy had fallen victim to an illusion. They thought that fascism, or at least something like it, might survive the fall of the Duce. Within minutes of the news reaching the public, they were shown their mistake. Fascism disappeared in a puff of smoke. Millions took lapel badges off, burned uniforms and concealed decorations. The demonstrations went on without interruption. Street names with fascist connotations were ripped from stands, and the streets given an impromptu antifascist baptism. By evening on the Monday, 26 July 1943, Grandi realized that the majority at the Grand Council had let a genie out of the bottle:

> 18.00 hours. Muti comes, Rotigliano. Bottai telephones me, Pareschi etc. All are worried because in many points of the city the *canaille* have taken charge. I do everything possible to obtain from the Ministry of Interior a service of protection. My 19 companions who risked their lives on Saturday in provoking the crisis, must they perhaps now lose their lives in an attack by the *canaille*?[57]

In his address to the nation, Marshall Badoglio had announced rather cryptically: 'the struggle continues', but Hitler was not fooled. His worst fears about the Italians had been realized and at the expense of his only friend, Benito Mussolini. He rushed through plans for the occupation of Italy (Operation Black), the arrest of the King and Badoglio (Operation Student) and for the freeing of Mussolini (Operation Oak). He was in a foul temper and showed his fury to his entourage:

> There can be no doubt about one thing: in their treachery they will announce that they are going to stick with us; that is perfectly obvious. But that is an act of treachery for they won't stick with us. . . . Sure that what's-his-name [Badoglio] declared right away that the war would be continued, but that changes nothing. . .get our hands on that rabble, especially Badoglio and the rest of the crew. Then you'll see they'll turn limp as a rag.[58]

Later that evening he decided to add the rabble in the Vatican to those whom he would arrest. German troops began to head south. At the headquarters of the Supreme Command South East in Salonica-Arsakli, Field Marshall Rommel had just arrived to begin to plan the transfer of command with General Löhr when at 11.15 at night the 'surprising transformation of the situation in Italy' was announced. The orders for reorganization were halted and the Field Marshall summoned to see the Führer.[59]

At 3.45 on the morning of Monday 26 July, while Ortona was lying on his bed in Rome, listening with a broken heart to the cries of 'Down with the Duce!', in Salonica General Löhr was awake and at his command post. Coded messages went out to all the commands in the Balkans, informing them of the events in Rome and issuing orders to prepare to take over Italian positions in Crete, the Peloponnese, the Islands and in Croatia: 'With respect to Italian service authorities these moves are to be concealed and if necessary to be explained on other grounds. Observation of the attitude of the Italians is to be carried out unobtrusively.' He gave precise orders for the event that

Italy might 'jump out' of the Axis; how the Italians were to be disarmed and rounded-up and how in the event of 'obstructions, weapons are to be used ruthlessly'. The code name was Operation Axis.[60]

The following morning General Löhr flew to Athens to discuss the new situation with his Italian opposite number. He requested that the Italian army accept the services of the German general staff which had just been set up as well as overall German command of the Axis forces. General Vecchiarelli, Geloso's successor in command of the Italian 11th Army, rejected both demands 'in a suitable manner' because he had received no instructions. The following day he received them, put his troops under Army Group E, and accepted the service of the German general staff.[61] In a short time the German forces in Greece and Yugoslavia had carried out the plans which in September would lead to the disarming and imprisoning of more than 300,000 Italian troops by German units of about a tenth of that strength, one of the most remarkable operations in the Second World War.

The mood of the German forces had become desperate. At the headquarters of Army group E in Salonica, Chief of Staff *Generalmajor* August Winter called his tired staff together at 9 a.m. on the morning of 26 July. They had been up most of the night getting the orders for Operation Axis to all the commands. The Chief of Staff analysed the situation and expressed his doubts about the sincerity of the Badoglio government's intentions. The war diary concluded:

We must be absolutely clear that the 25th and the 26th of July are the most serious and fateful days so far in the war. The Chief expresses absolute will: 'never to capitulate and if it is necessary to fight to an heroic end'.[62]

German divisions flooded into Italy. As Ambrosio bitterly remarked to Field Marshall Keitel when they met on 6 August at Tarvisio, 'At Feltre you told me that you could not spare even a division, now look how many you have sent down here!'[63] The mood of the invading troops was conveyed by German-born Baroness Carbonelli, whose nephew commanded a German tank unit. She told Ortona on 14 August that her nephew hated Italy and all Italians, understood perfectly that the war was lost but when that happened all the nations of Europe would be reduced to rubble first.[64] Hitler had no monopoly of the *Alles oder Nichts* mentality.

German troops had become jittery. Incidents occurred. On 1 August Operation Axis went off by mistake at the Greek air base of Kolanaki and the German unit defending the air base attacked and disarmed an Italian unit.[65] Headquarters had to reiterate that 'everything absolutely to be avoided which might lead to conclusions about preparations and alarm Italians. Previous orders for readiness positions still in force.'[66]

The Germans played a double game with the Italians but the new Italian government played it right back times two. Domestically the royal government stood between a vast apparatus of state more or less wholly integrated into and corrupted by fascism and the anti-fascist parties, groupings and underground movements, many of whom were communist or republican. As the brilliant journalist Paolo Monelli saw it from close up

> The King and Badoglio remained frightened and perplexed; like somebody who has consumed ingenuity and force to overcome a formidable obstacle and then finds himself in front of an unexpected vertiginous abyss.[67]

Colonel Montezemolo of the Italian general staff explained to the German General von Rintelen that no reprisals against former fascists had been planned and regretted that the press which had somehow got out of hand had gone too far in demanding the heads of the former big shots of the regime.[68] For a while Bastianini, Grandi and even Ciano wandered about the corridors of power waiting to be called to high office. Bastianini was temporarily named Ambassador to Turkey, but the wave of hatred and contempt could not now be contained. Ciano fled to Germany, Grandi to Portugal, others to hiding places and a few died in suspicious circumstances. The King, spattered with the stains of fascism, and Badoglio, covered with its decorations, were too compromised not to move cautiously towards anti-fascism. As the King himself put it in a memorandum to Badoglio, 'if the system initiated were to go on, one would arrive at the absurdity of implicitly judging and condemning the activity of the King himself.'[69]

There was no other way forward but to dismantle the fascist state, to abolish its special tribunals, its concentration camps and its paramilitary units, to rename places and institutions, to abrogate its legislation.

> The people enjoyed themselves as at a theatre when they see the house of the tyrant fall down and every new character on stage announces a further disaster for him.[70]

One bit of fascist legislation remained: the racial laws which turned Italian Jews into second-class citizens. On the night of 25 July, the Minister of the Royal Household, the Duke of Acquarone, asked Dino Grandi which were the most urgent steps to be taken by royal decree. Grandi replied: 'Suppression of the political tribunal for the defence of the state, suppression of the racial laws and the proclamation of a state of martial law until the emergency has passed.'[71]

The King did nothing then and Badoglio nothing later. On 27 July Carmen Senise, once again chief of police, dismissed prefect Antonio La Pera, head of the Ministry of the Interior's department of demography and race, arrested him and transferred him to Regina Coeli where the cells were beginning to fill with great figures from the regime, but 'Demorazza' itself continued to exist. On the 29th Senise ordered the liberation of political prisoners, except for communists, anarchists, spies and irredentists, and 'in addition those Jews must be liberated who are either interned or banished in forced residence who have not engaged in activities as enumerated above and have not committed acts of special gravity.'[72]

The King and Badoglio evidently regarded the abolition of the racial laws as too risky. Hitler had made no secret of his rage at the Italians. General Marras, the military attaché in Berlin, had been subjected to a torrent of abuse and menaces. As he said to Ortona on a visit to Rome, 'it's getting hot in every sense of the word'.[73] To cross the Führer unnecessarily on a matter so important to him seemed just too dangerous.

The Badoglio government had more important risks on its mind. A day after Raffaele Guariglia took office as Minister of Foreign Affairs, on 31 July, a cabinet meeting authorized him to begin to work for a separate peace. He tried to use the Vatican as intermediary and sent the Marchese Blasco Lanza d'Ajeta, former Chief of Cabinet to Ciano, to be new Secretary of Legation in Portugal with instructions to contact the Allies. Other emissaries, both political and military, followed him.[74] The month of August was tense with delicate and complicated negotiations. On 10 August Marshall Badoglio told General Ambrosio that he had now decided to deal directly and to send a military representative to learn the Allied terms. On 12 August General Giuseppe Castellano set out for Lisbon under a false passport and it was he who eventually signed the armistice on 3 September 1943, in Sicily.

The 'forty-five days' which ran between the fall of Mussolini on 25 July 1943 and the annnouncement of the Italian surrender on 8 September were days of intrigue, anxiety, sudden hopes and equally sudden disappointments but, above all, of great uncertainty. Nobody from King to road sweeper knew exactly what to do. The new Foreign Secretary found himself in an awkward position. He was nominally representative of an Axis power, engaged in a war to the death against Jewish Bolshevism and Anglo-American plutocracy; he was also privy to negotiations with the enemies of the Axis to reverse alliances. As he plaintively put it, 'Naturally I never thought for a moment that I should be able to talk openly . . . but I had hoped not to be forced to lie so totally.'[75]

This painful necessity was made worse by all the little difficulties of the forty-five days. When Hitler refused to see Badoglio and the King, Guariglia realised that he would have to confront Ribbentrop who eventually agreed to see him. On the evening of 5 August Guariglia summoned his immediate staff for a preparatory discussion for the meeting planned for the following day. Ortona who had been kept on as Guariglia's Head of Secretariat, recorded in his diary:

I put to him the problem of the dress we ought to wear. I observed that since we were going in order to tell the Germans 'the war continues', it's not the moment to show up in civilian clothes. (I remembered the encounter with Laval at Schloss Klessheim) It's better if we wear uniform. Guariglia asks me then: 'well how did you dress for the previous meetings?' I reply 'With Antonescu we went in the blue uniform of functionaries with white trousers'. So Guariglia replies with a typically neapolitan solution: 'we shall go then in white jackets and blue trousers'. I then point out that on our caps we have the insignia of the *fasces*. Acquarone advises us to adopt the beret of court gentlemen which only has an eagle. Finally I point out that based on my previous experiences Ribbentrop will lean out of the window well before the train stops and will make a long fascist salute. 'And you, Minister, what salute will you make in reply?'
'I'll improvise!'[76]

Those final words could stand as motto for the forty-five days: 'I'll improvise! I'll think of something!' At the last minute and with inadequate preparation and forethought, without coordination or planning, Italy slithered out of the Axis and stumbled toward something which would have to be 'unconditional surrender' but might be fiddled, fixed or improvised.

What could not be improvised was Jewish policy. Captain Merci in Salonica noticed after the fall of Mussolini 'that our ability to help the Jews will be greatly reduced'.[77] Dr Merten had deferred to them in the past because he believed that the Führer and the Duce had an understanding on the question. With the Duce out of the way the Germans could ignore Italian protests.

Jews in the occupied zone had become very anxious, as the Italian consul in Nice reported on 31 July, 'given the actual circumstances and foreseeing an occupation of the zone by German troops'. He asked permission to issue visas to allow Italian Jews to enter Italy without the time-consuming procedures of the immigration service of the Ministry of the Interior.[78] A few days later Senise authorized their repatriation.[79]

But what about the non-Italian Jews? The world now knew the situation of the Jews under Italian occupation. In early August the Italian legation in Stockholm reported that the Swedish press had been expressing its anxiety about the fate of the Jews in the Balkans. On 3 August the *Aftontidningen* discussed at length the fate of 'the only surviving Jews on Yugoslav territory' and quoted 'the German correspondent Hermann Ginsel who described with ill-concealed annoyance the normal lives that the Jews are conducting in the Italian-occupied zone'.[80]

The irritation of the SS in France was not concealed at all. Laval had begun to drag his feet on a law to 'rob Jews of their French nationality'. As he told *SS Gruppenführer* Oberg on 11 August, 'he could not open himself to the charge that he passed laws in order to drive Jews into our hands. The measure was so far-reaching that he would have to consult the Marshall [Pétain].'[81]

The Italians continued to obstruct the final solution in their zone as well. On orders from Oberg, *SS Sturmbannführer* Hagen went to see Lieutenant Malfatti at the Italian Embassy in Paris on 18 August to complain about the 'indecisive attitude of the Italian occupation forces' who had allowed Jews to flee from the German to the Italian zone of occupation and who had thus given the Laval regime a welcome excuse for not carrying out their promises. Hagen stressed how important a unified Axis policy in the matter was:

> Malfatti assured me that the standpoint of the present Italian government in the Jewish question was the same as that which had been laid down in the Italian laws on Jews. He pointed out quite specifically that of all the fascist legislation which had been revoked only the Jewish laws remained in force.[82]

It is hard to believe that the SS swallowed that line but they had little choice. Italy was still a member of the Axis and its anti-semitic legislation still in place. The Badoglio government added yet another twist to the tangle of paradoxes which characterized Italian policy toward the Jews. The failure to revoke the *leggi raziali* removed a possible handle which the SS could have used to force the Italians to surrender Jews. It allayed suspicion, and thus an obsolete anti-semitic measure ironically protected Jews for a little while longer.

During the middle of the month of August 1943 Italian diplomats and the Foreign Ministry exchanged telegrams on an almost daily basis on the Jewish question. Non-Italian Jews were to be allowed into the national territory; those Jews who had through exile or anti-fascism lost passports would get them back.[83] On 19 August Augusto Rosso, the new Secretary General of the Italian Foreign Ministry, sent a telegram to the Headquarters of the 2nd Army in

Croatia: 'It is to be avoided that the Croatian Jews be released or abandoned without any protection into foreign hands and exposed to reprisals, save in the case that they wish to be released outside our zone of protection.'[84]

When on 25 August the prefect of Lyons informed the Italian authorities that male Jews between 18 and 50 were to be handed over to the German 'Organization Todt' for forced labour, the *comando supremo*

> in relation to the previous opinion of the command to prevent the transfer of elements of the Jewish race into the German-occupied zone has given orders to the Command of the 4th Army not to adhere to the above-cited order.[85]

The Italian Foreign Ministry agreed entirely with that line and in order to coordinate Italian policy in all three zones of occupation a meeting of representatives of the army, the Foreign Ministry and the Ministry of the Interior was held on 28 August. All three ministries agreed that they would not allow the conscription of Jews for forced labour under German auspices but, as Ambassador Rosso observed in a telegram to *comando supremo*, 'given delicacy of material appears evident to proceed prudently with discretion reserving eventual possibility of employing Jewish elements for work in the Italian zone of occupation.'[86] The proven techniques of apparent compliance had become the 'agreed line of conduct' of the three ministries most concerned with the fate of the Jews. In the Italian zone of France Angelo Donati, the advisor to Police General Lospinoso, had evolved a more daring scheme to evacuate the Jews by boat to North Africa. In this too the Badoglio government agreed finally to help.[87]

What even the Secretary General of the Italian Foreign Ministry did not yet know, as most of the cabinet only learned much later, was the state of negotiations with the Allies. On 27 August General Castellano returned to Rome with the depressing news that the Allies demanded an unconditional surrender on a take-it-or-leave-it basis and, as if to emphasize the position, had unleashed the heaviest air offensive on Italian cities of the entire war.[88] By this stage the Italian peninsula was in effect in German hands. Ambrosio had no time to recall the Balkan and Greek divisions and with what Monelli calls the government's 'obsession with secrecy' could hardly do so.[89] The decision was bitter but unavoidable. On 3 September 1943, in a large tent in an olive grove at Cassibile near Syracuse, General Castellano signed the 'short armistice', as it came to be called.[90]

Barely a dozen people in Rome knew it, and the Germans in spite of intensive investigations never found out. They never knew that on the night of 7 September the American General Taylor arrived in

Rome secretly to coordinate the defence of the city at a time when Senise had calculated that there were already 5–6,000 German troops, some disguised in civilian clothes, in the city.[91] Even the ubiquitous Dollmann was caught out by the events, but then so was everybody by the way the armistice was proclaimed.

Eisenhower announced the armistice at 4.30 in the afternoon of Wednesday 8 September 1943, and Reuters put out a flash at 5.45. The Italian government was caught absolutely by surprise and hurriedly assembled at the royal palace. As Guariglia, who had been quietly walking in the Villa Borghese on the sunny September day, hurried in, he was met by Marshall Badoglio in the ante-chamber of the King's reception room: 'I ran to him anxious for news. He responded literally: "we're f– – – –d!"'[92]

Now that the news was out the Italians had either to confirm or deny it. No provision had been made for a broadcast. Badoglio had to rush to the studio and hurriedly read the following announcement, broadcast at 8 p.m.:

> The Italian government, recognizing the impossibility of continuing the unequal struggle against the overwhelming power of the adversary, with the intention of sparing the country further and much graver disasters, has requested an armistice of General Eisenhower, commander-in-chief of the Anglo-American allied forces. The request has been accepted. Consequently every act of hostility against the Anglo-Americans must cease on the part of Italian forces in every locality. They will react to eventual attacks from whatever other source.[93]

'Worse than this', wrote Alberto Pirelli, 'one could not have managed things.'[94] The statement was vague and confusing. Ambrosio had already issued orders to his commands under code name 'OP 44' which stipulated that the Italians were to react against the Germans 'with a decisive demeanour'.[95] What did that mean?

Confusion was complete in the 2nd Army. According to the Italian army's official 'Report on the Events Following the Armistice in the Balkan Peninusula' of 2 December 1943, the story unfolded in this way: General Mario Robotti and his entire command on the night of 9 September slipped away by boat and eventually made it to Italy. General Gambara, the commander of the XI Corps, remained in Sussak and surrendered without a fight to the German 71st Division. The worst muddle occurred in the Division 'Bergamo' which on the morning of 9 September received the order at 8.30 a.m. to 'actuate OP 44'. General Emilio Becuzzi ordered his men to resist the Germans and at 4 p.m. commanded 'resistance to the end'. At 16.52, XVIII Corps renewed the order to 'actuate OP 44 but without spilling blood'. General Becuzzi asked for clarification: 'how is one supposed to arrest the Germans under these new orders?' By the time the Division finally surrendered on 10 September the General was justly exasperated and reported that 'because of the mental confusion provoked by orders and counter-orders of the last few days, the mass of the officers and men would not have fired either at the Germans or at the partisans'.[96]

At least the Division 'Bergamo' had orders, even if contradictory. The commander of the *Lupi di Toscana* (the 'Wolves of Tuscany') had none. The regiment was being transferred by rail from France when the armistice was announced and hence detachments were strung out along the Italian peninsula. The commander General Ernesto Cappa and his chief of staff, Lieutenant Colonel Emiliano Scotti, had gone ahead by car to prepare for the arrival of the division as part of the defence of Rome. Lt Col Scotti kept a precise diary of the events and there is no mistaking his bitterness:

> Being without data about the destination and tasks of the division, the commander got into contact at once with the commander of the army corps 'territory Rome', with the commander of the armoured corps and with an officer attached to the general staff of the army but nobody was able to furnish indications of any sort.[97]

The only precise order the division received was General Badoglio's broadcast on the radio which they understood to mean: resist the Germans by force. As late as 6.55 p.m. on 10 September, nearly 48 hours after the announcement by Badoglio, the staff of the *Lupi* still could not get in touch with the operations room at the Army general staff 'because there was nobody in the office'.[98]

At Karlovac in Croatia, Captain Bruno Fiaschi had the same problem:

> Fiaschi wanted to break the isolation by calling the telephone operators at army and corps command headquarters. Nobody there; nobody responds. Spurred by the force of despair he tried to get a connection with Rome. Even at the Ministry of War no sign of life. Incredible the absenteeism of all the high commands on the night on which king, government, supreme command and commands of the large units ought to be securing respect for the armistice.[99]

Fiaschi in remotest Karlovac could not have known that staff officers in the ministry of war were not the only absentees. Early on the morning of 9 September, the King, the Queen, the top generals and members of the royal family slipped away to the coast where a

1 Mussolini and Hitler at the War Memorial in Berlin, 1937, reproduced by kind permission of Collins Publishers, London

2 Mussolini and Hitler visit Florence, 1938, reproduced by kind permission of Verlag Kurt Desch GmBH, Munich

3 Mussolini and Hitler in Germany, 1937, reproduced by kind permission of Verlag Kurt Desch GmBH, Munich

4 Italian fascist officers at the Lustgarten in Berlin, 1 May 1937, reproduced by kind permission of Verlag Kurt Desch GmBH, Munich

5 Pavelić and Mussolini, 18 May 1941, reproduced by kind permission of Verlag Kurt Desch GmBH, Munich

6 Pavelić and Ciano at the signing of the State Treaty between Croatia and Italy, 18 May 1941, reproduced by kind permission of Verlag Kurt Desch GmBH, Munich

7 The two dictators and the Italian royal family in Rome, 6 May 1938,
reproduced by kind permission of Verlag Kurt Desch GmBH, Munich

8 Fascist rally in Rome, 1938, reproduced by kind permission of Paul
Popper Ltd

9 Hitler and the leaders of the regime at the funeral of Hindenburg, 1934, reproduced by kind permission of Atlantis Verlag, Zürich

10 Deportation of Jews from Croatia, Summer 1941, reproduced by kind permission of Ufficio Storico, Stato Maggiore Italiano, Italy

11 Serb refugees and the Ustaši, Summer 1941, reproduced by kind permission of Ufficio Storico, Stato Maggiore Italiano, Italy

12 Italian officers with Serb peasants, reproduced by kind permission of Ufficio Storico, Stato Maggiore Italiano, Italy

13 General Mario Robotti, commander of the 11th Army corps in Yugoslavia 1941–42, reproduced by kind permission of Ufficio Storico, Stato Maggiore Italiano, Italy

14 Portrait of General Carlo
Geloso, commander of Italian
forces in Greece, 1941–43,
reproduced by kind permission
of Ufficio Storico, Stato
Maggiore Italiano, Italy

15 Fascists of Bergamo send greetings to the Duce, 1938, reproduced by kind
permission of the Archivio Centrale dello Stato

boat took them to Brindisi in the south. There is a fierce controversy which still rages about the propriety of the decision, but there can be no doubt that it robbed the capital of whatever political direction it had hitherto enjoyed. There is an equally fierce controversy about the failure to defend Rome properly, and about the muddle in commands everywhere.

The German plans, by contrast, went into instant and efficient operation. Orders went out minute by minute to each command. At 8.05 p.m., five minutes after Badoglio's radio statement, General Jodl at the Führer's headquarters signalled Supreme Command South East to implement Operation Axis.[100] By 9.35 General von Gyldenfeldt could report from Athens that he had arranged the surrender of the Italian 11th Army. General Hubert Lanz, the commander of the XXII Mountain Army Corps, wanted to try first 'with kindness and then with force'. The following conversation took place at five minutes to midnight between General Lanz and General Winter, Chief of Staff of Supreme Command South East/Army Group E:

General Winter: 'All weapons without exception are to be seized.'
General Lanz: 'That means fighting. Are you clear about the consequence of such measures?'
General Winter: 'Yes. We have been preparing "Axis" for weeks and months. If one says to the Italians, for them the war is over and they can go home, they will give up like sheep.'
General Lanz: 'That remains to be seen.'
General Winter: 'The Führer has commanded disarming them. We have to carry it out. We know what the difficulties are; if we cannot do it any other way, we shall have to carry out the disarming with force.'
General Lanz: 'Am I supposed to shed blood?'
General Winter: 'The order has been given to us and must be carried out'[101]

It was a fateful order and led General Lanz to command his men to storm the island of Kephalonia where General Antonio Gandin and the men of the Division 'Acqui' fought a bitter battle for nearly a week and were shot on the spot afterwards. It was the beginning of the process which would put General Hubert Lanz in the dock at Nuremberg as a war criminal.[102]

Field Marshall von Weichs in Belgrade was having his troubles with the Italians too but of a different sort. When Colonel Ricci, the Italian attaché at the HQ of German Army Group F, tried to reach Tirana in Albania where the newly constituted Italian Army Group (East) had been established, he had to confess to the Field Marshall that 'neither the commanding general nor his chief of staff were there. Both had gone for a walk.'[103]

That was too much for *Generaloberst* Lothar Rendulic, the commanding general of the 2nd Tank Army:

> In the morning [of 11 September], the commanding general with a paratroop company landed in Tirana and in a quick swoop seized the commanding general of the Italian Army Group(East) and his chief of staff. Thus the main source of existing Italian resistance was quelled.[104]

General Rendulic arrested them because of their 'anti-German attitudes'. A 56 year old Austrian general and a company of paratroops had been enough to seize the entire headquarters of an army of 250,000 men. No wonder Bruno Fiaschi reflected bitterly

> Isolated German sergeants with a bit of guts and a pistol in hand capture entire barracks of generals, colonels, officers and hundreds of soldiers of every rank. Without written orders, commanders of divisons, or regiments, of groups and of batteries, are not in a position to organize any form of resistance.[105]

The paradox is clear. The German army with its iron discipline and rigid structure of command allowed great liberty for individual initiative. Within that framework commanders and soldiers had freedom. The Italian army with its systematic disobedience, its rackets and disorder, could not function without written orders. This is one of the profoundest reasons for the different behaviour of the two armies to the Jews. General Lanz did not want to shoot Italians but obeyed orders as he did later in the round up of the Jews from the former Italian zone of Greece. The dialogue between General Winter and General Lanz illustrates the core of the German military tradition as does the daring raid by a full, four-star general, who dropped from the air with only a company of men and seized an entire Italian HQ. There was not a general in the Italian army who would have dared to try such a stunt and few in any army. On the other hand four stars could not prevent Rendulic or Löhr from becoming accomplices to crimes against humanity of which they disapproved. 'Hopeless subalterns!' Ulrich von Hassell called the German generals. They lacked the independence to resist immoral orders.[106] When the Yugoslavs were trying him as a war criminal in May 1945 General Löhr had only one answer on his role in the final solution of the Jewish question: Yes, he had heard that

> the Jews had been enclosed in ghettos and I also heard that many

had lost their lives, that gas chamber-lorries had been used by the police authorities to destroy Jews, allegedly in Poland. Whether these stories correspond to the truth or not I have not further investigated, since I was not competent to do so and had no possibility of doing it.[107]

That Jews were rounded up and murdered near his command, that a third of the population of Salonica had been transported underneath the windows of his office, that he provided the transportation for the round-up and extermination of the Greek Jews left in the former Italian zone and that, finally, he had actively urged General Geloso to cooperate in the extermination of the Jews of the Italian zone, he does not, of course, mention. The Yugoslavs were inclined to shoot him in any case; no need to supply them with additional grounds.

Yet Löhr was not a beast. Consul Zamboni, who did a great deal to save the Jews of Salonica, remembers him very clearly as an outspoken anti-Nazi. Richard Mitten who interviewed surviving officers in Löhr's command for a TV documentary on Waldheim told me that literally nobody on his staff had a bad word to say about him.[108] It is the language that is so chilling: *'da ich dafür nicht zuständig war'* – 'that I was not responsible for it', 'responsible' in the sense of duty, competence or bureaucratic jurisdiction. Separating the official from the human – *das Dienstliche* from *das Menschliche* – had led to a terrible disaster.

By now, as Guariglia noted,

it was not possible to provide adequately for the Jews who had fled to our zone of occupation in France and who with the retreat of the 4th Army would be abandoned to the Germans . . . the premature announcement of the armistice had spoiled everything.[109]

Jews fled from their places of confinement. Some headed for the mountainous border between France and Italy, where they joined columns of Italian troops straggling back in disorder themselves. Others headed down to the coast and got trapped in Nice when the black hordes of SS descended on the city, ripping down men's trousers on the street to see who was circumcised and combing every apartment room by room. Nice became the arena of one of the most brutal Jew-hunts of the war.[110] The Italian troops could no longer protect them.

In Rome, German troops poured into the city pushing the sporadic and ineffective defence out of the way. Even the Foreign Secretary Guariglia received no orders for several days and after a few vain attempts to maintain the authority of the cabinet, dissolved it and fled to the Spanish Embassy where he and his wife stayed cooped up for nearly nine months.[111]

Guariglia had known on 3 September that the armistice had been signed and had begun to destroy compromising documents at the Palazzo Chigi. Others he had shipped secretly to Lisbon and some he managed to conceal in Rome. Diplomats like Count Pietromarchi and Roberto Ducci knew that they too had better disappear; they must be on a list somewhere. As Roberto Ducci told Nicola Caracciolo in an interview shortly before he died, in the chaotic days after the armistice he was still at the Palazzo Chigi. There was one final thing to do:

> The files of the Jews in Croatia like the other later ones had the classification of absolute secrecy. I kept them locked in my armoured safe. It was from there that I took them on the 9th or 10th of September when we burnt the archives at the Palazzo Chigi. I decided not to burn that folder and to take it to my house because I thought it would be good if somebody in the future were to know that we had done something good in our lives.[112]

* * *

PART II
EXPLANATIONS

Why did the Nazi regime murder millions of Jews? Can any historian, can historians collectively, answer that question? For the past forty-five years they have tried and failed. No single work explains the holocaust. It may be that there are limits to what can be accomplished by the use of documents, accumulation of evidence and rational argument. Perhaps in the face of radical evil, reason ceases. During the Second World War serious thinkers. such as Denis de Rougement, tried to decide if Hitler was in fact the devil.

In this book I have asked a much smaller question: why did some Italian diplomats and soldiers save Jews at a certain time and place while their German colleagues helped to murder them? I believe that there are some answers to this double question and that they appear both through the story of the events as they unfolded and through a comparison of certain features of the two cultures, the two dictators, the two armies and the position of the Jews in Italian and German history. There are, of course, other comparisons that need to be made between, for example, the functioning of the two states, the operations of the two economies, the role of law and legality in Germany and Italy, and the two ideologies. A proper comparison would be a life's work, and, as Burckhardt once observed, a writer should bear in mind the brevity of the reader's existence. I offer these four comparisons as sketches of what the evidence seems to suggest in this case; I make no grander claims.

1

THE MATRIX OF VIRTUE
AND VICE

Roberto Ducci took the precious files on the Jews from Palazzo Chigi because he wanted the story to be told. It was a matter of life and death. The Gestapo were furiously searching Rome for evidence of Italian treachery. Had Ducci been caught with those files, he, Pietromarchi, Vidau, Vitetti, Lanza d'Ajeta, Castellani and many others would have been shot. For Ducci the secret files bore witness to his humanity and that of his fellow plotters. As Pietromarchi observed, the evidence would redeem them 'from many acts of baseness'. Does it?

Each of us will answer that question in his or her own way. Does a 'saving act' redeem members of a class who had co-operated in (and benefited from) twenty years of fascism? When Mussolini plunged Italy into war in 1940, who had dared to act then? Who resigned in protest? The German opponents of Hitler behaved better. General Beck resigned in 1938. Ulrich von Hassell, Carl Goerdeler, Adam von Trott, Helmuth von Moltke, Claus Count von Stauffenberg conspired against Hitler and died for their convictions after 20 July 1944. The Italian conspirators to save Jews lived to serve the post-war Republic of Italy, frequently in the highest of posts. Only Galeazzo Ciano, the good-for-nothing playboy, the son-in-law of Mussolini, the matinée idol, died for his part in opposing the Germans and betraying the Duce. He did so with great courage and composure.[1] A martyr, but to what?

That, in turn, depends on what the story of the Italian resistance to German brutality 'means', and. of course, it 'means' those contradictory and conflicting things that make human acts, even virtuous ones, so hard to interpret. Certainly there was an element of calculation. Ducci saved those files because, after all, as a high official of a discredited regime, he might find them handy witnesses for the defence. Indeed, in the summer of 1944, under the pseudonym 'Verax', he published an account of the way the Italian Foreign Ministry had excelled itself in saving Jews.[2] That was a useful thing to do when the air was filled with cries of revenge and when fascism lay in ruins. An Italian government which could show that it had not been 'that bad' might yet hope for co-belligerent status in the Allied war effort, a sort of remission of sentence for good behaviour.

Giuseppe Bastianini, who distinguished himself in 1943 as a defender of the Jews, had wanted to turn back Jewish refugees from Croatia in 1942 when they arrived at the borders of Italian-occupied Yugoslavia. The Carabinieri General Pièche, who received an award after the war from the Italian-Jewish community for his humanity, had recommended surrendering the Jews to the Croatians during it. He was converted when he learned their real destination. Count Ciano himself who thought that there was 'no Jewish problem' in Italy in 1937[3] did not oppose the 'racial laws' imposed by Mussolini in 1938. The 'meaning' of historical acts depends on timing.

By late summer 1942 General Roatta and his soldiers knew what Croatians had done to Jews and were beginning to suspect what the Germans were likely to do. Pietromarchi at the Italian Foreign Ministry had arrived at similar conclusions on his own. By a coincidence the months of September and October 1942 were months in which Mussolini's ill health and the struggle for power in the German Foreign Office immobilized both Italian and German decision-making. Those who might have acted quickly to frustrate the conspiracy to save Jews were paralysed. By November Rommel was in retreat in the Western Desert, the Allies had landed in Morocco and Algeria, the *Wehrmacht* had begun to fight the battle for Stalingrad, and the Italians faced for the first time the certainty that they at least would lose the war. November was also the month when the Italian authorities got hard evidence of the holocaust. By December Roatta had talked Mussolini out of his order to 'consign' the Jews of the occupied zones to the Germans. By 1943 the whole regime placed itself between the Jews and the SS and continued to do so until the armistice. Protecting Jews made sense for those who spun schemes to extricate Italy from the Axis. Mussolini wavered in late February and March 1943, under extreme pressure from Ribbentrop and the SS, but was soon talked back to the line of resistance.

There was, then, a considerable dose of calculation in Italian policy toward the Jews, but against that a peculiar national virtue is on display in this period. Of all the regimes conquered by, or part of, the Nazi new order, only Denmark can compare with Italy in its resistance to Nazi genocide. Let me cite again the passage in Hannah Arendt's *Eichmann in Jerusalem*:

What in Denmark was the result of an authentically political sense, an inbred comprehension of the requirements and responsibilities of citizenship and independence . . . was in Italy the outcome of the almost automatic general humanity of an old and civilized people.[4]

There is much evidence in these pages for the 'the almost automatic general humanity' of the Italians. We saw it in Major Prolo's draft regulations for the internment camp on Rab, when he insisted, with the approval of his superiors, that the Jews in the camp be given 'a treatment consciously felt to be "Italian"'.[5] We have seen it in Captain Merci's diaries in Salonica, and in the accounts of how young officers behaved in Croatia in 1941. Being Italian meant fellow-feeling for the oppressed.

Yet reality is more complicated than Hannah Arendt's broad brush allows. The primary virtue of humanity rested in a matrix of secondary vice. The disorder, disobedience and *menefreghismo* (I-could-not-care-less-ism) of Italian public life made the specific disobedience in the Jewish question easier. Slyness (*furberia*), the all-pervasive corruption of administration (*la bustarella*) and the casual carelessness of public officials (*pressapocismo*) made it easier for wealthy Jews to bribe guards, get the right forged papers and see the right official. It also made it easier for the conspirators to save Jews. After all, they wanted their state not to act, something which its natural ponderousness inclined it to do anyway.

In effect, the vices of Italian public life made the virtues of humanity easier to practise. The evidence presented in previous chapters makes that very clear. Habitual disobedience was so marked within Italian public bodies that even the army could not get its orders obeyed. There is a breathtaking entry in Marshall Cavallero's stenographic record for 14 January 1943, which I cite in its entirety:

10.05 hours: Receive Excellency Scuero [Under-Secretary for war] and Excellency Ambrosio [army chief of staff]. Topics –
– Repression of the mental habit of not obeying orders.[6]

An astonishing confession to find in the war diary of the chief of staff of a belligerent great power in the third year of a world war. The Italian generals could not make their men obey. Colonel Ravenni systematically disobeyed his commanding officer and got away with it, just as in every office in Italy bureaucrats acted or not as whim or the hope of profit moved them. This is not to diminish the virtue of what the conspirators did but it reduced the risk of doing it.

If Italian humanity rested on a matrix of secondary vice, German inhumanity lay deeply entangled in a system of secondary virtue. Cleanliness, punctuality, efficiency, dedication, honesty, sense of duty and responsibility, are German virtues and not to be despised. No sane person, who has ridden a German bus or used a German post office, would voluntarily choose to use the Italian equivalents. The civic virtues are precious because they are so rare. How many states in the world today are largely free of corruption? Would the list get to double figures? I doubt it.

Yet civic virtues are secondary virtues. They help us to live in an organized and efficient way. They are instruments to an end, not the end itself, and here the evidence of these pages and the research that went into it has crushing consistency. The uniformity of brutal behaviour in the German *Wehrmacht*, the absence of almost any expression of humanity in both public and private papers, makes exceptionally depressing reading. The little dialogue at midnight on 9 September 1943, between Generals Lanz and Winter on how to disarm the Italians speaks volumes. General Lanz did not want to shoot Italians and said so, but he had no way not to obey.

Although General Lanz and General Winter both ended up charged with war crimes of which they, together with Field Marshalls List and von Weichs and the other Balkan commanders, were undoubtedly guilty, they were, I am convinced, in no ordinary sense criminals. Their brutalities arose from the corruption on a primary level of what was an excellence on a secondary. As Eugen Dollmann said of Hans Georg von Mackensen, to understand his attitude to Mussolini one needed a short course in the history of Prussian, Lutheran culture.

Of all the documents I consulted for this study (by now a great many) the one reproduced overleaf is in some respects the most remarkable. An army staff officer tabulated the number of reprisals carried out in the Serbian zone up to December 1941, based on the number of German soldiers reported killed and wounded in each unit. He then worked out the number of hostages who ought to have been shot under the existing ratios, generously deducted enemy dead, and arrived at the sum of 20,174 persons not killed who ought to have been. It is the report of a bookkeeper on the underproduction of the *Wehrmacht*'s murder machine.[7] (See Document 3)

The language of the document is absolutely impersonal, the language of bureaucracy, the sentence structures of officialdom. The officer notes that the figures are not exact. The number executed amounts to a rough estimate. He concludes that new orders will be necessary to establish clear conditions in the matter of reprisal measures. The word *Menschen* (human beings) does not appear. General Böhme referred to persons he intended to shoot as being drawn from '*altserbischen Beständen*' (old Serbian supplies). Language in these documents turned people into 'matter','supplies', or 'stuff'. Immediately after the war the philologist Dolf Sternberger began to publish his *Aus dem Wörterbuch des Unmenschen* (the dictionary of the inhuman), in which he worked out the implications of such language,

A k t e n n o t i z .

zu den

seit Beginn der Aufstandsbewegungen i.Serbien
bis 5.12.1941 vollzogenen Sühnemaßnahmen.

1.) Mit Übergabe der Geschäfte des Bevollm.Kdr.Gen.i.Serbien vom
XVIII. auf das XXXXII.A.K. sollen mit Wirkung vom 5.12. die bis
zu diesem Zeitpunkt vollzogenen Sühnemaßnahmen zusammengefaßt
festgestellt werden.

2.) Grundlegende Befehle liegen im Qu.2 Akt (Bevollm.Kdr.Gen.i.S.
VIII 7) a.

3.) Auf Grund der Truppenmeldungen ergeben sich folgende Abschluß-
zahlen:

	J.R.125 + I./A.R.220	342.J.D.	Bfh.Serb. Verw.Stb.	113.J.D.	Höh.Kdo. LXV.	III/697
Eigene Verluste						
a)	11	32	--	--	117	--
b) verwundet	30	130	--	--	218	--
Feind Verluste						
a) im Kampf	369	923	24	--	2246	--
b) Sühne- maßnahmen	214	2685	3616	--	4649	-- 11.164

Bei den zugrunde liegenden Schlüssel von 1:100 bzw. 1:50 ergibt
sich als zu vollziehende Sühnmaßnahme:

$$160 \times 100 = 16\ 000$$
$$378 \times 50 = \underline{18\ 900}$$
$$34\ 900$$

Bev.Verjen.+5./6.i.Serbien
34476,5

172

- 2 -   **71**

4.) Durchgeführte Sühnemaßnahme = 11.164

  Abgerechnete tote Feinde   = 3.562
        Quote ./. tot Feinde-= 34.900
                    31 338

Damit waren noch zu sühnen: 31.338
                        ./. 11.164
                          20.174
                      ========

5.) Am 16.12. morgens fehlten zu dieser Meldung noch die Angaben
der 718.J.D. des III./I.R.697 und 113.J.D.

Hptm. von H a a c k e und Hptm. S c h u s t e r wurden zur
fernmündlichen Meldung aufgefordert. Für 718.J.D. ist nichts
veranlaßt.

6.) Es wird eindringlich festgestellt, daß die Meldungen der unter-
stellten Einheiten lückenhaft und ungenau sind, da vor allem
zu Beginn des Aufstandes die Exekutionen ohne schriftliche
Niederlegung erfolgen und nachträgliche Meldungen ungenau sein
mußten.

Die angegebene Zahl von 11.164 durchgeführten Exekutionen ist
als <u>Faustzahl</u> zu werten.

7.) Um auf dem Sachgebiet Sühnemaßnahmen klare Verhältnisse zu
schaffen, ist die Ausgabe eines neuen Befehls, der klare Melde-
verhältnisse schafft, unterläßlich. Er ist bereits ausgearbei-
tet und z.Zt. im Druck.

Document 3 German calculations of the number of hostages for execution,
1941

words drawn from the vocabulary of the totalitarian state, words like *Einsatz* (almost untranslatable but used to describe the insertion of units on a military front), *Menschenbehandlung* (people treatment) and *Zeitgeschehen* (contemporary happening or event).[8]

The holocaust depended on this dehumanized language. *Wehrmacht*, SS and bureaucracy concealed their actions in part from themselves by euphemisms for murder: *Sonderbehandlung* (special treatment), *Endlösung* (final solution) or, as in Turner's case, *Entlausung* (delousing). Finally, those sharp definitions of responsibility which divided the German bureaucracy into neat compartments allowed generals accused of war crimes to claim that it was not part of their *Zuständigkeit* (competence) to behave like human beings.

Yet even here there is a problem in understanding what the evidence means. General Edmund Glaise von Horstenau was hardly a Nazi and as an ex-Imperial Austrian General Staff Officer not even a Prussian. He served for three full years as General Plenipotentiary representing the *Wehrmacht* to the Independent State of Croatia. He knew everybody who counted in Berlin and conducted a voluminous correspondence, much of which survived the war. In public and private he protested against the savagery of the *Ustaši* butchers and against the indiscriminate execution of hostages. He wrote frankly and wittily to his fellow Austrian, the Supreme Commander South East, General Löhr. He did not use the language of euphemism nor surround the truth with bureaucratic abstraction. He said 'murder' when he meant 'murder' except if the victims were Jews. Then he said nothing. Indeed, in an ominous aside in a letter to Löhr in March 1943, he let slip that his best source of information in Berlin had been Martin Luther, the man inside the German Foreign Office who most closely resembled Eichmann in his relentless pursuit of Jews.[9] Why was Glaise silent?

In May 1944 Colonel Jäger, commandant on Corfu, argued against the deportation of the 2,000 Jews on the island because transport had become scarce and because the Jews were no threat but above all because it could

> only be carried out at the cost of a loss of ethical prestige; this latter because the unavoidable brutalities can only have a repellent effect. Besides the action cannot be carried out quickly and painlessly.
> *Proposal*: the action is to be postponed indefinitely.[10]

The action was, of course, not postponed. The Jews of Corfu were rounded up in June of 1944 and went to their death with the same relentless thoroughness that marked the extermination of the Jews of all the other Greek islands, no matter how small and harmless such communities were.[11] Yet Colonel Jäger deserves mention. His report to HQ the XXII (Mountain) Army Corps is the only document in the vast archives of Army Groups E and F in which the word 'ethical' appears. Words such as 'moral', 'ethical' or 'just' seemed to have no place in the service manuals of the German officer corps.

The contrast with Italian military files could not be more marked. Italian soldiers habitually used the language of Christian virtue in both public and private pronouncements. There was also a legacy of chivalric behaviour, a strong awareness of the dictates of honour and a determination to protect the weak and oppressed. The German army and state grew out of the same Western traditions. Why and how had such language been eliminated from German usage?

In 1928 the Weimar satirist Kurt Tucholsky summed the problem up in a prophetic little essay called '*Das Menschliche*' (the human):

> The '*Menschliche*' is something which elsewhere is self-evident. . . . To have made a separate department of it, which incidentally we should always write in quotation marks, has been reserved to the Germans who in contrast to more or less everybody else in the world seem to think that that there is something '*rein Dienstliches*' or even worse: '*rein Sachliches*'. If the gentlemen philologists would be kind enough to translate those words into any other language, I should be grateful. I cannot.[12]

Dienst is the word for service, such as service in the army, and *Sache* is the word for thing. German by placing a neuter *das* in front of these adjectives turns them into nouns and hence abstract categories. As Tucholsky continues:

> But that is the German view of life that makes understanding with other peoples so difficult. In this country *das 'Menschliche'* comes with the slatternly smell of disorder, of cheekiness, of uncontrollable chaos . . . *das 'Menschliche'* is what's left over when the harm has been done.[13]

The harm was done by concentration camp commanders, secretaries of Nazi bosses, businessmen with contracts to supply toxic gas or foremen working on crematoria who later pleaded '*das Dienstliche*' as their defence. The dry, impersonal language of the final solution grew out of two centuries of official language, stereotypical attitudes and rigid division of competence. Hannah Arendt called it 'the banality of evil' as she listened to the flat, pedantic responses of Adolf Eichmann in the glass cage in Jerusalem.

Evil is the perversion of good. The traditions of the German bureaucracy were not evils in themselves. The Prussians accomplished what few societies have; they abolished corruption in the civil service. They instilled a sense of duty in their servants and taught them to separate the self from the official position. Gianfranco Poggi sees in this process the very essence of the modern state: 'The moral ideal that ultimately legitimizes the modern state is the taming of power through the depersonalization of its exercise.'[14] The Italian state has yet to achieve this. There the citizen seeks to avoid the law by getting help from 'somebody who knows somebody'. He expects treatment not according to the law but according to his connections. The mafia calls itself 'friends of the friends'; the phrase emphasizes that personality supercedes law. The state yields to the power of the man in the white suit and dark glasses.

German bureaucrats served the state as an absolute with a sense of mission. They expected of themselves the highest possible competence. They took no bribes. It is remarkable how rarely rich Jews saved themselves by bribing Germans. They divided self from service. When service turned into murder of innocent men, women and children, their virtues trapped them and made them accomplices and facilitators of the worst crime in human history. Their inner world split into compartments, watertight areas, which prevented considerations of morality seeping into official acts.

The 'objectivity' expected of German officials, as Nietzsche noticed, led to 'the eternal loss of the subject' or, in effect, the disappearance of self. All official acts and documents were in theory to be interchangeable and like all other such acts and documents. No individual voice ought to be heard; it was the office talking. It may be that human beings cannot tolerate that level of personal suppression. Like a spring mechanism wound too tight the self snaps back. Certainly there was an equal and opposite explosion of self in the writings of Nietzsche and his ecstatic followers. He fought the deadening power of the bureaucratic ideal with a doctrine of youth, life, risk, and soul. History, he cried,

> belongs to the active and the mighty, to him who fights the great fight, who needs models, teachers, consolers and is unable to find them among his contemporaries in the present . . . he lives most beautifully who cares not for his existence.[15]

The great man stood beyond good and evil and beyond the petty, pedantic perfection of the state. Germany yearned for him as *Oberleutnant* Kurt Hesse put it in an extraordinary book of 1923:

> And so he will announce himself, he for whom we all wait full of yearning. . . . Whence he comes, none can say. Out of a prince's palace or a day labourer's hut. Yet each knows. He is the *Führer*. Each hails him; each obeys him. And why? Because he radiates a peculiar power. He is a ruler of souls.[16]

The power of the cult of the leader reflected the exasperation of the led. The Führer would somehow break the crust and free the soul. Spontaneity and blood would overcome bureaucracy. A flower would grow out of the drawers of the filing cabinet. And Hitler did not disappoint them. He too was an ecstatic, a Wagnerian, a visionary and dreamer of great dreams.

Nobody can measure how important these features of German culture were. If our scale went from zero to one hundred, no sensible student would place the impact of language, literature, values and customs at the bottom nor would anybody put them at the top. They belong somewhere in the middle and, alas, we don't know where.

The outcome of the First World War, the bitterness over the imposed peace of 1919, the madness of the worst inflation in human history when a lady left a basket with 60 million Reichsmarks on the pavement and came back to find the basket stolen but the money untouched, the fearful depression with its 6 million unemployed, what the other states in Europe did or did not do, the personality of Adolf Hitler, the course of the Second World War, all these realities shaped the outcome. Yet culture played a part in making Germans behave predictably as Germans.

German *Kultur* cannot escape the course of history. Auschwitz casts its shadow over the tomb of Frederick the Great and Wagner cannot be performed in Israel. German history is, as Count Kielmannsegg once observed, 'post-catastrophic', and that makes it even harder to assess the imponderable elements of Germanic culture. The brew of Hegel, romantic yearning, preoccupation with the absolute, bureaucratic efficiency and punctilious attention to performance was unstable and one day it might explode. That thought occurred to the German Jewish poet Heinrich Heine. In 1834 Heine published his remarkable history of religion and philosophy in Germany. In it there is a moment of vision, written a century before the 'night of the long knives' and Theresienstadt. I quote from it:

Christianity – and this is its greatest service – has to some extent soothed the brutal German lust for battle but has not destroyed it; but when one day the taming talisman, the cross, breaks, then the wildness of the old warriors will rattle forth, the mad beserk fury, of which the nordic sagas sing and say so much. The talisman is rotten and the day will come when it falls. The old stone gods will heave themselves out of the ancient debris and rub a thousand years of dust from their eyes. Thor with his giant hammer will spring up and shatter the gothic cathedral. . . . Smile not at my counsel, the counsel of a dreamer, who warns you of Kantians, Fichteans and natural philosophers. Smile not at

177

the fantasist who expects the revolution in the world of reality that has already taken place in the realm of the spirit. Thought precedes act like lightning the thunder. German thunder is, to be sure, German and not very agile. It comes rolling on very slowly. But come it will, and when you hear the crashing start, as it has never crashed in the history of the world, know that German thunder has at last reached its goal. At the sound eagles will fall dead from heaven and lions in the farthest deserts of Africa will pull in their tails and slink into their royal lairs. A piece will be played out in Germany which will make the French Revolution seem a harmless idyll.[17]

Heine got the history right but left us the problem of cause. For his generation, bred on the Hegelian dualism of matter and spirit, there was an inevitable logic in the argument that changes in the realm of the spirit would lead one day to changes in reality. Our generation has lost the certainties. We cannot say what caused what and with what force. I cannot prove it; I can only feel that Heine was right. The language, categories of thought and cultural attitudes which Heine saw as explosive seem to me to have exploded between 1933 and 1945.

They might not have. If Hitler had not gained power in 1933 – and it was touch-and-go right to the end – the explosion might never have occurred or, if it did, less violently. Yet the opposite is also true. Hitler embodied certain features of German *Kultur*, admittedly in a distorted and extreme version, which the addition of his fanaticism raised to the critical temperature. It was this chilling fanaticism which seemed most frightening and alien to Italian observers. Colonel Antonio Gandin*, who in March 1940 served as Chief of the Secretariat to Marshall Badoglio, then Chief of the General Staff, decided to get to know his Axis ally and read (in French) Hermann Rauschning's *The Revolution of Nihilism*: 'This book arouses in the reader – if he doesn't feel it already an irresistible sense of repulsion for Hitler and for the Germans, that is, especially if the reader is Italian.'[18]

German culture seemed incomprehensible to the Italians in both its guises: the efficiency and the romantic ecstasy. If the spirit of Hegel brooded over German culture, it was Machiavelli who represented Italian. To Germans Italians seemed corrupt and cynical, in touch with reality, but at the lowest level. Late in the war Marshalls Cavallero and Kesselring had a heated debate about command.

* Colonel Gandin, by then general and commander of the Division 'Acqui', was to die on 24 September 1943, as part of the massacre of officers and men who resisted the German demand to surrender the island of Kephalonia after the Italian armistice with the Allies. The massacre of the commanding officer and his men formed part of the so-called 'Hostages Trial' of German generals at Nuremberg.

Kesselring had called on Cavallero to tell him that the Führer had now decided that General Löhr was to have command of the combined Axis forces in case the Allies landed in the Balkans. Cavallero blew up:

> he cannot receive orders from the Führer nor can he say to the Duce that the Führer had given orders to the Supreme Command. The Führer had better speak to the Duce. He was not going to say to the Duce we are yielding the command of four armies (Greece, Montenegro, Dalmatia and Croatia). The Supreme Command cannot obey. . . . With the Italian people one has to respect the forms.[19]

There is in Italian the expression *fare una bella figura*. It is one of those cultural realities which cannot easily be translated from one language to another. It means much more than 'making a good impression' or 'creating the right image'. It can be seen in the amazement of Italians at the ill-fitting clothes and clashing colours worn by the English. It expresses itself in the automatic assumption that the visual arts belong at the centre of all primary and secondary curricula and in the excellence of Italian industrial design. How things look matter in Italy, and Marshall Cavallero who knew by late January that the war was lost and probably that he too was finished – Mussolini relieved him of his command a week later – still had to protest at the 'look' of Hitler's intention.

The German *Geist*, at least in its non-Catholic version, rejects show for substance. *Sein* (being) is more important than *Schein* (seeming). Goethe put this view into the mouth of one of the characters in his *Die Wahlverwandschaften* (Elective Affinities):

> *Das Höchste, das Vorzüglichste am Menschen ist gestaltlos und man soll sich hüten, es anders als in edler Tat zu gestalten.*[20]
> (The highest, most sublime qualities in mankind, are without form and one must beware of giving them any other form than in noble deeds.)

Nothing could be more alien from the Italian mentality than the 'formlessness of the sublime'. Sublimity reveals itself in form, shape, line and colour, in short, in the *bella figura*. The prickliness of Italian generals and diplomats about 'respecting forms' seemed to earnest Germans set on the achievement of their missions simply frivolous, childish or part of that general Italian 'inferiority complex' which German commanders used to explain all unsatisfactory Italian behaviour.

As the war headed inexorably towards an Axis defeat, and Italy's war effort collapsed, the Italian armed forces and state could only *fare*

179

una brutta figura, in effect, look 'bad'. All that remained amidst the shreds of Italian self-esteem were values: honour, humanity, compassion, *civiltà*. I cannot, of course, prove this but defeat, if anything, made Italian diplomats and soldiers even less willing to cooperate in the extermination of Jews than before. German virtues and vices represented the opposite of Italian: inwardness versus external form, substance versus show, rigour versus suppleness, the ideal versus the real, cold versus hot. Two more ill-fated and ill-suited allies could hardly be imagined.

The struggle to save the lives of a few thousand Jews turns out to depend on the extreme differences between two regimes so similar on the surface and so different beneath. Hitler's regime was serious in a way that Mussolini's was not. It dedicated its energies, its bureaucratic competence and efficient structures to try to conquer the world and to exterminate the Jews. At first the Italians found it hard to believe that anybody seriously contemplated either. By 1943 they had no doubt. Hitler would not bend. He would not negotiate. He would triumph or destroy himself and his entire regime. The Italians may have been frivolous and deluded but they were not mad. The Nazi state was deeply, inescapably and destructively mad. The two Axis partners were locked in an alliance of paradoxes and opposites. Nothing illustrated this better than the character of the two dictators.

2

TWO TYPES OF CHARISMA

It is exceptionally difficult to get Mussolini into focus. The absurdities of his posture, his jutting jaw and contemptuous lip, his hands on hips, chest thrown out, the cult of personality which required that the Duce know everything, see everything, hear everything, understand everything, which required that the light be on in his office so that passers-by would note that at any hour of the day or night the Duce was at work, provide the stuff of caricatures and gave Charlie Chaplin one of his most effective inspirations. Yet for Bottai and his generation in Italy, for the young men maddened by the experience of the trenches and disorientated by the chaotic world of peacetime, the encounter with Mussolini was 'destiny'. Antonio Salandra, sometime Prime Minister and one of the old-style politicians whom Mussolini outplayed and outmanoeuvred, offered this portrait of him:

> Enigmatic mixture alternatively of genius and vulgarity, of sincere profession of noble sentiments and of base instincts, of reprisal and vendetta, of rude frankness and badly dissimulated histrionics, of tenacious assertions and sudden changes, of effective and occasionally overwhelming eloquence adorned with culture and presumptuous ignorance expressed in plebeian language; at the core . . . an exclusive, I would say ferocious, cult of himself . . . no limits of discrimination between good and evil, no indication of a sense of the law, in general a force of nature containable only by greater forces.[21]

The image of a natural force recurs in many descriptions of Mussolini by those who knew him well, an uncontainable, explosive personality. The Russian Jewish socialist, Angelica Balabanoff, knew him in his down-and-out phase before the First World War and recalled an occasion in Lugano when Mussolini suddenly burst out, waving his arms at the well-to-do in the restaurants, 'Look, people eating, drinking and enjoying themselves. And I will travel third class, eat miserable cheap food. *Porca Madonna*! how I hate the rich! Why must I suffer this injustice? How long must we wait?'[22] Yet it was not the things of this world, riches and luxuries, that Mussolini desired. He was no Göring who accumulated rings and furs but a

181

frugal man who lived simply. What Mussolini craved was power. He said years later: 'I am obsessed by this wild desire. It consumes my whole being. I want to make a mark on my era with my will like a lion with its claws. A mark like that!'[23] With that he scratched the covering of a chair from end to end.

His sexual exploits assumed legendary proportions and a queue of countesses, movie stars, visiting lady journalists and diplomats' wives assisted him in them. His own sexuality, as he himself described it in a passage from his autobiography, was violent and unfeeling:

> I caught her on the stairs throwing her into a corner behind a door, and made her mine. When she got up weeping and humiliated, she insulted me by saying I had robbed her of her honour and it is not impossible that she spoke the truth. But I ask you, what kind of honour can she have meant?[24]

Brutality to women belonged to the expected tone among fascist leaders. Achille Starace, who served as secretary of the Fascist Party for years, used to arrive in Italian cities in full uniform covered with his medals and after strutting along the main streets would head for the principal brothel where he would demonstrate his potency by the number of times he had sex and by the brutality with which he treated prostitute and madam.[25]

The psycho-sexual aspect of the fascist movement deserves consideration. Women were there to be raped and men to be beaten or cowed. Fascist language reeks of machismo. Genital imagery can be found in Mussolini's private remarks and public speeches. Like Mozart's Don Giovanni, Mussolini had, and made sure that he was seen to have, his *mille e tre*, but he also had deep and lasting liaisons with intelligent women whom he presumably treated rather differently than the poor girl on the stairs. The journalist and biographer Margherita Sarfatti, who also happened to be Jewish, an irony in view of later events, wrote art criticism for the socialist paper *L'Avanti*, where she met and fell 'madly' for Mussolini who was then a socialist. Their relationship lasted for years and only ended when the anti-semitic racial laws made it embarrassing to the Duce.[26] He dedicated his final years to the socialite Clara Petacci, who shared his end in 1945, her corpse dangling by the feet next to his in a Milan piazza.

He also had a family and seems to have been by all accounts a concerned and attentive father. He had a particular affection for his eldest child, his daughter Edda, who married Galeazzo Ciano, later Foreign Minister. Goebbels met her on a visit to Berlin in April 1942: 'she impressed me this time as exceptionally serious and earnest. She is extremely intelligent and when one talks to her at length, she reveals herself as the real daughter of her father.'[27]

Mussolini presided over a society largely illiterate but thirsty for culture. To many of his followers he seemed an intellectual marvel, spouting Nietzsche, Sorel, Hegel, Baudelaire. He had the culture of the self-made, the insecure, the primary school headmaster in the days when the schoolmaster and the priest represented to the village the struggle between the modern world and superstition or the devil and god, depending on your view. It was to this generation that Benito Mussolini (born in 1883) belonged and appealed. He had attended (just) the necessary schools to get a teacher's training certificate and could certainly read. Above all, he could write. The brilliant journalist Paolo Monelli had fun (admittedly, after Mussolini had fallen and could not strike back) in his wonderful *Roma 1943* with Mussolini's prose.[28] Yet within months of founding his newspaper in Milan in November 1914, Mussolini's *Il Popolo d'Italia* was a commercial success.

One person whom he impressed was the equally lower middle class, equally insecure, Adolf Hitler. In one of his famous monologues during the war the Führer said:

It is a very special pleasure to meet with the Duce. He is a very great personality. Strange, that he was a building worker at the same time that I was. . . . If you walk in the Villa Borghese with him and see his head and those Roman busts before you, you feel he's one of the Roman caesars! Somehow he has the measure of a great man from that era in him. . . . When we received the Duce, we thought, that was fine, but our journey to Italy, our reception there – even with all the outmoded ceremonial – our visit to the Quirinale, that was really something else.[29]

The educated and secure were less impressed. The cultivated and well travelled Marshall Caviglia watched Mussolini strut and pretend at a reception to mark the state treaty between Italy and the new Independent State of Croatia in May 1941. He noted drily that Mussolini spoke German with Prince Bismarck, Minister of State at the German Embassy, 'to let us all see that he knows the language. The conversation between the two would have been less strained in French.'[30] A few days later Caviglia had an audience with the King:

At a certain point in the conversation he said 'the *Cavaliere* Mussolini'. And then as if talking to himself, '*Cavaliere* and so many other things'. In those few words there was the idea of his littleness of spirit and that of the charlatanism of Mussolini.[31]

Certainly, much about Mussolini may have been phoney but he was a phenomenal orator. In 1912 at the Socialist Party Convention in Reggio Emilia his violent attack on Italy's war in Libya made him nationally famous. Four months later at the age of 29, like some hero in one of F. Scott Fitzgerald's fantasies, he became editor of the main socialist party newspaper, *L'Avanti*, in Milan. He owed his success to the violence of his oratory, even if ironically it was violence against war. Mussolini spoke the extreme language of that generation of restless, half-educated, under-employed young men of the petty bourgeoisie who read little magazines, shouted at demonstrations, aroused the anger of their parents and put on celluloid collars to be clerks in insurance offices, young men who could write this sort of stuff:

What we need finally is a hot bath of black blood after all the tepid dampness of maternal tears. . . . There are too many of us. The loss of thousands of carcasses alike in the embrace of death, different only in the colour of their clothes, while not precisely a delight for the memory, will be compensated a thousand times over by the hundreds of thousands of odious, ballsed-up, crooks, idiots, wretches, bores, useless exploiters and brutes who would thus be removed from the world in a prompt noble, heroic and perhaps, who knows? even advantageous manner.[32]

Thus Giovanni Papini on 1 October 1914, as his contribution to the increasingly strident call for Italy to enter the First World War. Mussolini continued for a while to thunder the socialist party line against intervention but his impetuous nature – his enemies said French bribes – converted him. From a violent pacifist, he became a violent warmonger, betrayed his former socialist colleagues, and in a stormy meeting could be heard shouting above the din, 'You hate me . . . you hate me because you still love me!'[33]

Mussolini and Italy went to war in 1915, a war which turned from patriotic dream into bloody nightmare. The Italian army faced all the horrors of trench warfare, gas, barbed wire and the machine gun but had to do so uphill. Italy had only one serious war aim: to 'redeem' the lost Italian territories from Austrian rule. Most of these territories lay along the slopes of the mountains which ring the Italian peninsula and hence the Italo-Austrian front was one long battle from the plains up the mountains. Italian losses rank with the highest of any of the belligerents. 5,698,581 men of the age cohorts born between 1871 and 1900 served in the Italian armed forces, of whom 45.9 per cent were peasants. Of those 600,000 were killed in action and a further 100,000 died of their wounds. 946,000 were wounded.[34] In 1918 the fragile economy was wrecked, the country divided, much of its industry bloated and unproductive and the threat of Bolshevism hung over the turbulent cities. Out of this chaos, the fascist movement emerged and ultimately came to power.

In this sketch, which is, after all, meant to be background for a different story at a different time and place, I cannot say much about fascism and its rise to power in the years 1919 to 1922. Two things ought to be noted. Nobody could define its doctrine. Every time Mussolini was asked he had a different definition. It is said that one of his sons once asked him at the dinner table what fascism was and got the answer 'shut up and eat!', a not altogether misleading summary of what the movement later became. In May of 1919 Mussolini defined it this way: 'Prejudices are coats of mail or tin. . . . We don't have republican prejudices, nor monarchical ones. We don't have Catholic prejudices nor socialist or antisocialist. We are 'problemists', actualizers, realizers.'[35]

The rest of us might call Mussolini's 'prejudices' something else, principles, for example, or values, but for Mussolini the definition allowed him to be all things at all times, to move from his republican past to a monarchist future, from the exaltation of the collective to the cult of the individual, from atheism to catholicism and from socialism to capitalism. It would be a serious mistake to dismiss fascist doctrine as so much sand in the eye, a kind of intellectual shell game in which the hand is quicker than the eye. Beneath its verbiage there was an exaltation of the will as opposed to thought, and a self-conscious rejection of the ideals of the French Revolution, of liberty, equality and fraternity. Very clever people were fascists and wrote penetrating critiques of liberalism, democracy and capitalism. Mussolini understood how to use and direct them, to make them all look to him, the all-wise, for leadership. Fascism's very doctrinal flexibility made Mussolini's intellectual agility into a supreme virtue.

The other feature of fascism was violence. Unlike national socialism, which came to power by a combination of street agitation, Hitler's demagogy, skilled use of modern media, electoral success and upper-class intrigue, the fascists literally beat their way to power. From November 1920 on, little convoys of blackshirts would leap into lorries and depart to cities like Bologna, Florence or Trieste for some socialist-controlled village. There, armed with clubs and castor oil, watched benevolently by the carabinieri or the police, they would beat and humiliate the leaders and then sack the headquarters, reading rooms and union branches of the socialists. Socialists in rural communities had no weapons. Their transportation might be a rusty bicycle and, if they were lucky, there might be a telephone. They had no chance against the armed, violent ex-officers and commandos who flocked to join the fascists. Fascism clubbed its way to power in northern Italian villages and by 1922 in some cities as well. The blackshirts then decided to 'march on Rome', to make their revolution. Thirty thousand started out in late October 1922, in pouring rain and considerable disorder. The history of mankind would have been greatly improved if a single insubordinate Army commander had fired on them. A 'whiff of grapeshot' might have finished fascism in 1922 the way it seemed to have finished Hitler's Nazis on the streets of Munich a year later. But Mussolini gambled on the 'littleness' of the King and, in any case, had begun negotiations to become Prime Minister legally. In a speech in February 1921, he set out certain realities that Hitler needed a year in jail to realise:

> the revolution is not a 'jack-in-the-box' that springs up at will. . . . Now history, the collection of distant facts, teaches little to men but the chronicle of every-day events, history which takes place under our eye, ought to be more fortunate. Now, the chronicle says that revolutions are made with the army, not against the army, with arms, not without arms, with movements of organised units not with amorphous masses called out to demonstrate in the piazza.[36]

Mussolini's achievement in seizing power with a movement whose strength in the country was unknown and against the forces of order and the state whose strength was all too well known, ranks among the greatest feats of political wizardry in history. Mussolini was a remarkable man. The communist Angelo Tasca, one of the losers, knew perfectly well that he and the left had not been beaten by the hero of *The Great Dictator*: 'Mussolini was absolutely no genius; as Bolton King has justly observed, he only possessed "the inferior qualities of a statesman", but he possessed those to the highest possible degree.'[37]

Among those qualities was deep cynicism about his fellow human beings. Like Shakespeare's Caesar, he preferred 'men about me that are fat; sleek-headed men, and such as sleep o'nights'. A furious Leonardo Arpinati burst into the Duce's huge office in 1932 (one could still do that then) to protest about the appointment of Achille Starace. 'But he's a cretin!' 'I know', said the Duce without looking up from his papers, 'but a cretin who obeys'.[38]

Mussolini trusted nobody. He once remarked that he had never had a male friend,[39] and not even his closest and oldest collaborators knew his thoughts. They read of their dismissals in the newspapers. They were rarely thanked. Besides, he spied on them. In the huge empty-looking white marble palace which Mussolini intended for his museum of the armed forces in the Roman satellite city of EUR, the national archives are now housed. They include the voluminous secret correspondence of the Duce. There the student can read the reports of secret service agents who watched the movements and tapped the telephone conversations of literally everybody. They reported to the Duce that General Soddu had bought a fourteen room house and raised doubts about the sources of his funds.[40] They noted the rich lifestyle of General Cavallero, Chief of Staff, and recorded how often the general used staff cars for private business.[41]

On 20 January 1942, the Italian secret service reported on the scandalous behaviour of the Honourable Luigi Russo, from 1939 to 1943 Under-Secretary in the office of the President of the Council, the Italian equivalent of Sir Humphrey in *Yes! Prime Minister*:

> Among the functionaries of the presidency of the council lively discontent reigns because of the unserious behaviour of the Under Secretary Excellency Russo, who instead of dedicating himself during working hours to labour for the common good dedicates himself instead to personal cleanliness. In fact almost every day when he arrives at the office he takes a bath and in the bathroom has a radio and a telephone to respond to any urgent calls. In the bath he is shaved, has a manicure and takes certain injections. He receives many ladies there with whom he passes hours in long conversations.[42]

On that same day in a secluded villa on the shores of the Wannsee outside Berlin, Reinhard Heydrich of the SS called that infamous meeting to order which set the bureaucratic machinery in place for the 'final solution of the Jewish question'. Comment would be superfluous.

No wonder that even Mussolini turned from his entourage in disgust. On 25 July 1943, the morning after the Fascist Grand Council had voted a motion of no confidence in him, Mussolini turned to one of the few fascist leaders who had not betrayed him and observed bitterly:

> They have sniffed the contrary wind and felt the approaching storm, as happens with certain species of animals, and they fool themselves into creating an alibi. It never occurs to these pusillanimous creatures that when he who has raised them up on his own shoulders is no longer here, they will feel pretty miserable in the mortal dust.[43]

Mussolini too succumbed to the prevailing corruption of the regime. Surrounded by flattery and incense, he came in time to believe in his omnipotence and omniscience. Giuseppe Bottai was horrified on returning from the Ethiopian War to see what had happened to Mussolini: 'A terrible blow. . . . Not the man but a statue stood in front of me.'[44]

For years Mussolini took the great offices of state into his own hands. By 1929 he had eight of the thirteen ministerial portfolios; he presided over the fascist party, the Grand Council, the national council of corporations and the cabinet. He was Commandant General of the militia and by the outbreak of war Commander of the Armed Forces and Minister of War, the navy and the air force. He chaired or held the presidency of innumerable bodies, boards, corporations and committees.[45] Just to make sure that his creatures knew their place, he humiliated them in early 1941 by ordering all his most senior ministers (technically only under-secretaries), and the top echelon of the fascist party, to active military duty at the front.

Fascist government was chaos. Priorities were never set. The Duce concerned himself with trivia such as the day when Rome's traffic police changed from winter to summer uniforms. He spent precious hours reading and annotating reports in provincial newspapers. As always when too much power accumulates in one person, a *Camarilla* evolved. This was the word used by German observers in the late eighteenth century to describe how royal Prussian absolutism worked. It can be used to explain the American presidency under Richard Nixon or the Palazzo Venezia under Mussolini. What matters in government by *Camarilla* is not how high your office but how often you see the 'Great One'. Around Mussolini there grew up networks of favourites and friends of friends. Speculators watched the signs to see if Ciano, the son-in-law, was in the ascendant or descendant. They attached themselves to relatives of the Petacci clan, who used Clara's amorous liaison with the Duce to seek jobs and favours.

Show replaced substance. Under the egregious 'cretin' Achille Starace, the regime became obsessed by uniforms. Starace designed ever grander and more absurd uniforms and wore them himself on every conceivable occasion. One day he went to inspect an armoured unit and took a ride in a tank. As he stuck his head out of the turret, a wag cried, 'Look! There's Starace dressed as a tank.'[46] Starace designed new hats and caps for the party. One evening in 1940 during the first months of the war Piero Calamandrei, the writer, found himself staring into the window of a fashionable Roman hatter on the Corso Umberto:

The window was entirely draped in black like a funeral parlour in which twenty or so dress caps had been strung together and fixed on standing pegs also painted black. Some were Nazi types which had become modish in those years but with peaks even more sharply turned down and sullen and the crests even more protuberant and aggressive. Some were grey but most were black. On the black ones, as on funeral palls, the silver and gold of insignia and rank. At the base of each peg stood a little card indicating the rank of the hierarchy for which the appropriate head-covering was furnished: 'federal secretary', 'national councillor', 'minister', 'secretary of the party'. At each step up the hierarchy, the glitter of the stripes increased. But at the centre there was a kind of gigantic frying-pan manufactured to measure for an august macrocephalic cranium. It dominated the little frying pans of the satellites. Absolutely black, without a thread of rank but on the peak a very fierce bird of gold. Its little card explained: 'Duce'. The passers-by, still in front of the glass pane, looked at the display in silence and did not dare to look at each other.[47]

This was fascism as show, a make-believe world of marble and mannequins. Grandiose buildings went up with the dates of the regime engraved in Roman numerals to remind people that this was no government but a regime, an Empire, a world-historical cosmic phenomenon.[48] Mussolini half-seriously, and Starace wholly so, played with the idea of the 'new man', the new, aggressive, ascetic, disciplined, military man, a sort of Latin version of the Prussian general staff officer. Mussolini came back from Berlin in 1937 and immediately introduced the goose step, renamed the *passo romano*.

After the victories of the 1930s, if they can be called that, in Ethiopia and Spain, Mussolini began to make plans for the greatest show on earth, the exhibition of 1942 which would celebrate the year XX of the regime. At the same time he neglected preparations for war. It is true that the Italian state spent over a third of its budget on defence from 1936 onwards but between 1936 and 1939 the percentage of the budget allocated for the military only rose from 37.3 to 39.6 per cent.[49] At the same time, as Enrico Montovani has argued, 'the growth of productive capacity in the heavy industrial and chemical sectors was realised at the same time as there was a constant under-utilisation of the capacity of those same sectors.'[50]

Italy remained way behind the other great powers in manufacturing capacity. In 1937 the United States produced 4.11 times the Italian total in manufactured products per head of population, Great Britain 3.28 times, Germany 2.72 and France 2.11.[51] In 1938 Italy was behind Germany, Czechoslovakia, Great Britain, Sweden and Hungary in the proportion of gross national product derived from industry.[52] The Italian economy depended heavily on imported coal. In 1939 Italy imported a million tonnes of coal a month, three-quarters of which came by sea.[53]

Eighty years of bathos and rhetoric eroded the national ability to see such facts. The regime went to war with no serious war aims, no credible war machine and no reliable information. No assessment of 'national interest' had been made. Shrewdness in political fixing combined in varying proportions in the same person with effusions of empty phrases and false emotions. Indeed, one of the oddest aspects of Italy's war from 1940 to 1943 was the vagueness of its declared aims. Certainly there were territories to seize, nominally or historically Italian (that is, Venetian), factually Slovenian, Croatian, Montenegrin or Greek. But Italian soldiers rarely, if ever, spoke of the Second World War as a war of conquest. Sometimes generals like Geloso, in a plea for more troops for his Greek command, would speak of 'a territory which has been defined, and is, our vital space',[54] but nobody defined what 'vital space' meant. More common was to avoid discussing concrete war aims by clouding them in high-flown rhetoric. A not untypical example was the order of the day issued by General Vittorio Ambrosio on his assumption of the post as Chief of the General Staff of the Army in January 1942:

> Faith, passion, discipline in the vision of a greater fatherland, are the ideals from which each must draw in every contingency the force necessary to follow the road which will lead us to certain victory. I send a special and sincere greeting in this moment to those comrades who everywhere from the endless deserts of Africa to the gelid plains of Russia are fighting valorously to reaffirm, in a world purified by the blood of heroes, the imperishable grandeur of Rome.[55]

Ambrosio's order of the day owed more to Verdi than to Mussolini. There was no mention of the Duce, fascism or any ideology other than traditional nationalist romanticism. The alpini and bersaglieri who had to light candles to unfreeze their faces each time they came in from 'the gelid plains of Russia' would have been surprised to know that they were there to re-establish the Roman Empire.

It cannot be chance that for much of its modern history Italian foreign policy manoeuvred the country into 'unnatural' and dangerous alliances. There was built into Italian political life before 1940 an almost automatic mechanism of self-deception. Mussolini did not invent the politics of illusion and false grandeur. He inherited them from his liberal forebears, from Mazzini, Garibaldi, Balbo and Crispi. They too had rejected the world as it was for a world made new by rhetoric and will. Giuseppe Bottai, a fascist of 'the first hour', as original members of the party were called, and perhaps the most intelligent or, at least, most reflective of Mussolini's immediate entourage, recorded this truth in an extraordinary letter to his son, written in 1944 just before going off to 'expiate' by joining the French Foreign Legion at the age of 50:

Look, I and many of my generation . . . were raised to trust above all in ourselves, which is to say in our wills, that which made us consider our creative powers without limits more than in our consciences which would have revealed our limits. From that arose our voluntarism, our *arditismo* [a type of commando troop during the First World War], our combativeness, our 'Duce-ism'.[56]

Italy belonged among the underdeveloped or developing states of Europe throughout the years between 1870 and 1940. It depended on peasant agriculture like Russia or Spain and even as late as 1936 over 50 per cent of its people farmed either as landless peasants (16.2 per cent) or as direct cultivators (35.6 per cent).[57] It had the typical age structure of developing countries, with over 30 per cent of its population under 14 years of age,[58] and it exported surplus people to every corner of the world. Between 1901 and 1955 16,067,000 Italians emigrated, some several times, of whom 5,978,000 repatriated, leaving over 10 million Italians overseas – in the USA, Australia, Argentina, Chile, Canada and so on.[59]

Grand gestures by romantic nationalists could not conceal (or at least not entirely) the real Italy: poor, illiterate, hostile to an alien Piedmontese dynasty which had not even been able to win its wars by itself. True nationalists like Mazzini were disgusted. After the froth of the Garibaldian era, its red shirts, demonstrations and patriotic cries, there followed corruption, clients, mafia and impotence. As that great sceptic Pirandello observed in his political novel written in 1909, *I vecchi e i giovanni*, 'Ah, in truth, it's a terrible fate, that of the hero who does not die, of the hero who outlives himself. In fact the hero truly dies always, with the moment: the man survives and feels bad.'[60]

That was the Italian problem. It survived and 'felt bad', restless, dissatisfied and inferior. It constructed monuments in inverse proportion to the grandeur of daily life. At the end of the Corso in Rome in 1911 the kingdom of Italy built the 'Vittoriano', perhaps the most grotesque monument in Europe, to mark the fiftieth anniversary of unification. There it stands, a huge, hideous white slice of marble which overshadows the forum of the real Caesars, inflated rhetoric in stone. Then there is the '*palazzaccio*', the Palace of Justice on the Piazza Cavour, so laden with allegorical figures, marble ornaments and friezes that at one point it threatened to sink into the mud of the Tiber.

The regime was riddled with corruption topped by a kind of zany frivolity. Some incidents defy belief. The Chief of the Italian General Staff, Marshall Ugo Cavallero, refused to accept General von Horstig's offer of the new German Panther tank at 9.45 a.m. on Sunday 6 December 1942, because the Italian P40 was 'in programme of construction', only to be told by General Ago at 10.45 that 'in reality the P40 does not exist'.[61] This sort of incompetence, led the German Major Friedrich Karl von Plehwe, who served under Rintelen at the Italian Supreme Command, to remark:

The superficial and often corrupt fascist leadership was guilty of the fact that the Italian troops did not even get the few supplies that the country could have delivered. Year after year Italian officers looked enviously from a close angle of vision at the excellent equipment of the German forces. The majority of them rejected the fascist regime on these grounds alone. Out of rejection hate gradually grew and there was mounting tension between soldiers and blackshirts. This tension slowly eroded fascism from within.[62]

Early in December 1942 Bottai noted in his diary: 'The drama of a regime begins when it is not capable of finding the truth and finishes when it no longer has the will to seek it. The only question is whether we are in the first or the second phase.'[63]

Fascism had certainly reached Bottai's first phase well before the outbreak of the Second World War. The succession of defeats and the discovery of the holocaust shook the Italian leadership out of its dreams. During 1943 Mussolini and his henchmen had to face some very harsh realities. The little dialogue at Treviso in July 1943, when Mussolini explained why a separate peace made no sense, suggests that at the end the Duce regained his grip on the limits of the possible. Bolder spirits, such as Bastianini, could once again tell him the truth – too late to save the regime. Yet in the final analysis, when Mussolini fell from power in July 1943, he did so sane.

It is much less clear that Hitler was ever entirely sane. In May of 1905 the young Adolf Hitler arrived in Vienna. The city charmed him by its glitter and the splendour of its buildings. As he wrote in *Mein Kampf*

From morning until late at night I ran from one object of interest to another, but it was always the buildings that held my primary interest. For hours I could stand in front of the Opera, for hours I could gaze at the parliament. The whole Ring Boulevard seemed to me like an enchantment out of a 'Thousand-and-one-Nights'.[64]

Vienna had more than buildings to offer the young art student. There were plays at the *Burgtheater* and opera. At 'the mighty waves of sound', as he wrote to his friend Kubizek, and 'the fearful rush of billows of music', he felt 'sublimity',[65] the authentic transcendence of self which German prophets of cultural ecstasy had been preaching for a century. He absorbed the most dangerous element of German *Kultur*, its intoxication of reason.

There was much in Viennese culture to intoxicate. In art there was the Secession school of Klimt and Kokoschka; in architecture there was the modern school of Otto Wagner and Adolf Loos. This was the Vienna of the late Brahms, of Mahler, Richard Strauss, Schoenberg, Webern and Berg; of the writers Hofmannstahl, Schnitzler, Musil and Kraus; of the philosophers Mach, Brentano, Husserl and Buber; of the great Austrian school of economics of Menger, Böhm-Bawerk, Schumpeter and von Wieser. There was an Austro-Marxist school of socialism which included Victor Adler, Rudolf Hilferding, Karl Kautsky and Otto Bauer. Sigmund Freud and Alfred Adler practised the new psychiatry and read Vienna's best newspaper *Die Neue Freie Presse*, whose literary editor Theodor Herzl founded the Zionist movement. Vienna served its famous cakes covered in thick cream and gentlemen kissed hands. It was quite a place.

Yet Hitler never accepted the 'modern' side of Viennese culture. His own artistic tastes belonged to the neo-classical, the grandiose, the Wagnerian styles of the 1880s. He loved opera houses, their external pomposities and their internal plush. When the Germans overran France, he sent his agent Colonel Heim to purchase the library of the producer and critic Edward Gordon Craig, whose collection on opera houses was unique. He astonished his hosts in Paris by his knowledge of the structure of the Paris opera. The Vienna opera, its programme and its architecture, remained his ideal: a provincial petty bourgeois' dream of paradise.

Hitler associated the 'modern' aspects of Viennese culture with Jews, and not without some reason. In the first place Vienna had a great many Jews. By 1910 there were 175,318 Jews in Vienna, 8.6 per cent of a total population of 2,031,498 residents.[66] One-third of all the Jews lived in the Leopoldstadt district, usually Eastern European Jews with beards and caftans, people who had poured into the city from Galicia, one of the poorest and also, with sixty-nine inhabitants per square kilometre, one of the most thickly settled regions in Europe.[67] Jews played a prominent role in other cities of the Empire, in Budapest where they dominated the businesses and professions or Prague where one half of those who gave German, not Czech, as their native language in the pre-war censuses were Jews.[68]

Jews stood out in the sunburst of Viennese culture before 1914. Psychiatry was embarrassingly 'Jewish' in Freud's opinion which was why he welcomed Jung so heartily. The main newspaper of Vienna, *Die Neue Freie Presse*, had a Jewish owner and editor. Many leading journalists, playwrights, composers and authors were Jewish. The second generation of the Austrian school of economists was mainly Jewish and practically all of the leaders of Austrian socialism. Hitler began to notice that

> Vienna appeared to me in a different light than before. Wherever I went I began to see Jews, and the more I saw the more sharply they became distinguished in my eyes from the rest of humanity. Particularly the inner city and the districts north of the Danube Canal swarmed with a people which even outwardly had lost all resemblance to Germans . . . it became positively repulsive when, in addition to their physical uncleanliness you discovered the moral stains on the 'chosen people'. . . . Was there any form of filth or profligacy, particularly in cultural life, without at least one Jew involved in it? If you cut even cautiously into such an abcess, you found, like a maggot in a rotting body, often dazzled by the sudden light – a kike![69]

This passage tells us some important things. In the first place Hitler attacks Jews for their uncleanliness physically and by extension morally. Jews stain, corrupt and pollute culture. For him and many of his class and generation, the Vienna of the free spirit, of the new sexuality and new art, was profoundly threatening. The modern came in many forms, from the Jewish department store which threatened the small trader to the Jewish novelist who wrote about sex. Whereas Mussolini drew on, and allied with, futurism and other wilder forms of modern artistic activity, Hitler recoiled from it all and later had all such work removed from museums and declared 'degenerate'.

Nazism resembled in this respect the revolution in mores which swept America during the 1920s. Prohibition attacked the drinking habits of the alien immigrants and the Ku Klux Klan attacked them physically. Small-town Americans defended their Bible Belt morality with the same dread and tenacity that Hitler defended Germanic culture. Both feared and hated the city, the smart set, the modern woman and the Jew. The passage above was, of course, not written when Hitler was in Vienna but in 1924, when he spent time in prison after his abortive putsch in Munich, the very year in which an American democratic party convention could not bring itself to accept a Roman Catholic, cigar-smoking, big city politician as its candidate for president and took over a hundred ballots to say so.

The substitution of 'clean' for 'good' is a marked feature of SS documents and German army language. Areas are 'cleansed' of partisans and Jews. The *Obersturmbannführer* writes of his 'cleanliness' in the performance of his duties. *'Sauber'* (clean) is an adjective of high praise. Hitler shared those values, and paid particular attention until near the end to his personal appearance. Dr Henry Picker, who recorded his table talk, recalls that even on the morning of his suicide he shaved

with the same care as normal . . . and in general never failed to carry out his morning toilet with petty bourgeois pedantry: to put on his souvenir cuff-links with the coat of arms of the City of Danzig, his large silver, stem-wound pocket watch which he inherited from his father (which he always forgot to wind), and his wallet in which he always carried a picture of his father, his mother, his sister and himself (as a baby and as a boy with his father).[70]

Picker's description of Eva Braun makes the same point about her: 'she was always like an egg freshly peeled and in her intimate things scrupulously clean, punctual and accurate.'[71] Those three adjectives – *sauber*, *pünktlich* and *akkurat* – make a marked contrast with the 'dirty' sexuality of Italian values and they also show how secondary virtues had come in German thinking to replace primary. Cleanliness is supposed to be next to Godliness but is not Godliness itself. The virtues of love, compassion, fellow-feeling and warmth, disappear behind 'clean', 'punctual' and 'accurate'.

Jews became maggots, germs, dirt, rottenness, putrefaction. In Hitler's disordered fancy, he must wage a constant war against infection. In April 1943 he told Admiral Horthy: 'They had to be handled like tubercular baccili which could infect a healthy body. That wasn't horrible when one thought about the fact that innocent creatures of nature like hares and deer had to be killed to prevent damage.'[72]

The basic argument behind Hitler's madness was pure social darwinism. A few weeks after his talk with Horthy he told Goebbels:

One might well ask why there are any Jews in the world order? That would be exactly like asking why there are potato bugs? Nature is dominated by the law of struggle. There will always be parasites who will spur this struggle on and intensify the process of selection between the strong and the weak. The principle of struggle dominates also in human life. One must merely know the law of this struggle to be able to face it. The intellectual does not have the natural means of resisting the Jewish peril because his instincts have been badly blunted. Because of this fact nations with a high standard of living are exposed to this peril first and foremost. In nature life always takes measures against parasites; in the life of nations that is not always the case. From this fact the Jewish peril actually stems. There is therefore no other recourse left for modern nations except to exterminate the Jew.[73]

It's crazy but, like much paranoia, within its mad world utterly coherent. We don't know when Hitler first formulated these ideas but we do know he never changed them. Indeed, as Sebastian Haffner has pointed out, Hitler never changed in any way. He said the same things in 1920 as in 1945. There was no growth, no change, no learning from experience. As Haffner puts it:

> In his life there is no 'before' and 'after', everything which normally gives to human life its weight, warmth and worth. . . . [Hitler's was] a life without content, and therefore not exactly a happy life but a life curiously weightless, lightly thrown away. Constant readiness to kill himself accompanies Hitler's entire career and at the end there is a real, perfectly self-explanatory suicide.[74]

Hitler was certainly one of the strangest human beings ever to govern a great state. He had strange diet fetishes and nocturnal habits. He had no wife nor children and there is much debate about his sexual activity, if there was any. He had no friends during his adult life and certainly no equals. All his entourage feared him and in the entire history of the Nazi Party there is not one example of a serious attempt to oppose him. The behaviour of a Farinacci or an Arpinati would have been unthinkable in Hitler's case. He dominated his military advisers completely. Grand Admiral Dönitz summed it up as late as September, 1943:

> The enormous strength which the Führer radiates, his unswerving confidence, his far-sighted appraisal of the Italian situation, have made it utterly clear that we are all very insignificant in comparison with him. . . . Anybody who believes he can do better than the Führer is silly.[75]

Hitler appointed General, later Field Marshall, Wilhelm Keitel to the post of chief of the OKW. Keitel rapidly earned a variety of nicknames for his servility. To some he was the *Lackeitel*, a pun on *Lackei*, the German word for lackey; to others he was the *Nickesel*, the nodding donkey, a child's toy. He was, in any case, no threat to Hitler.

Hitler really commanded his troops in a way that Mussolini never could. He studied maps and received reports. He moved and removed field marshalls. He allocated units down to the divisional level. He made binding orders for his troops. And he was on the whole very good at it. Colonel General Alfred Jodl, later to be second to Keitel in the command structure, noticed in September 1938 that the generals 'cannot believe any more nor obey because they do not see the Führer's genius. In part it's because they see the corporal of the First World War and not the greatest statesman since Bismarck.'[76]

Jodl's reference to Bismarck brings us back in a sense to the origins of Prussia. The Prussian state emerged from the chaos of early modern Germany not by 'natural' means but through acts of will by remarkable individuals. The Great Elector, Frederick William I, Frederick the Great, Bismarck and now Hitler, a line of 'genius-statesmen', who could will the world to be what they desired. As in the case of Italian fascism, Prussian political culture suffered from voluntarism but in a much more extreme form. There was no tradition of collective decision-making, of give-and-take, of discussion at the highest level. In the three centuries from 1640 to 1945 which span the arc from the beginning to the end of Prussia, there were only fourteen years of more or less democratic government. No wonder that Hitler's diplomatic successes and lightning victories in 1940 earned him the title of 'Grösster Feldherr aller Zeiten', the greatest commander of all times.

History and self in Hitler's case had become intertwined. His sense of mission was so powerful that he came to believe that anything not accomplished in his own lifetime would never happen. Hence he had to hurry the process of history by his own titanic acts of will. He built no permanent structures and made no provision for his succession. His was the most extreme version of that Wagnerian tendency in German culture to see achievement as Alles oder Nichts, and, if nothing, then complete and utter destruction, bringing the Reich and all its works crashing down in a colossal Götterdämmerung.

As a military strategist Hitler was both genius and self-destructive. He commanded his armies directly. He ordered units to take positions and followed their activity down to divisional level. He imposed his will on the scions of the greatest military tradition in Europe and his early successes silenced the doubters. Yet his strategy, as Sir Harry Hinsley writes, reflected his temperament: 'desperate before it had need to be. . . . Frustration, moreover, the tendency to manufacture desperation, was only one side of his peculiar temperament; wilfulness and false confidence were the other, and logically complementary, characteristics.'[77]

His attitude to the German people was cool. He seems to have felt neither affection nor loyalty. As he said to his entourage at the end, the German people had proved itself to be weak, 'and would therefore cease to play a role among the peoples of the earth. . . . The weaker people no longer has any requirements of life.'[78] There was, therefore, no need to worry about its future. He would perish and the German people with him.

He inherited another tradition from his Prussian predecessors: an utter incapacity to organize decision-making. Around the greatest of Prussian kings there had always been cliques struggling for power.

Frederick the Great who trusted nobody multiplied agencies to watch each other. Under the Kaiser, decision-making had been a Hobbesian war of all against all. Under Hitler, as Ciano observed, there were 'at least four foreign policies – Hitler's, Göring's Neurath's, Ribbentrop's, without counting the minor ones.'[79]

The Hobbesian struggle of all against all swirled around Hitler's throne and had profound implications for the Axis. Von Ribbentrop declared Italy his turf and defended it against rivals, especially the SS. Early in the war he paid a state visit. It was not a great success, at least not on the Italian side. Ciano noted in his diary: 'In the last few days Ribbentrop has wanted to meet many people both inside and outside political circles. Everybody disliked him.'[80]

Poor von Ribbentrop never won the hearts of his Italian allies. He seemed to them garrulous, facile and always too optimistic. A dapper, grey-haired man, who had been a champagne salesman in an earlier incarnation, Ribbentrop owed his position to a capacity for intrigue and a leech-like devotion to Hitler's person. He understood perfectly the rules of survival at the court of the Führer, the chief of which was: 'stick close to the leader'. As the war went on, Ribbentrop spent more and more time riding in the armoured railway carriage which took the Führer from one gloomy lair to another. By late 1942 Ciano recorded how Ribbentrop spent his days:

> The atmosphere is heavy. To the bad news there should perhaps be added the sadness of that damp forest and the boredom of collective living in the Command barracks. There isn't a spot of colour, not one vivid note. Waiting rooms filled with people smoking, eating, chatting. Kitchen odour, smell of uniforms, of boots. All this is in great measure unnecessary at least for a mass of people who have no reason to be here. First among them is Ribbentrop, who compels the greater number of his employees to live a senseless troglodite life which, in fact, impedes his normal work as Foreign Minister.[81]

Clever as he was, Ciano missed a point that his friend Bottai noticed at the same time. In Europe at war and under German occupation there was not much scope for Herr von Ribbentrop to play statesman:

> In the progressive disappearance of the 'foreign' for the Ministry of Foreign Affairs, the latter tends to involve itself with the domestic affairs of the occupied countries. And since nobody remotely intends to restore those countries to any sort of autonomy, Ribbentrop and his men are kept busy in the new order, avoiding a constant emptying of their function. By now

there is a European 'domestic policy' which replaces the old 'foreign policy'.[82]

In the struggle to control occupied Europe's 'domestic policy', Ribbentrop, no matter how close he stuck to Hitler, could never win against the army and the black empire of the SS. Italy and Denmark became the only states on the European continent under Nazi control which had not been dissolved, annexed, reconstituted or rendered puppets, in effect the one sphere of foreign policy left in which von Ribbentrop could play Bismarck. Stockholm and Berne were not worthy of the attentions of a great imperial pro-consul like Foreign Minister von Ribbentrop, but Rome, now that was something, as Hitler put it, 'entirely different'. Von Ribbentrop visited Italy as frequently as he could and guarded it against his Nazi rivals in the murky world which surrounded Hitler. One reason that the Italian army could save Jews was that Ribbentrop had an interest in saving Italy.

Military matters were no more coherent. General Bader, commanding a big anti-partisan operation in the summer of 1942 in Yugoslavia, observed bitterly that 'the left hand does not know what the right hand is doing'.[83] General Alexander Freiherr von Neubronn, German general attached to the Vichy government, described the sheer number of overlapping military commands in France:

> Since the numerous agencies at the dictatorial summit constantly fought one another, there developed in government and the conduct of the war a chaos. . . . Without contact with one another the following agencies reported directly to the centre: Supreme Commander West, Military Commander France, Supreme Commander (Navy) France. Supreme Commander (Air) France, the Armistice Commission, the Embassy in Paris, the leader of the territorial unit of the Nazi Party, the SS, the Gestapo, the Organisation Todt, the representative of the Ministry of Propaganda, the Service Unit of Military Counter-Intelligence, the Border Patrol Command and so on.[84]

A world-historical genius-statesman cannot make decisions in committee. By definition he is great and the others, to use Dönitz's word, are 'insignificant'. Exactly the opposite happens under democracy. Churchill certainly dominated the British war machine but he had to listen to opponents and rivals in the cabinet. He had to go to the House of Commons, where, as his secretary John Colville recorded in his diary in 1944, he had to put up with 'hours of Parliamentary knock-about'.[85] The irony is that the apparent wastefulness of British procedure produced more efficient war planning. Churchill's aides were not 'insignificant'. He had to listen and in that give-and-take the wisest course was more likely to emerge.

The genius-statesman can be wrong and at Stalingrad was. Nobody had the nerve or standing to say so. The genius-statesman might not know something but unless he asked he would not find out. Absolute rule corrupts all subordinates. It compels them to lie to their lord in order to stay near power. Since their position rests on the whim of the All-Highest, they must fight to please. These characteristics repeated themselves at lower levels of the hierarchy. General von Neubronn remarked of his contemporaries:

> One of the most marked characteristics of Germans is the tendency to regard their own persons as particularly important, an attitude whose roots are, perhaps, to be sought in the inner insecurity of the normal German, in his 'uncertain arrogance', as a foreigner once shrewdly observed.[86]

Hitler's agencies could not co-operate since to co-operate meant to reduce one's importance or the importance of one's office relative to that of another. There was a grotesque and lengthy jurisdictional dispute between *Gruppenführer* (SS equivalent to *Generalmajor*) Meyszner and *Gruppenführer* Turner, two of the most brutal SS mass murderers in the Balkans. Both frequently appealed directly to Himmler. In a letter of 28 April 1942, Meyszner refuses to accept documents with Turner's notes on them:

> Be assured, my dear Turner, that I have no wish to lose myself in small matters . . . but on the other hand I can hardly avoid the feeling that, receiving documents with marginal comments by you written in blue crayon, I am merely your executive assistant. . . .
> I must, of course, make certain to keep my area of jurisdiction in my hands and to reserve to myself final decision-making power.[87]

The Meyszner-Turner correspondence went on for six months, involved at least twenty letters, and busied the SS hierarchy right to the top. The personal files of SS officers in the Berlin Document Centre are stiff with this kind of stuff. Jurisdictional battles are not random excrescences but part of the way the Hitler state had to operate. If all lines of authority are vertical, no horizontal agreement is conceivable. Traditions of Prussian bureaucratic clarity become horrid travesties in the struggle to gain areas of competence for the slaughter of human beings.

This makes the question of Hitler's role in the destruction of the Jews more problematical than it might at first appear. How could such a chaotic state have killed Jews apparently so systematically? No specific order by Hitler to destroy the Jews has ever been found. Two schools of historical argument have evolved. One which sees Hitler as the originator and moving force in the final solution, with or without a specific order, and the other which sees the destruction of the Jews as a response of the chaotic machinery of the Nazi state moving slowly in a general direction, certainly with Hitler's blessing but not entirely under his control. No serious historian denies that Hitler was ultimately responsible for the murder of the Jews; they debate his precise share in ordering it. Hitler's air adjutant, Major von Below, who spent eight years at the Führer's elbow, had no doubt:

> In any case I am absolutely convinced, even without a written order, that the destruction of the Jews has its source in an explicit order of Hitler, since it is unthinkable that Himmler or Göring would have undertaken something like that without his knowing it.[88]

Hitler's staff took pains to make sure that nothing went to him in writing. From the beginning of the murder operations, as Gerald Fleming has shown, Martin Bormann told Hitler's Chief of Chancellery that 'the Führer's Chancellery must under no circumstances be seen to be active in this matter'.[89] He and they used a variety of codes known as *Sprachregelung* (control of speech) to avoid saying to him and to each other exactly what they were doing. General Jodl told the Nuremberg judges that the final solution had been 'a masterpiece of secrecy'.[90]

The Italians simply could not fathom the fixity of Hitler's purposes. The psycho-historian, Peter Loewenberg, argues that the Jew played an important role in the structure of Hitler's ego:

> Hitler's anti-semitism was of a psychotic quality. All lustful, evil and sadistic parts of himself were projected onto Jews. He remained good, pure and righteous. The Jews were a projection of split off 'bad' feeling about himself. He had to get these feelings away from himself and out to where they could be destroyed. Hence the paranoid defence.[91]

Hitler was unique and uniquely responsible for what happened in Germany betwen 1933 and 1945, but he could not do everything himself. He had helpers at every stage. Reactionary generals like Ludendorff supported him in the early days. Later others from the elite assisted him to power in 1933. Almost without exception they underestimated him, but then insiders always do. The fact that insiders know the rules of the game makes them unfit to assess a Napoleon or a Hitler. What they can never envisage is how the

Napoleons and Hitlers intend to violate those rules. Hitler made foolish the wisdom of the wise.

On 4 May 1965, just over twenty years after Hitler's suicide, Albert Speer in Spandau prison tried to sum up Hitler's character:

Lately in these days full of memory I have been considering how after twenty years I would characterise Hitler today. I believe I know less than I did. Thinking about it increases the difficulties and makes him more impenetrable. Naturally I am fully clear about the judgement of history. But I wish I knew how to portray the man. Of course I could say that he was cruel, unjust, unapproachable, cold, uncontrolled, self-pitying and common, and he was, in fact, all those things. At the same time he was the exact opposite of practically all of them. He could be a thoughtful master, a considerate superior, charming, self-controlled and capable of enthusiasm for everything fine and great. Only two terms occur to me which cover all his characteristics and are the common denominator of these many contrasts: opaque and insincere. Today, in retrospect, I am still uncertain when and where he was really himself without acting, tactical considerations or sheer pleasure in lying for its own sake. I could not even say what he felt for me – real sympathy or mere considerations of my usefulness.

I don't even know what he felt for Germany. Did he love this country even a little bit or was it only an instrument of his plans? And what, I have asked myself many times since our discussions of my plans, did he really feel at the end of the Reich? Did he suffer?[92]

Speer had known Hitler well. For twenty years in Spandau Prison, where he served his time as a war criminal, he had thought of little else. If he could not make sense of Hitler, historians may be excused for not doing better. Yet one thing is clear: Hitler genuinely liked Mussolini. In July 1941 he told his entourage that 'a meeting with the Duce is always a special joy; he is a very great personality'.[93] *SS Obersturmbannführer* Eugen Dollmann, who was the German Embassy's expert on Roman high society, its translator and spy, often saw the two dictators together in the course of his duties:

The greatest political love of Hitler's life was undoubtedly Mussolini, a love which suffered under constant changes, but it was a sadness for the Führer that the one foreigner whom he really admired should belong to a nation . . . which in his heart he despised. . . . At the end there remained a limitless adoration of the Duce for the miracle achieved under such adverse conditions.[94]

They had, of course, much in common. Both suffered from what Paolo Monelli called the *'complesso del caporale'*, the corporal's complex,[95] that sense of inferiority and resentment at the generals, the diplomats, the royal princes, the elegant and upper-class members of the establishment who tittered behind gloved hands at the bad taste and habits of their new masters. Hitler and Mussolini would fume together at the perfidy of the upper classes and after 20 July Hitler had many of them filmed in their death throes to slake what von Hassell called his 'intensified hatred of the upper class'.[96] After he lost contact with his boyhood companions, Hitler never had a friend and certainly no equal. Mussolini was the only human being in the world with whom Hitler could share his experiences. They often met alone and no one knew what passed between them. Mussolini spoke goodish German but never good enough to follow Hitler's torrents of words. Still those summits often left Mussolini 'elated', as Ciano noticed, and mattered very much to Hitler.

In late November 1943 the Croatian Minister of Defence had an audience with the Führer. By then fascism had collapsed and Mussolini fallen. Hitler had kidnapped him from Italian imprisonment in one of the most daring feats of the war and set him up in a puppet regime on the shores of Lake Garda, the nasty little Repubblica Sociale Italiana. Mussolini had sunk to the level of a Pavelić, a Laval or a Quisling. The Croatian used the occasion to try to complain about the ridiculous Italian demands for Dalmatian territory and began to expatiate on the absurdity of Mussolini's policy. Hitler cut him off: 'He said more speaking to himself than to me, ". . . Mussolini helped me in difficult hours, I have certain obligations towards him."'[97] Acute observers noticed how Hitler went out of his way to spare Mussolini's feelings. Their 'cordial friendship', as General Ugo Cavallero called it,[98] was a fixed point in the relations between the Axis partners. Goebbels noted in his diary in March 1942 that

the Führer is very much attached to Mussolini and regards him as the only guarantor of German-Italian collaboration. The Italian people and Fascism will stick to our side as long as Mussolini is there. . . . The Führer really intended to present him with a new Condor plane but will refrain from doing so because he knows that Mussolini will immediately take the stick, and in case anything were to happen to him, he [Hitler] would never forgive himself.[99]

The following year Mussolini celebrated his 60th birthday three days after the Fascist Grand Council had ejected him from his office. His faithful friend Hitler stood by him in his moment of despair and to cheer him up sent him a carefully chosen present for his birthday: the complete works of Nietzsche bound in blue leather, ornamented with gold lettering and bearing the dedication on the title page in Hitler's hand: 'Adolf Hitler to his dear Benito Mussolini'.[100]

A normal human being with family, friends, ordinary eating habits and untroubled sleep cannot easily enter the distorted universe of Adolf Hitler. No writer has ever produced a satisfactory likeness and all biographies of Hitler fail to convey the full awfulness of the subject. But Hitler's relationship to Mussolini makes sense to me. In the cold loneliness of his 'mission', in the certainty of his genius and yet the urgent awareness of his own mortality, Hitler valued Mussolini above all men, the one human being able to share that isolation. There is an unforgettable photograph taken on 20 July 1944. Hitler, who had narrowly survived the explosion in the conference room at the *Wolfschanze* – his uniform spattered with stains, moustache and eye-brows singed and half-deafened by the pressure, went to greet Mussolini who had arrived for a visit. There they stand, both reduced, old before their years, two evil and destructive men but still tied to each other.

The 'brutal friendship' between Hitler and Mussolini, as F.W. Deakin called it, had profound consequences for the conduct of the war. As Mussolini's position weakened, Hitler propped him up and tolerated the incompetence and treachery of his henchmen. Mussolini gradually came to fear Hitler's power over him. By 1943 he would curse Hitler to his staff but emerge from conferences with him dazed and submissive. Marshall Caviglia in his bitter retirement summed up this aspect:

> There's no doubt that the war is lost but now it's no longer a nazi or fascist war. It's Hitlerian and Mussolinian. Hitler and Mussolini can never yield; if they yielded, they would be liquidated for ever. Therefore the war will continue and continue to the bitter end . . . as long as there's a table leg to burn, Hitler and Mussolini will want to continue the war.[101]

Another consequence arose from the nature of the Nazi state. In the midst of its chaos the 'Führer's wish' made law and guided action. The Führer wished to assist Mussolini, and all the satraps of the regime had to act accordingly. Even brutes like Martin Luther, the Foreign Office's man responsible for extermination of Jews, reminded his subordinates 'to be careful of Italian sensitivities'.[102] *Reichsführer SS* Heinrich Himmler made sure that his officials in the field recognized clear limits in dealing with Italians. In May of 1942 Himmler called *Gruppenführer* Meyszner, the police chief in occupied Serbia, to order:

Bear in mind that you are a Higher SS and Police Leader of Adolf Hitler's Reich, of the Führer, whom a close and cordial friendship unites with the congenial Duce Benito Mussolini. Of course we find a lot to complain about in the behaviour of individual Italians; in similar form they will object to things we do. That makes no difference. We are allies and only as such strong. Permit no jokes or other criticisms of the Italians but represent the line of the Axis to Germans and above all to foreigners.[103]

Hitler's affection for Mussolini gave the Italians some limited freedom to follow policies which frustrated German plans, irritated German field commanders, interfered with SS and Gestapo activities and from time to time produced an outburst of Hitler's legendary rage. Yet he stayed true to the 'congenial Duce' and accepted behaviour from the Italians which he tolerated nowhere else in his dark empire. The Italian army could save Jews in part because Hitler let them as he let them do other things of which he disapproved.

The two dictators shared a common fate and exercised power in ways which resembled each other so much that they gave rise to theories about totalitarianism and totalitarian states. They felt a kinship shared by nobody else. Hitler felt affection for Mussolini; Mussolini found Hitler repellent and yet exhilarating, hypnotically powerful, ultimately frightening. Yet on the cultural level they represented polar opposites. Mussolini, however violent, sensual, brutal and self-dramatizing, made contact with fellow human beings and remained firmly rooted in reality. Hitler, frigid, remote, isolated and strange, took leave of it. Mussolini belonged to the tradition of cynical and depraved *condottieri*, half Machiavelli and half Cesare Borgia. Hitler had no predecessors save, perhaps, in the wild imaginations of ecstatic philosophers of the irrational.

3

THE TWO ARMIES

The *Wehrmacht* and the *Regio Esercito Italiano* fought alongside each other in Africa, the Balkans and on the Russian front. As with the two regimes and the two dictators similarities tended to mask profound differences. The German army had a long tap root which reached back to the traditions of the Prussian state. It had a rich history and an exceptional record of military success. The Royal Italian Army had neither the one nor the other. Italy had been divided like Germany but none of its constituent states had been even remotely as dominant within the circle of Italian states as Prussia within Germany. The Kingdom of Piedmont under the House of Savoy had been too weak to unify Italy without foreign intervention, and the Piedmontese army had suffered humiliating defeats at the hands of the Austrians. It fought bravely during the First World War but then too had not escaped humiliation and near collapse.

Not much had changed by the 1930s. The Royal Italian Army had not distinguished itself in the Spanish Civil War and had lost a great deal of equipment as well as prestige. General von Rintelen, who visited the *scuola di guerra* in Turin, Italy's most famous staff college, came away depressed:

> Unlike the German military academy, which gave instruction in tactics priority as the most important subject, the Italian Army placed the problem of supply in the foreground of the lessons. The procedure of instruction in tactics was very schematic.[104]

Giolitti, the former Prime Minister, once called the Italian officer corps a bunch of 'black sheep and half wits'.[105] They were certainly too old. Italian senior officers were on average five to ten years older than their German counterparts. I made a comparison of the ages of the officers who appeared in the 'Events', which shows that on 1 May 1943 all the Italian army commanders and the Chief of the General Staff were in their 60s, while the German field marshalls and generals in the Balkan theatre or the Mediterranean were in their 50s. One or two German corps commanders like Hubert Lanz were still in their 40s.[106] Alberto Pirelli discovered to his horror that General Alfredo Dallolio was still at his post in 1939 as Chief of Procurement at the age of 87.[107] Promotion in the Italian Army was slow and cumbersome. In January 1943 Field Marshall Kesselring explained to Marshall Cavallero the new system of rapid promotion in the *Wehrmacht*. Cavallero noted that

> according to the new German law it happens that a captain can command a regiment and be promoted colonel if he does well for four months in battle. A lieutenant colonel can command a division and after four months under fire be promoted brigadier and after another four months be promoted major general. For us that would be a little strong as a point of departure.[108]

The German practice and General Cavallero's reaction are typical of the differences between the two armies. The Italians listened with interest to their German colleagues and did nothing. As to junior officers, their deficiencies became apparent early in the war. In August 1940 General Claudio Trezzani wrote to Marshall Pietro Badoglio, then Chief of Staff, as one Piedmontese to another, about the junior officers:

> As long as it is a question of risking one's skin, [they] are admirable; when, instead, they have to open their eyes, think, decide in cold blood, they are hopeless. In terms of reconnaissance, security, movement to contact, preparatory fire, coordinated movement and so on, they are practically illiterate.[109]

Nor had matters improved two years later when General Carlo Geloso, commanding officer of the Italian 11th Army in Greece, surveyed the results of some tactical exercises:

> short-range tactical reconnaissance . . . the exercise is proceeding when all it takes is a small burst of enemy fire on the flanks for our troops to forget and ignore the main reasons why they are there and their tactical responsibilities and to hurl themselves into combat.[110]

Italian generals and officers were extremely sensitive to what they saw as German tutelage and clashes on strategy and tactics were frequent and unpleasant. On the Russian front where the Italian 8th Army had been deployed on the great bend of the River Don, relations between the two armies became strained. General von Tippelskirch, German Staff Officer attached to the Italian army command, reported that the 'Italians regard the exchange of tactical experience as unwanted advice'.[111] A few months after his appointment the General had an exceptionally sticky encounter with Italian General Malaguti, Chief of Staff to the Italian 8th Army in Russia, on the issue of *Stützpunkte*, or what the Italians called *presidios* (strongholds or fortresses). The Italian preference for huddling in fortified places drove the Germans wild during the war in the Balkans; it was no more popular with the *Wehrmacht* in Russia. The war diary of General von Tippelskirch's liaison unit with the Italians records:

> In discussing this theme raised many times before, General von Tippelskirch once again emphasized with the aid of the situation map of the Alpine Corps the importance of the abandonment by the Italians of their fortress tactic and its replacement by a flexible line of fire. The impression was given that General Malaguti wanted to evade this tactical discussion. He admitted that he had not submitted the previous memorandum of General von Tippelskirch, which dealt with the same theme, to the G.O.C. He [Malaguti] had written on it 'has discovered America', whereupon the discussion became extremely heated.[112]

German observers, both those sympathetic and those hostile to their Axis partner, remarked on the poor discipline and poor saluting of Italian troops. German commanders and liaison officers frequently spoke of the Italian '*Minderwertigkeitsgefühl*' (inferiority complex) with regard to the Germans. Some of their contempt was pure racism. A counter-intelligence officer in Africa remarked with disdain that

> [Italian] soldiers come for the most part from members of the lower classes. These – mostly Southern Italians and Sicilians – are certainly not higher than the Arabs in behaviour and level of education. They think of themselves on the other hand as conquerors and try to play the victors. They prove their fitness as colonizers by their disdain for and mistreatment of the Arabs.[113]

With almost no exception, however, those Germans closest to the Italian troops in the field, the liaison units and attached officers, or at higher level the generals attached to Italian Supreme Command respected and admired their Italian counterparts. They recognized that much of the poor performance of the Italians could be explained by the inadequacies of supplies and the poor quality of weaponry. Occasionally, there was literally no equipment at all. On 17 March 1941 the Duke of Aosta, Viceroy of Italian East Africa, sent an absolutely furious telegram to Mussolini:

> Today the whole English force was concentrated against us. Our bombers in line have been reduced to three 79s, three 81s and nine 133s . . . the adversary uses dozens and dozens and bombs our lines without interruption . . . if you want, do something in time to help us; don't send one plane at a time but dozens. Since

2 February to today we have received one, I say one! 79 while we have sent crews to bring back twelve.[114]

Even before the war the Royal Italian Army had aroused Mussolini's suspicions. In 1938 or early 1939 (it's not possible to date the evidence more precisely) he ordered a report on the numbers of suspected anti-fascists in the principal Roman ministries. The report examined twelve ministries and listed by name those persons whose loyalty to fascism seemed doubtful. There were 2 in the Ministry of Colonies, 4 at the Ministry of Foreign Affairs, 9 at the Ministry of National Economy and so on. Only two ministries had more than 100 suspected cases: the Ministry of Public Instruction with 222 and the Ministry of War, that is, the army, with 375 names, by a very long way the most imposing list. By contrast the Navy list contained 33 names and the Air Force only 11. The Army's list showed the names of 25 generals, 33 full colonels, 44 lieutenant colonels, 58 majors, 107 captains, 90 first lieutenants and 18 civilians.[115]

These numbers need to be handled gingerly. They certainly cannot bear much historical interpretation. In the first place, the survey gives no numbers for total employment in the ministry concerned, just the names of 'anti-fascists'. There is no way to construct percentages nor to establish who carried out the survey. It is possible that the extraordinary numbers of 'anti-fascists' found in the Ministry of War reflects the zeal of the secret police in that ministry and the sloth of their colleagues in other ministries. It is possible that the officers on staff duty in the Ministry were untypical of the army as a whole.

Possible but unlikely. The army had taken little part in the fascist seizure of power, although it had watched benevolently the suppression of 'subversives' by fascist clubbing. Certainly some commanders had openly assisted fascist squads with arms and transport. Some had indicated that they would refuse to fire on young men recently discharged from the service, frequently much decorated and often commanded by former colleagues. The King and his bourgeois prime ministers had taken such rumblings seriously, forgetting the iron rule of armies in such circumstances: for every colonel whose principles prevent him from carrying out orders, there is a lieutenant colonel who wants to be colonel. In any case, the King refused to give the order to fire on the fascists 'marching on Rome', so the crisis was postponed but not averted.

The well-informed and observant German military attaché, General von Rintelen, attended a very large-scale manoeuvre in the Po valley in August of 1939. On that occasion he had a talk with the King:

With his small, unprepossessing figure King Victor Emanuele III created neither a royal nor a soldierly impression. If one had a chance to talk to him, one felt his shrewd and detached spirit. What he said had 'hand and foot'. In the army his prestige was great. They recalled that in 1917 he had saved the army on the Piave from collapse. As long as crown and fascism went hand in hand, there was no obedience question for the army, but I was convinced that in a conflict between the King and the Duce the officer corps would decide for the Monarch.[116]

Rintelen's deputy, Major von Plehwe, attributed the hositility to the army's impatience with a regime which could not deliver the materials to fight the war and used the word 'hatred' to describe relations between the army and the fascist blackshirts.[117] But there were other reasons less likely to be expressed openly. One was revealed to me in a chance remark during an interview in Rome with Dr G.C. Garaguso. Dr Garaguso had been a captain on the staff of the Italian 11th Army in Athens under General Carlo Geloso. He had known Geloso well socially since the General had been a friend of the young staff captain's parents and a neighbour in Rome. In passing, Dr Garaguso mentioned that Geloso had never been a freemason. I asked Dr Garaguso how he knew. He started, smiled and replied, 'One just knew, that's all.'[118]

This is not an insignificant matter. Dr Garaguso assured me that the great majority of senior commanders were freemasons and that everybody knew it. To be a freemason at any time is to participate in a secret society which arouses suspicion in the wider community. To be a freemason with its strong progressive, liberal and anti-clerical traditions in a Catholic country is a political assertion; to be a freemason in a Catholic, totalitarian society like fascist Italy in a culture thick with conspiratorial fact and fantasy was subversion. It was also illegal. In February 1923 Mussolini had declared that membership of a masonic order was incompatible with membership of the fascist party. Many leading fascists, including Ciano, Balbo, Rossoni, De Bono, Farinacci, Acerbo and Cesare Rossi were masons,[119] which in view of the anti-clerical, lay backgrounds of many fascists 'of the first hour' was not surprising.

In 1925 internal party struggles in Florence led to a mini-pogrom, the so-called 'fatti di Firenze', against well-known masons and symbols of masonry.[120] The question of who was or who was not a mason continued to swirl in the murky ambience of the great satraps of the regime. In 1926 Mussolini specifically warned Roberto Farinacci, his outgoing secretary of the party, 'above all, to avoid masonry'.[121] Finally, in 1929, as part of Mussolini's settlement of the dispute between state and church in the so-called 'Lateran Pacts', he outlawed freemasonry altogether.[122] Hence for an officer, especially a general, to remain a member of a masonic lodge amounted to a serious act of insubordination.

Loyalty to the Crown, to traditional values and to the inheritance of the Italian nationalist movement, of which freemasonry was in many ways a symbol, insulated the army from the regime. Like the peasants in the Italian south and organized workers in FIAT plants, soldiers lived in a world of their own. Mussolini's totalitarian urges foundered on his own lack of seriousness, the turgid resistance of the Italian bureaucracy and that tolerance of the half-completed which Italians sum up in the expression *pressapocismo*, loosely translatable as 'almost-ism'. There were no purges of senior generals nor tests of true fascist sympathy. On the whole fascism interfered very little in the career structures of professional officers and failed to do much about slow promotions. It provided several helpful small wars before 1939 which yielded new decorations and the chance to serve in exotic places overseas, but the army consistently fought those wars in the name of the 'Emperor-King', and of the House of Savoy, not in the spirit of the blackshirted revolution.

It may be that junior officers and NCOs were more strongly committed to the regime than senior officers. After all they had known, especially the younger men, nothing else. The figures from the Ministry of War enquiry suggest the contrary. The high number of junior officers listed as anti-fascist is impressive. As with the generals so with the lieutenants, impressionistic evidence supports the conclusion that the army remained outside the circle of fascist influence.

Nothing marked more clearly the army's relative immunity to fascism than its reaction to the 'Racial Laws' of 1938. Dan Vittorio Segre describes his own experiences as a young man:

In the military circles in which I roamed, either because my friends at school were the sons of officers or because around Udine there were many military bases where I could ride at will, it was almost a ritual to show loyalty to the King and a detachment from Fascism, together with open hostility to the Germans. On such occasions I felt part of a quasi-secret society, since in the presence of my mother and father somebody always found a pretext to speak in favour of the Jews and against the Germans. The fact that in those years the colonel of the most prestigious cavalry regiment in town was a Jew, was enough to cut short on anyone's lips – in our presence at least – any criticism he may have had of the Jews.[123]

It is no wonder that Goebbels was appalled by the Italian army. In May of 1943, after it had become clear to the Nazi leadership that the

Italian army was systematically sabotaging Hitler's destruction of the Jews, Goebbels wrote: 'The Duce, too, is now in a jam because he commands no formations like our SS. He must depend on his royalist army, which of course is not equal to such a brutal war of ideologies.' By 'war of ideologies' Goebbels clearly meant murdering Jews. 'War of ideologies' was one of many such euphemisms. A few lines further on he records that 'the Führer argued that the anti-semitism which formerly animated the Party and was advocated by it must again become the focal point of our spiritual struggle. . . . You just cannot talk humanitarianism when dealing with Jews. Jews must be defeated.'[124]

Anti-semitism seems to have been largely irrelevant in the Royal Italian Army. In Segre's Udine a Jewish colonel commanded a crack cavalry regiment. Indeed, when Mussolini began to prepare for his anti-semitic *leggi razziali*, he faced the embarrassing but characteristically Italian difficulty that nobody knew who the Jews were in the Italian Army. On 15 February 1938 a 'list of Jewish officers' had to be compiled based on the unsteady foundations of a sensationalist text called 'Behind the Mask of Israel' by a certain Gino Sottochiesa. As the covering note to the Under-Secretary at the Ministry of War observes, 'To be able to carry out a real control it would be necessary that Your Excellency authorize verification based on a census taken at the Central Institute of Statistics.'[125]

The survey was carried out on the hit-or-miss basis of presumed 'Jewish' surnames. This was a tricky business since Italian Jewish surnames are frequently the names of the principal cities and on a list of officers prepared on 25 February 1938 Colonels 'Bologna', 'Modena' and 'Fiorentino' appear. The compilers felt safer with the General in the Engineers, Ugo Levi, and the General of the Quarter-master Corps, Edoardo Sacerdote, whose father's name was 'Abramo'. Certain famous Italian Jewish family names like De Benedetti and Mortara appear on the list along with the brothers Rodriguez (both colonels) and the improbably named Colonel Domenico Chirieleison (an Italianized version of 'kyrie eleison', the first words of the mass!).[126] The list contained the names of 6 generals and 14 full colonels, and whether this particular list was correct or not it reflected a remarkable, uniquely Italian, state of affairs. Nowhere else in Europe were there so many Jews in senior commands in the army. I have no equivalent list for the navy, but there were several flag officers in that service too. As early as 1902, Italy had a Jewish Minister of War, General Giuseppe Ottolenghi.

In the final section of this part I shall try to explain the very different circumstances of Jews in Italy and Germany but even without further comment it is clear that the Royal Italian Army really did constitute a 'state within the state', something often said to be true of the *Wehrmacht*. Alternatively one can take Goebbels' line and say that fascism showed itself to be superficial precisely because it failed to instil a proper anti-semitism in its soldiers. My own reading would be to say that the fascist regime never fully established itself. It erected a façade of total control behind which the institutions of pre-fascist Italy went on as before. The Crown, the Army and the Church were never *gleichgeschaltet*, as the Nazis described their radical transformation of Germany's institutions, and, as Himmler noted in conversation with Mussolini, the Duce lacked an SS. Indeed, he lacked a reliable party as well and the fascist militia, even those units on active service, enjoyed a low reputation among professional soldiers. Certainly they were no match for the *Waffen-SS*.

The traditional, liberal, masonic, philo-semitic culture of the Royal Italian Army provided a framework within which a conspiracy to save Jews from the Germans, French or Croatians would be applauded. As Hitler and the German High Command suspected, many senior officers had pro-Allied sentiments and believed that they were fighting on the wrong side, as, indeed, in spite of fascism, they were. Hence when Roatta said, 'the thing is just not possible', he could count on an officer corps which had already, loudly and frequently, said the same thing.

Nothing more dramatically illustrates the difference between the two armies than their attitude towards Jews. On 30 November 1942, three days after General Roatta visited the Jews in the internment camp at Kraljevice to promise them the protection of the Italian armed forces, Major General Hermann Foertsch, Chief of Staff at German Army Group E in Salonica-Arsakli, conducted the weekly *Chefbesprechung*, a kind of informal review of the situation in the Army Group's zone of operations.[127] At the end of the meeting, 'The Chief announced that on 1 December the cut in daily rations will apply to us. In addition the Chief drew attention to the regulations of the High Command of the Army/Personnel Office about attitude to the Jew.'[128]

The minutes end there. Clearly the final items about rations and Jews were merely administrative announcements, routine stuff, for information only. I tracked down the content of the regulations. I found that such regulations formed part of the quarterly instruction which all commands at division level and above were to give officers in order to provide 'guidelines for personal conduct of the officer corps and for promulgation of the decisions of the military courts of justice'.[129] The document, printed and official, was sent out to several hundred commands and was headed

refr: attitude of the officer to Jewry   Berlin, 31 October, 1942
                                    secret

The following cases are hereby brought to the attention of the officer corps:

An officer has in the last few years, if in admittedly loose form, maintained a link to a Jew, former school comrade and childhood friend, through a regular exchange of birthday greetings. He has even continued this exchange while commanding a regiment on the Eastern Front and has attempted to reach the Jew by sending a letter, without a return address, using as intermediary a junior officer under his command who was going on leave.

Another officer has been seen on several occasions in uniform on the streets of a German city with a Jew, who, to be sure, was an officer during the First World War, now however was marked as a Jew by the wearing of the Star of David.

These incidents make it necessary to make clear once again the attitude to Jewry expected of the officer.

Each officer must be filled with the conviction that in the first place the influence of Jewry opposes the German people's claim to living space and prestige in the world and in the second place compels the *Volk* to spill the blood of its best sons in the struggle to maintain itself in a world of enemies. . . . There is no difference between the so-called 'decent' Jew and the others.

The regulation concludes by explaining that no relations of any kind may be maintained at any level and for any purpose between the German officer and '*das Judentum*' and concludes by reminding the officer corps of the severe disciplinary consequences of failing to observe these regulations.[130]

Commanding officers frequently reinforced such attitudes by specific references to the 'Jewish Question'. On 16 March 1944 General Lanz, the commanding general of the XXII (Mountain) Army Corps, issued 'Corps Order Number 1 for Operation "Margarete"', the occupation of Hungary which took place on 19 March. The orders, which went out to all commanders explained the political objectives of the operation as follows:

For some time it has been clear to the Führer and the government of the Reich that the Hungarian government of Kallay intended to betray its European allies. Jewry, which controls everything in Hungary as well as individual, reactionary, Jew-related or corrupt elements of the Hungarian aristocracy, has brought the friendly

Hungarian people to this position. . . . Above all Jewry [*das Judentum*] has understood how to maintain its position in spite of racial laws. It has entirely subverted the spiritual and cultural life of Hungary, known how to suppress social reform movements and destroy the spirit of self-defence.[131]

As General Geloso revealed in his report of July 1943, *Generaloberst* Löhr himself had intervened, during the mass evacuation of the Jews of Salonica in the spring of 1943, to urge the Italians to do the same thing with the Jews of their zone, a request reinforced by Löhr's Chief of Staff Winter in conversation with his Italian opposite number.[132] With the exception of the case of Corfu, there is no evidence that any commander in the Balkan theatre or, for that matter, any NCO showed the slightest objection to the deportation and murder of Jews. Typical is this report from *Unteroffizier* Bergmayer of the *Geheime Feldpolizei* (Secret Field Police) from late March 1944, about the evacuation of the Jews of Joannina in north-western Greece. The GFP arrived at three in the morning outside the ghetto. The heads of the Jewish community were informed that by 8 a.m. every man, woman and child must be assembled in the square. Anybody not there and later found would be shot. The operation went smoothly. The *Unteroffizier* notes:

> The Greek population in the meantime had assembled in the streets and squares. With silent joy that one could read in their expressions they followed the departure of the Hebrews from their city. Only in a very few cases did a Greek permit himself to wave farewell to a member of the Jewish race. One could see clearly how the race was hated by old and young alike. Sympathy with their plight or unfavourable reactions to the action were not observed. . . . Altogether 1,725 members of the Jewish race were deported.[133]

It is hardly surprising that the Greek population watched the Jews leave in silence. By 1944 German destruction of Greek villages and mass shootings of Greek hostages had reached such proportions that the puppet Prime Minister of Greece J.D. Rallis had protested to General Speidel, the Military Commander in Athens, and Speidel himself had become so worried that he wrote a long report for Löhr in which he spoke of the 'growing hate for the German forces . . . the continuous decline in discipline among the troops themselves and their sinking prestige.'[134]

The army itself had begun to draw back from its own excesses. In December 1943 Löhr called a meeting at Army Group E in Salonica to which all corps and divisional commanders as well as the Chief of

Staff of the Military Commander in Greece were summoned. The issue of reprisals was discussed and Army Group E established a new set of guidelines:

> The principle: it is simply not permissible to behead everybody. If one is to carry out reprisal measures, one must stick to the truly guilty and genuine hostages and not raze completely uninvolved villages to the ground, That merely leads to an increase in the number of guerrillas. Minimum quota for shootings are to become maxima: 1:50 for every death; 1:10 for wounded.[135]

The massacres did not stop but, if anything, got worse. Ambassador Neubacher, the German Plenipotentiary for the Greek economy, wrote to Field Marshall von Weichs on 5 April 1944, to protest:

> It is sheer insanity to shoot babies, children, women and old people because heavily armed reds had been quartered for one night in their houses and had shot two German soldiers in the neighbourhood. The political consequences of such deeds may be very serious. It is obviously easier to kill quite harmless women, children and old men than to hunt down an armed band. I demand a thorough investigation of the matter.[136]

As the Nuremberg Military Tribunal remarked, the massacres in Greece 'give the lie to one of the most important single myths that the *Wehrmacht* seeks desperately to perpetuate – that the terrible crimes of troops in the field were committed by SS units over whom the *Wehrmacht* had no control.'[137]

The Nuremberg Tribunal began a debate which shows no sign of ebbing. In the years immediately after the war senior German commanders continued to deny that the army had been involved in the murders but with less and less success. In 1978 Christian Streit published his *Keine Kameraden. Die Wehrmacht und die sowietischen Kriegsgefangenen* which traced what he described as the 'inclusion of the *Wehrmacht* in the Nazi extermination policies'. German generals did not merely go along with the extermination of whole categories of people but actively promoted such policies. Hitler injected an ideological component into the war by attacking Russia which won the genuine consent of the German officer class:

> The attraction of Hitler's concept of the war in the East rested to a very great extent on the fact that by citing as the enemy 'Jewish Bolshevism' he made those enemy groups – that is, Jews and Socialists – into a single enemy and hence focused on precisely those scapegoats who had served as integrating factors in

216

domestic politics since Bismarck's time. The equation 'Jews = Bolsheviks' could move certain groups to a passive tolerance of the extermination policy who would have considered themselves otherwise too good for the 'vulgar' anti-semitism of the Streicher type.[138]

Hence, Streit argues, the *Wehrmacht* did more than tolerate orders which from the beginning of the Russian campaign required German soldiers to violate all existing rules of war. They did so voluntarily and made themselves accomplices in appalling crimes. Streit cites a speech by *Ministerialdirektor* Mansfeld, leader of the working party on labour deployment in the Four Year Plan, on 'general issues of the employment of labour' which he delivered to the Reich Chamber of Commerce:

The present difficulties in labour deployment would never have arisen, if it had been decided in good time to make extensive use of Russian prisoners of war. There were 3.9 million Russians available, of whom only 1.1 million remain. Alone between November, 1941, and January, 1942, 500,000 died. The number of presently employed Russian prisoners of war (400,000) is hardly likely to rise. If deaths from typhus decline, another 100 to 150,000 Russians might be employed in our economy.[139]

In other words, 2 million human beings had been killed or allowed to die in just eight months. Many hundreds of thousands more were to follow. Herr Mansfeld merely mentions these statistics in the way we saw the staff officer in Belgrade calculate his 'kill' ratios. Something ominous, astonishing and ultimately unfathomable seems to have happened to the entire bureaucratic and military establishment of the Hitler Reich. In June 1942 the SS noted that the introduction of the new 'gas wagons' had been entirely successful:

Seit Dezember 1941 wurden beispielsweise mit 3 eingesetzten Wagen 97,000 verarbeitet, ohne dass Mängel an den Fahrzeugen auftraten.'
(Since December 1941, for example, with the employment of three wagons, 97,000 have been processed without any defects in the vehicles occurring.)[140]

The 97,000 'processed' were, of course, human beings but the text gives no hint of that. Omer Bartov in his *The Eastern Front 1941–45*, published in 1985, has tried to explain this barbarization by doing 'history from below', that is, by studying the lives of ordinary soldiers and junior officers in three German divisions on the Russian front. He examines in detail the impact of the hardships of the front, the social mix and age of the officer corps, the high proportion of Nazi party members within the cohort, but concludes that the barbarization of the *Wehrmacht* depended fundamentally on 'belief', especially the 'Hitler myth' and, above all, on the fact that 'the underlying National Socialist *Untermenschen* ideology regarding the population of Russia played an important role in the barbarization of of the troops'.[141]

Bartov has been attacked for overestimating the impact of ideology in what was in any case a brutal war. Critics cite other brutalities by other armies not saturated by Nazi ideas of racism. In his fascinating study of German-occupied territories, published in 1989, Theo Schulte shows convincingly how ideology tended to be filtered and diluted by the inertia of army life and the boredom of occupation duty. Far from being fierce ideologues, some of troops were *Pantoffelsoldaten* (slipper soldiers), as an inspecting officer reported in late 1942:

> My impressions by the inspections of these strong points were as follows: the men do not budge from inside their fieldposts and strongpoints for the entire day. As a result of this inactivity the soldiers have become sluggish and unsoldierly [*lahm und unsoldarisch*]. I have encountered men on guard duty who were wearing slippers and who, when they saw me, put on a jovial face, and gave their report as if they were civilians. If one entered a strongpoint, in most cases no notice whatever was taken of what one was doing. Calls to attention or for the men to assume an attitude of quiet were out of the question. The men remained lying on their beds or sitting on stools. I would like to mention that this was not the case everywhere but it can be considered fairly standard.[142]

That account reminds me more of MASH than of the *Wehrmacht*, but, as Schulte rightly observes, any organization which engaged millions of people and put them down in all sorts of environments is bound to be less than uniform. Yet Schulte's evidence from Army Rear Areas suggests that with regard to Jews the arguments remained the same everywhere. In a situation report dated 1.1.1942, the local commander in a rear area observed:

> The Jews who gad about in the district constitute a particular menace. They serve as communications personnel for the partisan bands, convey reports and act as recruiters for the partisans. In this respect, Jewish women and young girls are active in numerous places.[143]

There are countless other examples of this argument being used from the French coast to the Greek islands. Himmler used it on a visit to Mussolini. Every German agent in the Italian zone of Yugoslavia used it. Glaise von Horstenau used it in reports to Berlin. Ironically, the Italians themselves used it in the spring of 1943 to explain to the Germans the need to intern the Jews in the Italian zone of southern France. It grew out of the apparently universal conviction at every level of German military activity that the Jews were always, everywhere, a separate category. A Greek Jew was just a Jew, never a Greek. This mental *Absonderung*, or separation, prepared the ground for the physical separation of Jews and finally for their eradication.

In this respect the research behind my account supports the 'revisionist' historians such as Streit, Browning, Bartov and Schulte. No German officer or civilian at any stage or in any kind of document or informal conversation ever saw *das Judentum* in other than absolute categorical terms. None expressed approval or understanding of Italian behaviour towards them. Whether the German army had or had not become an ideological army, how far and in which ways it participated in crimes against humanity, are still questions to be debated. On one point there can no longer be any doubt: in their attitudes to Jews the two Axis allies inhabited different moral universes.

4

GERMANS, ITALIANS AND JEWS

Does it follow, therefore, that Germans hated Jews and Italians did not? There does seem to have been remarkably little Italian anti-semitism. Jewish communities on Italian soil had, of course, an ancient lineage. The Roman Jewish community can trace its continuous existence with some certainty to the days of the Roman Republic when Jews were called 'liberti', the 'freed', because they were so difficult to enslave.[144] In the ensuing 1,800 years they had suffered all the persecutions, forced conversions, exclusions and deprivations which are common to Jewish history everywhere. What made Italian Jews different from co-religionists elsewhere was not the Jews but the environment in which they lived.

From the end of the Roman Empire to the middle of the nineteenth century Italy was, to use Prince Metternich's famous phrase, 'a geographical expression'. Divided and contentious, the Italian states fought each other until they fell prey to foreigners. The key to stability in Italy and the permanent focus of the power balance was the international position of the Popes. The Popes saw themselves with some justice as the heirs of the Caesars and ruled not only in Rome but in a huge slice of territory stretching across the centre of the peninsula. No scheme to unify Italy and to drive out the foreigners could ignore the sovereignty of the Papacy. Hence Italian liberalism and nationalism necessarily made an enemy of the Pope.

The Popes responded in kind. Even before the French Revolution unleashed a frightening wave of secularism and anti-clericalism, the Holy See had been tightening its censorship and restricting behaviour. At the very moment when American patriots were about to fire 'the shot heard round the world' and proclaim the great 'self-evident truths' of modern liberalism, Pius VI (1775–1799) re-issued on 5 April 1775 a strengthened 'Edict concerning the Jews', which reinforced all the medieval restrictions on Jewish life. It tightened the stipulations concerning the ghettos. It limited Jewish residence, property-owning, physical movement and, among its forty-eight articles, reimposed the *segno*, the mark which distinguished Jews from Gentiles. As Attilio Milano says in his great book on the history of the Jews in Italy,

Italian Jewry was literally 'petrified' in 1789 where it had been two centuries before.[145]

Nationalists, liberals and Jews had a common enemy: the Papacy. When the French came and swept away what they saw as medieval superstitions, they, of course, abolished ghettos while they closed and secularized monasteries, broke up the commons and introduced private property. They reorganized Italian politics into large, modern units and introduced the latest achivements of the Napoleonic code: civil rights and political freedom.

As soon as Napoleon fell, the Popes and the restored monarchies got busy turning the clocks back, almost literally in the case of the King of Piedmont, Victor Emanuel I, who on 25 May 1814 revoked every decree, promotion, appointment or other act of government which had taken place after 23 June 1800, as if those years had never occurred. On the same day, the ghetto in Turin was reconstituted. On 1 March 1816 the liberal professions in the Kingdom of Piedmont were again barred to Jews. In the Duchy of Modena, not only was the ghetto restored with all the old restrictions but the *segno*, in the case of Modena, a red ribbon on the hat, was reimposed.

The Italian states returned to the blackest of reaction. Pope Gregory XVI opposed the introduction of gas lights on the streets of Rome and other cities in the Papal States because it might encourage people to walk about at night and spread seditious ideas. He opposed railways on the same grounds. The English essayist Hazlitt fell foul of the Piedmontese reactionaries in 1825:

We proceeded to the Custom-House. I had two trunks. One contained books. When it was unlocked, it was as if the lid of Pandora's box flew open. There could not have been a more sudden start or expression of surprise, had it been filled with cartridge paper or gun-powder. Books were the corrosive sublimate that eat out despotism and priest-craft . . . a box full of them was contempt of the constituted authorities. . . . It was not till I arrived at Turin that I found it [the box] was a prisoner of state, and would be forwarded to me anywhere I chose to mention, out of his Sardinian majesty's dominions.[146]

In such a world Jews and liberal nationalists had a common cause. As a pamphlet of 1831 addressed to fellow-Jews put it

Italian Israelites! The time has come in which the Italian arises to take again his lost dignity . . . that fire which burns for other Italians must burn also in our bosoms, for Italy is our fatherland and not the sterile territory of Palestine.[147]

All the great leaders of the Italian movement of national regeneration known as the *Risorgimento* wrote on the 'Jewish Question'. Massimo D'Azeglio put it most precisely in his 'Concerning the Civil Emancipation of the Jews' written in the revolutionary year of 1848: 'The cause of Jewish regeneration is strictly united to the cause of Italian regeneration because there is only one justice.'[148]

Jews became patriotic Italians and took part in the wars of national liberation. The architect of unification, Count Cavour, employed the Jew Isaaco Artom as his private secretary and Jews fought on the barricades and in the services. Jews became propagandists for the new Italy. German-speaking Jews who were Austrian subjects in cities like Trieste turned themselves into Italian-speaking patriots. One of them Hector Schmitz became one of Italy's greatest novelists under the name Italo Svevo. Felice Venezian founded the Dante Alighieri Society, the Italian equivalent of the British Council or US Information Service. Jews identified strongly with the Italian monarchy. As the great historian Arnaldo Momigliano noted in a lecture at Brandeis, in 1984, 'It explains why my grandmother used to cry every time she listened to the *Marcia Reale* – the Royal Hymn of the Italian Monarchy – and if you can cry at such atrocious music, you can cry at anything.'[149]

It helped to integrate Jews that there were few of them. Momigliano reckons that there were barely 30,000 at the beginning of the nineteenth century. De Felice in his massive and authoritative history of the Jews under fascism has used the records of the fascist regime's own department of Demography and Race to arrive at figures such as these for the Jewish population in 1938:

	Main Cities	Other Communes
Italian Jews	41,224	4,137
Foreign Jews	7,767	1,975
	48,991	6,112 [150]

They made up less than 1 per cent of the Italian population and blended easily into the surrounding Italian environment. In Rome the Jews of the ghetto and Trastevere spoke the *Romanesco* of other slum dwellers mixed with the occasional Hebrew phrase and had their distinctive cuisine and habits. Elsewhere, as in Ferrara and cities further north, Jews divided into three distinctive groups, symbolized by the three different synagogues: *la scola tedesca* (ashkenazic), *la scola spagnola* (sephardic) and *la scola italiana* (Italian) but, as any reader of Giorgio Bassani's wonderful *The Garden of the Finzi-Contini* will recall, ashkenazic Jews in Ferrara had become by the 1930s no less Italian than their sephardic or Judaeo-Italian co-religionists.[151]

To Jews from northern Europe, then and now, Italian Jews, like the countless jokes about Jews in China and Japan, 'did not look Jewish'. As Primo Levi remarked in his last book, this fact cost many of them their lives in the Nazi death camps. They could not communicate; they spoke no Yiddish: 'The Polish, Russian, Hungarian Jews were stupefied that that we Italians did not speak it; we were suspect Jews, not to be trusted . . . it was not comfortable to be an Italian Jew.'[152]

Jewish identity had become attenuated by the twentieth century. Dan Vittorio Segre recalls that knowledge of Hebrew, the rituals and practices of Judaism had become little more than symbolic acts of identity in his well-to-do north Italian family.[153] Nello Rosselli, one of the founders of the anti-fascist movement *Giustizia e Libertà*, summed up the situation of many Italian Jews in a speech of 1924: 'I am a Jew who doesn't go to temple on the sabbath, who doesn't know Hebrew, and who doesn't observe any part of the religion. . . . I am not a zionist and am not, therefore, an integral Jew.'[154]

Jewishness for well-educated Italian Jews had become the smile of the Cheshire Cat, just visible as it disappeared. Mixed marriages between Jews and non-Jews had become extremely common. In practice, according to the census of 1938, 43.7 per cent of marriages involving Jews were marriages in which one partner was not Jewish. Even the office for Demography and Race was struck by the figure and commented: 'The percentage of Jews of both sexes who marry persons of other races and religions in Italy is markedly higher than in other countries of Europe.'[155]

Jews spread out into various professions and activities but nowhere achieved that prominence in, say, banking or the professions, as in Hungary, the type of prominence which provoked anti-semitic comment or defensive measures. Certainly, as H. Stuart Hughes notes in his *Prisoners of Hope. The Silver Age of the Italian Jews*,[156] there were many important writers who were Jews, but nothing in Alberto Moravia's work or Carlo Levi's is specifically 'Jewish'. Even Primo Levi, who has become for our generation the very symbol of Jewish survival in the holocaust, saves his soul in Auschwitz not by Torah but by Dante. *If This Be a Man* explores the dilemma of Italian Jewry. A man with the most Jewish of names, 'Levi', finds himself in a Nazi concentration camp for no other reason than his Jewishness, but his Jewish identity has become so tenuous that he turns to the supreme Christian poetic work for solace at his moment of need. Italian Jews, in truth, 'did not look Jewish'.

Partly for that reason and partly for others less easy to understand, certain inflammations of public awareness never occurred in Italy. A common source of anti-semitism in other European countries was modern marketing. The department store and the mail order catalogue threatened the small shop, the artisan and the local trader. Jews came to be symbolic of that transformation. During the 1890s in places as diverse as Dijon and Vienna 'don't buy from the Jews!' began to appear on walls. In Milan, Italy's most advanced trading city, Jews took part in the commercial life of the city in numbers out of proportion to their share of the population, but a recent study by Jonathan Morris of lower middle-class politics in Milan from 1885 to 1905, based on an extensive cull of the archives of the city and the journals of the small traders, has uncovered not one single instance of anti-semitism.[157] Count Ciano was right when he argued in 1937 that there was no 'Jewish question' in Italy:

> The problem does not exist here. There are not many Jews and, with some exceptions, there is no harm in them. And then Jews should never be persecuted as such. That produces solidarity among Jews all over the world. There are so many other pretexts for attacking them. But, I repeat, the problem does not exist here.[158]

Jews fanned out across the political spectrum. One, Umberto Terracini, was, along with Antonio Gramsci, Palmiro Togliatti and Angelo Tasca, a founder of the New Order in Turin and of the Italian Communist Party. Another, Aldo Finzi, joined the fascist party at the beginning and rose to be Under-Secretary at the Ministry of the Interior in the first years of the regime. Dante Almansi, a Jew, became Vice-Chief of the Fascist Police. The two Rosselli brothers founded the principal, non-marxist resistance group. Dan Vittorio Segre's family supported the Fascist Party in Udine as did the Finzi-Continis in Bassani's novel. There was no Jewish problem as such in Italy.

When Italy joined Nazi Germany in the Anti-Comintern Pact of 6 November 1937 Jews began to get nervous. A month after the treaty was signed, Ciano wrote in his diary: 'The Jews are flooding me with insulting anonymous letters, accusing me of having promised to persecute them. It's not true. The Germans have never mentioned this subject to us.'[159] The rumours reached such a level that the Italian Foreign Ministry issued an official denial on 14 February 1938:

> the recent polemics in the press have been such as to arouse the impression in certain foreign circles that the Fascist government is on the point of initiating an anti-semitic policy. Responsible circles in Rome are in a position to affirm that such impressions are completely erroneous.[160]

That was simply false and many people knew it. At precisely the same time the Ministry of War had begun to make lists of Jews in the officer corps. Some time in 1937–38 Mussolini changed his attitude to the Jews. People at the time, and some scholars after the event, assumed that the introduction of anti-semitic legislation had been a condition of the establishment of the Axis. Meir Michaelis, whose *Mussolini and the Jews* investigates this question, states categorically that 'the entire ample documentation in this field, in fact, contains not the least hint of German interference in Italy's domestic Jewish question during the period under review [that is, 1936–38].'[161]

Mussolini hated the impression that he, the master in such matters, had become Hitler's pupil, and by August the fascist press, as Bottai noted in his diary on 10 August 1938

> were engaged in a journalistic attempt to show a continuity in the racist thinking of the Duce. But people remember the pages of his conversation with Ludwig. They remember that the writer, chosen to receive historic confidences, is a Jew, that the first biographer of Mussolini was a Jewess and that he has nominated many Jewish senators.[162]

The elderly General De Bono, who led one of the columns in the 'march on Rome', was a kind of fascist patriarch complete with white Vandyke beard. He was appalled by the new turn of fascist politics even though, as he wrote in his diary on 4 September 1938, 'I have always been an anti-semite':

> It seems that they're doing everything to make enemies. This business with the Jews has exploded like a bomb. But if you say that you realised for a long time the deleterious influence of the Jews, why haven't you said anything before? Why have you waited for the German example? That's the way the public thinks – how will they excuse so many inconsistencies? I feel like an idiot whose heart is breaking. It's Mussolini's fault but also those who surround him who instead of moderating his impulses urge him on. . . . There's no measure, never any equilibrium. The deleterious person is Starace.[163]

This inconsistency combined with the general unpopularity of the alliance with Nazi Germany put Mussolini in an embarrassing position. He grew irritable and increasingly strident. In a characteristic outburst at the Fascist Grand Council on 6 October 1938 he tried to convince sceptical councillors that he had always been a strong, consistent anti-semite. As Bottai recorded in his diary

> Mussolini 'attacks' with polemical force. It's an internal polemic which goes its way with harsh words for probable opponents present and absent. 'I have been thinking about this problem since 1908', he asserts. 'If you want, you can document that.

Look, for example, at my speech of the 3rd of April 1921 where I speak of "this our aryan and mediterranean stock".[164]

But it was hard going for Mussolini. Not even the most enthusiastic supporters of the new anti-semitic measures believed him and some like Italo Balbo, the boss of fascism in Ferrara with its rich, frequently pro-fascist, Jewish landowners (like the Finzi-Continis), openly opposed him. Balbo, the flyer and war hero, had the charisma and independent status to defy Mussolini. Even Farinacci, the boss of fascism in Cremona and the most vocal of the fascist anti-semites, refused to fire Joele Foà, his Jewish private secretary.[165]

If the Germans cannot be directly blamed for Mussolini's sudden conversion to the Nuremberg Laws, they and the atmosphere they created in Europe certainly played a part. In May 1938 the Hungarian regime of Prime Minister Bela Imredy passed the first of several discriminatory laws which step by step first segregated the rich, powerful and fiercely loyal Magyar Jewish community and ultimately destroyed it.[166] Early in 1939 Hungary, too, signed the Anti-Comintern Pact. Meir Michaelis may be right that no proof exists that the Germans intervened to force Mussolini to promote anti-Jewish legislation, but they had no need to intervene. Everybody in Europe knew what Nazism meant for the Jews. To ally with that state was at the very least to condone racial persecution. Respectability in the Anti-Comintern club required commitment and the Horthy regime in Hungary, the Antonescu regime in Rumania and the Duce's regime in Italy met that requirement. The Jews paid the dues for the regime's new association.

On 6 October 1938 the Fascist Grand Council approved the text of the racial laws which as Royal Decree Number 1728 became law on 17 November. Jews suddenly turned into second-class citizens, forbidden to serve in the armed forces or the state bureaucracy, to teach in state schools and universities, to own or manage companies engaged in military production or employing more than a certain number of employees, to have 'aryan' domestic servants and so on.[167] These were Nuremberg Laws but Italian-style, that is, shot through with inconsistencies and riddled with exemptions for this or that category of persons 'who deserved well of the state', such as the families of those killed in battle, holders of high decorations for valour and the like. A committee of the Department of Demography and Race in the Ministry of the Interior met to consider the thousands of applications for 'discrimination', the term for honorary exemption from the burden of Jewishness.

The files of 'Demorazza', as the department was called, make depressing reading. Jewish generals, admirals, distinguished lawyers

and bankers, war widows, semi-literate tradespeople, all wrote begging petitions on the special *carta bollata* (officially stamped paper),
which the citizen has to use to approach the Italian state. The
anonymous letter, a peculiar vice of Italian public life, added to the
misery of the Jews by raising all sorts of unsubstantiated charges.
Files filled up with letters of support or opposition. But the main
impression was of a pervasive moral degradation. A full admiral,
whose family fought for Italy in 1848, and who was a former inspector general of naval armaments, submitted a humble petition begging
for the restoration of his Italian citizenship because as an engineer
officer in the First World War he had not received the 'War Cross',
a medal which conferred automatic exemption under the law of 17
November 1938. He adds that his wife and children are Catholic but
he is of *la religione ebraica*.[168] I only found one example of backbone.
A young air force lieutenant resigned his commission and returned
his decorations.[169] The rest outdid themselves in servility and professions of loyalty to a regime which had betrayed and humiliated
them.

The Jewish fascists were doubly desperate, deprived at a stroke of
the King's pen of their party and their state. Susan Zuccotti gives the
number of Jewish members of the fascist party at nearly 5,000, which
would amount to 10 per cent of the Jewish population.[170] Just as not
all Jews were equally Jewish, so there were fascists and fascists. By
1938, as Camillo Boitani explained to me, a party membership had
become a document like a birth certificate, a piece of evidence one
needed to be admitted to competitions for state employment or for
certain careers in the armed services. Nobody checked if dues were
paid or if membership had been renewed.[171] It had come to be
known as the *tessera del pane*, the bread ticket. Certainly one did not
have to join, but many did. It made life more convenient and
involved no great sacrifice of principle for most people. After all, had
not 'He' (i.e. Mussolini) saved Italy from bolshevism?

Some Jews were committed fascists. Among them was a cousin of
the Segre family, Ettore Ovazza, an early and enthusiastic supporter
of the movement, As Dan Vittorio Segre describes it in his memoirs,
'on a cold, grey autumn day' Ovazza and two others arrived at the
family estate:

> We received them in the dining room, with my mother in a state
> of nerves serving tea and small cakes, apologizing all the time for
> not having a maid (because of the 'laws'). After a while with her
> eyes full of tears she left the room.[172]

Ovazza's proposal was simple and monstrous: to lead a punitive
expedition of the sort that had helped fascism club its way to power

in 1921 and 1922, against the little Jewish periodical *Israel* published in Florence:

> The operation would also remind Mussolini of the heroic days prior to the March on Rome during which the Jews had so ardently supported him. Such an action should be carried out by people of unstained Fascist faith and of recognized national stature. My father was one of these. By joining the punitive action he would add lustre to the initiative.[173]

Signor Segre refused. Ettore Ovazza departed with his companions and a few weeks later they burned the offices and printing press of *Israel*. Ovazza's grotesque gesture changed nothing nor did his 'unstained Fascist faith' save him or his family from the Germans. On 9 November 1943 the Germans found Ovazza, his wife and 15 year old daughter hiding at Gressoney and, having literally butchered them, burned their still living bodies in the furnace at a local school.[174]

The 'Laws' ruined lives and brought misery to thousands of patriotic Italian Jews, but often, as Evi Eller told me, the behaviour of the local population 'mitigated' the force of the 'Laws'. The Ellers had migrated from Hungary in 1925 and settled at Orano near Fiume, a region that today belongs to Yugoslavia. Her father, who ran a small garage, became an Italian citizen in 1937. The following year the 'Laws' deprived him of his citizenship and forced Evi, then 20, to give up her university course in classics and Italian at Padua. Mr Eller was forced to sell his business and Evi, as a Jew, was immediately dismissed from her job as supply teacher at the *liceo* in near-by Abbazia. The local people helped them in whatever way they could. Tradesmen somehow never got round to sending the Ellers a bill. The grocer gave them free vegetables. When Evi began to offer private coaching for school exams, her first pupil was the nephew of the captain of the fascist militia: 'When the others saw that, they too found the courage to send their children to me for lessons.'[175]

Thousands of Jews, Italian and foreign, tell similar stories: acts of kindness here, moments of courage there, gratuitous assistance from total strangers somewhere else. Without that remarkable practical compassion many more Jews would have perished when the holocaust hit Italy than actually did. Nicola Caracciolo made a programme for Italian TV on Jews under fascism, and interviewed a group of Jewish survivors in a restaurant in Jerusalem. Each had his or her special Italian, the police officer who helped get false papers, the doctor who hid a total stranger in his apartment for nearly two years, the village mayor who hid a family on his farm and so on. Blanka Stern, who escaped to Italy from Yugoslavia, made a more general point:

I want to add something. It's well known how the Germans had psychological ways of making us Jews into an inferior race, not human anymore, people without rights. When we arrived in Italy the people gave us back our sense of being human. They gave us back our sense of humanity, in short, that we were again part of the human race.[176]

The officials who controlled the Jewish concentration camp at Ferramonti in Calabria turned it into the largest kibbutz on the European continent. Barracks were divided into kosher and non-kosher and the *maresciallo* of the carabinieri even learned some Yiddish to communicate with the prisoners. Prisoners were addressed as *signore* and the Jewish doctors provided clinics for the surrounding peasant villages. The commandant risked his life in 1943 to get permission to allow his prisoners to go free before the German troops retreating from Sicily fell upon the Jews and destroyed them.[177]

Jews were not the only beneficiaries of the humanity of the Italian people. After Mussolini's regime collapsed and the Badoglio government made its peace with the Allies on 8 September 1943, a new, much nastier, fascist puppet republic ruled the north under tight control of the German occupiers. Allied prisoners and airmen found refuge among the peasantry of the northern Italian hills and mountains. Roger Absalom estimates that at one point, in spite of the death penalty which threatened those who got caught, Italian peasants were hiding as many as several divisions' worth of Allied officers and men.[178]

Not all Italians behaved this way and there are stories of betrayal, denunciation and treachery. Italian humanity was selective. Jews were often extremely badly treated by the regime. Mussolini encouraged the spread of anti-semitic propaganda and made fanatics like Telesio Interlandi, editor of a paper called *La Difesa della Razza* (the Defence of the Race) into respected figures. Institutes published racist studies and professors who should have known better gave lectures. Italy was not free of anti-semitism, either clerical or racial, but somehow it never seized the imagination of the Italian people.

No explanation of the Italian attitude to the Jews from 1938 to 1945 can ever be satisfactory. Most end by citing aspects of what we loosely call national character. National character certainly exists. The rich compound of language, habits, tradition, architecture, social structure, laws, history, climate and geography that give a place its specificity is undeniably 'out there' in reality. Every traveller senses such differences expressed in the details of daily life – from the size of the tablespoons to the sounds of the streets.

Jews in Germany had, like their Italian co-religionists, not been full citizens of the Germanic states until well into the nineteenth century. The Prussian establishment tolerated but never liked them. In the late eighteenth century, Prussia, Austria and Russia carved up Poland and with his new territories Frederick the Great inherited a large number of Polish Jews. He was not pleased. He had always hated Jews. In his Testament of 1768 he wrote:

> We have too many Jews in the cities. On the borders of Poland they are necessary because in that land only the Jews are traders. As soon as a town is distant from Poland the Jews become harmful because of the usury they practise, the smuggling that goes through their hands and the thousand rascalities that work to the disadvantage of *Bürgers* and of Christian merchants. I have never persecuted the members of this sect or anyone else. However I think it wise to watch that their number does not increase too greatly.[179]

Prussia and its landowning class survived into the twentieth century and with it the attitudes of Frederick the Great. To the Junker establishment, however enlightened, certain things were axiomatic. No Jew could be an army officer. That was perfectly clear. They took the same view about the other pillar of the Prussian state, the civil service. Since university and school teachers were then as now civil servants, the teaching professions were consequently closed as well. As Ludwig Philippson complained in 1853, 'one grants us Jews full rights in commercial matters but denies us Jews public effectiveness in public office.'[180]

Even when full civil rights were finally granted under the German Empire after 1871 or in the Weimar Republic after 1919, Jews hesitated to accept high public office. The banker Max Warburg declined the Finance Ministry in the 1920s because 'a Jew would have been out of the question'.[181] There were no Jewish generals or staff officers and a Jewish Minister of War would have been a contradiction in terms. Why was this? There are many possible answers but one which seems persuasive to me is the general weakness of liberalism. It goes like this: liberalism was weak; the position of the Jews depended on the strength of liberalism. Hence the weakness of liberalism led to a weak position for the Jews.

The German states of the eighteenth and early nineteenth centuries left little room for the growth of political liberalism. The state in Prussia preceded the people. Liberalism as an ideology of the middle class rested on a social group which in both Germany and Austria never got to power. The Austrian bourgeoisie built marvellous university buildings, a neo-classical parliament and a splendid opera and strung them along the Ring Boulevard which surrounds the old city of Vienna. Symbols of Greek democracy, even ones in marble, could not conceal the reality that power in Austria rested, as it always had, in the Hofburg, in the Emperor's hands and in those of the great magnates. Bismarck ran Germany after 1862 and, while he had a soft spot for clever Jews, employed a Jewish house physician, a Jewish banker and a Jewish broker, he never lost the prejudices of his class and culture. No Jews held high office in his time.

Liberalism had a troubled passage in the Germanic states. Free trade was introduced by an unfree bureaucracy and freedom of speech and assembly were concessions warily made by authority, never rights. There was no radical republican tradition as in France, nor the *risorgimento* version of liberalism as in Italy, no Whig tradition as in England and no inheritance of natural rights as in the American colonies. There was certainly the enlightened philosophy of Immanuel Kant but Kant lived under Frederick the Great. As he explained in his essay 'What is Enlightenment', free-thinking took place most safely in the well-ordered state under the motto: 'reason as much as you like and over whatever you like but obey.'[182]

Liberalism suffered two other disabilities in Germany, both, paradoxically, legacies of her greatest cultural achievements. In the first place, the impact of Goethe and German romanticism left as an inheritance the idea that fulfilment takes place within the soul. It rejected the public for the private. It elevated the inner life to the detriment of the outer and thus disdained that open forum which liberalism demanded. The other legacy which in my view had literally fatal consequences for Jews was the impact of Hegel. Two properties of Hegelian philosophy matter here. The first was his concept of history.

History was not, as it was for Gibbon, 'little more than the register of the crimes, follies and misfortunes of mankind' but a deeply satisfying spectacle, the march to freedom. The World-Spirit moves in a stately progress to its own cosmic form of *Bildung*. We know how it works: by the process of self-reflection or reconciliation of opposites. Things are not just there but work in constant opposition to each other. The cosmos moves by contradiction, by what Hegel saw as a triangular evolution of thesis, antithesis and synthesis. That synthesis in turn bears within it new theses and antitheses. Reality and philosophy progress together as the World-Spirit comes to know itself through history.

Hegelianism intoxicated a whole generation; it had all the answers. Even today nobody should read Hegel on an empty stomach. Hegelianism moulded German culture and pushed it in certain directions. In the first place Hegel gave history a purpose and within that purpose a special role for the Germanic peoples and the Prussian state. Secondly he transformed the study of history from 'one damned thing after another' into a deep form of philosophy which had a direction and end. Peoples – and this is really important – were not studied for themselves, for amusement, instruction or melancholy reflection as in the eighteenth century, but as embodiments of stages in the World-Spirit's thought processes. Finally, history's laws lay *inside* reality, knowable by philosophy but not refutable by evidence. There is no way to disprove an act of the World-Spirit or to deny that the Greeks embody some principle or other.

Of course, if you don't believe in the existence of the World-Spirit the whole edifice crumbles like a gothic façade made of powdered chalk. If, on the other hand, something scientific, 'real' and non-metaphysical could replace the operations of the World-Spirit, the system could go on running but without the need for an imaginary mind to think it.

It was into that system that Germans, almost unconsciously, inserted biology. Darwin had discovered the 'laws' of the evolution of species. It was obvious, wasn't it, that those laws applied to human species, peoples, races? . . . all too obvious. A version of Darwin's ideas swept Germany in the last third of the nineteenth century and became what the socialist Karl Kautsky called 'the marxism of the middle class'. Darwinian ideas explained everything: why blacks were poor and backward and why, therefore, Europeans had to rule them; why Germanic peoples had free institutions and Asiatics did not; why northern peoples were more enterprising than Latins and so on.

Hitler's table talk and his view on the Jewish problem now fall into place. To minds accustomed to thinking of history in Hegel's way the laws of racial struggle were irresistible and were, indeed, not resisted. From the murder of the feeble-minded by so-called 'euthanasia' actions in 1940 to the ethnic policies of the German army in the Balkans, the fatal Hegelian legacy can be traced.

Hegel's system required the World-Spirit to work through peoples which he converted into abstract entities embodying principles. This habit had nasty consequences for the Jews. It became easy, indeed philosophically unavoidable, to speak not of *die Juden* (the Jews) but of *das Judentum* (untranslatable). Hegelianism and the Jewish problem came together in one of the most anti-semitic essays of the nineteenth centry, Karl Marx's *Zur Judenfrage*. The circumstances were these. In 1843 Bruno Bauer, a prominent left-wing disciple of Hegel (Hegel could be read either from left to right or vice versa), published a book called *Die Judenfrage*. Bauer argued the standard progressive case. The Jews had to be emancipated from their medieval religion; democracy had to be introduced in the German states; and the Jewish problem would be solved.

Marx did not like the book and in his reply the 26 year old philosopher worked out some of the first stages of his scientific socialism. He began by refuting Bauer's faith in democracy. He took a close look at the politics of the American states of New Hampshire and Pennsylvania and concluded that democracy on its own can never cure the ills of society. If anything, democracy by opening civil society to individual intiative makes the triumph of greed and egotism inevitable.

As a good Hegelian, he asks 'what social element must be overcome in order to abolish *das Judentum*, that is, what principle does Jewry embody?

> Let us observe the real, worldly Jew, not the sabbath Jew as Bauer does, but the every-day Jew. We must seek the mystery of the Jew not in his religion but the mystery of the religion in the real Jew. What is the worldly basis of Jewry? Practical need, self-interest. What is the worldly culture of the Jews? Usury. What is his worldly God? Money. . . . We perceive in Jewry a general, contemporary, antisocial element. . . . Emancipation of the Jews is in the last instance the emancipation of humanity from Jewry.[183]

Hitler could not have said it better than the young Jewish doctor of philosophy from Trier, but it is the form not the sentiment I want to consider. Note first the Hegelian play of opposites. Marx proceeds by reversing each subject and predicate. Everything becomes its opposite. Closer examination suggests that by the same device any nonsense sounds profound. To illustrate, here is a paragraph of Hegelian nonsense which I made up:

> The contact with reality must be transformed by the reality of contact. Hence all objects of sense perception become the sense of perceived objects. The authority of knowledge then becomes the knowledge of authority.

This little exercise in do-it-yourself-Hegel illustrates the perils of Hegelian philosophy. Any charlatan can write profound-sounding twaddle. Worse still the charlatan can mistake it for serious philosophy. Schopenhauer put it well:

> The greatest cheek in serving up plain nonsense, in smearing together senseless, empty, raving word-tangles of the kind that one had only heard before in madhouses came to light in Hegel and became the tool of the most shameless mystification that there has ever been.[184]

Marx used Hegelian categories, great abstractions that begin with the definite article. He wrote *das Judentum* and like all good Hegelians ignored the variety of individuals. Hegel made it impossible for Germans to say 'some', 'a few', 'maybe not all'. The language of the final solution is in this sense Hegelian for it lumps all Jews into *das Judentum* and opposes them to *das Germanentum* or *das Ariertum* or any of the other phrases that end up in Dolf Sternberger's *Wörterbuch des Unmenschen*, the dictionary of the inhuman.

This is not far-fetched, academic nonsense. The dualistic form of thought found constant expression in Hitler's *Alles oder Nichts*, in the rigour of SS distinctions, in the orders of generals and colonels and in people's heads. Besides, the political process as such, the give-and-take so beloved of liberal theory, seemed degrading to minds steeped in Hegelian absolutes, aristocratic values and authoritarian habits. Politics was *Kuhhandel*, vulgar cattle dealing, precisely the sort of low activity in which Jews engaged.

Hence the liberal intelligentsia in Germany and Austria found themselves in a dilemma. Culture was a matter of the soul, to be protected from the vulgar crowd. Politics was degrading and not 'ideal'. Power remained firmly in the hands of pre-industrial aristocracies, kaisers and counts. Even men such as Freud or Max Weber feared and distrusted the 'masses'. One of the reasons why Freud kicked Alfred Adler out of his psychoanalytic inner circle in 1911 was that Adler would insist on practising social democracy. The tragedy of German liberalism arose because it hesitated in the middle, unacceptable to the aristocratic elites and fearful and contemptuous of what it considered the masses. By 1932 the two great German parties of liberalism which had been co-founders of the German Empire had dwindled to just over 1 per cent of the vote each. The disappearance of German liberalism cleared the way for the elimination of the Jews.

In theory, liberalism knows no race nor colour. The actor in the traditional liberal model has no individuality. 'We hold these truths to be self-evident', wrote Jefferson, 'that all men are created equal', all men, irrespective of who they might be. The Jews posed a problem because their identity remained stubbornly collective. To be a Jew meant to be part of a community sanctified by religion and tradition, to stand out in dress, eating habits, daily observance and language. Enlightened Prussian bureaucrats, influenced both by Kant and Adam Smith, had trouble imagining how the Jews could be absorbed as a collective body. Freiherr von Schrötter, a distinguished, enlightened and progressive Prussian civil servant, put it this way: 'The purpose must be to undermine their nationality and bring them to the point where they no longer constitute a "state within the state".'[185]

There was nothing particularly Prussian in that. All enlightened reformers on the continent assumed that the Jewish problem could only be solved by the disappearance of Jews as a religious community. The same rationalism which made them attack the church as a bastion of superstition made them assume that traditional Judaism belonged to the Dark Ages too.

Assimilation seemed to be the answer. Jews would become like Germans, shave their beards and forget the sabbath. The trouble was that, even as Germans, Jews could never be typical. Their history had given them characteristic skills and a special social structure. They had no peasantry nor landowning class. They were urban, commercial and even in Germany unusually literate. In 1871 there were approximately 500,000 Jews in Bismarck's empire. Two-thirds of them lived in Prussia and a quarter of those in Berlin. Sixty per cent of all Jews (as opposed to 20 per cent of the population as a whole) lived in towns. By 1926, of the 564,000 Jews in Germany (under 1 per cent of the population), most lived in cities and were grossly over-represented in trade and the professions. They made up 13 per cent of all doctors, 16 per cent of all lawyers, and 40 per cent of all scrap metal dealers. Jews owned one-fifth of all private banks and four-fifths of all department stores.[186]

They stood out by their wealth. Werner Mosse has traced the Jewish economic elite from the beginning of the nineteenth century to 1935 and has worked out that roughly one-fifth of the business elite throughout the entire period was Jewish. The evolution of the modern corporation had little effect. Jews (of course not always the same people) made the change from counting house to corporation board room in about the same proportions. In 1908, of the twenty nine families with aggregate fortunes of 50 million marks or more, nine (31 per cent) were Jewish. The Rothschilds (including the Gold-schmidts) came second, the Speyers sixth and the Mendelssohns (including the Mendelssohn-Bartholdys) eighth.[187]

Jews distinguished themselves in characteristically 'modern' sectors of the economy. They introduced modern marketing through the department store, a sector which aroused great resentment among small traders and shopkeepers. It is no accident that small traders were over-represented as Nazi voters. Tom Childers has shown that the Nazi vote of 1930, roughly 18 per cent, had been there in the 1920s ready to be mobilized but divided among small 'Christian' protest parties or economic pressure groups.[188]

Publishing and what we now call the media seemed to be dominated by Jews. Although the biggest film producer, Alfred Hugenberg, was right-wing and very distinctly not Jewish, the cultural section of the Nazi party trumpeted statistics that 'Jews' owned 70 per cent of all film companies and financed two-thirds of all films.[189] The two most important liberal newspapers, the *Berliner Tageblatt* and the *Frankfurter Zeitung*, were 'Jewish' papers, and Jews were prominent in the world of publishing. Think of the contribution of Fischer and Ullstein.

Paranoids exist in all societies. There are in any mental hospital or on any street corner persons who will tell you how the Jews or the Masons or the Catholics conspired to ruin their marriages. The influence such fantasies have depends on the general health of society and the attitude of the elites. In the German case both worked against the integration of German Jewry no matter how patriotic German Jews were.

In political and social terms Jews, even assimilated Jews, shared the fate of the German middle classes as a whole. Like Gentile members of the bourgeoisie, even after Bismarck, they could not get into the fancy regiments or the right clubs. Even the Krupps, Thyssens and Haniels, none of whom were Jewish, could not break into the aristocratic circle that surrounded the throne and guarded its values. Ralf Dahrendorf has likened German society in the late nineteenth century to a set of distinct, geological layers.[190] It was a much more rigid, less fluid society than late Victorian or Edwardian England. On the eve of the First World War, Britain had a liberal government some of whose members were high aristocrats like Churchill, others utterly self-made like Lloyd George or Viscount Morley. German cabinets had no such figures and in any case could not be said to govern the country.

Jews were middle class, liberal but above all they were Jewish. The distrust and hatred of liberal institutions and practices affected them twice over. In November 1907 the Bavarian military attaché in Berlin reported to his Minister of War that he had discussed with the Prussian Minister whether Jews might become officers in the reserve, 'this admittedly very democratic institution'. The Prussian Minister of War told him that 'all those officials questioned on the matter were unanimously against it'.[191]

The First World War drove Germany mad. The late Herr Wolfgang von Tirpitz, son of the admiral, told me a characteristic story. Captured in the first great sea battle of the war on 28 August 1914, when he went down with his ship but survived, Herr von Tirpitz spent a gentlemanly three years in captivity in a country house on the Welsh border, complete with batman and good cigars. In 1917 he was exchanged for a British prisoner and returned to a Germany he no longer recognized. The brutalities of war had, he told me, turned it into 'a madhouse'.

The Prussian elite which had chosen to go to war faced a terrible dilemma. To win it had to mobilize the masses, literally to move them physically and spiritually, but it had to do so without allowing the masses any rights. When in 1917 Chancellor Bethmann Hollweg suggested tentatively that the Prussian voting system be democratized as a sign of good will to those dying in the trenches, General Wild von Hohenborn wrote to his wife: 'If the Kaiser's army should threaten to turn into a parliament's army then only a new Bismarck and a new Roon can help. Maybe I see it too black.'[192]

By 1917 there was no Kaiser's army in any case.The fiction that the Kaiser commanded his troops like a latter-day Frederick the Great had been forgotten and from 1916 to 1918 Germany was ruled by a military dictatorship under Hindenburg and Ludendorff. The Chancellor's office, the position Bismarck designed for himself, was still there and Theobald von Bethmann Hollweg still held it as he had since 1909. The parliament was growing noisier and less servile. The army had to break its power and destroy the Chancellor. Lieutenant Colonel Max Bauer, chief of operations at Army High Command, had no doubt that Bethmann Hollweg 'has lost the favour of the parties supporting the state . . . through his servility to the parties fighting against a strong monarchy (Jewish liberalism and social democracy).'[193]

The longer the war went on the more the upper classes saw the Jew as the symbol of all those odious liberal demands which threatened the hegemony of the old Prussian elite. In July of 1918 Lieutenant Colonel Bauer wrote a lengthy memorandum on the consequences for the army of changes in domestic politics. The Crown Prince was so impressed that he sent a copy to the Kaiser and to General Ludendorff. Here is Bauer's view of the position of the Jews:

A terrible rage has broken out everywhere against the Jews and justly so. When one is in Berlin and goes through the economic offices or along the Tauentziehenstrasse, one can quite easily believe that one is in Jerusalem. On the front on the other hand one hardly ever sees a Jew. Almost every thinking person is outraged at the modest contribution made by Jews but nothing can be done. To get at the Jews, that is, capital, which has both press and parliament in its hand, is impossible.[194]

Paranoia had spread from the mental hospitals to the general staff and the throne room. Jews, or to be accurate, *das Judentum*, threatened the Prussian status quo. It stood for liberalism, capital, press, social democracy and parliament, the very forces that the Junker establishment had vanquished in 1815 and 1848. As Bauer was writing his memorandum, the German General Staff was in the midst of its final *Alles oder Nichts* operation on the Western front, the infamous Ludendorff offensive, in which more men were to die than at Verdun. On 29 September 1918 General Ludendorff confessed that the 'Supreme Army Command and the German Army are at an end', but not so reduced that Ludendorff was prepared to take the blame. As he told his staff on taking leave of them, 'it was time to bring those circles into government whom in the main we have to thank that things have come to this. . . . Let them eat the soup that they have prepared for us.'[195]

A month later, Heinrich Class, head of the extreme right-wing Pan-German league, made it clear to the executive committee of the organization precisely how that was to be done. The true responsibility was to be pushed on to others: 'The situation to be used for fanfares against *das Judentum* and the Jews to be made into lightning rods for everything wrong.'[196]

Kaiser Wilhelm II himself in his bitter exile knew who to blame for the end of the Hohenzollern dynasty. On 2 December 1919, a few weeks after his abdication and flight, he wrote a private letter to Field Marshall August von Mackensen, in which he poured out his hatred of Jews:

> The deepest, vilest disgrace, which any people in all of history has ever suffered, the German people has brought upon itself . . . urged on and seduced by the hateful tribe of Juda who enjoyed rights as guests among them. That was its thanks! May no German ever forget it and not rest until these parasites have been crushed and exterminated; this poisonous fungus on the German oak.[197]

The German ruling class in 1918-19 fell upon and blamed the Jews for their own failings. The Jew stood for modernity, progress, democracy and ultimately the bankruptcy of their reactionary regime. Hitler did not have to invent the 'stab-in-the-back' legend. The Kaiser, German general staff and its allies delivered it to him ready-made, nor was he the first to cry 'the Jews are to blame for everything'. Wilhelm II's language, full of biological imagery and threats of extermination, was already in the air long before Hitler stood up in a beer hall for the first time.

Germans who believed it were not stupid nor brutal, just shocked. How were they to know the real situation? In 1918 there were no radios in private use. Yes, there were hardships on the home front, unrest and strike threats. Yet in 1918 the Germans seemed to have won the war in the East. The German army had destroyed Tsarist Russia and occupied huge chunks of Russian territory. Nobody, not even members of parliament, was prepared for the collapse of Imperial Germany. Suddenly there was no Kaiser and Germany had accepted an armistice. In Berlin the socialists seized power and one of them in a moment of euphoria had proclaimed a republic from the balcony of the Reichstag. Somebody must be to blame.

It was easy to blame the Jews. In 1917 the Bolsheviks had seized power in Russia. Trotsky, Kamenev, Zinoviev, Radek and countless other Russian Bolsheviks were Jews. For all the horrified German burgher knew, so was Lenin. The international Jewish capitalist-communist conspiracy had gained power in St Petersburg and now seemed to be reaching for Berlin. To minds maddened by the brutalities of the trenches and seared by hunger and loss of loved ones, it was not an implausible view. Hence the ground had been laid for the ideological consensus which Christian Streit and Theo Schulte have identified on the Russian front, and I have found in the Balkans. The equation Jew=Bolshevik=Enemy made it difficult for German officers in the Second World War to act as their Italian colleagues did or even to understand their motives.

Not all Germans held such views. The Nazis never got more than about one-third of the vote in a free election. Nor was Germany (including Austria) more anti-semitic than other zones of Europe. Far from it. Poland, Rumania, the Ukraine, areas of economic backwardness and peasant agriculture, developed a popular anti-semitism of terrible, murderous ferocity. Historians have found little evidence that persecution of Jews between 1933 and 1945 enjoyed wide support in Germany. As late as October 1941 the US Embassy in Berlin reported to Washington:

> The revival of the Jewish question by the required wearing of the Star of David has met with almost universal disapproval by the people of Berlin and in some cases with astonishing manifestations of sympathy with the Jews in public. The reaction has become increasingly obvious to all observers. ... The party organization has now begun distributing leaflets to households urging people to avoid all contact with Jews and to shun the Star of David with disdain when they meet it on the street.[198]

Albert Speer recorded the same phenomenon:

> At the end of 1941 I took part in a boring and endless lunch in the Reich Chancellery. In the course of conversation Goebbels began suddenly to complain to Hitler about the behaviour of the Berliners: 'The introduction of the Jewish star has produced the opposite of what it was supposed to do, my Führer! We wanted to exclude the Jews from the community. But ordinary people don't avoid them. On the contrary! They show sympathy for them everywhere. This people is simply not ripe and is infected with sentimentality.' Embarrassment. Hitler stirred his soup in silence. Seated at the huge round table, we would have preferred to hear about the advances on the eastern front. The majority of

us were not anti-semites. Even Dönitz and Raeder not really. But we just passed over the matter in silence.[199]

Michael Marrus in his study of recent writing on the holocaust sums up the present consensus among historians this way:

Informed theories about the centrality of anti-semitism in Nazism do not rest upon claims that anti-Jewish ideology was a predominantly German doctrine or a constant preoccupation of the leaders of the Third Reich. Research on the background to the Holocaust, indeed, has suggested the opposite.[200]

Jews in Germany were certainly vulnerable in a way that Jews in Italy were not. They were prominent, numerous, identifiable, and concentrated. Italian Jews were almost literally the opposite. Germans had a set of attitudes and values which heightened imagined distinctions between Gentile and Jew; Italian values minimized them. Germans despised trade and commerce and political fixing as *Kuhhandel* (horse-trading), activities at which Italians excelled. Germany had a very brief experience of constitutional democracy; Italy had a rooted, liberal tradition, however corrupt and deformed. The German aristocracies had social and economic power, especially embodied in the Junker class and the great East Elbian estates. After all, one of them, Paul Ludwig Hans Anton von Beneckendorff und von Hindenburg, was the President of the German Republic who named Adolf Hitler – the 'Bohemian Corporal', as he contemptuously called him – Chancellor of the Reich in 1933. The Italian aristocracy broke into local groupings lacking homogeneity and divided by the struggle between church and state. The upper German social strata excluded Jews; the Italian did not. Finally, the single most characteristic institution in the history of Prussia-Germany had been the army. As Georg Heinrich von Behrenhorst had put it in the eighteenth century, 'The Prussian monarchy is not a country which has an army, but an army which has a country, in which – as it were – it is just stationed.'[201] The single most characteristic institution in Italy was the church.

The smaller question – why did Italian officers and diplomats refuse to co-operate in the holocaust while their German opposite numbers did? – can, I hope, now be answered. The two strands of the argument, the 'events' as they unfolded and the 'explanations' which have compared structures, behaviours and beliefs, converge at this point. Italian officers behaved as they did because they served in a traditional, monarchist, liberal, gentlemanly, masonic, philo-semitic and anti-fascist service. The professional diplomats, even those who had come from the fascist movement, shared those values, and, then, there was always in the background the church. The worse the war went the more they asserted those values of *civiltà italiana* against the monstrous demands of their Axis partner. German officers acted as they did because traditions of obedience and rigidities of thought made any other action unthinkable, because by 1941–42 Hitler's ideology had fused with their own prejudices and assumptions, because their culture had an almost Manichaean dualism which excluded Jews and other *Untermenschen* from the human race, because the Nazi regime had a dark apparatus of repression and terror from which nobody, not even a four-star general, could feel exempt. Ambassador Guelfo Zamboni told me that in Salonica even *General-oberst* Löhr, Supreme Commander South East, trembled when the SS came.[202] Italian officers and diplomats could conspire because the risks were less. Nobody obeyed in Italy anyway; because Mussolini could, even at the end, still hear a human voice and react, because they knew that their conspiracy made sense nationally.

German opponents of Hitler faced the opposite problem. The risks were certain; the chances of succeeding poor. Nazi Germany was a serious totalitarian state; fascist Italy was a façade. Hitler bore in his demented head deformed, monstrous, but still recognizable values which German culture had bequeathed to him. The madder he got the more poisonous they became. Mussolini believed in nothing; his contempt for humanity and its noises blinded him to moral issues but he could see the real world. Hitler spent his final days bent over Wagnerian projects for dream cities of the future and reading Carlyle's *Frederick the Great*, while bombs turned his capital into rubble and shook even the subterranean bunker in which he eventually died. These and many other elements help to explain why a few good men in a bad time were willing and able to do something good, and, if my explanations do not convince, I can at least claim to have told their story.

CONCLUSION

Visitors to Berlin used to climb observation platforms on the Western side of the Wall and look eastwards across Hitler's divided capital. The wall was in reality two walls separated by a no-man's land and guarded by watch towers. The area between the two walls looked uncannily like a concentration camp as if a bit of Auschwitz had been scratched across the face of the Reich capital. From the platform near what was once the Potsdamer Platz they could see the bunker in which Hitler died. Its massive concrete slabs resisted post-war attempts to blow it up and huge fragments of concrete pushed the soil into large mounds. There was something deeply right about the isolation of that bunker; a symbol which the destruction of the wall has inadvertently removed. Hitler's last monument rested in a place where nobody went. His tomb, cut off from humanity, was sur-rounded by the symbols of fear and oppression which his regime brought to mankind, a pile of rubble in an empty field.

Hitler inflicted more misery on his fellow human beings than anybody in the history of the human race. He may not have been more vicious than some great evil-doers in the past but he had more terrible means at his disposal. Yet, as I have tried to show, it is more than naive, it is dangerous to see Hitler as uniquely guilty. While he was undoubtedly mad, his madness came in forms which seemed attractive and right to millions of his fellow countrymen. His resent-ments were theirs; his prejudices and preferences like their own. He used the engines of a modern state to murder and enslave millions, but that engine functioned smoothly to the end. In the SS files, I found pay-slips complete with the correct deductions and provision for pensions dated 30 April 1945. The Nazi state ticked over until there were no typewriters to pound or gas to put in gas chambers.

Something went terribly wrong in Germany, and historians have long been poring over the remains to try to see where, when and how. Immediately after the war they wrote books about the mind of Germany which set Germany apart from 'the West' from Martin

Luther's time to the present. Others saw the decisive moments in the rise of Prussia, the reign of Frederick William I or Frederick the Great. In the 1960s a school emerged in Germany which saw the turning point in and during the First World War. That was followed by one which pushed it back to Bismarck's time and latterly, in our torpid, conservative age there are those who claim it was all the fault of the Bolsheviks anyway and Germany was just reacting to 'prior' Soviet terror or waging preventive war on Russia before Russia attacked Germany.

Something went terribly wrong in Italy too and the rise of fascism was really 'prior' to the emergence of Nazism. Hitler always acknowledged his debt to Mussolini and rightly. Mussolini invented the modern mass movement of the right. He learned his techniques from Lenin and drew his ideology from the accumulating detritus of irrationalism, voluntarism, futurism and anti-modernism in all its poisonous variants. The fascist regime had secured its power, jailed its enemies and begun to build its great Roman monuments while Hitler's party lurked in the shadows of the Weimar Republic, not able to collect 3 per cent of the votes.

The two regimes had much in common. The Axis was less 'unnatural' than many Italians wished to believe. They differed less in structure than in thoroughness and purpose. Hitler never wavered in his determination to destroy Jewry. Mussolini never fixed his attention on anything for very long. Hitler's views on politics remained constant from 1920 to the last days in the bunker; Mussolini changed his direction with each passing wind. For Mussolini power itself seemed to be the end; for Hitler it was but a means.

I cannot answer the big question: how was the holocaust possible? But I offer two final reflections which this book suggests. The evils of fascism and national socialism became possible when one human being could write about another:

> With the Führer leading us, we shall always be victorious. He unites in his person all the virtues of the great soldier: courage, discretion, flexibility, a capacity for sacrifice and a lordly contempt for his own comfort. It can only be an honour to fight under him. . . . The Führer is deeply religious, though completely anti-Christian. He views Christianity as a symptom of decay. Rightly so. It is a branch of the Jewish race. This can be seen in the similarity of religious rites. Both (Judaism and Christianity) have no point of contact with the animal element, and, thus, in the end, they will be destroyed. The Führer is a convinced vegetarian, on principle. His arguments cannot be refuted on any serious basis. They are totally unanswerable.[1]

Thus, Joseph Goebbels in his diary for 1939 and he meant it. He too died in the bunker. A world without Hitler had no meaning for him. He poisoned himself and his wife and the brood of little girls whose names all began with H. The ruins of the bunker are his also, loyal beyond the grave but to what? To another human being. Goebbels, Bottai and all other hypnotized followers of the two great dictators forgot the deep truth in the law of Moses:

> Thou shalt have none other gods before me. . . . Thou shalt not bow down thyself unto them nor serve them: for I the Lord thy God am a jealous God, visiting the iniquity of the fathers upon the children unto the third and fourth generation of them that hate me. (*Deuteronomy* 5, 7–9)

You don't have to be religious to see what went wrong. The fanatical followers of Hitler and Mussolini made men into gods and suffered for it. Nobody is always right. No arguments are 'unanswerable'.

As Bottai admitted in his letter of 'expiation' to his son,[2] he and his generation had gloried in the will. They scoffed at reason and experiment. Rationality was cold, lifeless, old. They were young, vital, forceful, virile. In 1944, in his 50s, Bottai saw the results. In a great work on the destruction of reason, György Lukacs wrote: 'Hitler and Rosenberg dragged the irrational pessimism of Nietzsche and Dilthey, of Heidegger and Jaspers, that had been preached from lecterns and talked of in salons and cafés, and let it loose on the streets.'[3]

Unreason knows no limits. It cannot measure profit against loss or assess means and ends. It rejects the liberty of the mind and threatens the person of the thinker. It cannot tolerate free speech, blasphemous books, satire and irreverence. It mobilizes the turbulent energies, emotions and wishes inside each of us and hurls them against the limits of the human condition. In doing so it destroys itself and lays waste its surroundings. Behind the martial façades of fascism and national socialism its acolytes were afraid. They feared and hence tried to escape the judgement of reason. The ruins of Europe and the piles of skeletons were the outcome.

As Edward Gibbon wrote two centuries ago, the person called to rule over us should approach the task with awe:

> The man who presumes to reign should aspire to the perfection of the divine nature; he should purify his soul from her mortal and terrestrial part; he should extinguish his appetites, enlighten his understanding, regulate his passions, and subdue the wild beast which, according to the lively metaphor of Aristotle, seldom fails to ascend the throne of the despot.'[4]

SOURCES AND BIBLIOGRAPHY

1. ORAL HISTORICAL SOURCES

Mr Paul Bandler, 28 March 1988, Rome
Avv. Camillo Boitani, 2 April 1988, Rome
Gen. Carlo Casarico, 7 April 1988, Rome
Mrs Evi Eller, 4 April 1988, Rome
Dott. Giacomo Cristiano Garaguso, 26 March 1988, Rome
Professor Salvatore Loi, 26 March 1988, Rome
His Excellency Ambassador Guelfo Zamboni, 9 April 1988, Lido dei Pini

2. PRIMARY AND UNPUBLISHED SOURCES

German

BERLIN DOCUMENT CENTRE

Personal files of:
Abetz, Otto, Ambassador *SS Brigadeführer*
Dollmann, Eugen, *SS Obersturmbannführer*
Glaise von Horstenau, Edmund, *Generalleutnant SS Brigadeführer*
Hildebrandt, Richard, *SS Obergruppenführer*
Kasche, Siegfried, Ambassador *SA Obergruppenführer*
Knochen, Helmut, *SS Standartenführer*
Meyszner, August, *SS Gruppenführer*
Oberg, Carl Albrecht, *SS Gruppenführer*
Rintelen, Enno von, *General der Infanterie*
Schimana, Walter, *SS Gruppenführer*
Turner, Harald, *SS Gruppenführer*
Wolff, Karl, *SS Obergruppenführer*

Other files:
SS HO 649
SS HO 1478
SS HO 1479
SS HO 1642
SS HO 2471
SS HO 4410

BUNDESARCHIV-MILITÄRARCHIV:

Archive series numbers	Name of the series	Folder numbers
RH 1/v.58	Oberkommando der Wehrmacht: Politische Einzelfälle	
RH 31 III	Bevollmächtigter deutscher General in Agram	1–13
RH 31 VI	Deutscher General beim Haupʾquartier der ital. Wehrmacht	1,2.3. 4k
RH 31 VII	Deutscher General des OB West in Vichy	1–15,24,28,30
RH 31 IX	Deutscher General beim ital. Armeeoberkommando 8	1,9,10,20,26, 35,36,37
RH 31 X	Deutscher Generalstab beim ital. Armeeoberkommando 11	1–5
RH 21 2	Panzerarmeekommando 2	590–92,614–16
RH 23	Kommando des rückwärtigen Armeegebiets 559 Gruppe/Afrika	112,128–31
RH 24 15	Generalkommando XV(Gebirgs-) Armeekorps	5–7,8,11–12, 44–8
RH 24 22	Generalkommando XX(Gebirgs-) Armeekorps	7,9–11,19–22 23
RH 26 392	392.(Kroat.)Inf.Div.	1–4
RH 28 1	1. Gebirgs-Division	107–11,117–19
RW 4	Oberkommando der Wehrmacht/ Wehrmachtsführungsstab	508,573,574, 587–88,662,682 744–5,749,752 757
	Kommandierender General und Befehlshaber in Serbien	11–12,23,79, 79
	Militärbefehlshaber Griechen- land	126–7,128–31 146–9

Protokol über den Verhör des kriegsgefangen deutschen Generals Alexander LÖHR, verfasst am 24. Mai 1945 in der Kanzlei des Lagers Banjica-Belgrad. Anwesend: Bojović Radosav, Dr Albert Weiss, Nada Bogićević.

Italian

ARCHIVIO CENTRALE DELLO STATO, ROME

Segreteria Particolare del Duce, Carteggio Riservata

B. 191:	Bolletini giornalieri f.103–104 1.3.43–31.4.1943
	Comando Supremo, Stato Maggiore Generale Ufficio Operazioni: messagi in arrivo
f. 290	30.3.1943–3.4.1943

f. 291	4.4.1943–6.4.1943
B. 144 f. 144	Ebrei: Segrè, Guido Ammiraglio
B. 145 f. 39	Ministero della Guerra
B. 1 f. 10	Pariani, Alberto
B. 23 f. 223	Cavagnari, Domenico Ammiraglio
B. 34 f. 242	Riunioni del Direttorio del Partito Nazionale Fascista: 1942–43
B. 44 f. 242	Badoglio, Pietro, Maresciallo d'Italia
B. 60 f. 278	Pricolo, Francesco
B. 61 f. 349	Favagrossa, Carlo
B. 62 f. 364	Antifascismo: Sf. 5 Ministero degli Esteri Sf. 8 Ministero della Guerra Sf. 11 Ministero della Marina
B. 67 f. 389 f. 390	Badoglio, Pietro Cavallero, Ugo
B. 71 f. 461	Pavelić e Regno di Croazia
B. 73 f. 463 f. 489 f. 525	Gambara, Gastone Mackensen, Hans Georg von Roatta, Mario
B. 86 W/R1	Guzzoni, Alfredo
B. 92 W/R	Russo, Luigi
B. 93 W/R	Soddu, Ubaldo Sorice, Antonio

Ministero dell'Interno. Direzione Generale Pubblica Sicurezza: Affari Generali

B. 7 f. 27	Ovra Zona IX (Dalmazia) 1941–43 Ufficio Rapporti Germania:
B. 5 f. 28	richeste dalla Gestapo – razzismo 1938
B. 5 f. 53	richieste dalla Gestapo 1941
B. 44 f. C11/48	Germania – Polizia

Ministero dell'Interno Direzione Generale Demografia e Razza

B. 2 f. 10	Francia occupata durante la guerra
B. 3 f. 12	Francia occupata durante la guerra
B. 4 f. 15–17	Affari Generali (discriminazioni ecc)
B. 5 f. 24	Israeliti militari
B. 9 f. 38	Precettazione civile per lavoro
B. 11 f. 41	Mobilitazione totale degli ebrei
B. 13 f. 43	Censimento e situazione ebraica

Ministero dell'Interno Direzione Generale Pubblica Sicurezza
Affari Generali Categoria GI Associazioni

B. 329 f.1439   Legione Dalmatica 1942–43

Ministero dell'Interno Direzione Generale Pubblica Sicurezza Affari
Generali Riservati

B. 1	A5	Notizie dall'estero 1942: Croazia
B. 56	J4	Movimento sovversivo all'estero
B. 3		Notizie all'estero 1943:
	f. 3	Croazia
	f. 16	Francia
	f. 49	dissidi fra soldati italiani e tedeschi nel fronte Russo
	f. 50	situazione della Slovenia tedesca
	f. 63	Grecia
	f. 64	Polonia
	f. 65	Francia
B. 17		Notizie dall'estero:
	f. 84	Croazia

Ministero dell'Interno Direzione Generale Pubblica Sicurezza Affari
Generali Riservati Gtg A5G II Guerra Mondiale

B. 19	Attività degli ebrei
B. 412	Propaganda disfattista fra le truppe
B. 415	Croazia
B. 423	Ebrei mobilitazione civile

Ministero dell'Interno Divisione Polizia Politica:

B. 329 f. 350   Unione Israelitica Italiana

MINISTERO DEGLI AFFARI ESTERI-ARCHIVIO STORICO DIPLOMATICO

Francia: 1940–43

B. 50	f. 11	Sionismo (1941)
B. 55		Rapporti politici (1942)
B. 64	f. 8	Sionismo (1942)
B. 68		Rapporti politici (1943)
B. 77		Notizie militari (1943)
B. 80		Rapporti politici (1943)

Grecia

B. 22   Rapporti politici

Jugoslavia (Croazia)

B. 114   f. 4   Sionismo (1941)
B. 133   f. 8   Sionismo (1942)
B. 138   f. 8   Deportazione degli ebrei croati (1942–43)

Jugoslavia (Montenegro)

B. 122   f. 5   Sionismo (1941)

Santa Sede

B. 65   Rapporti (1943)

Relazione sull'opera svolta dal Ministero degli Affari Esteri per la tutela delle comunità ebraiche (1938–1943), 43854, riservato, settembre, 1946

STATO MAGGIORE DELL'ESERCITO V REPARTO UFFICIO STORICO

Comando Supremo Regio Esercito

B. 1442   Diario Storico settembre-dicembre 1942
B. 1443   Diario Storico gennaio–aprile 1943
B. 1481   Diario Storico: Allegati 1–20 dicembre 1942
B. 1048   Servizio Informazioni Esteri agosto 1942
B. 1356   Novità operative del SMRE Ufficio Operazione I ottobre–novembre 1942

Comando Superiore Slovenia Dalmatia ('Supersloda') Seconda Armata

B. 993   Frontiera Orientale 1942
B. 1222   Frontiera Orientale ottobre-novembre 1942
B. 1358   'Notiziario vario' maggio-giugno 1942
B. 1359   'Notiziario vario' luglio-agosto 1942
B. 1360   'Notiziario vario' settembre 1942 – febbraio 1943
B. 1363   'Operazioni' 1943
B. 1371   'Bosnia: Situazione' gennaio–giugno 1942
B. 1372   'Montenegro: Situazione' gennaio–giugno 1942
B. 736   'Albania' marzo–aprile 1942

B. 1393A   Diario Storico: Grecia-Relazioni Varie
1) 'Due anni di guerra al comando dalla 11a Armata'
   Generale Carlo Geloso;
2) Relazione Generale Umberto Broccoli

Comando Forze Armate Grecia (11a Armata)

B.   634   Diario Storico gennaio 1942
B.   635   Diario Storico febbraio 1942
B.   737   Diario Storico marzo–aprile 1942
B.   839   Diario Storico maggio 1942
B.   840   Diario Storico giugno 1942
B.   966   Diario Storico luglio 1942
B. 1054   Diario Storico settembre–ottobre 1942
B. 1098   Diario Storico novembre–dicembre 1942
B. 1226   Diario Storico gennaio 1943

Comando Quarta Armata (Francia)

B.   741   Diario Storico giugno–luglio 1942
B.   813   Diario Storico agosto–settembre 1942
B. 1099   Diario Storico ottobre–novembre 1942
B. 1127   Diario Storico gennaio–febbraio 1943

Corpi d'Armata

B. 1100   I Cd'A (Francia) gennaio–febbraio 1943
B. 1186   I Cd'A (Francia) marzo–aprile 1943
B. 1312   I Cd'A (Francia) maggio–giugno 1943
B. 1083   XV Cd'A (Francia) gennaio–febbraio 1943
B. 1101   XX Cd'A (Francia) ottobre–dicembre 1942
B. 1102   XX Cd'A (Francia) gennaio–febbraio 1943
B. 1217   XX Cd'A (Francia) marzo-aprile 1943
B. 1249   XX Cd'A (Francia) maggio-giugno 1943

Divisions, Regiments, Battalions

B.   258   32 Div. Ftr 'Marche' luglio–agosto 1941
B.   706   Div. Alpini 'Pusteria' aprile–maggio 1942
B.   821   Div. Alpini 'Pusteria' giugno–luglio 1942
B.   989   2. Div. Celere 'Emanuele Filiberto Testa di Ferro' novembre–febbraio 1942–43

B. 1186	2. Div. Celere 'Emanuele Filiberto Testa di Ferro' marzo–aprile 1943
B. 1253	2. Div. Celere 'Emanuele Filiberto Testa di Ferro' maggio–giugno 1943
B. 2225	Div. Ftr 'Lupi di Toscana' gennaio–settembre 1943
B. 783	55 Regt.Ftr. Div. 'Marche' giugno–luglio 1942
B. 859	154 Regt.Ftr. Div. 'Murge' agosto–ottobre 1942
	259 Regt.Ftr. Div. luglio–agosto 1942
	260 Regt.Ftr. Div. luglio–agosto 1942

Carabinieri reali

B. 446	Sussak: 23 Btg CCRR Mobilitato 1942
	Spalato 9 Btg CCRR Autonomo 1942
	Knin 16 Btg CCRR Autonomo 1942
B. 824	Reparti CCRR maggio–dicembre 1942

Miscellaneous

| SP 58/36 | Elenco diplomatici e militari italiani che hanno aiutati ebrei durante la 2a Guerra Mondiale |
| SP 59/13 | Problemi ebrei francesi nei territori occupati dalla 4a Armata (Francia) |

NATIONAL ARCHIVES WASHINGTON, DC

Comando 2a Armata

T–821	Item: 5283a-d Microfilm Roll 405
	5283e-m Microfilm Roll 406
	5283n Microfilm Roll 407

3. PRINTED PRIMARY SOURCES

Actes et Documents du Saint Siège Relatifs à la seconde guerre mondiale, 'Le Saint Siège et les victimes de la Guerre Janvier-Décembre 1943' (Libreria Editrice Vaticana, 1975)

Akten zur Deutschen Auswärtigen Politik Series E, 1941–45:

Bd. 1 12 Dezember 1941 – 28 September 1942 (Göttingen, 1969)
Bd. 2 1 März 1942   – 15 Juni   1942 (Göttingen, 1972)
Bd. 3 16 Juni 1942   – 30 September 1942 (Göttingen, 1972)
Bd. 4 1 Oktober 1942   – 31 Dezember 1942 (Göttingen, 1975)
Bd. 5 1 Januar 1943   – 30 April   1943 (Göttingen, 1977)
Bd. 6 1 Mai 1943   – 30 September 1943 (Göttingen, 1979)

Alfieri, Dino, *Dictators Face to Face*, trs. David Moore (London and New York, 1954)

Anfuso, Filippo, *Roma Berlino Salò* (Carnusca sul Naviglio, 1950)

Artom, Emanuele, *Diario: Gennaio 1940–Febbraio 1944*, Centro di documentazione ebraica contemporaneo (Milan, 1966)

Below, Nicolaus von, *Als Hitlers Adjutant 1937–1945* (Mainz, 1980)

Bottai, Giuseppe, *Diario 1935–1944*, a cura di Giordano Bruno Guerri (Milan, 1982)

Carpi, Daniel, 'Nuovi documenti per la storia dell'Olocausto in Grecia. L'attegiamento degli italiani', *Michael on the History of the Jews in the Diaspora*, vol. VII, (Tel Aviv, 1981)

Cavallero, Ugo, *Comando Supremo. Diario 1940–1943 del Capo di S.M.G.* (Rocca S. Casciano, 1948)

Caviglia, Enrico, *Diario 1925–1945* (Rome, 1952)

Ciano, Count Galeazzo, *Diaries 1937–39* (London, 1952)

Ciano's Diary 1939–1943, ed. Malcolm Muggeridge (London, 1947)

Documenti diplomatici italiani, Nona Serie, 1939–43, vol. IV, 9 aprile 1940–10 giugno 1940 (Rome, 1960)

Dorian, Emil, *The Quality of Witness. A Romanian Diary, 1937–1944*, ed. Marguerite Doran and trs. Marci Soceanu Vamos (Philadelphia, Pa, 1982)

Ebrei in Italia: Deportazione, Resistenza, Centro di documentazione ebraica contemporaneo (Florence, 1974)

Die Endlösung der Judenfrage in Frankreich, Deutsche Dokumente 1941–44, ed. Serge Klarsfeld (Paris, 1977)

The Goebbels Diaries 1939–41, trans. and ed. Fred Taylor (London, 1982)

The Goebbels Diaries 1942–43, ed. Louis P. Lochner (Garden City, NY, 1948)

Grandi, Dino, 'Pagine di diario del 1943', *Storia Contemporanea* anno XIV, no. 6 (December, 1983)

Guariglia, Raffaele, *Ricordi 1922–1946* (Naples, 1950)

Hassell, Ulrich von, *Vom andern Deutschland* (Frankfurt/Main, 1964)

Hitlers Tischgespräche im Führerhauptquartier, ed. Henry Picker (Stuttgart, 1976)

The Holocaust. Selected Documents in eighteen volumes, ed. John Mendelsohn (New York, 1982)

Das Kreigstagebuch des Oberkommandos der Wehrmacht, ed. P.E. Schramm with A. Hillgruber, W. Hubatsch, H.-A. Jacobson (Frankfurt/Main, 1961 ff)

'Excerpts from the Salonika Diary of Lucillo Merci (February-August 1943)' compiled by Joseph Rochlitz with introduction by Menachem Shelack. *Yad Vashem Studies*, vol. XVIII (Jerusalem, 1987)

Mussolini, Benito, *Memoirs 1942–43*, trs. Frances Lobb, (London, 1949)

Ortona, Egidio, 'Il 1943 da Palazzo Chigi. Note di Diario' *Storia Contemporanea*, anno XIV, no. 6 (December, 1983)

Ortona, Egidio, 'Diario sul Governo della Dalmazia (1941–43)', *Storia Contemporanea*, anno XVIII, no. 6 (December, 1987)

'Extracts from the Private Diary of Count Luca Pietromarchi' from *The Righteous Enemy. The Italians and the Jews in Occupied Europe 1941–43*. A collection of notes and research materials for the documentary film by Joseph Rochlitz (Rome, 1988)

Pirelli, Alberto, *Taccuini 1922–1943* (Bologna, 1984)

Poliakov L., *La condition des Juifs sous l'occupation italienne*, Centre de Documentation Juive Contemporaine. Serie 'Documents' no. 3 (Paris, 1946)

Poliakov L. and Sabille, Jacques, *Jews under the Italian Occupation* (Paris, 1955)

Reichsführer! Briefe an und von Heinrich Himmler, ed. Helmut Heiber (Stuttgart, 1968)

Rinser, Luise, *Gefängnistagebuch* (1946, reprinted Frankfurt/Main, 1973)

Speer, Albert, *Spandauer Tagebücher* (Frankfurt/Main, 1975)

Stato Maggiore dell'Esercito. Ufficio Storico
  La campagna di Grecia, 3 vols. By Mario Montanari (Rome, 1980)
  Dalmazia. Una Cronaca per la storia. By Oddone Talpo (Rome, 1985)
  Le operazioni delle unità italiane in Jugoslavia (1941–43) By Salvatore Loi
  (Rome, 1978)
*Topographie des Terrors. Gestapo, SS und Reichssicherheitshauptamt auf dem
  'Prinz-Albrecht-Gelände'*. Eine Dokumentation, ed. Reinhard Rürup (Berlin,
  1987)
*Trials of War Criminals before the Nuremberg Military Tribunal under Control
  Council Law No. 10*, Nuremberg, October 1946–April 1949, 15 volumes,
  (Washington, DC, US Government Printing Office, 1951–52)
  Vol. XI 'The High Command Case'
       'The Hostages Case'
Verbände und Truppen der deutschen Wehrmacht im Zweiten Weltkrieg, Georg
  Tessin (Osnabrück, 1972–79)
World War II German Military Studies. A collection of 213 special reports on the
  Second World War prepared by former officers of the *Wehrmacht* for the
  United States Army, ed. Donald S. Detweiler, assoc. eds Charles B.
  Burdick and Jürgen Rohwer, 24 vols (New York, 1979)

4. Secondary Sources:

Absalom, Roger 'Ex prigionieri alleati e assistenza popolare nella zona della
  linea gotica, 1943–44' in *La Linea Gotica 1944. Esercito, popolazioni, partigiani*,
  ed. G. Rochat, E. Santarelli, P. Sorcinelli, Istituto pesarese per la storia del
  movimento di liberazione (Milan, 1986)
Adler, Jacques, *The Jews of Paris and the Final Solution, Communal Response and
  Internal Conflicts 1940–44* (Oxford, 1987)
Alvaro, Corrado, 'Prefazione', Pirandello, Luigi *Novelle per un anno*, 2 vols,
  5th edn (Milan, 1964)
Amé, Cesare, *Guerra segreta in Italia 1940–43* (Rome, 1946)
Arendt, Hannah, *Eichmann in Jerusalem. A Report on the Banality of Evil*
  (London, 1963)
Ascarelli, Attilio, *Le Fosse Ardeatine* (Bologna, 1964)
Baccino, Renzo, *Fossoli* (Modena, 1961)
Baranowski, Shelly, 'Consent and Dissent: The Confessing Church and
  Conservative Opposition to Hitler', *Journal of Modern History*, vol. 59, no. 1
  (1987)
Barbagli, Marzio, *Educating for Unemployment. Politics, Labor Markets and the
  School System, Italy 1858–1973*, trs. Robert H. Ross (New York, 1982)
Bartov, Omer, *The Eastern Front, 1941–1945, German Troops and the
  Barbarization of Warfare* (Basingstoke and London, 1985)
Bassi, Michele, *Cotignolo: un Approdo di Salvezza per gli ebrei e per i perseguitati
  politici durante la guerra (1943–45)* (Faenza, 1985)
Bastianini, Giuseppe, *Uomini, cose, fatti* (Milan, 1959)
Behrens, C.B.A., *Society, Government and the Enlightenment. The Experiences of
  Eighteenth-century France and Prussia* (London, 1985)
Bennett, Ralph, *Ultra and Mediterranean Strategy 1941–1945* (London, 1989)
Berend, I.T. and Ranki, G., *Economic Development in East Central Europe in the
  nineteenth and twentieth centuries* (New York, 1974)
Bericht der Internationalen Historikerkommission (Waldheim Commission), *Profil*,
  no. 7 (Vienna, 15 February 1988)

Bertoldi, Silvio, *Badoglio* (Milan, 1982)

Bethel, Nicholas (Lord), *The War Hitler Won. September 1939* (London, 1972)

Bonjour, Edgar, 'Die Schweizer Juden in Frankreich 1942/43', *Schweizerische Zeitschrift für Geschichte*, vol. 33, no. 2 (1983)

Bosworth, R.J.B., *Italy. The Least of the Great Powers: Italian Foreign Policy before the First World War* (Cambridge, 1979)

Bowman, Steven, 'Greek Jews and Christians During World War II', *Remembering the Future: Jews and Christians During and After the Holocaust*, Oxford Conference, Theme 1 (1988)

Bowman, Steven, 'Could the Dodekanisi Jews Have Been Saved?' in, The Jewish Museum of Greece *Newsletter*, no. 26 (Winter, 1989)

Bracher, K.D. *The German Dictatorship. The Origins, Structure and Consequences of National Socialism* (London, 1971)

Braham, R.L. (ed.), *Hungarian Jews in Modern Times* (New York, 1966)

Braham, R.L. *The Politics of Genocide. The Holocaust in Hungary*, 2 vols (New York, 1980)

Brett-Smith, Richard, *Hitler's Generals* (London, 1976)

Brichetti, Giuseppe Gerose, *Il generale Vincenzo Cesare Dapino* (Mignano di Montelugo, 1982)

Broucek, Peter, *Ein General im Zwielicht. Die Lebenserinnerungen Edmund Glaises von Horstenau*, 2 vols (Vienna, 1980 and 1983)

Browning, Christopher R., *The Final Solution and the German Foreign Office. A Study of Referat DIII of Abteilung Deutschland 1940–43* (London and New York, 1978)

Browning, Christopher R., 'Wehrmacht Reprisal Policy and the Mass Murder of the Jews of Serbia', *Militärgeschichtliche Mitteilungen*, vol. 33, no. 1 (1983)

Browning, Christopher R., *Fateful Months. Essays on the Emergence of the Final Solution* (New York/London, 1985)

Caffaz, Ugo, *L'antisemitismo italiano sotto il fascismo* (Florence, 1975)

Campbell, John and Sherrard, Philip, *Modern Greece* (London, 1968)

Capogreco, Carlo Spartaco, *Ferramonti. La vita e gli uomini del più grande campo d'internamento fascista (1940–1945)* (Florence, 1987)

Caracciolo, Nicola, *Gli ebrei e l'Italia durante la guerra 1940–1945* (Rome, 1986)

Caracciolo, Nicola, *Tutti gli uomini del Duce* (Milan, 1982)

Carpi, Daniel, 'The Rescue of Jews in the Italian Zone of Occupied Croatia', *Rescue Attempts during the Holocaust*, Second Yad Vashem International Conference (Jerusalem, 1977)

Carsten, F.L., *The Reichswehr and Politics 1918–1933* (Oxford, 1966)

Chadwick, W.O., 'Weizsäcker, the Vatican and the Jews of Rome', *Journal of Ecclesiastical History*, vol. 28, no. 2 (April 1977)

Chadwick, W.O., *Britain and the Vatican during the Second World War* (Cambridge, 1986)

Childers, Thomas, *The Nazi Voter. The Social Foundations of Fascism in Germany 1919–1933* (Chapel Hill, N.C. and London 1983)

Ciocca, Pierluigi, 'L'Italia nell'economia mondiale' in *L'Economia italiana nel periodo fascista*, Quaderni Storici 29–30, (May–December 1975)

Clausen, Detlev, *Grenzen der Aufklärung. Zur gesellschaftlichen Geschichte des modernen Antisemitismus* (Frankfurt/Main, 1987)

Cohen, Gary B., 'Jews in Liberal Politics: Prague, 1860–1914', *Jewish History*, vol. 1, no. 1 (Spring, 1988)

Cohen, Richard, *The Burden of Conscience. French Jewry's Response to the Holocaust* (Bloomington, Ind., 1987)

Colville, John, *The Fringes of Power: Downing Street Diaries*, 2 vols. (London, 1987)

Conot, Robert, *Justice at Nuremberg* (London, 1983)

Conway, John S., 'How shall the Nations Repent? The Stuttgart Declaration of Guilt, October, 1945', *The Journal of Ecclesiastical History* vol. 38, no. 4 (1987)

Craig, Gordon, *The Politics of the Prussian Army 1640–1945* (Oxford, 1955)

Craig, Gordon, *Germany 1866–1945* (Oxford/New York, 1978)

Crampton, R.J., *A Short History of Modern Bulgaria* (Cambridge, 1987)

Dahrendorf, Ralf, *Gesellschaft und Demokratie in Deutschland* (Munich, 1968)

Davidowicz, Lucy, *The War Against the Jews 1933–1945* (London, 1975)

Deakin, F.W., *The Brutal Friendship. Mussolini, Hitler and the Fall of Italian Fascism* (London, 1962 and Penguin edn 1966)

De Felice, Renzo, *Storia degli ebrei italiani sotto il fascismo* (Turin, 1972)

De Felice, Renzo, *Mussolini il Duce: Lo stato totalitario 1936–1940* (Turin, 1981)

De Felice, Renzo and Goglia, Luigi, *Mussolini. Il Mito* (Bari, 1983)

Deist, Wilhelm, *Militär und Innenpolitik im Weltkrieg 1914–1918*, Quellen zur Geschichte des Parlamentarismus und der politischen Parteien, 2 vols (Düsseldorf, 1970)

Deist, Wilhelm, 'Der militärische Zusammenbruch des Kaiserrechs: zur Realität der Dolchstoslegende', in Büttner, Ursula (ed.), *Das Unrechtsregime. Internationale Forschung über den Nationalsozialismus*. Festschrift für Werner Jochmann (Hamburg, 1986)

Deist, Wilhelm, 'Die Reichswehr und der Krieg der Zukunft', conference paper at 'Kontinuität und Wandel' (Hamburg 18–19 March, 1988)

della Peruta, Franco, 'Quando in Italia c'erano i ghetti', *Storia illustrata* no. 339 (Milan, February, 1986)

De Mauro, Tullio, *Storia linguistica dell'Italia unita* (Bari, 1972)

Das Deutsche Reich und der Zweite Weltkrieg:
　　Vol. 1 *Ursachen und Voraussetzungen der deutschen Kriegspolitik* by Wilhelm Deist, Mannfred Messerschmidt, Hans-Erich Volkmann, Wolfram Wette (Stuttgart, 1979)
　　Vol. 2 *Die Errichtung der Hegemonie auf dem europäischen Kontinent* by Klaus A. Meier, Horst Rohde, Bernd Stegmann, Hans Umbreit (Stuttgart, 1984)
　　Vol. 3 *Der Mittelmeerraum und Südosteuropa* by Gerhard Schreiber, Bernd Stegmann, Detlef Vogel (Stuttgart, 1984)
　　Vol. 4 *Der Angriff auf die Sowjetunion* by Horst Boog, Jürgen Förster, Joachim Hoffmann, Ernst Klink, Rolf-Dieter Müller, Gerd R. Ueberschär, (Stuttgart, 1983)

Djilas, Milovan, *Wartime* (London, 1977)

Dollmann, Eugen, *Roma Nazista* (Milan, 1949)

Dragoni, Ugo, *Fiaschi in Jugoslavia. Ricordi polemici della campagna di guerra, 1941–43* (Alessandria, 1983)

Ebrei a Torino. Ricerche per il centenario della Sinagoga 1884–1984 (Chieri-Turin, 1984)

'L'Economia italiana nel periodo fascista', *Quaderni Storici* no. 29–30, Ancona (May–December 1975)

Epstein, Adam, 'Primo Levi and the Language of Atrocity', *Bulletin of the Society for Italian Studies*, no. 20 (1987)

Evans, Richard J., 'The New Nationalism and the Old History. Perspectives on the West German "Historikerstreit"', *The Journal of Modern History*, vol. 59, no. 4 (1987)

Favez, Jean-Claude, *Une Mission Impossible? Le CICR les déportations et les camps de concentration nazis* (Lausanne, 1988)

Fest, Joachim C., *Hitler*, trs. Richard and Clara Winston (London, 1974)

Fleischer, Hagen, *Im Kreuzschatten der Mächte. Griechenland 1941–1944*, 2 vols (Frankfurt/Main, Bern, New York, 1986)

Fleming, Gerald, *Hitler and the Final Solution* (London, 1985)

Foot, M.R.D. *S.O.E. in France. An Account of the Work of the British Special Operations Executive in France 1940–44* (London, 1966)

Galli de' Paratesi, Nora, *Le brutte parole. Semantica del eufemismo* (Milan, 1969)

Gestro, Stefano, *La divisione italiana partigiana 'Garibaldi'. Montenegro 1943–45* (Milan, 1981)

Gilbert, Martin, *The Holocaust. The Jewish Tragedy* (London, 1986)

Goethe, J.G. von, *Die Wahlverwandschaften* (Insel Tascherausgabe) (Frankfurt/Main, 1978)

Guerri, Giordano Bruno, *Galeazo Ciano. Una vita, 1903–1944* (Milan, 1979)

Haffner, Sebastian, *Anmerkungen zu Hitler* (Munich, 1979)

Heine, Heinrich, *Zur Geschichte der Religion und Philosophie in Deutschland* (1834) in *Heinrich Heine's Sämtliche Werke* (Hamburg, 1876)

Heller, Joseph, *Catch 22* (London, 1962)

Herzstein, Robert Edwin, *Waldheim. The Missing Years* (London, 1988)

Hibbert, Christopher, *Benito Mussolini* (London, 1962, rev. 1975)

Hilberg, Raul, *The Destruction of the European Jews*, rev. and definitive edn, 3 vols (New York and London, 1985)

Hildebrand, George H., *Growth and Structure in the Economy of Modern Italy* (Cambridge, Mass., 1965)

Hildebrand, Klaus, *The Foreign Policy of the Third Reich* (London, 1973)

Hinsley, F.H., Thomas, E.E., Ransom, C.F.G. and Knight, R.C., *British Intelligence in the Second World War* (London, Her Majesty's Stationery Office, 1979–88)

Hinsley, F.H., *Hitler's Strategy* (Cambridge, 1951)

Hitler, Adolf, *Mein Kampf* trs. Ralph Mannheim (New York, 1943)

Hoffmann, Peter, 'Roncalli in the Second World War: Peace Initiatives, the Greek Famine and the Persecution of the Jews', *The Journal of Ecclesiastical History*, vol. 40, no. 1 (1989)

Holborn, Hajo, *A History of Germany*, 3 vols (London, 1965)

Hoppe, Hans-Joachim, *Bulgarien. Hitlers eigenwilliger Verbündete. Eine Fallstudie zur nationalsozialistischen Südosteuropapolitik* (Stuttgart, 1979)

Hughes, H. Stuart, *Prisoners of Hope. The Silver Age of the Italian Jews 1924–1974* (Cambridge, Mass., 1983)

Iatrides, J.O. (ed.), *Greece in the 1940s. A Nation in Crisis* (Hanover, N.H. and London, 1981)

Irico N. and Municelli, A., 'Vittime della Speranza. Gli ebrei a Saluzzo dal 1938 al 1945', *Notiziario dell'Istituto Storico della Resistenza in Cuneo e Provincia* no. 28 (1985)

Jäckel, Eberhard, *Hitlers Herrschaft* (Stuttgart, 1986)

Jäckel, Eberhard, and Rohwer, Jürgen (eds), *Der Mord an den Juden im zweiten Weltkrieg* (Stuttgart, 1985)

Jarausch, Konrad, *The Enigmatic Chancellor, Bethmann Hollweg and the Hubris of Imperial Germany* (New Haven and London, 1973)

Jeserum, Stefano, *Essere Ebrei in Italia nella testimonianza di ventuno protagonisti* (Milan, 1987)

Kant, Immanuel, *Was ist Aufklärung? Aufsätze zur Geschichte und Philosophie* (Göttingen, 1985)

Katzburg, Nathaniel, *Hungary and the Jews, 1920–1943* (Ramat Gan, 1981)

Kent, Peter C., 'A Tale of Two Popes: Pius XI and Pius XII and the Rome-Berlin Axis', *Journal of Contemporary History*, vol. 23, no. 4 (October 1988)

Kitchen, Martin, *A Military History of Germany from the Eighteenth Century to the Present Day* (London, 1975)

Kitchen, Martin, 'Winston Churchill and the Soviet Union during the Second World War', *The Historical Journal*, vol. 30, no. 2 (1987)

Klarsfeld, Serge (ed.), *Die Endlösung der Judenfrage in Frankreich. Deutsche Dokumente* (Paris, 1977)

Klarsfeld, Serge, *Vichy-Auschwitz: le rôle de Vichy dans la solution finale de la question juive en France*, 2 vols (Paris, 1983 and 1985)

Knox, Macgregor, *Mussolini Unleashed 1939–1941. Politics and Strategy in Fascist Italy's Last War* (Cambridge, 1982)

Koelbing, H.M. 'Zur Befreiung des Konzentrationslagers Buchenwald. Ein Dokument.' *Schweizerische Zeitschrift für Geschichte*, vol. 35, no. 4 (1985)

Kogon, Eugen, Langbein, Hermann, Rückert, Adalbert *et al.*, *Nationalsozialistische Massentötungen durch Giftgas* (Frankfurt, 1983)

Kolossa, Tibor, 'Statistische Untersuchung der sozialen Struktur der Agrarbevölkerung in den Ländern der oesterreichischungarischen Monarchie' in *Die Agrarfrage in der oesterreichischungarischen Monarchie* (Bucharest, 1965)

Komlos, John, *The Habsburg Monarchy as a Customs Union: Economic Development in Austria-Hungary in the Nineteenth Century* (Princeton, 1983)

Landes, David, *The Unbound Prometheus. Technological Change and Industrial Development in Western Europe from 1750 to the Present* (Cambridge, 1969)

Levi, Carlo, *Cristo si è fermato a Eboli* (1945; 19th reprinting, Turin 1975)

Levi, Primo, *Se questo è un uomo/La tregua* (Turin, 1958 and 1963)

Levi, Primo, *I sommersi e i salvati* (Turin, 1986)

Loewenberg, Peter, *Decoding the Past. The Psychohistorical Approach* (Berkeley, 1985)

Loewenberg, Peter, 'Nixon, Hitler and Power: An Ego Psychologcal Study', *Psychoanalytic Inquiry*, vol. 6, no. 1 (1986)

Lukacs, G., *Die Zerstörung der Vernunft. Der Weg des Irrationalismus von Schelling zu Hitler* (Berlin, 1955)

Lyttleton, Adrian, *The Fascist Seizure of Power. Fascism in Italy, 1919–1929* (London, 1973)

Mack Smith, Denis, *Mussolini* (London, 1981)

Malaparte, Curzio, *Kaputt* (Rome/Milan, 1948)

Manuel, A.R., and Frankel, H. *The German Cinema* (London, 1971)

Marini, Margherita, *Treno Ospedale 34* (Modena, 1976)

Marrus, M.R., *The Holocaust in History* (Hanover, N.H./London, 1987)

Martin, B. and Schulin, E., *Die Juden als Minderheit in der Geschichte* (Munich, 1981)

Martini, Lucifero, *I protagonisti raccontano. Diari, ricordi e testimonianze di combattenti italiani nella lotta popolare di liberazione della Jugoslavia* (Fiume/Pola, 1983)

Mayda, Giuseppe, *Ebrei sotto Salò. La persecuzione antisemita 1943–45* (Milan, 1978)

Meinecke, Friedrich, *Die deutsche Katastrophe. Betrachtungen und Erinnerungen*, 6th edn (Wiesbaden, 1965)

Mendelsohn, E., *The Jews of East Central Europe Between the Wars* (Bloomington, Ind., 1983)

Meyer-Zollitsch, Almuth, *Nationalsozialismus und Evangelische Kirche in Bremen* Verlag des Staatsarchivs der Freien Hansestadt Bremen, Bd. 51 (Bremen, 1985)

Michaelis, Meir, *Mussolini and the Jews: German-Italian Relations and the Jewish Question in Italy 1922–45* (Oxford, 1978)

Milano, Attilio, *Storia degli ebrei in Italia* (Turin, 1963)

Milward, A.S., *The German Economy at War* (London, 1965)

Minniti, Fortunato, 'Dalla "non belligeranza" alla "guerra parallela"', *Storia Contemporanea*, Anno XVIII, no. 6 (December 1987)

Momigliano, Arnaldo Dante, 'The Many Worlds of Vito Volterra', Lecture, Brandeis university, 30 April 1984

Monelli, Paolo, *Roma 1943* (Rome, 1946)

Montovani, Enrico, 'Dall' economia di guerra alla ricostruzione' in *L'Economia italiana nel periodo fascista*, Quaderni Storici, nos 29–30 (May–December 1975)

Morris, Jonathan, *The Political Economy of Shopkeeping in Milan 1885–1905* (unpublished Ph.D. University of Cambridge, 1988)

Müller, Klaus Jürgen, *The Army, Politics and Society in Germany 1933–1945* (Manchester, 1987)

Namier, Lewis B., *Conflicts. Studies in Contemporary History* (New York, 1943)

Palumbo, Michael, *The Waldheim Files. Myth and Reality* (London/Boston 1988)

Pandolfi, Paola, 'Ebrei a Firenze nel 1943. Persecuzione e Deportazione', *Argomenti storici*, Quaderno V (Florence, 1980)

Paris, Edmond, *Genocidio nella Croazia satellite* (Milan, 1976)

Passerini, Luisa, *Fascism in Popular Memory. The Cultural Experience of the Turin Working Class* (Cambridge, 1987)

Pastorelli, Pietro, 'I Documenti Diplomatici Italiani', *Affari Esteri*, XVIII, no. 70 (Spring 1986)

Pavlowitch, Stevan K., *Yugoslavia* (London, 1971)

Peukert, Detlev J.K., *Inside Nazi Germany. Conformity, Opposition and Racism in Everyday Life* (New Haven/London, 1987)

Picciotto Fargion, Liliana, 'Gli ebrei in Italia tra persecuzione e sterminio 1943–1945', *Notiziario dell'Istituto della Resistenza in Cuneo e Provincia*, no. 28, 2nd semester (1985)

Pieri, Piero and Rochat, Giorgio, *Pietro Badoglio* (Turin, 1974)

Pirandello, Luigi, *I vecchi e i giovani* (1909; Verona, Gli Oscar, 1973)

Plehwe, Friedrich Karl von, *Als Die Achse zerbrach. Das Ende des deutsch-italienischen Bündnisses im zweiten Weltkrieg* (Wiesbaden and Munich, 1980)

Poggi, Gianfranco, *The Development of the Modern State. A Sociological Introduction* (London, 1978)

Potočnik, Franc, *Il Campo di sterminio fascista: L'Isola di Rab* (Turin, 1979)

Prato, David, *Dal Pergamo della comunità di Roma* (Rome, 1950)

Preradovich, Nikolaus von, *Die militärische und soziale Herkunft der Generalität des deutschen Heeres* (Osnabrück, 1979)

Rabinbach, Ansen G., 'The Migration of Galician Jews to Vienna 1857–1880', *Austrian History Yearbook*, 11 (1975)

Rasero, Aldo, *Tridentina Avanti. Storia di una divisione alpina* (Milan, 1982)

Rintelen, Enno von, *Mussolini als Bundesgenosse. Erinnerungen des deutschen militärattaches in Rom 1936–1943* (Tübingen and Stuttgart, 1951)

Ritter, Gerhard, Staatskunst und Kriegshandwerk. Das Problem des 'Militarismus' in Deutschland, vol. 3, 'Die Tragödie der Staatskundt Bethman Hollweg als Kriegskanzler (1914–1917)' (Munich, 1964)

Roatta, Mario, *Otto Milioni di Baionette. L'esercito italiano in guerra dal 1940 al 1944* (Milan, 1946)

Rocca, Gianni, *Fucilate gli ammiragli. La tragedia della Marina italiana nella seconda guerra mondiale* (Milan, 1987)

Rochat, Giorgio and Massobrio, Giulio, *Breve storia dell'Esercito italiano dal 1861 al 1943* (Turin, 1978)

Röhl, J.C.G., *Kaiser Wilhelm II. 'Eine Studie über Cäsarenwahnsinn'*, Schriften des Historischen Kollegs: Vorträge 19 (Munich, 1989)

Roskill, S.W., *The Strategy of Sea Power. Its Development and Application* (London, 1962)

Rosenblitt, Marsha L., *The Jews in Vienna 1867–1914. Assimilation and Identity* (Albany, NY, 1983)

Sala, Teodoro, 'Guerriglia e controguerriglia in Jugoslavia nella propaganda per le truppe occupanti italiane (1941–1943)', *Il Movimento di Liberazione in Italia*, July–September 1972

Salvatorelli, Luigi and Mira, Giovani, *Storia d'Italia nel periodo fascista*, 2 vols, Gli Oscar (Milan, 1972)

Salvatores, Umberto, *Bersaglieri sul Don*, 3rd edn (Bologna, 1965)

Schopennhauer, Arthur, *Die Welte als Wille und Vorstellung*, Sämtliche Werke, vol. 1 (Stuttgart and Frankfurt, n.d.)

Schreiber, Gerhard, 'Italien im machtpolitschen Kalkül der deutschen Marineführung 1919 bis 1945', *Quellen und Forschungen aus italienischen Archiven und Bibliotheken* herausgegeben vom Deutschen Historischen Institut, Rome. no. 60 (1982)

Schreiber, Gerhard, 'Sul teatro mediterraneo nella seconda guerra mondiale', *Rivista marittima* (March 1987)

Schröder, Josef, *Italiens Kriegsaustritt 1943. Die deutschen Gegenmassnahmen im italienischen Raum: 'Fall Alarich' und 'Fall Achse'* (Zürich/Frankfurt/Main, 1969)

Schulte, Theo J., *The German Army and Nazi Policies in Occupied Russia* (Oxford/New York/Munich, 1989)

Scotti, Giacomo, *'Bono Taliano': Gli italiani in Jugoslavia (1941–43)* (Milan, 1987)

Scotti, Giacomo and Viazzi, Luciano, *Le Aquile delle Montagne Nere. Storia dell'occupazione e della guerra italiana in Montenegro (1941–1943)* (Milan, 1987)

Segre, Dan Vittorio, *Memoirs of a Fortunate Jew. An Italian Story* (London, 1987)

Senise, Carmen, *Quando ero capo della polizia* (Rome, 1946)

Serpieri, Arrigo, *La guerra e le classi rurali italiane* (Bari, 1930)

Serra, Enrico, *La diplomazia italiana e la ripresa dei rapporti con la Francia, 1943–45* (Rome, 1984)

Seton-Watson, Christopher, *Italy from Liberalism to Fascism 1870–1925* (London, 1967)

Shelach, Menahem, *Heshbon Damim. Hatzlat Yehudi Croatiah al yiday ha-italkim 1941–43* (Blood Account. The Rescue of Croatian Jews by the Italians) (Tel Aviv, 1986)

Shirer, William L., *The Rise and Fall of the Third Reich. A History of Nazi Germany* (New York, 1960)

Sorrani, Settimo, *L'Assistenza ai profughi ebrei in Italia, 1933–1941* (Rome, 1983)

Speer, Albert, *Spandauer Tagebücher* (Frankfurt/Main, 1975)

Spinosa, Antonio, *Starace* (Milan, 1981)

Spurber, Nicholas, 'Changes in the Economic Structures of the Balkans, 1860–1960' in *The Balkans in Transition. Essays on the Development of Balkan Life and Politics since the eighteenth century* eds Charles and Barbara Jelavich (Berkeley and Los Angeles, 1963)

Steinberg, Jonathan, 'Fascism in the Italian South: the Case of Calabria' in David Forgacs (ed.), *Rethinking Italian Fascism. Capitalism, Populism and Culture* (London, 1986)

Steinberg, Lucien, *The Jews against Hitler (Not as a Lamb)*, trs. Marion Hunter (Glasgow, 1978)

Sternberger, Dolf *et al.*, *Aus dem Wörterbuch des Unmenschen*, 2nd edn (Hamburg, 1957)

Stoianovich, Traian, 'The Social Foundations of Balkan Politics, 1750–1941' in *The Balkans in Transition. Essays on the Development of Balkan Life and Politics since the eighteenth century*, eds Charles and Barbara Jelavich (Berkeley and Los Angeles, California, 1963)

Streit, Christian, *Keine Kameraden. Die Wehrmacht und die sowjetischen Kriegsgefangen en 1941–1945* (Stuttgart, 1978)

Sweets, John F., *The Politics of the Resistance in France, 1940–1944* (DeKalb, Illinois, 1976)

Sweet-Escot, Bickham, *Greece. A Political and Economic Survey 1939–1953* (London, 1954)

Sylos Labini, Paolo, *Saggio sulle classi sociali* (6th edn Bari, 1976)

Tamaro, Attilio, *Due Anni di Storia* 3 vols (Rome, 1948)

Tamir, Vicki, *Bulgaria and her Jews. The History of a Dubious Symbiosis* (New York, 1979)

Tasca, Angelo, *Nascita e avvento del fascismo* 2 vols. 5th edn (Bari, 1974)

Toniolo, Gianni, *L'Economia dell'Italia fascista* (Rome and Bari, 1980)

Toscano, Mario, 'Gli ebrei in Italia dall'emancipazione alle persecuzioni'. *Storia Contemporanea*, Anno XVII, no. 5 (October 1986)

Tucholsky, Kurt, 'Das Menschliche' (1928) in *Panter Tiger & Co* (Hamburg, 1954)

Tyler, Maud, *The Forgotten Solution: Some Interpretations of Federalism in Piedmont and Lombardy before 1850* (unpublished Ph.D. dissertation, University of Cambridge, 1985)

Uffreduzzi, Marcello, *Il Viale dei Giusti. Solidarietà verso gli ebrei e persecuzione nazista* (Rome, 1985)

Valeri, Nino, *Da Giolitti a Mussolini. Momenti della crisi del liberalismo* (Florence, 1956)

'Verax' (Roberto Ducci), 'Italiani ed ebrei in Jugoslavia', *Politica estera*, vol. 1, no. 9 (1944)

Warburg, Max M., *Aus meinen Aufzeichnungen*, private printing (New York, 1952)

Weinberg, Gerhard L., *World in the Balance: Behind the Scenes of World War II* (Hanover, N.H./London, 1981)

Woodhouse, C.M., *Apple of Discord. A Survey of Recent Greek Politics in their International Setting* (London, 1948)

Woodhouse, C.M., *The Story of Modern Greece* (London, 1968)

Woodhouse, C.M., *The Struggle for Greece 1941–49* (London, 1976)

Wuescht, Johann, *Jugoslawien und das Dritte Reich. Eine dokumentierte Geschichte der deutsch-jugoslawischen Beziehungen 1933–1945* (Stuttgart, 1969)

Yahil, Leni, *The Rescue of Danish Jewry. Test of a Democracy* (Philadelphia, Pa., 1969)

Zeman, Z.A.B., *Nazi Propaganda* (Oxford, 1964)

Zuccotti, Susan, *The Italians and the Holocaust. Persecution, Rescue and Survival* (New York and London, 1987)

HOLOCAUST CHRONOLOGY

EVOLUTION OF POLICY

From 30 January 1939 to 8 September 1943

1939

30 January 1939, Adolf Hitler announces in the Reichstag that a war will bring the destruction of the Jewish race in Europe (E. Kogon *et al.* *Nationalsozialistische Massentötungen*, p. 326)

1 September 1939, GERMAN TROOPS INVADE POLAND

1 September 1939. Hitler order establishes 'Aktion T 4', the euthanasia programme (Karl A. Scheuness in Jäckel, *Mord*, pp. 70 ff.)

21 September 1939, Heydrich Memo on making the incorporated territories of greater German Reich *'Judenfrei'* (Browning, Appendix, p. 214)

12 October 1939, First transports to Lublin reservation (Browning, Appendix, p. 214)

1940

15 February 1940, Stettin deportation (Browning, Appendix, p. 214)

3 March 1940, Himmler explains 'ich tue nichts was der Führer nicht weiss' [I do nothing that the Führer does not know] (Jäckel, *Herrschaft*, 106)

12 March 1940, Schneidenmühl deportation (Browning, Appendix, p. 214)

23 March 1940, Göring bans further deportation to general government [Poland] (Browning, Appendix, p. 214)

18 June 1940, Hitler and Ribbentrop mention Madagascar plan to Mussolini and Ciano (Browning, Appendix, p. 215)

16 July 1940, Jews of Colmar in Alsace 'shoved' into unoccupied France (R. Hilberg, *The Destruction*, p. 614)

27 September 1940, General von Stülpnagel signs decree requiring that all French Jews register as such in German-occupied zone (R. Hilberg, *The Destruction*, p. 616)

15 November 1940, Warsaw ghetto sealed (Browning, Appendix, p. 215)

20 November 1940, Hitler and Pal Teleki discuss Jewish question in Berlin on occasion of Hungary's signing Anti-Comintern Pact. H. thinks in terms of a French colonial possession (text in N. Katzburg, *Hungary and the Jews*, p. 217)

1941

21 January 1941, Iron Guard launch pogrom against Jews of Bucharest (Dorian, *Quality*, pp. 137–39, Diary entry, 24 January, 1941)

21 January 1941, 'Law for the protection of the nation' in Bulgaria forbids intermarriage between Jews and non-Jews, limits travel by Jews without authorization and imposes other restrictions (R. Hilberg, *The Destruction*, p. 749)

13 March 1941, OKW issues *'Richtlinien auf Sondergebieten zur Weisung "Barbarossa"'* giving SS *'Sonderaufgaben'* in territory taken in future war against Russia. (Krausnick in Jäckel, *Mord*, pp. 88–89)

29 March 1941, Vichy government establishes a commissariat of Jewish affairs with Xavier Vallet in charge (R. Hilberg, *The Destruction*, p. 624)

2 May 1941, Rosenberg appalled at what he heard from Führer: 'was ich heute nicht niederschreiben will aber nie vergessen werde' (Jäckel, *Herrschaft*, p. 108)

6 June 1941, *Kommissarbefehl*: OKW orders the 'elimination' of Red army commissars taken prisoner after Russian invasion. (Klaus Hildebrand, *The Foreign Policy of the Third Reich*, (London, 1973, p. 110)

17 June 1941, Heydrich briefs leaders of SS *Einsatzgruppen* in Berlin, (Krausnick in Jäckel, *Mord*, pp. 92 ff.)

22 JUNE 1941, GERMANY INVADES RUSSIA

2 July 1941, Heydrich issues orders to SS in East specifying which categories to be executed at once (Krausnick in Jäckel, *Mord*, p. 90)

31 July 1941 Göring signs order empowering Heydrich to deal with Jewish problem in newly conquered areas of Russia: *Staatsanwaltschaft*'s comment that the bureaucratic execution of policy already established (Jäckel, *Mord*, p. 201)

3 August 1941, Cardinal Count Galen preaches sermon against euthanasia programme and on 24 August programme halted. (Scheuness in Jäckel, *Mord*, pp. 75 ff.)

14 August 1941, Benzler's first request to deport Serbian Jews (Browning, Appendix, p. 216)

24 August 1941, Hitler orders the halting of 'Aktion T4' (euthanasia). 70,273 persons listed as killed in the action. (Kogon *et al. Nationalsozialistische Massentötungen*, p. 328)

30 August 1941, General Hauffe and Rumanian Chief of Staff General Tataranu sign the 'Tighina agreement' that no Jews in Rumanian-occupied Russia ('Transnistria') be driven across the Bug into German killing zone. Rumanian killings begin. (R. Hilberg, *The Destruction*, pp. 770 ff.)

1 September 1941, Jews in Germany compelled to wear the yellow star (R. Hilberg, *The Destruction*, pp. 177–8)

3 September 1941, first experiments with Zyklon B gas carried out in Auschwitz. (Kogon *et al. Nationalsozialistische Massentötungen*, p. 328)

9 October 1941, *Wehrmacht* begins the killing of Serbian Jews (R. Hilberg, *The Destruction*, p. 686)

11 November 1941, German Foreign Office receives the reports of *Einsatzgruppen* massacres, numbers 1 through 5 (Browning, Appendix, p. 217)

25 November 1941, '*Erste Verordnung*' to the Reich citizenship law of 15 September 1935, deprives German Jews living outside Germany of their citizenship (*Reichsgesetzblatt*, Teil I, nr 133)

25 November 1941, German Foreign Office receives *Einsatzgruppen* report number 6 (Browning, Appendix, p. 217)

5 December 1941, First Jewish transports arrive at Kulmhof, where gas wagons are used. (Kogon *et al. Nationalsozialistische Massentötungen*, p. 328)

16 December 1941, Hans Frank tells highest officials in the *Generalgouvernement* in Poland that Jews are to be 'annihilated'. (R. Hilberg, *The Destruction*, pp. 482–83)

30 December 1941, Under State Secretary Martin Luther of German Foreign Office argues that all Anti-Comintern states must adopt the German model in the Jewish question (ADAP, E, Bd I, no., 72, p. 132)

1942

6 January 1942, German Ambassador in Copenhagen reports Danish refusal to carry out anti-Jewish measures (ADAP, E, Bd I, nr 100, pp. 185–86)

10 January 1942. Luther tells Eichmann that the Rumanian, Croatian and Slovakian governments have agreed that Jews with their citizenship may be deported with the German Jews (ADAP, E, Bd. I, no. 108, pp. 198–99)

20 January 1942. Conference am Grossen Wannsee Nr 56–58 establishes *Endlösung der Judenfrage* (ADAP. E, Bd. I, no. 150, pp. 267–75)

10 February 1942, Councillor Franz Rademacher writes to Minister Harald Bielfeld that the war has provided 'other territories for the *Endlösung*' and that the Führer has decided to abandon Madagascar in favour of deportation to the east (ADAP, E. Bd. I, no. 227, p. 405)

11 February 1942, Under State Secretary Luther complains that Rumanians' 'wild' expulsions of Jews to Transnistria must be stopped and coordinated with foreign ministry (ADAP, E, Bd. I, no. 230, p. 405)

14 February 1942, Goebbels records a conversation with Hitler in which the 'Führer once more expressed his determination to clean up the Jews in Europe pitilessly. There must be no squeamish sentimentalism about it. . . . The Führer expressed this idea vigorously and repeated it afterwards to a group of officers.' (*The Goebbels Diaries 1942–43*, ed. Louis P. Lochner, Garden City, NY, 1948, p. 86)

6 March 1942, Eichmann chairs Second *Endlösung* conference on compulsory sterilization of half-Jews (R. Hilberg, *The Destruction*, pp. 420–21)

7 March 1942, Goebbels receives ' a detailed report from the SD and police regarding a final solution of the Jewish question. . . . There are 11,000,000 Jews still in Europe. They will have to be concentrated later, to begin with,

in the East; possibly an island such as Madagascar can be assigned to them after the war.' (*Goebbels Diaries 1942*, pp. 115–16)

17 March 1942, Beginning of the transport of the Jews of Lublin to Belzec concentration camp. (Kogon *et al. Nationalsozialistische Massentötungen*, p. 328)

20 March 1942, Foreign office replies to Eichmann's letter of 9 March about the *Abtransport* of 1,000 Jews from France to Auschwitz (11 March: number raised to 6,000) by stating 'no objection' (ADAP. E. Bd. IV, no. 56, p. 97)

26 March 1942, Deportations of Slovak Jews begin (Browning, Appendix, p. 218)

27 March 1942, Goebbels records that 'beginning with Lublin, the Jews in the General Government are now being evacuated eastward. The procedure is a pretty barbaric one and not to be described here more definitely. Not much will remain of the Jews. . . . No other government and no other regime would have the strength for such a global solution of this question. Here too the Führer is the undismayed champion of a radical solution necessitated by conditions and therefore inexorable. Fortunately a whole series of possibilities presents itself to us in wartime that would be denied us in peacetime.' (*Goebbels Diaries 1942*, pp. 147–48)

28 March 1942, First French trains deport Jews to Auschwitz (Browning, Appendix, p. 218)

17–20 April 1942, Ghetto of Lublin cleared of Jews and destroyed (R. Hilberg, *The Destruction*, p. 490)

6 June 1942, General Roatta hints at *note consequenze* of the surrender of the Jews (n. 13, p. 275)

11 July 1942, SS *Sturmbannführer* F. Suhr of the *Reichssicherheitshauptamt*, Section IV B 4 (Eichmann's unit) urges German foreign ministry to convince the Italians to take measures against Jews in Greece like those proposed by Germans, especially the marking of all Jews with the yellow star. (Carpi, *Nuovi Documenti*, Doc. no. 2, pp. 172–74)

11 July 1942, *Generalleutnant* von Krenzki assembles 6–7,000 Jewish men between 18 and 45 in Liberty Square, Salonica, for forced labour. (R. Hilberg, *The Destruction*, p. 693; Carpi, *Nuovi Documenti*, p. 127 and n. 17)

15 July 1942, First trains carrying Jews leave Holland (R. Hilberg, *The Destruction*, p. 585)

22 June 1942, SS asks if foreign ministry objects to the deportation of 40,000 Jews from occupied France, 40,000 from the Netherlands and 10,000 from Belgium (ADAP, E, Bd. 3, no. 26, p. 43)

22 July 1942, First trains carrying Warsaw Jews leave for Treblinka (R. Hilberg, *The Destruction*, p. 491)

24 July 1942, Under state secretary Luther reports that Croatian government agrees to the deportation of Jews from its territory but that Italians remain difficult. Argues for proceeding and dealing with expected difficulties in Italian zone (ADAP, E, Bd. III, no. 131, p. 224)

11 August 1942, French government agrees to deportation of 30,000 stateless Jews from the unoccupied zone. (ADAP, E, Bd. II, no. 178, p. 301)

13 August 1942, Train DA 60/1 leaves Zagreb for Auschwitz with 1,300 Jews (R. Hilberg, *The Destruction*, pp. 714–15)

13 August 1942, Representative in Netherlands tells German foreign ministry that Jews now know what 'work employment in the east' is really about and are escaping into Belgium (ADAP, E. no. 188, p. 315)

18 August 1942, Prince Bismarck hints to Ciano that *eliminazione* the fate of deported Jews (n. 26, p. 276)

21 August 1942, Mussolini writes 'Nulla Osta' and orders Jews to be consigned, (p. 2)

4 September 1942, Councillor Rademacher reports the objection of the Italian plenipotentiary in Athens to application of yellow star to Greek Jews (ADAP, E, Bd. III, no. 266, p. 454)

11 September 1942, Ciano instructs Italian ambassador to Bulgaria to 'defend' Jews of Italian nationality, 'not so much as Jews but simply because they constitute Italian interests abroad'. (Carpi, *Nuovi Documenti*, Doc. no. 3, p. 175)

24 September 1942, Ribbentrop orders the acceleration of Jewish evacuation from Europe and instructs representatives to approach Bulgarian, Hungarian and Danish governments (ADAP, E, Bd. III, no. 307, p. 526)

10 October 1942, György Ottlik, editor of the *Pester Lloyd*, reports that Baron Sztójay, Hungarian ambassador in Berlin, explained that 'resettlement' of Jews meant execution. (Katzburg, *Hungary*, pp. 220–1, no. 20)

12 October 1942, Under state secretary Luther warns Turkish government 'for reasons of courtesy' that it has to the end of the year to evacuate its Jews living under German occupation. Thereafter, they will be deported. (ADAP, E, Bd. IV, no. 42, p. 72)

13 October 1942, Rumanian government halts deportations and releases Bucharest Jews from internment (Dorian, *The Quality*, pp. 234–35)

14 October 1942, Ambassador in Croatia informs German foreign ministry that Croatian government prepared to pay Germans RM30.– for every Jew deported. (ADAP, E, Bd. IV, no. 49, p. 83)

20 October 1942, Perić, Croatian ambassador, hints to Ciano that deported Jews to be killed (n. 88, p. 278)

20 October 1942, German ambassador in Croatia reports that Italians offered Croatian government to take Jews from 2nd zone (ADAP, E, Bd. IV. no. 72, p. 120)

23 October 1942, Italian foreign ministry aware of *eliminazione* of Jews (n. 90, p. 278)

26 October 1942, Norwegian secret police begin rounding up all Jewish men between 15 and 65 (R. Hilberg, *The Destruction*, p. 656)

3 November 1942, 2nd Army knows what will happen to Jews (cf. n. 99, p. 279)

4 November 1942, General Pièche reports that deported Croatian Jews being gassed in the railway carriages. Marked *Visto dal Duce* with note by Vidau: *evidenza* (p. 78)

8 November 1942. AMERICAN AND BRITISH FORCES LAND IN NORTH AFRICA

11–12 November 1942, GERMAN AND ITALIAN TROOPS OCCUPY UNOCCUPIED FRANCE

14 November 1942, General Pièche says that deportation of Jews *equivalente alla condanna a morte* (n. 107, p. 279)

20 November 1942, German Ambassador in Croatia reports that Italians are interning Jews in camps and refusing all outside interference (ADAP, E, Bd. IV, no. 204, p. 351)

2 December 1942, Hungarian government rejects German demand that Jews be deported on grounds of technical difficulty (Katzburg, *Hungary*, p. 221)

13 December 1942, Goebbels notes: 'The Italians are extremely lax in the treatment of Jews. They protect the Italian Jews both in Tunis and in occupied France and won't permit their being drafted for work or compelled to wear the Star of David. This shows once again that Fascism does not really dare to get down to fundamentals.' (*Goebbels Diaries 1942*, p. 241)

21 December 1942, Himmler sends Hitler *Bericht Nr 51* which reports activities of *Einsatzgruppen* in Soviet territory from August to November, 1942: 336,211 Jews murdered (Jäckel, *Mord*, p. 37)

1943

6 February–14 March 1943, SD in Salonica segregates Jews in ghettos, requires them to wear yellow star, to observe curfew, etc (Carpi, *Nuovi Documenti*, p. 141)

2 March 1943, Goebbels reports that 'we are now definitely pushing the Jews out of Berlin. They were suddenly rounded up last Saturday and are to be carted off to the East as quickly as possible.'; notes with distaste that some 'tipped off prematurely' and hence hid. (*Goebbels Diaries, 1942*, p. 241)

15 March 1943, First transport leaves Salonica for Auschwitz. Germans issue Jews with Polish currency (Carpi, *Nuovi Documenti*, p. 142)

12 April 1943, Captain Merci appalled at the 'tragedy' of Jews of Salonica, hurled into box cars sixty at a time. 'It is clear that these people will not reach their destination alive.' (Rochlitz and Shelach, *Salonika Diary*, p. 308)

17 April 1943. Hitler tells Horthy that Jews a bacillus to be eliminated like culling animals (Jäckel, *Mord*, pp. 59–60)

17 April 1943, Mussolini admits in speech to the Fascist Party Directorate that 'all kinds of rumours are abroad. Now there is talk of atrocities happening in Russia. . . . The Party must stop this kind of talk.' (F.W. Deakin, *The Brutal Friendship*, p. 320)

19 April 1943, Battle of Warsaw ghetto begins (R. Hilberg, *The Destruction*, pp. 551 ff.)

13 May 1943, Hitler explains to Goebbels that Jews the parasites of the social organism who intensify the process of racial selection, hence no other way but to exterminate Jews. . . . The Jew was also the first to introduce the lie

into politics as a weapon. Aboriginal man, the Führer believes, did not know the lie. (*Goebbels Diaries, 1942*, p. 377)

16 May 1943, General Jürgen Stroop reports that the Warsaw ghetto 'is no longer in existence'. The end of the rising in the ghetto (Martin Gilbert, *The Holocaust*, p. 566)

26 May 1943, The SS in Marseilles report that Police Inspector Lospinoso has established himself and his staff at the Villa Surany in Nice and that the Italians intend to make the coastal strip to a depth of 50km 'Jew free'. (Serge Klarsfeld, *Die Endlösung*, no. 122, p. 199)

25 June 1943, German foreign office representative in the Netherlands reports 102,000 of the 140,000 Dutch Jews 'have been removed from the body of the people'. (*Topographie des Terrors*, Text 61, p. 149)

2 July 1943, SS *Gruppenführer* Müller writes that resumption of deportation of Jews from France is 'very welcome' especially since the *Reichsführer* has ordered an 'acceleration of the action'. (Serge Klarsfeld, *Die Endlösung*, no. 125, p. 204)

25 JULY, MUSSOLINI REMOVED AS PRIME MINISTER AND ARRESTED; NON-FASCIST GOVERNMENT UNDER MARSHALL BADOGLIO APPOINTED

18 August 1943, SS in Paris make another attempt to get the Italian authorities to 'recognise the German standpoint . . . in the Jewish question' by urging it on Lieutenant Mafatti of the Italian embassy. He replies that the only fascist laws not abrogated are the racial laws which shows that 'the standpoint of the present Italian government as laid down in the Italian laws on the Jews'. (Serge Klarsfeld, *Die Endlösung*, no. 130, p. 214)

8 SEPTEMBER 1943, GENERAL EISENHOWER ANNOUNCES THAT ITALY HAS SIGNED AN ARMISTICE WITH THE ALLIES: KING AND ROYAL GOVERNMENT FLEE TO BRINDISI

NOTES

THE PROBLEM

1 'Estratti dal diario del Conte Luca Pietromarchi', in Joseph Rochlitz, *The Righteous Enemy. The Italians and Jews in Occupied Europe 1941–43*, a collection of notes and documents for the documentary film (Rome, 1988) p. 7, 13 September 1942

2 'Appunto per il Duce', 21 August 1942, Ministero degli Affari Esteri (MEA), Archivio Storico Diplomatico (ASD) Gab AP 35. 'Croazia'. Cf Daniel Carpi, 'The Rescue of Jews in in the Italian Zone of Occupied Croatia' in *Rescue Attempts During the Holocaust*, proceedings of the second Yad Vashem international conference, Jerusalem, 1977, pp. 474–75 and p. 512; 'Verax' (Roberto Ducci, head of the 'Croatian office' in the MEA) 'Italiani ed ebrei in Jugoslavia', *Politica estera*, vol. 1, no. 9 (Rome, 1944), p. 23

3 'Appunto per il Duce', 21 August 1942, MEA ASD Gab Ap 35, 'Croazia'

4 'Appunto-Visto dal Duce', MEA ASD Gab A.P. 35 'Croazia', 4 November 1942

5 Pirelli, Alberto, *Taccuini 1922–1943* (Bologna, 1984) p. 365

6 Zoppi to Ministero degli Affari Esteri (MEA), Paris, 14 January 1943, MEA, Archivio Storico Diplomatico (ASD), 'Francia Affari Generali', B. 80 (1943), f. 8 'Sionismo'

7 Giordano Bruno Guerri, *Galeazzo Ciano. Una Vita 1903–1944* (Milan, 1979) p. 536

8 Interview with Mr Imre Rochlitz, Cambridge, 11 February 1988

9 Schossberger, Hermann, Slavko Herak, Dott. Vladimir Vranic, Ing. Arthur Lothe and Milan Singer, signatories, Porto Re, 28 November, 1942, MEA ASD 'Jugoslavia (Croazia)' B. 138 (1943) F. 8. 'Deportazione degli Ebrei' (1942–43)

10 Interview with Mr Imre Rochlitz, 11 February 1988

11 Hilberg, Raul, *The Destruction of the European Jews*, rev. and definitive edn, 3 vols (New York and London, 1985) p. 715

12 Gilbert, Martin, *The Holocaust. The Jewish Tragedy* (London, 1986) p. 410

13 RAM von Ribbentrop to von Mackensen, German ambassador in Rome, 9 March 1943, and von Mackensen to Ribbentrop, 17 March 1943, *Akten zur Deutschen Auswärtigen Politik 1918–1945* (ADAP) Serie E: 1941–45 Bd V. 1. January 1943–30 April 1943, nos. 189, p. 368 and no. 215, p. 243. Also von Mackensen, telegram 20 March 1943, Bundesarchiv, Koblenz, NS 19, nr. 37669 (provided by the kindness of Dr Gerhard Schreiber, Militärgeschichtliches Forschungsamt, Freiburg im Breisgau)

14 Schneerson, Isaac, 'Avant-Propos' to L. Poliakov, *La Condition des Juifs en France sous l'occupation italienne* (Paris, 1946) p. 10

15 In Israel, Daniel Carpi has written, in addition to the article on the Jews of Croatia (cf. note 8 above) an important article in Italian 'Nuovi documenti per la storia dell'Olocausto in Grecia. L'Attegiamento degli Italiani (1941–43)', *Michael on the History of the Jews in the Diaspora*, vol. VII, Tel Aviv, 1981 and (in Hebrew) 'The Italian Government and the Jews of Tunisia in the Second World War (June 1940–May 1943)', *Zion. A Quarterly for Research in Jewish History*, vol LII (1987) no. 1. Menachem Shelach has written in Hebrew a lively and readable account of the rescue of the Jews of Croatia in his *Heshbon Damim (Blood Account)*, (Tel Aviv, 1986). Meir Michaelis in *Mussolini and the Jews: German-Italian Relations and the Jewish Question in Italy, 1922–1945* (Oxford, 1978) treats the issue as part of a much larger study as does Renzo de Felice, *Storia degli ebrei italiani sotto il fascismo* (Turin, 1972), still the single most authoritative work on the Jews during fascism. Joseph Rochlitz has made an exceptional documentary television film called *The Righteous Enemy* which traces the story of the Jews under Italian protection and includes interviews with many of the principal Italian diplomats who took part in the matter and has, together with Menahem Shelach, published excerpts from the diaries of Captain Lucillo Merci, who was liaison officer with the German forces in Salonica and hence eye-witness to the tragedy of the Jews there, cf. Joseph Rochlitz with introduction by Menachem Shelach, 'Excerpts from the Salonika Diary of Lucillo Merci (February–August 1943), *Yad Vashem Studies*, XVII, Jerusalem (1987). Serge Klarsfeld, who in Joseph Rochlitz's film describes his own experiences as a young man under Italian protection in southern France, has published several important documentary collections which contain evidence on the question, cf. his *Vichy-Auschwitz: Le Rôle de Vichy dans la solution finale de la question juive en France*, 2 vols. (Paris, 1983 and 1985) and an extremely important collection of German documents, *Die Endlösung der Judenfrage in Frankreich. Deutsche Dokumente 1941–44*, which he published at his own expense in 1977 in an attempt to bring some of the surviving mass murderers to justice. He provided addresses and telephone numbers of former SS and SD officers in France now living in West Germany and elsewhere. There is also a brief treatment of the matter in Giusepe Mayda, *Ebrei sotto Salò: la persecuzione antisemita 1943–45* (Milan, 1978)

16 Zuccotti, Susan, *The Italians and the Holocaust. Persecution, Rescue and Survival* (New York and London, 1987) p. 99. Zuccotti's chapter five, 'Italians and Jews in the Occupied Teritories', gives a very readable account of what happened to the Jews under the protection of the Italian army.

17 *Actes et Documents du Saint Siège relatifs à la Seconde Guerre Mondiale*, (ADSS) vol. 9 'Le Saint Siège et les Victimes de la Guerre, Janvier–Décembre 1943', ed. Pierre Blet, Robert A. Graham, Angelo Martini, Burkhart Schneider (Libreria Editrice Vaticana, 1975) p. 34

18 Deakin, F.W., *The Brutal Friendship. Mussolini, Hitler and the Fall of Fascism* (London, 1962 and Penguin edn 1966)

19 Arendt, Hannah, *Eichmann in Jerusalem. A Report on the Banality of Evil* (London, 1963), p. 161

20 *Akten zur Deutschen Auswärtigen Politik*, Series E, 1941–45, vol. 1, no. 230, p. 405, Vortragsnotiz des Unterstaatssekretärs Luther, 11 February 1942

21 Braham, R.L., 'The Destruction of the Jews of Carpatho-Ruthenia' in R.L. Braham, *Hungarian-Jewish Studies*, (New York, 1966) p. 231
22 Picciotto Fargion, Liliana, 'Gli ebrei in Italia tra persecuzione e sterminio 1943–1945', *Notiziario dell'Istituto Storico della Resistenza in Cuneo e Provincia*, no. 28, 2nd semester, 1985, p. 33
23 Levi, Primo, *Se questo è un uomo La tregua* (Turin, 1963) p. 103 (translation, JS)
24 Auden, W.H., 'In memory of W.B. Yeats (d. Jan 1939)' in *W.H. Auden The Collected Poems*, ed. Edward Mendelson (London, 1976) p. 197

EVENTS: PHASE ONE

1 Rochat, Giorgio and Massobrio, Giulio, *Breve storia dell' Esercito italiano dal 1861 al 1943* (Turin, 1978) p. 271
2 Minniti, Fortunato, 'Dalla "non belligeranza" alla "guerra parallela"', *Storia Contemporanea*, anno XVIII, no. 6 (December, 1987) p. 1143
3 Pieri, Piero and Rochat, Giorgio, *Pietro Badoglio*, (Turin, 1974) pp. 731–32
4 *Ciano's Diary 1939–1943*, ed. Malcolm Muggeridge (London, 1947) p. 79, 29 April 1939
5 Quirino Armellini, *Diario*, cited in Pieri and Rochat, *Pietro Badoglio*, p. 746
6 Minniti, Fortunato, 'Dalla "non belligerenza"', p. 1131.
7 ibid., pp. 1159 and 1164
8 Riunione, 29 May 1940, *Documenti diplomatici italiani*, 9th series 1939–43 (Rome, 1960) nr. 642, p. 495 (abbreviated as *DDI*)
9 De Felice, Renzo, *Mussolini il Duce. Lo stato totalitario 1936–1940* (Turin, 1981) p. 835
10 *Das Deutsche Reich und der Zweite Weltkrieg*. Bd. 3 'Der Mittelmeeraum und Südost Europa'. By Gerhard Schreiber, Bernd Stegemann and Detlef Vogel, prepared by the Militärgeschichtliches Forschungsamt (Stuttgart, 1984) p. 223 (abbreviated as *MGFA*)
11 Rochat, Giorgio and Massobrio, Giulio, *Breve storia*, p. 273
12 *Ciano's Diary 1939–1943*, 16 July 1940, p. 277
13 *MGFA*, vol. iii, pp. 368 ff.
14 Verbale, *DDI*, 9 series, vol v, no. 677, p. 655; *MGFA*, iii, p. 201
15 *MGFA*, III, p. 372
16 Riuione, 15 October 1940, *DDI* 9th ser. v, no. 728, p. 699
17 SME US *Grecia* T.2 Doc. 157, p. 465
18 *MGFA*, iii, p. 408
19 Salvatorelli, L. and Mira, G., *Storia d'Italia nel periodefasasta*, 2 vols, Gli Oscar (Milan, 1972) (Cambridge, 1951), ii, p. 487
20 *MGFA*, iii, pp. 205, 374, 381
21 Hinsley, F.H., *Hitler's Strategy*, p. 101
22 *The Goebbels Diaries 1939–41*, trans. and ed. Fred Taylor (London, 1982) p. 185
23 Rintelen, Enno von, 'The German-Italian Cooperation During World War II', *World War II. German Military Studies*, vol. 14 (New York, 1979) p. 15
24 ibid., p. 33
25 Löhr, Alexander, *Protokoll*, p. 6
26 *MGFA*, iv, pp. 233 ff.
27 BAMA OKW/Wfüst RW 4/ 588 'Weisung nr. 20: Unternehmen Marita' Führerhauptquartier, 13 December 1940
28 Rintelen, Enno von, *Mussolini als Bundesgenosse*, p. 120

29 *MGFA*, iii, pp. 599 ff.; Rintelen, *Mussolini als Bundesgenosse. Erinnerungen des deutschen militärattaches in Rom 1936–1943* (Tübingen and Stuttgart, 1951), p. 120

30 Knox, Macgregor, *Mussolini Unleashed 1939–1941. Politics and Strategy in Fascist Italy's Last War* (Cambridge, 1982), p. 261

31 SME US *Grecia* T.2, Doc. no. 297, pp. 836–42

32 *Ciano's Diary 1939–43*, p. 328, 17 January 1941

33 ACS SPD CR B. 86 w/R1 f.2 'Guzzoni, Alfredo, generale', 25 January 1942

34 Rintelen, Enno von, *Mussolini als Bundesgenosse*, p. 124

35 *Ciano's Diary 1939–43*, p. 330, 18 January 1941

36 *Hitlers Tischgespräche in Führehauptquarter*, ed. Henry Picker (Stuttgart, 1976), p. 57, 21 July 1941

37 *MGFA*, iii, pp. 597–98

38 SME US *L'esercito italiano*, p. 240

39 *The Goebbels Diaries 1939–1941*, p. 231

40 Caviglia, Enrico, *Diario 1925–1945* (Rome, 1952), p. 326, 14 April 1941

41 *MGFA*, iii, pp. 459 ff.; *Kriegstagebuch des Oberkommandos der Wehrmacht (Wehrmachstführungsstab)* kept by Helmuth Greiner and Percy Ernst Schramm, vol. 1, 1 August 1940–31 December 1941 (Frankfurt/Main, 1965) (abbreviated as *KTB*) pp. 1200 ff.

42 *MGFA*, iii, p. 473 ff.

43 ibid. p. 483

44 BAMA OKW/Wfüst RW 4/ 588, Chef d Wfüst to Chef L, 12 May 1941, reports the Führer's orders given at meeting on 10 May.

45 *The Goebbels Diaries 1939–1941*, p. 339, 29 April 1941

46 Roatta, Mario, *Otto Milioni di Baionette. L'esercito italiano in guerra dal 1940 al 1944* (Milan, 1946) pp. 166–67

47 Pirelli, Alberto, *Taccuini*, p. 299

48 Diary entry in Peter Broucek, *Ein General im Zwielicht. Die Lebenserinnerungen Edmund Glaise von Horstenau*, 2 vols (Vienna, 1980 and 1983) vol. 2, p. 696

49 Glaise to OKW, 18 May 1941, BAMA 'bev. dt. General in Agram' RH 31 III /1

50 Hassell, Ulrich von, *Vom andern Deutschland* (Frankfurt/Main, 1964) p. 183

51 Ambrosio to all commands, 1.05 p.m. 19 May 1941, SME US DS 'Comando 9 Btg Auton CCRR' B. 446, allegato 23,

52 Ortona, Egidio, 'Diario sul Governo della Dalmazia (1941–1943)' *Storia Contemporanea*, anno XVIII, no. 6 (December 1987) 14 June 1941, p. 1367

53 Glaise to OKW (telegram) BAMA 'Bev. dt. General in Agram' RH 31 III/1

54 Hilberg, Raul, *The Destruction of the European Jews*, rev. and definitive edn, 3 vols (New York and London, 1985) vol. 2, pp. 710–11

55 *KTB*, vol. 1, p. 393, 6 June 1941; BAMA 'Bev. dt General in Agram', RH 31 III/1 Glaise to OKW, 6 June, reported that the visit had 'given the greatest possible satisfaction to the Croatians'.

56 SME US DS 'Comando 9 Btg Auton CCRR' B. 446, Split, 4 June 1941

57 BAMA 'Bev. dt General in Agram' RH 31 III/1, Glaise to OKW, 28 June 1941

58 MEA ASD Jugoslavia (Croazia) AAPP B. 138(1943) 'Note relative all' occupazione italiana in Jugoslavia' contains 50 pages of photographs so awful that they seared themselves on my memory as if etched. Not all are *Ustaši* atrocities; there are Serb reprisals, *cetnik* atrocities on partisans,

partisans on *cetniks* and terrible pictures of mutilated and disfigured Italian corpses. Prisoners were frequently castrated, made to chew their genitals and then tortured to death. There is in Menahem Shelach's *Heshbon Damim. Hatzalat Yehudi Kroatiah al yiday Ha-italkim 1941–43*, (Tel Aviv, 1986) pp. 35–37 an account of the *Ustaši* massacre of the largely Jewish inmates of the concentration camps of Metajna and Slano on the island of Pag in the summer of 1941. When the Italians ordered the exhumation of the bodies thrown into mass graves, they found 791 bodies including those of 91 children, the youngest of whom was five months old. Many had been shot but many had been literally butchered with knives and axes. Shelach speculates that the official reports reached the highest levels of Italian society and shows that one reached the Duke of Spoleto who had been nominated as a potential king of the new Croatian state but sensibly never went near the place.

59 MEA ASD Jugoslavia (Croazia) AAPP B. 138(1943) 'Note relative all' occupazione italiana' p. 46
60 Shelach, Menachem, *Heshbon Damim*, p. 30
61 ibid., p. 31, note
62 Stoianovich, Traian, 'The Social Foundations of Balkan Politics, 1750–1941', in *The Balkans in Transition. Essays on the Development of Balkan Life and Politics since the eighteenth century*, ed. Charles and Barbara Jelavich (Berkeley and Los Angeles, California, 1963) pp. 334–35
63 BAMA 'bev. dt. General in Agram' RH 31 III/1, Glaise to OKW Abteilung Ausland, 7 July 1941
64 ibid. Glaise to OKW 10 July 1941
65 ibid. Glaise to OKW 19 July 1941
66 ACS MI DGPS AAGGRR. B. 17 f.84 Croazia, Casertano to ministry of foreign affairs (copy to ministry of the interior), 10 June 1941
67 SME US DS 32 Regg. ftr. 'Div Marche' B. 258
68 ibid. allegato 24, 28 June 1941
69 SME US *Dalmazia Una Cronaca per la storia (1941)*, by Oddone Talpa, (Roma, 1985) allegato no. 7, pp. 477–79
70 Jäckel, Eberhard and Rohwer, Jürgen (eds) *Der Mord an den Juden im zweiten Weltkrieg* (Stuttgart, 1986), p. 16
71 Gilbert, Martin, *The Holocaust. The Jewish Tragedy* (London, 1986) pp. 173–74
72 BAMA 'Kdr Gen. u Befh Serbien' RW 40/79 Aktenvermerk, 24.11.1942
73 Hassell, Ulrich von, *Vom andern Deutschland*, p. 192
74 ibid., p. 187
75 Scotti, Giacomo and Viazzi, Luciano, *Le Aquile delle Montagne Nere. Storia dell'occupazione e della guerra italiana in Montenegro (1941–43)* (Milan, 1987), p. 93
76 SME US *Dalmazia*, p. 503
77 ibid. p. 504
78 ibid. p. 506, Pietromarchi to Casertano, private, 29 July 1941
79 Browning, Christopher, 'Wehrmacht Reprisal Policy and the Mass Murder of Jews in Serbia', *Militärgeschichtliche Mitteilungen*, vol. 33, no. 1(1983), p. 32
80 ibid. p. 33
81 ibid. p. 34
82 SME US DS 'Notiziaro Vario 2ª Armata' B. 1361, Roatta to SMRE il Capo di SM: 'Oggetto: Ispezione eseguita in Slovenia e Dalmazia' 10 January 1942

83 Browning, Christopher, 'Wehrmacht Reprisal Policy', p. 35

84 Scotti, Giacomo and Viazzi, Luciano, *Le Aquile*, p. 139

85 Potočnik, Franc, Il *Campo di sterminio fascista: L'isola di Rab* (Turin, 1979) 'Verbale della riunione a Kočevje il 2 agosto 1942' p. 47

86 ibid., p. 48

87 ibid., p. 49

88 SME US 'CCFFAA Grecia (11ª Armata)' B. 966, 'oggetto: op. controllo del banditismo', 22 July 1942

89 SME US DS 'Comando 1/XXIII Btg Guardia alla frontiera' B. 783, allegato 21, Comando XI Corpo d'Armata, 21 July 1942

90 BAMA 'bev. dt General in Agram' RH 31 III/1 'Aufzeichnung für den deutschen Gesandten', 9 December 1941

91 *Trials of War Criminals, Nuremberg Trials under Control Council Law No 10*. case No 7, 'The Hostages Case', p. 766

92 Browning, Christopher, 'Wehrmacht Reprisal Policy', p. 38

93 BDC SSO 'Hildebrandt, Richard', Turner to Hildebrandt, 17 October 1941; translated in Browning, Christopher, 'Wehrmacht Reprisal Policy', p. 39

94 BDC SSO, 'Turner, Harald', Turner to Wolff, 11 April 1942

95 Löhr, Alexander, *Protokoll*, p. 9

96 BAMA 'W Bfh Südost (AOK 12) 1a' RH 20–12/150 'Zusätze zum Füherbefehl 003830/42 18.10.1942'

97 Salvatores, Umberto *Bersaglieri sul Don*, 3rd edn (Bologna, 1965) p. 19

98 ibid. p. 21

99 Interview with Professor Salvatore Loi, 26 March 1988; see also Salvatores, Umberto, *Bersaglieri*, pp. 19–20

100 Interview with Professor Loi. ibid.

101 Ortona, Egidio, 'Diario', pp. 1371, 10 August 1941

102 ibid. p. 1372, 11 August 1941

103 SME US *Le Operazioni delle Unità italiane in Jugoslavia (1941–1943)* by Salvatore Loi, (Rome, 1978) pp. 177–78

104 Scotti, Giacomo, *'Bono Taliano': Gli italiani in Jugoslavia (1941–43)* (Milan, 1977) p. 116, Kardelje to Tito, 14 December 1942

105 SME US *Le Operazioni*, pp. 191–92; SME US *Dalmazia*, p. 888

106 SME US DS 'Comando 55 Rgt ftr ''Marche''' B. 783, allegato No. 9, 'Relazione sulle operazioni di rastrellamento effettuato dal reggimento nei giorni 8–12 giugno', 16 June 1942

107 Caviglia, Enrico, *Diario*, p. 356, 20 January 1942

108 Plehwe, Friedrich Karl von, *Als die Achse zerbrach. Das Ende des deutsch–italienischen Bundnisses im zweiten Weltkreig* (Wiesbaden/Munich, 1980), p. 39 and pp. 170–71

109 BAMA 'bev. dt General in Agram' RH 31/III/12, Glaise to Löhr, 13 January 1943

110 ACS SPD CR 1922–1945, B. 73, f. 525, 12 February 1942

111 Steinberg, Lucien, *The Jews Against Hitler (Not as a Lamb)*, trs. Marion Hunter (Glasgow, 1978) p. 303

112 BAMA 'bev.dt. Gen in Agram' RH 31 III/3 'zur Lage in Kroatien', 6 March 1942

113 SME US DS. B. 1361, 'Notiziario vario 2ª Armata' 'Oggetto: ispezione eseguita in Slovenia e Dalmazia', 10 January 1942, p. 3

114 ibid. p. 4

115 ibid. p. 7

116 BAMA 'bev. dt. General in Agram' RH 31 III/3 'Bericht über die Lage in Kroatien. 2. Hälfte Februar 1942', 25 February, 1942, pp. 10–11

117 Scotti, Giacomo and Viazzi, Luciano, *Le Aquile*, pp. 79–80

118 SME US DS B. 1361 'Notiziario vario 2ª Armata', Ambrosio to Comando Supremo, 4 February 1942

119 SME US. DS 'Divisione ''Pusteria''' B. 82. Comando Div. 'Pusteria' to CT Montenegro, 12 June 1942

120 SME US DS 'Supersloda' B. 1222, 'Sunto degli argomenti trattati nel convegno di Zagabria del 19 settembre 1942'

121 Cavallero, Ugo, *Comando Supremo. Diario 1941–1943 del capo di S.M.G.* (Rocca S. Casciano, 1948), p. 421, 20 December 1942

122 Deakin, F.W., *The Brutal Friendship. Mussolini, Hitler and the Fall of Italian Fascism* (London 1962 and Penguin edn 1966), pp. 190–91 and 196–97

123 BAMA 'Gen Kdo XV(Geb.) AK' RH 24 – 15/3, OB Südost to Befh Kroatien, 26 June 1943

124 Cavallero, Ugo, *Comando Supremo*, p. 429, 3 January 1943

125 SME US *Le operazioni delle unità italiane in Jugoslavia (1941–1943)* 'Proclama alla Popolazione' 7 September 1941, doc. no. 66, p. 394

126 NA T-821 R. 405 It 5283a 'Comando 2a Armata' Ufficio Affari Civili, 26 October 1942

127 BAMA 'bev. dt. General in Agram' RH 31 III/1, Glaise to OKW Wfüst, Abt. L, 9 August 1941

128 Siegfried Kasche was an *Obergruppenführer* in the SA, a violent anti-semite and opponent of the Italians, who because of his party connections had the reputation of being all-powerful. The SS hated and feared him because, as SS *Obergruppenführer* Berger of the SS main office explained in a letter to Himmler, he 'belonged to those who can never forget the 30th of June 1934' (the 'night of the long knives' when the SS murdered eighty-eight of the top SA leadership) and whom an SS observer called 'cold and incalculable'. (BDC SS – HO 1642, Berger to Himmler, 13.7.1943 and BDC SA 'Kasche')

129 BAMA 'bev. dt. General in Agram' RH 31 III/8, 'Vermerk über Gespräch mit Bürgermeister Dr Deak aus Karlovac', 22 August 1941

130 ibid. 'Bericht des Professor Dr. von Loesch, Leiter des Instituts für Grenz-und Auslandskunde in Berlin', 30 September 1941

131 ibid. 'Mitteilung des deutschen Oberleutnants Weis, Sachbearbeiter des Deutschen Wehrwirtschaftsoffiziers Agram für Tabakfragen in Dubrovnik', 22 December 1941

132 BAMA 'bev. dt. General in Agram' RH 31 III/8 'Bericht des Polizeiattachés bei der deutschen Gesandtschaft in Zagreb' 30 May 1942

133 ibid. 'Schreiben des Ministerialrates Schnell im Reichsministerium für Bewaffnung und Munition an das Auswärtige Amt', 18 July 1942. Menachem Shelach reproduces the full German text of Schnell's report in *Heshbon Damim*, p. 58

134 Interview, Mr Imre Rochlitz, 5 February 1988

135 NA T-821, R. 405 'Comando 2ª Armata' Ufficio Affari Civili, 'Situazione ebrei', 27 August 1942

136 ibid. p. 2

137 SME US, *Le Operazioni*, p. 192; and Glaise to OKW, 16 December 1942, BAMA 'bev. dt. General in Agram', RH 31 III/1

138 Cavallero, Ugo, *Comando Supremo*, p. 227; BAMA 'bev. dt. General in Agram' RH 31 III/2 'Verbalnote', 13 March 1942; *Bericht der Internationalen Historikerkommission (Waldheim Commission)* (Vienna,

15 February 1988), p. 27, for a list of the participants at the 3 March 1942 meeting
139 SME US *Le operazioni*, pp. 204–08; *Bericht der Internationalen Historikerkommission*, pp. 27–28
140 BAMA 'bev. dt. Gen. in Agram' RH 31 III/3 Glaise to OKW Abt. Ausland (FS) 26 April 1942
141 Raul Hilberg, *The Destruction of the European Jews*, pp. 401–406 and for a discussion of its significance, see Lucy Davidowicz, *The War Against the Jews 1933–1945* (London, 1975), pp. 168 ff.; Gerald Fleming, *Hitler and the Final Solution* (London, 1985), pp. 92–94; Eberhard Jäckel, *Der Mord an den Juden*, for a vigorous podium discussion on the steps which led to the Wannsee conference, pp. 179. The full text can be found in ADAP, Series E, vol. 1, no. 150, pp. 267–275

EVENTS: PHASE TWO

1 Fleming, Gerald, *Hitler and the Final Solution* (London, 1985), p. 22
2 *The Goebbels Diaries 1942–43*, ed. Louis P. Lochner (Garden City, NY, 1948), pp. 147–48, 27 March 1942
3 Interview with Dr Evi Eller, Rome, 4 April 1988
4 Zuccotti, Susan, *The Italians and the Holocaust Persecution, Rescue and Survival* (New York and London, 1987), p. 158
5 Roatta to Comando Supremo, 22 September 1942, draft of the document on the notepaper of the Ufficio Collocamento, probably the work of Castellani who was active in planning the 2nd Army's response to the Jewish question. NA T -821 R. 405 It 5283a 'Comando 2a Armata'
6 Browning, Christopher, *The Final Solution and the German Foreign Office. A Study of Referat DIII of Abteilung Deutschland 1940–43* (London and New York, 1978), Appendix, p. 218
7 Hilberg, Raul, *The Destruction of the European Jews*, rev. and definitive edn, 3 vols (New York and London, 1985) p. 490
8 MEA ASD Gab. AP 3 B. 64 Francia(1942) f. 8 Sionismo, Buti to ministry of foreign affairs, 30 May 1942
9 ACS MI DGPS GG RR B.5 f. Razzismo, Bastianini to Presidenza Consiglio Ministri, 15 May 1942
10 MEA ASD Gab AP – 42 AG Croazia 35, B. 133 (1942) f. 8 Sionismo, Ciano to Bastianini, 1 June 1942
11 Ortona, Egidio, 'Diario', 24 May 1942, p. 1375
12 MEA ASD Gab AP – 42 AG Croazia 35 B. 133 (1942) f. 8. 'Sionismo', Bastianini to ministry of foreign affairs, 1 June 1942
13 ibid. Roatta's reply sent in full in Bastianini to MEA, 16 June 1942
14 ibid,, 'Appunto', 23 June 1942
15 ibid. Castellani to MEA, 23 July 1942
16 The Italian government first learned of the 'thirty pieces of silver' in ibid., Casertano to MEA, 22 August 1942. Cf ADAP, E, vol. IV, no. 49, p. 83, Kasche to foreign office, 14 October 1942
17 NA T – 821 R.405 It 5283a 'Comando 2a Armata', Bastianini to Roatta, 7 July 1942
18 Ortona, Egidio, 'Diario sul Governo della Dalmazia (1941–1943)', *Storia Contemporanea*, anno XVIII, no. 6 (December, 1987) p. 1382, 15 July 1942
19 SME US DS B. 1358 'Notiziario Supersloda A.C.' 17 June 1942 and ibid., 31 July 1942

20 Cavallero, Ugo, *Comando Supremo Diario 1940–1943 del Capo di S.M.G.* (Rocca S. Casciano, 1948), pp. 287–88
21 SME US DS 'SMRE SIE' B. 1048, 'Notiziario Mensile Stati Esteri' no. 7, 31 July 1942, pp. 96–98. The 'Specchio di distribuzione mensile', or the list of those to receive the document, shows that it went out in an edition of over 150 copies and went to the King, the Royal Family and all senior commanders.
22 MEA ASD Gab AP – 42 AG Croazia 35, Bastianini to MEA, 19 August 1942
23 Hassell, Ulrich von, *Vom andern Deutschland* (Frankfurt/Main, 1964), p. 154
24 Dollmann, Eugen, *Roma Nazista* (Milan, 1949), p. 370 tells the story that when Reinhard Heydrich visited Rome in 1939 he was furious that Otto von Bismarck should represent Germany in the eternal city since he was a half-Jew. His mother, the wife of Herbert Bismarck, was first married to Count Hoyos, a Hungarian grandee, but had been born more humbly as the daughter of a Trieste Jewess. Heydrich apparently tried to get Bismarck removed but Arturo Bocchini, chief of the Italian secret police, told him that the Führer himself had ordered Otto von Bismarck's 'achille's heel' to be left unmentioned.
25 'Verax', 'Italiani ed ebrei in Jugoslavia', *Politica estera*, anno 1, no. 9 (1944) p. 25. 'Verax' was the pseudonym used by Roberto Ducci, chief of the Croatian department under Count Pietromarchi in the Italian foreign ministry.
26 MEA ASD Gab Ap – 42 AG Croazia 35, Appunto, 18 August 1942, with the marginal comment in pencil 'retype this but for the Chief of Cabinet who will sign' initialled V and D, for Luigi Vidau, chief of 'Ufficio IV' the office of 'reserved affairs' (i.e. secret) and Roberto Ducci, the desk officer on the Croatian desk.
27 ibid.
28 Pietromarchi, Luca, 'Estratti del diario privato' in Joseph Rochlitz, *The Righteous Enemy. The Italians and Jews in Occupied Europe 1941–43.* A collection of notes and research materials for the documentary film (Rome, 1988), p. 7, 20 August 1942
29 MEA ASD Gab Ap – 42 AG Croazia 35, consul general, Sarajewo to MEA, 24 August 1942
30 ibid., 'Appunto per il Duce', 21 August 1942 (cf. document reproduced on p. 2)
31 Pietromarchi, Luca, 'Estratti del diario', p. 7, 24 August 1982
32 MEA ASD Gab AP- 42 AG Croazia 35, Casertano to MEA, 22 August 1942, arrived at ministry 24 August.
33 NA T – 821 R. 405 It 5283a 'Comando 2a Armata', Capo Gabinetto Lanza d'Ajeta to Comando Supremo, 28 August 1942
34 SME US DS B. 1359 'Notiziario Vario 2a Armata', 31 August 1942
35 ADAP, Series E vol. III, no. 266, p. 454 'Aufzeichnung des Legationsrats Rademacher', 4 September 1942
36 Pietromarchi, Luca, 'Estratti del Diario', p. 8, 28 August 1942
37 NA T – 821 R. 405 It 5283e 'Comando 2a Armata', VI Corpo d'Armata, Ufficio Affari Civili, 'Situazione ebrei', 27 August 1942
38 MEA ASD Gab – 42 AP Croazia 35, attached to Castellani to Pietromarchi, 11 September 1942
39 ibid. Castellani to Pietromarchi, 11 September 1942
40 NA T – 821 R. 406 It 5283e 'Comando 2a Armata', Consul Mammalella to General Clemente Primieri, 20 January 1943

41 Pietromarchi, Luca, 'Estratti del Diario', p. 8, 13 September 1943

42 SME US DS B. 1442 Comando Supremo, 13 September 1942

43 SME US DS B. 993 Supersloda, Roatta to Comando Supremo, 18 September 1942

44 Fleischer, Hagen, *Im Kreuzschatten der Mächte. Griechenland 1941–1944*, 2 vols. (Frankfurt/Main/Bern/New York, 1986) pp. 48 ff. and pp. 134 ff.; see also John L. Hondros, 'The Greek Resistance 1941–1944: A Re-evaluation' in Iatrides, John O. (ed.), *Greece in the 1940s. A Nation in Crisis*, (Hanover and London, 1981)

45 SME US DS B. 1054 CCFFAA Grecia (11a Armata), diary entry, 19 September 1942

46 ibid. diary entry, 22 September 1942, allegato

47 Ortona, Egidio, 'Diario', p. 1382, 10 July 1942

48 Pirelli, Alberto, *Taccuini 1922–1943* (Bologna, 1984), p. 347, 10–11 September 1942

49 Deakin, F.W., *The Brutal Friendship*, p. 48

50 Bottai, Giuseppe, *Diario*, p. 327, 7 October 1942

51 Ortona, Egidio, 'Diario', p. 1387, 8 October 1942

52 ibid. p. 1387, 10 October 1942

53 Deakin, F.W., *The Brutal Friendship. Mussolini, Hitler and the Fall of Italian Fascism* (London, 1962 and Penguin edn, 1966), p. 58

54 NA T – 821 R. 405 It 5283e 'Comando 2a Armata', Roatta to Comando Supremo, 22 September 1942

55 MEA ASD AP – 42, AG Croazia 35, Castellani to Pietromarchi, 24 September 1942

56 Ciano particularly disliked Cavallero's 'servile attitude' to the Germans and thought of him as a man 'who lies, consorts with the Germans and steals all he can', *Ciano's Diary 1941–1943*, ed. Malcolm Muggeridge (London, 1947), pp. 532, 534 and 548, and also Guerri, G.B., *Galeazzo Ciano Una vita, 1903–1944* (Milan, 1979), pp. 497–99. For his contacts with industry see Pirelli, Alberto, *Taccuini*, pp. 297 and the *Dizionario biografico degli Italiani*, vol. 22, p. 702. Cavallero was a director of Pirelli and Ansaldo between the wars and was involved in a procurement scandal which forced him to resign. See also, Rocca, Gianni, *Fucilate gli ammiragli. La tragedia della Marina Italian nella seconda guerra mondiale* (Milan, 1987), p. 274

57 Rintelen, Enno von, *Mussolini als Bundesgenosse. Erinnerungen des deutschen militärattaches in Rom 1936–1943* (Tübingen and Stuttgart, 1951), pp. 190–91

58 Dollmann, Eugen, *Roma nazista*, p. 139

59 SME US DS B. 1442 Comando Supremo 1–15 December 1942. The war diary shows that Kesselring saw Cavallero every day except Wednesday, 2 December during the first half of the month, generally in the late afternoon. Kesselring took part in internal discussions among the chiefs of staff of the three services and with the chiefs of naval operations, especially on matters involving convoys to Africa.

60 A vivid account of Cavallero's last day is to be found in Paolo Monelli, *Roma 1943* (Rome, 1946), pp. 192–93, who inclines to the view that Cavallero was murdered. The Marshall's son denies it in the introduction to his father's diaries, Cavallero, Ugo, *Comando Supremo*, pp. xvii ff.

61 SME US DS B. 1443 Comando Supremo, diary entry, 26 January 1943. It is interesting that he should telephone General Vercellino who commanded the Italian 4th Army in France, because on 21 January, *The*

Times had published an article on Italian protection of the Jews in southern France. The Germans, as we shall see, had been pressing hard to get their hands on the Jews in that zone. Which was uppermost in Cavallero's mind? The loyalty to the Axis or the realization that the world had begun to hear about the 'final solution'? If the latter, he might have called Vercellino to encourage him; if the former, to discourage him.

62 Caviglia, Enrico, *Diario 1925–1945* (Rome, 1952), p. 341
63 Deakin, F.W., *The Brutal Friendship*, p. 138
64 ibid., p. 71
65 Pirelli, Alberto, *Taccuini*, p. 372, 5 November 1942
66 ACS MI DG 'Demorazza' B. 9, f. 38 Padre Pietro Tacchi Venturi to Excellency Guido Buffarini Guidi, under-secretary of the interior, 12 July 1943, in which he again includes a letter from Cardinal Maglione protesting about the inclusion of Jews in mixed marriages in the forced labour system, dated 8 June 1942, and complains about the 'slowness of the Ministry of Interior' and 'absolutely absurd' regulations.
67 BAMA RH III/7, Gesandte Kasche to Ambassador Ritter, 20 January 1943, Anlage, 18.1.1943, 'Besprechung mit Generaloberst Löhr, Agram, Hotel Esplanade'
68 BAMA RH 20 -12/149 AOK 12, 'Aktennotiz über Reise OB nach Belgrad und Agram', 28 August–1 September 1942, pp. 2–3 and p. 9
69 BAMA RH 20 -12/150 W Bfh Südost (AOK 12) KTB 1a Geh. Kdosache, 'Betr.: Unstimmigkeiten mit Italienern vom 1.8–22.9'
70 ADAP Series E, vol. III, no. 310, 'Aufzeichnung über die Unterredung zwischen dem Führer und dem Poglavnik', 25 September 1942, pp. 532 and 536–37
71 BAMA RH 31 III/7 'Aufzeichnung für den Führer' Zagreb, 1 October 1942, p. 6
72 MEA ASD Gab AP – 42 AG Croazia 35, Appunto, Rome, 3 October 1942
73 Carpi, Daniel, 'The Rescue of Jews in the Italian Zone of Occupied Croatia', in *Rescue Attempts during the Holocaust* (Jerusalem, 1977) p. 480
74 ibid., p. 480
75 ibid., p. 481
76 ADAP Series E, vol. IV, no. 91, 'Niederschrift über meinen Empfang beim Duce Benito Mussolini am Sonntag, dem 11.10.1942 in Rome in Palazzo Venezia, 17 Uhr', p. 150
77 Pietromarchi, Luca, 'Estratti del diario', p. 2, 14 October 1942
78 ADAP Series E, vol. IV, no. 38, p. 38, von Mackensen to foreign office, 11 October 1942
79 ibid. no. 69, p. 110, Ribbentrop to Kasche, 17 October 1942
80 ibid. no. 70, p. 117 'Aufzeichnung des Unterstaatssekretärs Luther: Grundsätze und Richtlienien für die deutsche Italienpropaganda', 10 October 1942
81 ibid. no. 89, p. 144, 'Aufzeichnung des Unterstaatssekretärs Luther. Betrifft: Italien und die Judenfrage' 22 October 1942
82 Browning, Christopher, *The Final Solution and the German Foreign Office. A Study of Referat DIII Of Abteilung Deutschland* (London and New York, 1978), p. 137
83 Dorian, Emil, *The Quality of Witness. A Romanian Diary 1937–1944*, ed. Marguerite Dorian and trs. Mara Soceanu Vamos (Philadephia, Pa, 1982) p. 235, 14 October 1942
84 Malaparte, Curzio, *Kaputt*, (Rome/Milan, 1948) p. 34
85 ADAP Series E, vol. I, no. 230, p. 405 'Vortragsnotiz des Unterstaatssekretärs Luther', 11 February 1942

86 BAMA RH 31 III/12 'bev. dt Gen Agram', Glaise to Löhr, 2 March 1943
87 Browning, Christopher, *The Foreign Office*, p. 135
88 MEA ASD Gab AP – 42, AG Croazia 35, 'Appunto', 20 October 1942
89 ibid. Appunto, p. 2, 23 October 1942
90 ibid. p. 2, the text reads: "According to what the Counsellor [Perić] confided then in his personal capacity, such "collaboration" would consist almost certainly in the definitive "elimination" of such Jewish groups.'
91 ibid. Appunto, 28 October 1942. Ducci writes: 'Analagous communication has been made by the Chief of Cabinet to Minister Bismarck, 28/X'
92 ADAP Series E, vol. IV, no. 110, pp. 196–97, von Mackensen to foreign office, 28 October 1942, 9.10 p.m.
93 NA T -821 R. 407 It 5283m Comando 2a Armata, Comando Supremo to Supersloda, 28 October 1942
94 ibid. 'Questione ebrei' 24 October 1942, signed Primieri
95 ibid. 'Aspetto morale', 26 October 1942
96 ibid. Telescritto, 29 October 1942
97 *Relazione sull' opera svolta dal Ministero degli Affari Esteri per la tutela delle comunità ebraiche (1938–1943)* riservato (Rome, 1946) p. 20; 'Verax' (Roberto Ducci) 'Italiani ed ebrei in Jugoslavia', *Politica estera*, anno 1, number 9 (1944), p. 26; see also the interview that Ducci gave to Nicola Caracciolo published in Caracciolo, Nicola. *Gli ebrei e l'Italia durante la guerra 1940–1945* (Rome, 1986) pp. 114 ff. in which Ducci argues that all the foreign ministry officials were agreed that the policy of *consegna* had to be sabotaged. He also argues 'not to defend Mussolini but to explain what happened then . . . that "*nulla osta*" is an Italian expression to say "for my part I have nothing against it"; in other words, it was not exactly an order to consign the Jews'. See Rochlitz, Joseph, *The Righteous Enemy* TV documentary for an interview with Ducci in which he makes similar statements. None of this impugns Ducci's intentions, but simply says that memory often fools us especially on things we want to believe anyway.
98 Carpi, Daniel, *The Rescue*, p. 488
99 MEA ASD Gab AP – 42 AG Croazia 35, il Comando, Bataglione Mitraglieri Autocarro di Corpo d'Armata, 6 November 1942
100 ibid. attached to a letter from Castellani to the foreign ministry, 18 November 1942
101 SME US DS B. 1442 Comando Supremo, 29 September 1942 and ibid. B. 1443, 14 January 1943 in which Cavallero, Scuero (under-secretary at the ministry of war) and General Ambrosio met to discuss a 'new commandant for the arm of the carabinieri. Candidates: General Hazon and General Pièche'. Hazon got the job but died on 19 July. His successor at that point was not Pièche but General Angelo Cerica from the Forest Militia (see Deakin, F.W., *The Brutal Friendship*, p. 479)
102 Interview with General Carlo Casarico, Rome, 7 April 1988
103 NA T -821 R. 405 It 5283a Comando 2a Armata 'Relazione sulla Croazia' 1 November 1942. The report is to be found in the files of the civil affairs office of 2nd Army HQ together with the report of 14 November. Both signatures have been marked 'illegible' but over the 14th is written 'Pièche'. Since the signature is the same, the former must also be by Pièche.
104 ibid. p. 4

105 ibid. p. 5
106 MEA ASD Gab AP – 42 AG Croazia 35 'Appunto' 4 November 1942
107 NA T -821, R. 405 It 5283a Comando 2a Armata, Pièche to MEA, 14 November 1942
108 Pirelli, Alberto, *Taccuini*, p. 365
109 Interview with Mr Imre Rochlitz, 5 February 1988
110 SME US DA B. 1001 Comando Div. 'Murge' Sezione U.I.S., Allegato 156, 9 November 1942
111 ibid, Allegato 169, 22 November 1942 and Allegato 170, 23 November
112 ibid. Allegato 169, 22 November 1942
113 MEA ASD Gab AP – 42 AG Croazia 35, Guariglia to Ciano, 5 November 1942
114 BAMA RH 20 -12/150 W Bfh Südost (AOK 12) *Chefbesprechung*, 24 September 1942
115 BAMA RH 31 III/ 5 'bev. dt Gen. in Agram' *Fliegermajor* Josef Donegani to Glaise, 7 October 1942
116 BAMA RH 31 III/12 'bev. dt Gen. in Agram', Glaise to Löhr, 2 March 1943
117 Capogreco, Carlo Spartaco, *Ferramonti. La vita e gli uomini del più grande campo d'internamento fascista (1940–1945)* (Florence, 1987) pp. 80–81 and 173. The visits took place on 22 May 1941 and on 27 May 1943.
118 *Actes et Documents du Saint Siège relatifs à la seconde guerre mondiale* vol. 9 'Le Saint Siège et les victimes de la Guerre Janvier–Decembre' (Vatican, 1975), no. 49, p. 124, Maglione to Borgoncini Duca, 13 February 1943. Bastianini, Giuseppe, *Uomini, cose, fatti* (Milan, 1959) p. 89 and Guariglia, Raffaele, *Ricordi 1922–1946* (Naples, 1950) pp. 535–36 who records the cardinal secretary of state complaining in February 1943 that whereas the Nuncio Borgoncini Duca had been in post with the Italian government since 1929, ambassadors of Italy to the Holy See kept changing which did not correspond 'to the seriousness and importance of the mission in itself'.
119 Hoffmann, Peter, 'Roncalli in the Second World War: Peace Initiatives, the Greek Famine and the Persecution of the Jews', *The Journal of Ecclesiastical History*, vol. 40, no. 1 (1989)
120 *Actes et documents*, vol. 9, p. 34
121 Chadwick, W.O., *Britain and the Vatican during the Second World War* (Cambridge, 1986) gives a vivid description of the lives of the Allied diplomats penned up precariously inside the Vatican during the war.
122 Kitchen, Martin, *A Military History of Germany from the Eighteenth Century to the Present Day* (London, 1975) pp. 320–21.
123 SME US DS B. 1442 Comando Supremo, 4 November 1942, 7.15 p.m.
124 Deakin, F.W., *The Brutal Friendship*, pp. 84–85
125 SME US DS B. 1442 Comando Supremo, 8 November 1942
126 BAMA RH 19 VII/7 OB Sudost/ Okdo Herresgruppe E KTB 1(a) Chefbesprechung, 31 May 1943
127 SME US DS B. 1442 Comando Supremo, 1 September 1942
128 ibid. B. 1099 Comando 4a Armata, 10 November 1942
129 Cavallero, Ugo, *Comando Supremo*, p. 386, 11 November 1942
130 Cohen, Richard I., *The Burden of Conscience. French Jewry's Response to the Holocaust* (Bloomington, Ind., 1987) p. 40
131 Ortona, Egidio, 'Diario', p. 139, 10 November 1942
132 BAMA RH 20 -12/153 W Bfh Südost (AOK 12) Löhr to OKW, 21 November 1942; see also SME US DS B. 1442 Comando Supremo,

18 and 19 November 1942. Roatta remained in Rome until 21 November. In a meeting with Cavallero he repeated what he had said to Löhr that there was no use carrying out grand operations against the partisans. Success can only be temporary 'like the water which a boat divides'.

133 MEA ASD Gab AP – 42 AG Croazia 35 'Appunto per il Gabinetto AP' signed Vittorio Castellani, 3 December 1942

134 SME US DS B. 1001 Allegato 150 F/E Comando Div. 'Murge' Sez. U.I.S., 3 November 1942

135 MEA ASD Gab AP – 42, AG Croazia 35, Hermann Schossberger and others to Roatta, Porto Re, 28 November 1942

136 Jean-Claude Favez has worked out that it was in the autumn of 1942 that the International Committee of the Red Cross in Geneva received incontrovertible proof that Jews were being murdered in special camps. On 14 October 1942, the Committee met to consider the launch of an international appeal against Nazi genocide and under the influence of the Swiss Government decided to remain silent. Cf. Jean-Claude Favez. *Une Mission Impossible? Le CICR, les déportations et les camps de concentration nazis* (Lausanne, 1988) pp. 160–64 for the full minutes of the discussion.

EVENTS: PHASE THREE

1 Pietromarchi, Luca, 'Estratti del diario privato' in Joseph Rochlitz, *The Righteous Enemy, The Italians and Jews in Occupied Europe* (Bologna, 1984), 27 November 1942, p. 8

2 Pirelli, Alberto, *Taccuini, 1941–43* A collection of notes for the documentary film (Rome, 1988), p. 377, 4 December 1942

3 Pietromarchi, Luca, 'Estratti del Diario', 10 December 1942 in J. Rochlitz, *The Righteous Enemy*, p. 8

4 Malaparte went to see Pietromarchi to tell him what he had seen, and Pietromarchi recorded one or two particularly gruesome incidents in the entry of 27 November.

5 Deakin, F.W., *The Brutal Friendship. Mussolini, Hitler and the Fall of Italian Fascism* (London, 1962 and Penguin edn 1966), p. 320 (in the original, hardback edition published in 1962; the Penguin edition of 1966 omits this interesting citation)

6 SME US Cartella no. 1393 Geloso, Carlo, 'Due Anni in Grecia al commando dell 11a Armata', 2 July 1943, pp. 174–75. The *'relazione'* was written, as was customary when a senior commander left post, at some length because Geloso had been dismissed. It constitutes a form of defence. There is just a possibililty that Löhr may have made the suggestion before the deportations because the one file missing of all the documents attached to the war diary of the command headquarters of the 11th Army is that for 4 December 1942, when the diary itself records that General Geloso 'had gone to Salonica to meet General Löhr for an exchange of ideas . . . on local political questions'. (SME US DS B.1098 CS FFAA Grecia (11a Armata) 4 December 1942). It is tantalizing that the file should be missing and to be unable to find out what 'local political questions' were discussed.

7 Roatta, Mario, *Otto Milioni di Baionette* (Milan, 1946), p. 176

8 Deakin, F.W., *The Brutal Friendship*, (Penguin edn) p. 111

9 *The Goebbels Diaries 1942–43*, ed. Louis P. Lochner (Garden City, NY, 1948), p. 241, 13 December 1942

10 Cavallero, Ugo, *Comando Supremo Diario 1941–1943 del Capo di S.M.G.* (Rocca S. Casciano, 1948), p. 404, 1 December 1942

11 SME US DS B. 1442 Comando Supremo, 6 December 1942

12 Bottai, Giuseppe, *Diario 1935–1944*, a cura di Giordano Bruno Guerri (Milan, 1982), p. 342, 6 December 1942

13 ibid., p. 343

14 Bracher, K.D., *The German Dictatorship. The Origins, Structure and Consequences of National Socialism* (London, 1971) pp. 422–23

15 BA MA RH 31 XIV/7 'Deutscher Verbindungstab beim ital. 2 AOK' Oblt Salazer, 'Gefechtsbericht über Division 'Cosseria' für die Zeit vom 9. bis. 18. Dezember. 1942'

16 ibid. p. 4

17 ibid. Oblt Otto Joos, 'Rückzugskämpfe der ital. Division 'Sforzesca' vom Don. Mitte Dezember 1942 bis Anfang Januar 1943', 19 November 1943, p. 3

18 BA MA RH 31 XIV/ 8 Deutscher Verbindungstab, KTB, p. 6, 21. 1 1943. There is a vivid description of the retreat from the Don written by an Italian army nurse (originally under her serial number not her name) who worked on a hospital train and kept a diary. In addition to recording the horrors of the battle, she also noted the concentration camps. As she sat writing her diary while the train stopped near such a camp, the chaplain said to her, 'watch well, sister, and write!' and then in the same harsh and bitter tone,'This is an edifying spectacle!' Marini, Margherita (Matricola CRI 15408) *Treno Ospedale 34* (Milan, 1982) p. 26

19 ibid. 'Auszug und Schlussfolgerungen aus den Gefechtsberichten der verschiedenen deutschen Verbindungskommandos bei den ital. Div ''Celere'', ''Torino'', ''Pasubio'' ''Ravenna'' ''Cosseria''. XXIX deutsches A.K., XXXV ital. A.K., ital. Alpini und deutsches XXIX Pz. Korps, Alpini Div. ''Julia'', 12 April, 1943'

20 *Ciano's Diary 1939–1943*, ed. Malcolm Muggeridge (London, 1947), p. 535, 16 December 1942

21 ibid. p. 536, 18 December 1942

22 SME US DS B. 1481 Comando Supremo 1–20 December 1942, Allegati, 18 December 1942, 12 noon

23 ibid. B. 1442, 19 December 1942 9.30 a.m.

24 ibid. 6.30 p.m.

25 ibid. 20 December 1942, 9.00 a.m.

26 SME US DS B. 1442 Comando Supremo, 22 December 1942, 11.35 a.m.

27 ibid. 23 December 1942, 6.00 p.m.

28 SME US DS B. 1443 Comando Supremo, 6 January 1943

29 Fest, Joachim C., *Hitler*, trs. Richard and Clara Winston (London, 1974) p. 665

30 ibid. p. 665

31 ibid. p. 677

32 Jäckel, Eberhard, *Hitler's Herrschaft* (Stuttgart, 1986), pp. 119–20

33 ibid. p. 122

34 Fleischer, Hagen, *Im Kreuzschatten der Mächte. Griechenland 1941–1944*, 2 vols, p. 179

35 SME US DS B. 1443 Comando Supremo, 20 January 1943, 9.45 a.m.

36 Bastianini, Giuseppe, *Uomini, cose, fatti* (Milan, 1959), p. 88

37 Pietromarchi, Luca, 'Estratti del Diario', 2 February 1943, in J. Rochlitz, *The Righteous Enemy*, p. 9

38 *Ciano's Diary*, p. 553, 31 January 1943

39 Ortona, Egidio 'Diario sul Governo della Dalmazia (1941–43)', *Storia Contemporanea*, anno XVIII, no. 6 (December, 1987), p. 1402, 2 February 1943

40 *Ciano's Diary*, p. 544, 5 February 1943

41 'THRACE (THRAKI)' by Steven Bowman, *Encyclopedia of the Holocaust*, Yad Vashem (Jerusalem, forthcoming)

42 Tamir, Vicky, *Bulgaria and her Jews. The History of a Dubious Symbiosis* (New York, 1979), p. 189, Beckerle to Foreign Office, 22 January 1943

43 ibid., pp. 200–02

44 For a good introduction to the war period, se Fleischer, Hagen, *Im Kreuzschatten der Mächte*, pp. 37 ff.

45 ACS MI DG PS AA GG RR(1942) b.8 f. 63 Grecia, R. Console in Salonica to foreign ministry, 2 December 1941

46 Fleischer, Hagen, *Im Kreuzschatten der Mächte*, pp. 117–18

47 Thomadakis, Stavros B., 'Black Markets, Inflation and Force in the Economy of Occupied Greece', in Iatrides, J.O. (ed.), *Greece in the 1940s. A Nation in Crisis* (Hanover, N.H. and London, 1981), Tables 1–3, pp. 67 and 71–72

48 ADAP, Series E, vol. III, no. 122, p. 213. Mussolini to Hitler, 22 July 1942

49 'SALONICA (THESSALONIKI)' by Steven Bowman, *Encyclopedia of the Holocaust*

50 Bowman, Steven, 'Greek Jews and Christians During World War II', *Remembering the Future. Jews and Christians During and After the Holocaust*, Oxford Conference, Theme 1 (1988), p. 219

51 ibid. p. 218–19

52 For a complete series of weekly reports on the situation in Salonica in 1942–43, see the weekly bulletins of Consul Zamboni in J. Rochlitz, *The Righteous Enemy*, pp. 110–228

53 ADAP, Series E, vol. III, no. 136, pp. 232–33, Altenburg to foreign office, 27 July 1942

54 BA MA RH 23/112 Korpsrück Afrika A.O.III 'Betr. Verhältnis des Juden- und Arabertums zu den italienischen Behörden in Tripolis', 7 February 1942 p. 2

55 ibid. p. 4

56 MEA ASD AAPP Francia B. 8(1943) f.8 Sionismo, Levi Vittoria to foreign ministry

57 'SALONICA (THESSALONIKI)' by Steven Bowman, *Encyclopedia of the Holocaust*; Carpi, Daniel, 'Nuovi documenti per la storia dell'Olocausto in Grecia. L'attegiamento degli italiani', *Michael on the History of the Jews in the Diaspora*, vol. VII (Tel Aviv, 1981) pp. 138–40

58 MEA ASD AAPP Grecia B. 20 (1942) ministry of foreign affairs to embassy, Athens, 24 November 1942

59 Interview with Ambassador Guelfo Zamboni, Lido dei Pini, 9 April 1988. Ambassador Zamboni, who was 92 at the time of the interview saluted Joseph Rochlitz and myself when we had finished, announced that it was time for his daily exercise, leapt on to a bicycle and pedalled off into the distance.

60 Interview with Professor Salvatore Loi, 26 March 1988

61 'Excerpts from the Salonika Diary of Lucillo Merci (February–August 1943)' compiled by Joseph Rochlitz with introduction by Menachem Shelach. *Yad Vashem Studies* vol. XVII (Jerusalem, 1987)

62 ibid. pp. 299–301, 19 February 1943

63 ibid p. 301
64 ibid. p. 304, 30 March 1943
65 Carpi, Daniel, 'Nuovi documenti', p. 142
66 'Excerpts from the Salonika Diary of Lucillo Merci', p. 303, 10 March 1943
67 Berlin Document Centre, SS Officers, 'Meyszner, August' Himmler to Meyszner, 9 May 1942
68 BA MA RH 20-12/445 WB Südost (AOK 12) Geh. Feldpolizei 611, 'Bericht', 19 August 1941
69 SME US B. 1393A Geloso, General Carlo, 'Due Anni in Grecia' pp. 164–71
70 Interview with Dr G.C. Garaguso, Rome, 26 March 1988. Dr Garaguso was not only a captain of Geloso's staff for two years but a neighbour in Rome. His parents and the Gelosos were old friends and the general acted as a kind of military patron of the young officer.
71 SME US DS B. 1443, Comando Supremo, 24 January 1943
72 Interview with Dr Garaguso
73 SME US B. 1393A Geloso, General Carlo, 'Due Anni', p. 42
74 BA MA RH 19 VII/53 OB Südost/ OKdo Herresgruppe E 'Betr:. Italienische Säuberungsmassnahmen in Griechenland', 21 May 1943, p. 3
75 For a good account of the 'bust' see Fleischer, Hagen, Im Kreuzschatten der Mächte, pp. 174 ff. and Thomadakis, Stavros B., 'Black Markets, Inflation, and Force in the Economy of Occupied Greece', pp. 74–76
76 Heller, Joseph, Catch 22 (London, 1962) p. 123
77 Dragoni, Ugo, Fiaschi in Jugoslavia. Ricordi polemici della campagna di guerra 1941–43 (Alessandria, 1983) p. 175
78 Heller, Joseph, Catch 22, p. 124
79 SME US DS B. 1054 CSFFAA Grecia (11a Armata) Geloso to Ambrosio, 19 October 1942
80 The German reaction can be found in BA MA RH 20 – 12/154 WBfh Südost (AOK 12) 'Tätigkeitsberichte 1a' of 15 December 1942, in which the chief of staff, Major General Herman Foertsch, suggests using the civil population to guarantee the safety of the railway: 'If a mine explodes or tracks are loosened, the civilian patrol responsible is to be called to reckoning and eventually shot. If an attack takes place near a village, punish the village! Take hostages! Arrest anybody not native to the place! Practise the widest possible and most ruthless deployment of the civil population to do repairs.' For the British role in the destruction of the Gorgopotamos bridge, see Clogg, Richard, 'The Special Operations Executive in Greece' in Iatrides, J.O., Greece in the 1940s, p. 116; Woodhouse, C.M., The Struggle for Greece, 1941–49 (London, 1976), p. 26
81 Pirelli, Alberto, Taccuini, p. 352, Giovanni Pirelli to Alberto Pirelli, 12 October 1942
82 Deakin, F.W., The Brutal Friendship. Mussolini, Hitler and the Fall of Italian Fascism (London, 1962 and Penguin edn 1966), p. 82
83 Roskill, S.W., The Strategy of Sea Power. Its Development and Application (London, 1962) p. 171
84 Rocca, Giovanni, Fucilate gli ammiragli. La tragedia della Marina italiana durante la seconda guerra mondiale (Milan, 1987)
85 Bennett, Ralph, Ultra and Mediterranean Strategy, 1941–1945 (London, 1989) p. 148
86 Die Endlösung der Judenfrage in Frankreich. Deutsche Dokumente 1941–44, ed. Klarsfeld, Serge (Paris, 1977); totals are listed on the bottom of the documents; see also pp. 11–12

87 BA MA RW 40/ 79 Kdr Gen u Befh Serbien, Führerbefehl Nr. 383/42, 9 March 1942

88 BA MA RW 4v/752 OKW/WfüStab 'Besondere Anordnung Nr 1 für das neubesetzte franz. Gebiet', 16 November 1942

89 BDC SS HO 2471 Oberg to Himmler, 16 November 1942

90 SME US SP 59/13 Comando 4a Armata, S.M. Ufficio Informazioni, 1 December 1942

91 SME US DS Comando Supremo S.I.M. Allegato 6, No. 5357/CS 'Promemoria', 2 January 1943

92 MEA ASD AAPP Francia B. 80(1943) f.8 Sionismo, Ciano to Italian ambassador at Vichy, 5 December 1942; copies to *comando supremo*

93 ibid. Barranco to Calisse, 6 January 1943

94 BDC SSO 'Knochen, Helmut': 'Beurteilungsnotizen über die Führer beim Stab des HSS PoF, 2 June, 1943'; Oberg's file contains a very different assessment: 'not entirely open character, tries to push himself into the foreground. Will: conscious of goals, egotistical in his essence, must always have a firm leadership. Does not always find the right tone in dealing with his subordinates' (BDC SSO 'Oberg')

95 Klarsfeld, Serge, *Die Endlösung*, p. 100, Knochen to Müller, 13 January 1943

96 ME ASD AAGG 'Francia' B. 80(1943) f.8 Sionismo, Zoppi to ministry of foreign affairs, 14 January 1943

97 SME US DS B. 1099 Comando 4a Armata 'Dislocazione', 13 November 1942

98 BA MA RH 31 VII/7b 'Deutscher General beim OB West in Vichy' Bericht über die Reise 22–30 March 1943

99 Neubronn, Alexander von, 'Ein Soldat blickt zurück', p. 102

100 ibid, p. 102

101 BA MA RH 31/VII/5 'Deutscher General beim OB West in Vichy', 'Besprechung des Herren Inspekteurs in Bourges', 18 November 1942

102 SME US DS B. 1442 Comando Supremo, 12 November 1942. Cavallero reported a conversation with Vacca Maggiolini to the Duce. Vacca Maggiolini used the expression 'long face'.

103 BAMA RW 4/v. 752 'OKW WfüSt' 'Besprechung über Fragen des neubesetzten franz. Gebietes', 23 December 1942, p. 13. The meeting was a large one, twenty-two participants, representing the High Command, foreign office, armistice commission, *Wehrmacht* propaganda office, counter-intelligence, etc. Warlimont took the chair. Interestingly there was no SS representation.

104 BA MA RH 31 VII/12 'Deutscher General des OB West in Vichy', Deutscher Verbindugsoffizier bei der italienischen Kontroll Delegation in Toulon, 2 May 1943

105 MEA ASD AAPP Francia B. 68(1943) Francia, f. 3, consul general, Marseilles, to chief of police, 5 February 1943

106 BA MA RH 31 VII/8 'Deutscher General des OB West in Vichy', 'Lagebericht Stand: Anfang Februar 1943' Oberst von Rost, p. 2

107 BA MA RH 31 VII/24 'Deutscher General des OB West in Vichy', 5 June 1943.

108 SME US B.1127 Comando 4a Armata, Allegato 23, Comando Supremo to General the duke of Avarna, 16 January 1943

109 *The Times*, London, 21 January 1943. 'From our special correspondent, French frontier, January 20'

110 Hinsley, F.H. with E.E. Thomas, C.F.G. Ransom, R.C. Knight, *British*

Intelligence in the Second World War, London: Her Majesty's Stationery Office, 1979–88) vol. III, pt 1, p. 147. Churchill had been given a summary of the conflict between the Germans and Italians. He also knew from Enigma that the Germans were decrypting *cetnik* signals which revealed Mihailović's intention to turn Italian arms against the Germans. He had, in addition, the texts of Löhr's letters of 5 and 10 March 1943, in which Löhr stated that he would regard the *cetniks* as enemies in compliance with orders from Berlin.

111 SME US B. 1443 Comando Supremo, 26 January 1943
112 Klarsfeld, Serge, *Die Endlösung*, p. 267, Aschenbach to Röthke, 11 February 1943
113 ME ASD AAPP Francia B. 68(1943) f. 3, consul general, Marseilles, to foreign ministry, 6 February 1943
114 SME US DS B. 1100 Comando I Corpo d'Armata, 14 February 1943
115 Interview with Mr Albert Sharon, J. Rochlitz, *The Righteous Enemy*.
116 SME US DS B. 110 Comando I Corpo d'Armata, Allegato 39, 14 February 1943
117 SME US SP 59/13 and also SME US DS B. 1127, Comando 4a Armata, Allegato 56, 22 February 1943
118 ME ASD AAPP Francia B. 68(1943) C.I.A.F., 28 February 1943
119 ibid. B. 80 (1943) f. 8 Sionismo, Cremese to foreign ministry, 1 March 1943
120 ibid. same date. See also SME US SP 59/13, telegram Comando Supremo to Comando 4a Armata, 1 March 1943 in which the intention to take steps in Vichy is announced. The telegram closes with the words: 'I ask you in the meantime to postpone arrest of prefects'.
121 SME US SP 59/13 'Stralcio dal DS del CS.' B. 1443, Allegato 14
122 BA MA RH 31 VII/7a 'Deutscher General beim OB West' von Neubronn to OB West, 4 March 1943
123 Klarsfeld, Serge, *Die Endlösung*, pp. 173–74, Knochen to Müller, 12 February 1943
124 ADAP, Series E, vol. V, no. 155, pp. 283–84. Gesandter I. Klasse Bergmann to special train 'Westfalen', 24 February 1943
125 ibid. no. 158, pp. 286 ff, 'Aufzeichnung des Gesandten I. Klasse Schmidt', Rome, 27 February 1943. The cited passage can be found on pp. 296–97
126 Pietromarchi, Luca, 'Estratti del Diario', 1 March 1943 in J. Rochlitz, *The Righteous Enemy*, p. 9
127 Bastianini, Giuseppe, *Uomini, cose, fatti*, p. 86
128 Guerri, G.B., *Galazeo Ciano. Una Vita, 1903–1944* (Milan, 1979), p. 536
129 Bottai, Giuseppe, *Diario*, p. 363, 1 March 1943
130 Pietromarchi, Luca, 'Estratti del Diario', p. 4, 11 March 1943
131 *Actes et Documents du Saint Siège*, vol. 9, no. 82, p. 170, bishop of Berlin von Preysing to Pope Pius XII, Berlin, 6 March 1943
132 ibid, no. 85, pp. 175–77, The chargé d'affaires in Pressburg, Monsignor Burzio to Cardinal Maglione, 7 March 1943
133 ibid. no. 86, pp. 178–79, notes of the secretariat of state, 8 March 1943
134 Chadwick, W.O., *Britain and the Vatican during the Second World War* (Cambridge, 1986), p. 220
135 ibid. p. 216
136 *The Goebbels Diaries*, p. 261–62, 2 March 1943
137 Hassell, Ulrich von, *Vom andern Deutschland*, p. 197, 20 August 1941

138 ADAP, Series E, vol. V, no. 181, pp. 347–48, von Mackensen to foreign office, 5 March 1943

139 ibid., no. 189, pp. 368 ff., the Reich foreign minister to embassy, Rome, 9 March 1943

140 *The Goebbels Diaries*, p. 282, 9 March 1943

141 Poliakov, L. and Sabille, J., *Jews under the Italian Occupation* (Paris, 1955), pp. 147–48

142 MEA ASD Gab AP – 42 AG Croazia 35 'Appunto', 9 March 1943 and ibid. AG. IV (copy) 'Appunto', 9 March 1943

143 Quoted in Plehwe, Friedrich-Karl von, *Als die Achse*, p. 20

144 *Actes et Documents du Saint-Siège*, vol. 9, p. 183, 'Notes du Cardinal Maglione', 13 March 1943

145 ibid. no. 104, p. 195, Cardinal Maglione to Father Tacchi Venturi, 17 March 1943

146 ibid. no. 105, p. 196, 'Notes de Monsignor Montini', 18 March 1943

147 Even Captain Merci knew that the fate of the Jews was being decided in Rome. 'In the meantime negotiations are under way between Rome and Berlin and the agreement is still pending' (See 'The Salonika Diary', p. 304, 21 March 1943)

148 ADAP, Series E, vol. 15, no. 215, pp. 413–14, The ambassador in Rome to foreign office, telegram, 18 March 1943, 9 a.m.

149 Rintelen, Enno von, *Mussolini als Bundesgenosse*, p. 138

150 Pirelli, Alberto, *Taccuini*, p. 402

151 Caviglia, Enrico, *Diario*, p. 395

152 Bastianini, Giuseppe, *Uomini, cose, fatti*, p. 88

153 Senise, Carmen, *Quando ero capo della polizia* (Rome, 1946), p. 62. There is a vivid portrait of the petty bourgeois Senise in his black suit going home each night to family dinner in Dollmann, Eugen, *Roma Nazista*, pp. 76 ff.

154 Pietromarchi, Luca, 'Estratti del Diario', 31 March 1943 in J. Rochlitz, *The Righteous Enemy*, p. 10

155 Bastianini, Giuseppe, *Uomini, cose, fatti*, pp. 88–89

156 *Actes et Documents du Saint Siège Relatifs à la seconde guerre mondiale*, Le Saint Siège et les victimes de la guerre Janvier–Décembre 1943 (Liberia Editrice Vaticana, 1875), vol. 9, no. 105, p. 196, note 3, 19 March 1943. Pietromarchi records in his diary that when the nuncio heard that the Italians had not yielded to German pressure, he told Bastianini that the Holy Father would bless the Italian government and added that the Russians had allowed Italian prisoners of war to write home because the Italian government had treated Jews humanely. (See Pietromarchi, Luca, 'Estratti del Diario', 31 March 1943 in J. Rochlitz, *The Righteous Enemy*, p. 10)

157 MEA ASD *Relazione sull'opera svolta*, p. 30

158 Pietromarchi, Luca, 'Estratti del Diario', 31 March 1943 in J. Rochlitz, *The Righteous Enemy*, p. 10

159 Reprinted in J. Rochlitz, ibid, p. 49

160 Bundesarchiv Koblenz NS 19 Aktenbestand 3766, ambassador in Rome to foreign office, 20 March 1943 (This document was found by *Kapitän* Dr Gerhard Schreiber of the Militärgeschichtliches Forschungsamt, Freiburg im Breisgau, in the course of his own research and he kindly let me have a copy. It is oddly not included in the official ADAP Series E, volume 5)

161 Dollmann, Eugen, *Roma Nazista* (Milan, 1949), p. 361

162 Zuccotti, Susan, *The Italians and the Holocaust. Persecution, Rescue and Survival* (New York and London, 1987), p. 86

163 ACS MI DG Demorazza B. 9, f. 38. Both *Il Giornale d'Italia* and *Il Messagero* headlined the story with pictures of the 132 Jews at work on the banks of the river by Castel Sant'Angelo. The *Messagero* offered the particularly nasty comment in a front-page opinion column that 'Jews had always despised manual labour and considered it a low occupation destined for inferior classes and foreigners'. The history of the *'precettazione civile al lavoro'* (the civil conscription for labour) of 1942 will make an interesting and necessary footnote to the story of Italian Jews. Susan Zuccotti uses Emanuele Artom's delightful diary to give some account of what it felt like to be on the receiving end in Turin (Zuccotti, Susan, *The Italians*, pp. 61–64) but until De Felice's final volume appears we are unlikely to know who authorized this move and why. The files of 'Demorazza' make interesting reading. It was clear that the overwhelming majority of prefects thought the measure absurd, counter-productive or both. 78 replied that 'the necessity to direct Jews to forced labour had not manifested itself'. As far as I can tell only in Turin and Rome were serious efforts made to conscript and employ substantial numbers of Jews at hard labour. There is an obsequious telegram in the files from Dr Dante Almansi, Cavaliere of the Grand Cross and former vice-chief of police, in which he, as the head of the Union of Jewish Communities, thanks the Duce for conscripting Jews and adds that the 'Jews are happy to have been called to give their labour while all the forces of the nation are engaged for the victory. I express to you, Duce, our profound gratitude for the announced civil conscription for labour.' Comment is superfluous.

164 Lospinoso in J. Rochlitz, *The Righteous Enemy*, p. 51. Lospinoso denied very strongly suggestions made during the Eichmann trial that Mussolini had, in fact, confided in him: 'It is grotesque to imagine that Mussolini would lower himself from his high seat to confide in a dependant and to hold so unworthy a conversation as if two equals were plotting together to play a trick on a third.' (ibid. p. 55)

165 Zuccotti, Susan, *The Italians*, p. 86

166 Klarsfeld, Serge, *Die Endlösung*, no 122, p. 199, Moritz to commander of the security police, 26 May 1943

167 NA T 821 R. 405 Comando 2 Armata, Ufficio Affari Civili, 'Sistemazione ebrei', 18 February 1943

168 ibid. the elders of Kraljevice to Excellency Roatta, 4 February 1943.

169 ibid. Senise to prefects, 18 May 1943

170 ibid. Petition, 13 April 1943, agreed by General Primieri, 28 April 1943

171 SME US DS B. 446, Comando XII Btg CCRR, 23 October 1942

172 NA T -821 R.405 Comando XI Corpo d'Armata, 'Relazione Mensile', 18 February 1943

173 Potočnik, Franc, *Il Campo di sterminio fascista. L'isola di Rab* (Turin, 1977) p. 41, circular no. 36, Comando 2a Armata, 1 March 1942

174 SME US DS B. 446 '23 Btg CCRR Mobilitato' 23 February 1942

175 Potočnik, Franc, *Il Campo*, p. 95, Comando del 14 Btg RRCC, 17 January 1943

176 ibid., p. 23

177 ibid. p. 119

178 NA T – 821 R. 407, It 5283L Comando 2a Armata, 'Situazione internati civili alla Data del 1 luglio 1943'

179 ibid. Ufficio Affari Civili 'Trattamento degli ebrei nel campo di Arbe', 10 July 1943
180 *Actes et Documents du Saint Siège*, vol. 9, no. 122, p. 213, Notes de la Secrétairerie d'Etat, 30 March, 1943. Cardinal Maglione asked for further information to justify the assertion, and Monsignor Montini replied on 1 April that it had come from an army chaplain, Father Ottorino Marcolini, returned from the Russian front, 'who heard such a rumour from a source believed to be credible but not otherwise documented'. See also Note 155 above for Bastianini's version of the story.

EVENTS: THE LAST ACT

1 *The Goebbels Diaries 1941–43*, ed. Lous P. Lochner (Garden City, NY, 1948), p. 271, 3 March 1943
2 Deakin, F.W., *The Brutal Friendship. Mussolini, Hitler and the Fall of Italian Fascism* (London, 1962 and Penguin edn 1966) p. 274
3 Bastianini, Giuseppe, *Uomini, cose, fatti* (Milan, 1959) p. 92
4 ibid., p. 96
5 Dollmann, Eugen, *Roma Nazista* (Milan, 1949) p. 161
6 Bastianini, Giuseppe, *Uomini, cose, fatti*, p. 99
7 Dollmann, Eugen, *Roma Nazista*, p. 164
8 Senise, Carmen, *Quando ero capo della polizia* (Rome, 1946), pp. 110 and 113
9 *The Goebbels Diaries*, p. 352, 7 May 1943
10 ACS SPD CR 1922-45 B. 73, and Deakin, F.W., *The Brutal Friendship*, pp. 320–21. Scorza belonged to the generation of Bastianini, Farinacci, Suardo and Bottai. A poor Calabrian he had risen via the brutality of the squads to become the boss of the province of Lucca. There he had been involved in the war of all against all typical of provincial fascism and had ended on the wrong side. Like many early fascists he had been a journalist as well. His nomination marked a return to the older generation and a further sign of the bankruptcy of the movement.
11 Deakin, F.W., *The Brutal Friendship*, p. 264
12 ADAP, Series E, vol. V, no. 336, p. 676, von Mackensen to foreign office, 22 April 1943
13 BA MA RW 40/131 WB Südost (Okdo H Gr E) 1C/AO 'Politische Lage', signed Speidel, 19 April 1943, pp. 6–7
14 BA MA RH 19 VII/ 23b OB Südost/H Gr E, Der Bevollmächtigte des Reiches für Griechenland, Athen, 3 Mai 1943
15 ACS SPD CR 'Bollettini e Informazioni' (bb 148–341) Com. Gen dei RRCC B. 174, 1942–43 'Promemoria per il Duce: Relazione sullo spirito delle truppe', 13 May 1943, pp. 1–2
16 BA MA RH 31 III/12 'bev. deutscher General in Agram' 'persönliches' Glaise to Chef OKW, 6 May 1943
17 ibid., Glaise to Löhr, 26 May 1943
18 Deakin, F.W., *The Brutal Friendship*, (Penguin edn) p. 368
19 ibid., pp. 368–69
20 BA MA RH 31 VI/ 3 Der deutsche General beim Hauptquartier der ital. Wehrmacht, Hauptmann Beck, 'Gedanken zum Einsatz Sizilien', 25 May 1943
21 Plehwe, Friedrich-Karl von, *Als die Achse zerbrach. Das Ende des deutsch–italienischen Bundnisses im zweiten Weltkrieg* (Wiesbaden and Munich, 1980), pp. 62–64
22 Bottai, Giuseppe, *Diario 1935–1944*, a cura di Giordano Bruno guerri (Milan, 1982), pp. 400–01, 19 July 1943

23 Rintelen, Enno von, *Mussolini als Bundesgenosse Erinnerungen des deutschen Militätaches in Rom 1936–1943* (Tübingen and Stuttgart, 1951), pp. 204 ff.; Alfieri, Dino, *Dictators Face to Face*, trs. David Moore (London and New York, 1954) p. 234, 237–38; ADAP series, no. 146, p. 246, Mackensen to foreign office, 13 July 1943; ibid. no. 155, pp. 260–61, Dollmann, Eugen, 'Aufzeichnung für Herrn Botschafter H.G. von Mackensen', 18 July 1943

24 Alfieri, Dino, *Dictators*, p. 234

25 Rintelen, Enno von, *Mussolini*, p. 212

26 Ortona, Egidio, 'Il 1943 da Palazzo Chigi. Note di Diario', *Storia Contemporanea*, anno XIV, no. 6 (December 1983) p. 1126

27 Alfieri, Dino, *Dictators*, p. 238

28 Ortona, Egidio, 'Il 1943', pp. 1126–27

29 Mussolini, Benito, *Memoirs 1942–43*, trs. Frances Lobb (London, 1949) pp. 50–51

30 Ortona, Egidio. 'Il 1943', p. 1127

31 Alfieri, Dino, *Dictators*, p. 246

32 Caviglia, Enrico, *Diario 1925–1945* (Rome, 1952), p. 399, 18 February 1943

33 BAMA RH 31 X/1 Deutscher Generalstab beim 11. ital. AOK, Kriegstagebuch Nr 1, 19 July 1943. The war diary was kept by *Oberleutnant* Waldheim from 19.7.1943 to 21.8.1943

34 BA MA RH 19/9 Ob Südost/Okdo HGrE KTB Führungsabteilung (Arsakli) 'Befehlsregelung im Südostraum' 22 July 1943

35 Bottai, Giuseppe, *Diario*, p. 401, 20 July 1943

36 Grandi, Dino 'Pagine di diario del 1943'. *Storia Contemporanea*, anno XIV, no. 6 (December 1983), p. 1039, 25 March 1943

37 ibid. p. 1062, 21 July 1943

38 ibid. p. 1063, 22 July 1943

39 Ortona, Egidio, 'Il 1943', p. 1129, 21 July 1943

40 ADAP, Series E, vol. 6, p. 166, p. 287, von Mackensen to Ribbentrop, telegram, 22 July 1943

41 Bottai, Giuseppe, *Diario*, p. 404, 23 July 1943

42 Grandi, Dino, 'Pagine', p. 1064, 23 July 1943

43 Alfieri, Dino, *Dictators*, p. 280

44 Grandi, Dino, 'Pagine', p. 1065, 24 July 1943

45 Bottai, Giuseppe, *Diario*, p. 405, 24 July 1943

46 ibid., pp. 405–06, 24 July 1943

47 Deakin, F.W., *The Brutal Friendship*, (Penguin, edn) p. 486

48 Mack Smith, Denis, *Mussolini* (London, 1981), p. 295

49 Alfieri, Dino, *Dictators*, pp. 282–83

50 ibid., p. 286

51 Deakin, F.W., *The Brutal Friendship*, (Penguin edn) p. 492

52 ibid., p. 498

53 Grandi, Dino, 'Pagine', p. 1067, 25 July 1943

54 Mack Smith, Denis, *Mussolini*, p. 298

55 Ortona, Egidio, 'Il 1943', p. 1132, 25 July 1943

56 Grandi, Dino, 'Pagine', p. 1067, 25 July 1943

57 ibid., p. 1069, 26 July 1943

58 Fest, Joachim C., *Hitler*, trs. Richard and Clara Winston (London, 1974) p. 692

59 BA MA RH 19 VII/9 OB Südost/ Okdo HGrE KTB Führungsabteilung, 25 July 1943, 11.15 p.m.

60 ibid, 26 July 1943, 3.45 a.m.

61 BA MA RH 31 X/1 Deutscher Generalstab beim 11, ital AOK, KTB, 26 July 1943 and 27 July 1943
62 BA MA RH 19 VII/1 OB Südost/HGrE *Chefbesprechung*, 26 July 1943, 9 a.m.
63 Monelli, Paolo, *Roma 1943* (Rome, 1946) p. 220
64 Ortona, Egidio, 'Il 1943', p. 1142, 14 August 1943
65 BA MA RH 31 X/1 Deutscher Generalstab beim 11. ital. AOK KTB, 1 August 1943
66 BA MA RH 24 – 15/5 Gen Kdo XV(Geb)AK Chefsachen, FS 3 August 1943
67 Monelli, Paolo, *Roma 1943*, p. 156
68 ADAP, Series E, vol. VI, no. 195, p. 339, embassy in Rome to foreign office, 29 July 1943
69 Monelli, Paolo, *Roma 1943*, p. 157
70 ibid., p. 158
71 Mayda, Giuseppe, *Gli ebrei sotto Salò. La persecuzione antisemita 1943–45* (Milan, 1978) p. 51
72 ibid., p. 52
73 Ortona, Egidio, 'Il 1943', p. 1135, 31 July 1943
74 Guariglia, Raffaele, *Ricordi 1922–1946*, (Naples, 1950) pp. 587 ff.;Monelli, Paolo, *Roma 1943*, pp. 220 ff.; Salvatorelli, L. and Mira, G. *Storia d'Italia nel periodo fascista*, 2 vols, Gli Oscar (Milan, 1972) vol. 2, p. 539
75 Guariglia, Raffaele, *Ricordi*, p. 617
76 Ortona, Egidio, 'Il 1943', p. 1137, 5 August 1943
77 'Excerpts from the Salonika Diary of Captain Merci (February–August, 1943)', compiled by Joseph Rochlitz with introduction by Menachem Shelach. *Yad Vashem Studies* vol. XVIII (Jerusalem, 1987) p. 323, 30 July 1943
78 MEA ASD AAPP Francia B. 80 (1943) f.8 Sionismo, consul general in Nice Spechel to foreign ministry, 31 July 1943.
79 ibid. Senise, ministry of the interior, to foreign ministry, A.G. IV, 4 August 1943
80 MEA ASD Gab. A.P. – 42, AG Croazia 35 B. 138 (1943) f. 8 'Deportazione degli ebrei', legation, Stockholm to ministry of foreign affairs, 3 August 1943
81 Klarsfeld, Serge, *Die Endlösung der Judenfrage in Frankreich. Deutsche Dolumente* (Paris, 1977), no. 128, p. 209, Hagen to Higher SS and Police Leader, 11 August 1943
82 ibid., no. 130 p. 214, Hagen to Higher SS and Police Leader, 18 August 1943
83 MEA ASD AAPP Francia B. 80 (1943)f. 8. Sionismo, consul general in Nice to foreign ministry, 7 August 1943; Vidau to royal delegate for repatriation, 10 August 1943 in which Vidau gives the 'nulla osta' to repatriation without 'preventive authorization' of the ministry of the interior. See also Ghigi to ministry, 13 August 1943 in Carpi, Daniel, 'Nuovi Documenti', no. 26, p. 200
84 MEA ASD Gab. A.P. – 42, AG Croazia 35 B. 138 (1943) Rosso to Ufficio Collegamento of the Comando Supremo, 19 August 1943. The first paragraph was published in his 1944 essay by Roberto Ducci under the pseudonym 'Verax' in *Politica estera*, vol. 1 no. 9 (1944) p. 28
85 MEA ASD AAPP Francia B.80(1943) f. 8 Sionismo, Gen di Brigata Bartiromo to foreign ministry, 25 August 1943
86 ibid., 'Promemoria su accordi presi in riunione mattino 28 agosto fra rappresentanti Ministero Esteri, Ministero Interni (presente il Capo

Polizia) e Stato Maggiore', and Rosso to *comando supremo*, 6 September 1943

87 Zuccotti, Susan, *The Italians and the Holocaust. Persecution, Rescue and Survival* (New York and London, 1987) pp. 88–89

88 Salvatorelli. L. and Mira, G., *Storia d'Italia*, vol. 2, p. 539–40; Monelli, Paolo, *Roma 1943*, pp. 210–11

89 ibid., p. 222

90 Salvatorelli, L. and Mira, G., *Storia d'Italia*, vol. 2, p. 541 and Monelli, Paolo, *Roma 1943*, pp. 214–15

91 Guariglia, Raffaele, *Ricordi*, p. 652

92 ibid., p. 704

93 Salvatorelli, L. and Mira, G., *Storia d'Italia*, vol. 2, pp. 541–42

94 Pirelli, Alberto, *Taccuini 1922–1943* (Bologna, 1984) p. 476

95 Monelli, Paolo, *Roma 1943*, p. 224

96 SME US DS B. 1222 Comando 2 Armata, 'Relazioni degli avvenimenti successivi all'armistizio nella penisola balcanica' by Gen A. Mariotti, 2 December 1943

97 SME US DS B. 1253, Allegato Nr. 7 Comando Div. fant. 'Lupi di Toscana' 8 September 1943.

98 ibid., 10 September 6.55 p.m. It is agreeable to recall that both officers were released by the Germans, although elsewhere officers who had ordered Italian troops to resist were summarily shot, because the German commander thought the Lupi were 'una bella divisione'.

99 Dragoni, Ugo, *Fiaschi in Jugoslavia. Ricordo polemico della campagna di guerra, 1941–32* (Alessandria, 1983) p. 190

100 BA MA RH 19 VII/10 OB Südost/HGrE, Kriegstagebuch 1(a), 8 September 1943, 8.05 p.m.

101 ibid. 8 September 1943, 11.35 p.m.

102 TWC NMT CC 10, Vol. XI, 'the hostages case'. (case no. 7, count 3 j) 'on or about 24 September 1943, the Commander of the XXII Mountain Corps (Lanz) [gave orders] to execute the captured Italian General Gandin, and all officers of his staff'.

103 BA MA RH 19 VII/10 OB Südost/HGrE, Kriegstagebuch 1(a), 8 September 1943, 9.55 p.m.

104 BA MA RH 21 – 2/v.590 Pz AOK 2, Kriegstagebuch Nr. 4, 11 September 1943

105 Dragoni, Ugo, *Fiaschi in Yugoslavia*, p. 201

106 Hassell, Ulrich von, *Vom andern Deuschland* (Frankfurt/Main, 1964) p. 187

107 Protokol über den Verhör des Kriegsgefangenen deutschen Generals Alexander Löhr, verfasst am 24. Mai 1945 in der Kanzlei des Lagers Banjica, Belgrad, p. 9 (kindly supplied by Mr Richard Mitten, Vienna).

108 Interview with Ambassador Guelfo Zamboni, Lido dei Pini, 9 April 1988; conversation with Mr Richard Mitten, Cambridge, 18 April 1988

109 Guariglia, Raffaele, *Ricordi*, p. 699

110 Zuccotti, Susan, *The Italians*, p. 89

111 Guariglia, Raffaele, *Ricordi*, pp. 714–18

112 Caracciolo, Nicola, *Gli ebrei e l'Italia durante la guerra 1940–45* (Roma, 1986), p. 122

EXPLANATIONS

1 Guerri, Giordano Bruno, *Galeazzo Ciano. Una vita, 1903–1944* (Milan, 1979) pp. 620–21; Mack Smith, Denis, *Mussolini* (London, 1981) pp. 303–04

2 'Verax' (Roberto Ducci) 'Italiani ed ebrei in Jugoslavia', *Politica estera*, vol. 1, no. 9 (1944)
3 Cited in Michaelis, Meir, *Mussolini and the Jews: German–Italian Relations and the Jewish Question in Italy 1922–1945* (Oxford, 1978) p. 140
4 Arendt, Hannah, *Eichmann in Jerusalem. A Report on the Banality of Evil* (London, 1963) p. 161
5 See note 179 on p. 133
6 SME US DS Comando Supremo B. 1443, 14 January 1943
7 BA MA RW 40/29 'Kdr Gen. u. Befh. Serbien KTB 1a', 20 December 1941
8 Sternberger, Dolf *et al. Aus dem Wörterbuch des Unmenschen*, 2nd edn (Hamburg, 1957)
9 BA MA RH 31/III/12 'bev. dt. General in Agram – persönliches', Glaise to Löhr, 2 March 1943
10 BA MA RH 24 – 22/23 Oberst Jäger to Gen. Kdo XXII(Geb.)A.K. 14 May 1944
11 Bowman, Steven, 'Could the Dodekanesi Jews Have Been Saved?', The Jewish Museum of Greece *Newsletter*, no. 26, winter 1989, p. 2
12 Tucholsky, Kurt, 'Das Menschliche' (1928) in *Panter Tiger & Co* (Hamburg, 1954) pp. 174–75
13 ibid., p. 175
14 Poggi, Gianfranco, *The Development of the Modern State. A Sociological Introduction* (London, 1978) p. 101
15 Nietzsche, Friedrich, *Vom Nutzen und Nachteil der Historie*, Werke in Zwei Bänden, ausg. August Messer (Leipzig, 1930) pp. 35–36
16 Hesse, Kurt, *Der Feldherr Psychologos*, (Berlin, 1922) cited in Wilhelm Deist. 'Die Reichswehr und der Kreig der Zukunft', conference paper at 'Kontinuität und Wandel', Hamburg, 18–19 March 1988, pp. 4–5
17 Heine, Heinrich, *Zur Geschichte der Religion und Philosophie in Deutschland* (1834) in *Heinrich Heines Sämtliche Werke* (Hamburg, 1876) pp. 266–68
18 Cited in Piero Pieri and Giorgio Rochat, *Pietro Badoglio* (Turin, 1974) p. 733
19 SME US DS B. 1443 Comando Supremo 20 January 1943, 9.45 a.m.
20 Goethe, J.G. von, *Die Wahlverwandschaften* (Insel Taschenausgabe) (Frankfurt/Main, 1978) p. 166
21 Tasca, A., *Nascita e avvento del fascismo*, 2 vols. 5th edn (Bari, 1974) p. 588
22 Hibbert, Christopher, *Benito Mussolini* (London, 1962, rev. 1975) p. 25
23 ibid., p. 47
24 Mack Smith, Denis, *Mussolini* (London, 1981) p. 4
25 Spinosa, Antonio, *Starace* (Milan, 1981) p. 40
26 Mack Smith, Denis, *Mussolini*, p. 20
27 *The Goebbels Diaries 1942–1943*, ed. Louis P. Lochner (New York, 1948), 25 April 1942, p. 185
28 Monelli, Paolo, *Roma 1943* (Rome, 1946) pp. 34–35
29 Picker, Henry, *Hitlers Tischgespräche im Führerhauptquartier 1941–42*, 3rd edn (Stuttgart, 1976) pp. 57–59
30 Caviglia, Enrico, *Diario 1925–1945* (Rome, 1952) p. 336
31 ibid., p. 350
32 Valeri, Nino, *Da Giolitti a Mussolini. Momenti della crisi del liberalismo* (Florence, 1956) p. 21
33 Hibbert, Christopher, *Mussolini*, p. 37
34 Serpieri, Arrigo, *La guerra e le classe rurali italiane* (Bari, 1930) pp. 41–42 and p. 51

35 Salvatorelli, L. and Mira, G., *Storia d'Italia nel periodo fascista*, 2 vols. 4th edn (Milan, 1972) vol. 1, p. 56
36 Tasca, Angelo, *Nascita*, p. 230
37 ibid., p. 551
38 Spinosa, A., *Starace* (Milan, 1981) p. 63
39 Mack Smith, Denis, *Mussolini*, p. 4
40 PS report, 4 January 1942, ACS, SPD CR 1922–45 B. 93 f w/r Sf. 2 'Soddu Ubaldo'
41 PS report, 10 January 1942, ACS SPD CR 12922–45 B.67 f.390/R 'Cavallero, Ugo'
42 PS report, ACS SPD CR B. 92 f W/R Sf. 2 20 January 1942
43 Deakin, F.W., *The Brutal Friendship: Mussolini, Hitler and the Fall of Italian Fascism* (London, 1962 and Penguin edn 1966) p. 465
44 Bottai, Giuseppe, *Diario 1935–1944* a cura di Giordano Bruno Guerri (Milan, 1982) p. 10
45 Mack Smith, Denis, *Mussolini*, p. 127
46 Monelli, Paolo, *Roma 1943* (Rome, 1946) p. 32
47 Quoted in Spinosa, A., *Starace*, p. 199
48 Bottai, Giuseppe, *Diario*, 2 December 1942, p. 340
49 Ciocca, Pierluigi, 'L'Italia nell'economia mondiale', in *L'Economia italiana nel periodo fascista*, Quaderni Storici, 29–30 (May–December 1975) table 2, p. 363
50 Montovani, Enrico, 'Dall'economia di guerra alla ricostruzione' in ibid., p. 654
51 Toniolo, Gianni, *L'Economia dell'Italia Fascista* (Rome and Bari, 1980) table 1.2, p. 8
52 ibid, table 1.5, p. 15
53 Knox, Macgregor, *Mussolini Unleashed 1939–1941. Politics and Strategy in Fascist Italy's Last War* (Cambridge, 1982) p. 70
54 Geloso to Ambrosio, 19 October 1942, SME US DS 'Comando Superiore Forze Armate Grecia (11ª Armata)' B. 1054 Allegato 6
55 'Oggetto: Assunione di Incarico [Capo di SME]' Vittorio Ambrosio. SME US DS ibid., B. 635, Allegato 5
56 Bottai, Giuseppe, *Diario*, p. 526
57 Sylos Labini, Paolo, *Saggio sulle classi sociali*, (6th edn Bari, 1976) p. 157
58 Hildebrand, George, H., *Growth and Structure in the Economy of Modern Italy* (Cambridge, Mass., 1965) p. 115
59 ibid., p. 117
60 Pirandello, Luigi, *I vecchi e i giovani* (1st edn 1909; Verona, Gli Oscar, 1973) p. 267
61 SME US DS Comando Supremo B. 1442. There may be sceptical readers who refuse to believe this little episode. Here is the complete text of the diary:

Ore 9.45 riceve il General von Horstig
Offerta del nuovo carro 'Pantera' tedesco
Informa che noi abbiamo il P 40 ch'è in programma di costruzione. Aggiunge che si dichiara per l'unità di armamento e, in quanto all M 15 è previsto di diminuire la sua produzione man mano subentra il P40

Ore 10.45 riceve l'Ecc. Ago. Argomenti:
– Offerta del carro Pantera da parte dei Tedeschi

– sua richiesta di avere l'attrezzatura per costruirlo e guadagnare tempo

– Ecc. Ago informa che in realtà il P40 non esiste ancora e che sono da esaminare ancora tutti i problemi inerenti alla trasformazione del motore a benzina e dell'adattamento del motore T4 al carro.

62 Plehwe, Friedrich-Karl von, *Als Die Achse zerbrach. Das Ende des deutsch-italienischen Bündnisses im zweiten Weltkrieg* (Wiesbaden and Munich, 1980) p. 40
63 Bottai, Giuseppe, *Diario*, 2 December 1942, p. 340
64 Hitler, Adolf, *Mein Kampf*, trs. Ralph Mannheim (New York, 1943) p. 19
65 Fest, Joachim C., *Hitler*, trs. Richard and Clara Winston (London, 1974) p. 23
66 Rozenblitt, Marsha L., *The Jews of Vienna 1867–1914. Assimilation and Identity* (Albany, NY, 1983) p. 17
67 Rabinbach, Anson G., 'The Migration of Galician Jews to Vienna 1857–1880', *Austrian History Yearbook* 11 (1975) p. 48. In some of the eastern cities of the empire such as Cracow, Lemberg and Czernowitz, in 1910 Jews made up 21.3, 27.8 and 32.8 per cent of the population and in the little market town of Brody over two-thirds. (cf. Rabinbach, table III, p. 46)
68 Cohen, Gary B., 'Jews in German Liberal Politics: Prague, 1860–1914', *Jewish History*, vol. 1, no. 1 (spring, 1986) p. 58
69 Hitler, Adolf, *Mein Kampf*, pp. 56 ff.
70 Picker, Dr Henry, *Hitlers Tischgespräche*, pp. 24–25
71 ibid., p. 23
72 Jäckel, Eberhard, *Hitlers Herrschaft* (Stuttgart, 1986) pp. 131–32
73 *The Goebbels Diaries 1942–43*, 13 May 1943, p. 377
74 Haffner, Sebastian, *Anmerkungen zu Hitler* (Munich, 1978) p. 9
75 Quoted in F.H. Hinsley, *Hitler's Strategy* (Cambridge, 1951, p. 230)
76 Jäckel, Eberhard, *Hitlers Herrschaft* p. 166, note 25
77 Hinsley, F.H., *Hitler's Strategy*, pp. 120–21
78 Below, Nicolaus von, *Als Hitlers Adjutant 1937–45* (Mainz, 1980), p. 417
79 Ciano, Count Galeazzo, *Diaries 1937–39* (London, 1952) 21 November 1937, p. 35
80 ibid., 21 September 1940, p. 292
81 ibid., 18 December 1942, p. 536
82 Bottai, Giuseppe, *Diario*, 9 December 1942, p. 344
83 Col. Umberto Fabbri to Comando Superiore 2ª Armata, 29 January 1942, SME US DS B.1361, 'Notiziario Vario 2ª Armata' in which Fabbri, the Italian attaché wih *Kampfgruppe* Bader, reports a dinner conversation with the German general Paul Bader, its commander.
84 von Neubronn, *Generalleutnant* a.D. Alexander Freiherr, *Ein Soldat Blickt Zurück. Erinnerungen aus den Jahren 1939–1945* (typescript, dated 1949) in BAMA RH 31/vii/30, pp. 65–66
85 Colville, John, *The Fringes of Power. Downing Street Diaries* 2 vols, vol. 2: 1941–April 1955 (London, 1987) pp. 154–55, 6 October 1944
86 Neubronn, Alexander von, *Ein Soldat*, p. 66
87 *Gruppenführer* August Meyszner to *Gruppenführer* Harald Turner, 28 April 1942, BAMA Kdr Gen.u.Befh. in Serbien, RW 40/79
88 Below, Nicolaus von, *Als Adjutant*, p. 291
89 Fleming, Gerald, *Hitler and the Final Solution* (London, 1984) p. 20
90 ibid., p. 22

91 Loewenberg, Peter, 'Nixon, Hitler and Power: An Ego Psychological Study', *Psychoanalytic Inquiry*, vol. 6, no. 1 (1986) p. 45
92 Speer, Albert, *Spandauer Tagebücher* (Frankfurt/Main, 1975) pp. 633–63
93 Picker, Henry, *Hitlers Tischgespräche* pp. 57–59
94 Dollman, Eugen, *Roma Nazista* (Milan, 1949) p. 106
95 Monelli, Paolo, *Roma 1943*, pp. 39–40
96 Hassell, Ulrich von, *Vom andern Deutschland* (Frankfurt/Main, 1964) p. 15
97 BAMA RH 31 III/9 'Audienz beim Führer' 23, 11, 1943
98 Cavallero, Ugo, *Comando Supremo. Diario 1940–1943 del Capo di S.M.G.* (Rocca S. Casciano, 1949) p. 417
99 *The Goebbels Diaries 1942–43*, 20th March, 1942, p. 135
100 Rintelen, Enno von, *Mussolini als Bundesgenosse*, pp. 228–229
101 Caviglia, Enrico, *Diario 1925–1945* (Rome, 1952) p. 395
102 ADAP, Series E., vol. IV, no. 70, p. 117, 'Aufzeichnung des Unterstaatsekretärs Martin Luther', 10 October 1942
103 BDC SSO, 'Meyszner File', Himmler to Meyszner, 9 May 1942
104 Rintelen, Enno von, 'The German-Italian Connection', p. 4
105 Knox, Macgregor, *Mussolini Unleashed 1939–1941. Politics and Strategy in Fascist Italy's Last War*. (Cambridge, 1982) p. 16
106 Compiled from Nikolaus von Preredovich, *Die militärische und soziale Herkunft der Generalität des deutschen Heeres 1 Mai 1944* (Osnabrück, 1978) and Ministero della Guerra, Gabinetto, *Ruolo degli Ufficiali Generali del R. Esercito in s.p.e. e fuori quadro*, 5 October 1937
107 Pirelli, Alberto, *Taccuini*, 30 August 1939, p. 227
108 SME US DS Comando Supremo B. 1443, 16 January 1943
109 Knox, Macgregor, *Mussolini Unleashed*, p. 154
110 Gen. Carlo Geloso 'Oggeto: Addestramento', 25 March 1942, SME US DS B. 736
111 'KTB des deutschen Generals beim ital. AOK 8' 17.9.1942, p. 30 BA MA RH 31 IX – 1
112 ibid., 14 October 1942
113 AO III '*Betr* Verhältnis des Juden- und Arabertums zu den italienischen Behörden in Tripolis' 7.2.1942 BA MA RH 23/112 'Korpsrück Afrika'
114 Vicerè al Capo di Governo, 17 March 1941, in SME US *L'esercito italiano*, p. 247
115 'Elenco degli ufficiali, funzionari ed agenti antifascisti divisi per ministri' (no date but in a sequence from late 1938? early 1939) ACS SPD CR 1922–1945 B. 62, f. 364, sf. 8
116 Rintelen, Enno von, *Mussolini als Bundesgenosse. Erinnerungen des deutschen Militärattachès in Rom 1936–1943* (Tübingen, 1951) p. 66
117 von Plehwe, Friedrich-Karl, *Als die Achse zerbrach*, p. 40
118 Interview with Dr Giacomo Cristiano Garaguso, Rome, 26 March 1988
119 Seton-Watson, Christopher, *Italy from Liberalism to Fascism 1870–1925* (London, 1967) pp. 632–33
120 Lyttleton, Adrian, *The Fascist Seizure of Power. Fascism in Italy 1919–1929* (London, 1973) pp. 280–82 for a vivid account of the intertwining of freemasonry, factional strife and principle in the fascist movement in the mid-1920s.
121 ACS SPD Cart. Ris. B. 37, f. 2, Mussolini to Farinacci, 10 July 1926
122 Mack Smith, Denis, *Mussolini*, p. 159
123 Segre, Dan Vittorio, *Memoirs of a Fortunate Jew. An Italian Story* (London, 1987) pp. 61–62
124 *The Goebbels Diaries*, pp. 356–57

125 'Elenco di ufficiali ebrei' 15 February 1938 and 'Cognomi di razza ebraica di Generali, Colonelli, Ten. Colonelli (compresi nel quadro d'avanzamento)' 25 February 1938, ACS SPD CR 1922–1945 480R B. 145 f. 390 Sf.9; Cf. also 'Censimento personale di razza ebraica' 6 September 1938, which contains a note from Mussolini to Sebastianini, his private secretary 'What does Pariani [then under-secretary of war] intend to do about the Jewish officers?' ibid.

126 ibid.

127 Herzstein, R.E., *Waldheim. The Missing Years* (London, 1988) pp. 113–14. Cf. *Der Bericht der internationalen Historikerkommission* (The Waldheim Report) *Profil*, Vienna, nr 7, 15 February 1988 pp. 8–12 for a detailed account of the functioning of the staff of Army Group E.

128 'Chefbesprechung am 30.11.1942', Bundesarchiv-Militärarchiv (BA MA) RH 20 – 12/158 'Beilagen zum Tätigkeitsbericht November 1942 1a'

129 'Vierteljahres Belehrung des Offz. Korps des Stabes über OKW-Befehle betr. Lebensführung des Offz.-Korps und Bekanntgabe kriegsgerichtlicher Urteile'. BA MA RH 24 – 15/7 Gen Kdo XV(Geb.) AK KTB 26.8.1943–31.12.1943

130 Oberkommando des Heeres, Heerespersonalamt Amt, Berlin, 31 October 1942, BA MA RH 15/ 186

131 BA MA RH 24 – 22/9 'Korpsbefehl Nr. 1 für das Unternehmen "Margarete"', K.H.Qu. 16.3.1944, initialled 'L'

132 Geloso, Carlo, Generale d'Armata, 'Due Anni in Grecia al Commando dell 11ª Armata, 23 aprile 1941–3 maggio 1943', 2 July 1943, Stato Maggiore dell'Esercito, Ufficio Storico (SME US) Cartella No. 1393 bis. The sources of conflict listed by Geloso were the formation of the Greek government, police services, the taking and shooting of hostages, the question of Greek possession of radio sets, forced labour and the Jewish question, pp. 162–77

133 BA MA RH 24 – 22/23 Gruppe Geheime Feldpolizei 621, Bericht betr. Evakuierung der Juden aus Joannina, Unteroffizier Bergmayer, 27.3.1944

134 BA MA RH 19/VII/1 OB Südost/Hr Gr E KTB Der Militärbefehlshaber Griechenland to OB Südost, 8.1.1944

135 ibid. *Chefbesprechung* 9–10 December 1943

136 TWC NMT CC 10, p.831, Neubacher to von Weichs; cf. Waldheim, *Bericht*, p. 40.

137 TWC NMT CC 10, p. 833

138 Streit, Christian, *Keine Kameraden. Die Wehrmacht und die sowjetischen Kriegsgefangenen 1941–1945* (Stuttgart, 1978) p. 57

139 ibid., p. 128

140 Kogon, Eugen, *et al.*, *Nationalsozialistische Massentötungen durch Giftgas. Eine Dokumentation* (Frankfurt, 1983) p. 84 and appendix for a photocopy of the document itself.

141 Bartov, Omer, *The Eastern Front 1941–45, German Troops and the Barbarization of Warfare* (Basingstoke and London, 1985) p. 152

142 Schulte, Theo J., *The German Army and Nazi Policies in Occupied Russia* (Oxford/New York/Munich, 1989) p. 146

143 ibid., p. 230

144 Milano, Attilio, *Storia degli ebrei in Italia* (Turin, 1963) p. 9

145 ibid., p. 336

146 Quoted in Maud Tyler, *The Forgotten Solution: Some Interpretations of Federalism in Piedmont and Lombardy before 1850* (unpublished Ph.D. dissertation, University of Cambridge, 1985) p. 3

147 della Peruta, Franco, 'Quando in Italia c'erano i ghetti', *Storia illustrata*, n. 339 (Milan, February 1986) p. 85

148 ibid.

149 Momigliano, Armando Dante, 'The Many Worlds of Vito Volterra', lecture delivered Brandeis University, 30 April 1984, p. 8 (typescript copy given to me by the author)

150 de Felice, Renzo, *Storia degli ebrei italiani sotto il fascismo* (Turin, 1972) p. 13

151 Momigliano, A.D., 'The Many Worlds', p. 3

152 Levi, Primo, *I sommersi e i salvati* (Turin, 1986) p. 78

153 Segre, Dan Vittorio, *The Memoirs*, pp. 27–29

154 Cited in Renzo De Felice, *Storia*, p. 89

155 ibid., p. 17

156 Hughes, H. Stuart, *Prisoners of Hope. The Silver Age of the Italian Jews 1924–1974* (Cambridge, Mass., 1983) especially pp. 9 ff. where Hughes very sensitively poses the question 'what is left of identity when language and religion are gone?'

157 Morris, Jonathan, *The Political Economy of Shopkeeping in Milan 1885–1905* (unpublished Ph.D. dissertation, University of Cambridge, 1988)

158 *The Ciano Diaries*, 3 December 1937, cited in Meir Michaelis, *Mussolini and the Jews. German–Italian Relations and the Jewish Question in Italy, 1922--1945* (Oxford, 1978) p. 140

159 ibid.

160 'Informazione Diplomatica', no. 14, 14 February 1938, in Meir Michaelis, *Mussolini*, p. 141

161 ibid., p. 158

162 Bottai, Giuseppe, *Diario*, p. 129, 10 August 1938

163 De Bono, E., 'Diario' in Renzo De Felice, *Storia*, p. 240

164 Bottai, Giuseppe, *Diario*, p. 136, 6 October 1938

165 Mayda, Giuseppe, *Ebrei sotto Salò. La persecuzione antisemita 1943–45* (Milan, 1978) p. 17

166 Katzburg, Nathaniel, *Hungary and the Jews 1920–1943* (Ramat-Gan, 1981) pp. 101–04 and Randolph L. Braham, *The Politics of Genocide. The Holocaust in Hungary*, 2 vols (New York, 1981) vol. 1, pp. 122–27

167 The most complete account of the racial laws of 1938 is to be found in Renzo De Felice's *Storia degli Ebrei sotto il fascismo* in which all the most important documents are published in an appendix. Susan Zuccotti in *The Italians and the Holocaust* offers an excellent and readable account in English of the laws and their application in chapter 3, pp. 28–51

168 Guido, Segre, ammiraglio di squadra, 2 November 1938, ACS SPD CR 1922–45 480R B. 144, f. 315

169 Valfredo, Segre, to S.E. Valle, 5 September 1938 with Mussolini's marginalia, ibid.

170 Zuccotti, Susan, *The Italians*, p. 27

171 Boitani, Camillo, interview, Rome, 2 April 1988. See also Paolo Monelli, *Roma 1943*, pp. 23 ff. for an entertaining account of the fraudulence of party membership.

172 Segre, Dan Vittorio, *Memoirs*, p. 79

173 ibid., p. 81

174 De Felice, Renzo, *Storia*, p. 454

175 Eller, Evi, interview, Rome, 4 April 1988

176 Caracciolo, Nicola, *Gli ebrei e l'Italia durante la guerra 1940–45* (Rome, 1986) pp. 42–43

177 Bandler, Paul, interview, Rome, 28 March 1988; see also the fascinating account of the concentration camp in Calabria by Carlo Spartaco Capogreco, *Ferramonti. La vita e gli uomini del più grande campo d'internamento fascista (1940–1945)* (Florence, 1987). Dr Capogreco, who is Calabrian, not Jewish, was intrigued by the ruins of the camp and decided to reconstruct this forgotten chapter of the history of Calabria. It is a fine, humane and moving work.

178 Absalom, Roger, 'Ex prigionieri alleati e assistenza popolare nella zona della linea gotica 1943–44', in *La Linea Gotica 1944. Esercito, popolazioni, partigiani*, ed. G. Rochat, E. Santarelli, P. Sorcinelli, Istituto pesarese per la storia del movimento di liberazione (Milan, 1986) pp. 453–56 and notes pp. 467–68.

179 Craig, Gordon, 'Frederick the Great and Moses Mendelssohn: Thoughts on Jewish Emancipation', lecture, Leo Baeck Society (New York, 28 December 1985) p. 10

180 Holeczek, Heinz, 'Die Judenemanzipation in Preussen' in *Die Juden als Minderheit in der Geschichte*, eds Bernd Martin and Ernst Schulin (Munich, 1981) p. 154

181 Warburg, Max M., *Aus meinen Aufzeichnungen?*, private printing (New York, 1952) p. 122

182 Kant, Immanuel, *Was ist Aufklärung. Aufsätze zur Geschichte und Philosophie* (Göttingen, 1985) p. 61

183 Marx, Karl, 'Zur Judenfrage' (1843) *Marx-Engels Gesamtausgabe* (Frankfurt/Berlin, 1927–32) Erste Abteilung, Bd.1 1.Halbband, p. 601

184 Schopenhauer, Arthur, *Die Welt als Wille und Vorstellung*. Sämtliche Werke (Stuttgart/Frankfurt) vol. 1, pp. 579–80

185 Holeczek, Heinz, 'Die Judenemanzipation', p. 147

186 Zmarzlik, Hans-Gunther, 'Antisemitismus im Deutschen Kaisserreich, 1871–1918' in *Die Juden als Minderheit*, pp. 251–52. See also Thomas Nipperdey, *Deutsche Geschichte*, pp. 248 ff. for statistics on the rapid growth of wealth among German Jews.

187 Mosse, W.E., *Jews in the German Economy. The German-Jewish Economic Elite 1820–1935* (Oxford, 1987) pp. 202–03

188 Childers, Thomas, *The Nazi Voter. The Social Foundations of Fascism in Germany, 1919–1933* (Chapel Hill, N.C. and London, 1983) pp. 142 ff. and pp. 211 ff. and Thomas Childers, 'Interest and Ideology: Anti-System Politics in the Era of Stabilization 1924–1928' in Gerald D. Feldman (ed.) *Die Nachwirkungen der Inflation auf die deutsche Geschichte 1924–1933* (Munich, 1985) pp. 1–20. Childers also points out how much the sudden end of hyperinflation alienated small businessmen and traders. The Weimar republic could, for these people, do no right.

189 Manvel, A.R., and Frankel, H., *The German Cinema* (London, 1971) p. 68

190 Dahrendorf, Ralf, *Gesellschaft und Demokratie in Deutschland* (Munich, 1968) pp. 72ff.

191 Gen.d.K. Ludwig Frhr von Gebsattel to Bavarian ministry of war, 14 January 1907, in Wilhelm Deist, *Militär und Innenpolitik im Weltkrieg 1914–1918*, Quellen zur Geschichte des Parlamentarismus und der politischen Parteien, 2 vols (Düsseldorf, 1970) p. xvi, n. 11

192 *Generalleutnant* Wild von Hohenborn to his wife, Document 283, 13 April 1917 in Wilhelm Deist, *Militär und Innenpolitik*, vol. 2, pp. 712–13. See also Konrad Jarausch, *The Enigmatic Chancellor. Bethmann Hollweg and the Hubris of Imperial Germany* (New Haven and London, 1973) pp. 357 ff. and Gerhard Ritter, *Staatskunst und Kriegshandwerk. Das Problem des*

'*Militarismus*' *in Deutschland*, vol. 3. 'Die Tragödie der Staatskunst Bethmann Hollweg als Kriegskanzler (1914–1917)' (Munich, 1964) pp. 546 ff.

193 Deist, Wilhelm, *Militär und Innenpolitik* I, p. 574

194 ibid, vol. 2, document no. 464, p. 1243

195 Deist, Wilhelm, 'Der militärische Zusammenbruch des Kaiserreichs. Zur Realität der "Dolchstosslegende"', in Ursula Büttner (ed.), *Das Unrechtsregime. Internationale Forschung über den Nationalsozialismus* (Hamburg, 1986) p. 121

196 ibid., pp. 121–22

197 Röhl, J.C.G., *Kaiser Wilhem II. 'Eine Studie über Cäsarenwahnsinn'* Schriften des Historischen Kollegs: Vorträge 19 (Munich, 1989) pp. 16–17

198 U.S. embassy to department of state, 14 October 1941, in *The Holocaust. Selected Documents in Eighteen Volumes* ed. John Mendelsohn (New York, 1982) vol. 8, 'Deportation of the Jews to the East', document no. 7, p. 19

199 Speer, Albert, *Spandauer Tagebücher* (Frankfurt/Main, 1975) pp. 400–01

200 Marrus, Michael R., *The Holocaust in History* (Hanover, NH, 1987) p. 9

201 Cited in Christian Graf von Krockow, *Warnung vor Preussen* (Berlin, 1981) p. 213, n. 5; C.B.A. Behrens, *Society, Government and the Enlightenment. The Experiences of Eighteenth-century France and Prussia* (London, 1985) pp. 182–83

202 Interview with Ambassador Guelfo Zamboni, Lido dei Pini, 9 April 1988

CONCLUSION

1 *The Goebbels Diaries 1939–1941*, ed. Fred Taylor (London, 1982) pp. 18 and 77

2 Bottai, Giuseppe, *Diario 1939–1944*, a cura di Giordano Bruno Guerri, p. 526. Cf. note 56, p. 302

3 Lukacs, György, *Die Zerstörung der Vernunft. Der Weg des Irrationalismus von Schelling zu Hitler* (Berlin, 1955) p. 70

4 Gibbon, Edward, *The Decline and Fall of the Roman Empire*, 7 vols. ed. J.B. Bury (London, 1909) vol. II, p. 442

INDEX

301